The Reader's
Bathroom Reader

The Reader's
Bathroom Reader

Literary treasures for your private moments

SWEETWATER
PRESS

SWEETWATER
PRESS

The Reader's Bathroom Reader

ISBN-13: 978-1-58173-683-0
ISBN-10: 1-58173-683-5

Cover design by Miles G. Parsons
Book design by Sarah Robins Powell and Scott Fuller
Contributors: Julie Steward, Megan Roth, and Holly Smith

Printed in the United States of America

really short first lines

Can a major novel start with ten words or less? These authors thought so. Here are the first lines of famous long books for people with short attention spans.

"TOM!"
The Adventures of Tom Sawyer,
Mark Twain

124 was spiteful.
Beloved, Toni Morrison

Call me Ishmael.
Moby Dick, Herman Melville

Call me Jonah.
Cat's Cradle, Kurt Vonnegut Jr.

Mother died today.
The Stranger, Albert Camus

There was a wall.
The Dispossessed, Ursula Le Guin

Who is John Galt?
Atlas Shrugged, Ayn Rand

Amoebae leave no fossils.
Even Cowgirls Get the Blues,
Tom Robbins

I was a child murderer.
Expensive People, Joyce Carol Oates

She's looking at me.
Shiloh, Phyllis Reynolds Naylor

Elmer Gantry was drunk.
Elmer Gantry, Sinclair Lewis

It was a dark and stormy night.
A Wrinkle in Time, Madeline L'Engle

It was a pleasure to burn.
Fahrenheit 451, Ray Bradbury

We called him Old Yeller.
Old Yeller, Fred Gipson

In a sense, I am Jacob Horner.
The End of the Road, John Barth

It was like so, but wasn't.
Galatea 2.2, Richard Powers

Kino awakened in the near dark.
The Pearl, John Steinbeck

Lolita, light of my life, fire of my loins.
Lolita, Vladimir Nabokov

Where now? Who now? When now?
The Unnamable, Samuel Beckett

I get the willies when I see closed doors.
Something Happened, Joseph Heller

The day broke gray and dull.
Of Human Bondage,
W. Somerset Maugham

Now what I want is Facts.
Hard Times, Charles Dickens

A screaming comes across the sky.
Gravity's Rainbow,
Thomas Pynchon

There was no possibility of taking a walk that day.
Jane Eyre, Charlotte Brontë

This is the saddest story I have ever heard.
The Good Soldier,
Ford Madox Ford

May in Ayemenem is a hot, brooding month.
The God of Small Things,
Arundhati Roy

I am an invisible man.
Invisible Man, Ralph Ellison

Last night I dreamt I went to Manderly again.
Rebecca, Daphne du Maurier

No one remembers her beginnings.
Rubyfruit Jungle, Rita Mae Brown

To whom it may concern: It is springtime.
Slapstick, Kurt Vonnegut Jr.

You better not never tell nobody but God.
The Color Purple, Alice Walker

"He is very ugly," said his mother.
Great Lion of God, Taylor Caldwell

Elihu B. Washburne opened his gold watch.
Lincoln, Gore Vidal

Miss Jane Marple was sitting by her window.
The Mirror Crack'd, Agatha Christie

The beet is the most intense of vegetables.
Jitterbug Perfume, Tom Robbins

It was Wang Lung's marriage day.
The Good Earth, Pearl Buck

How do people get to this clandestine Archipelago?
The Gulag Archipelago, Aleksandr Solzhenitsyn

"Smell that air," said Major Mann.
Catch a Falling Spy, Len Deighton

I write this sitting in the kitchen sink.
I Capture the Castle, Dodie Smith

It was love at first sight.
Catch 22, Joseph Heller

I was born in Bombay—once upon a time.
Midnight's Children, Salman Rushdie

What's it going to be then, eh?
A Clockwork Orange, Anthony Burgess

When they write my obituary.
The History of Love, Nicole Krauss

We slept in what had once been a gymnasium.
The Handmaid's Tale, Margaret Atwood

really, really long first lines

On the other hand, some novelists love to linger on their lovely first lines. Here is a list of really, really, really, really long first lines of books. The shortest is an already hefty 62 words, and the longest weighs in at a whopping 396 words.

· · · · ·

Ages ago, Alex, Allen and Alva arrived at Antibes, and Alva allowing all, allowing anyone, against Alex's admonition, against Allen's angry assertion: another African amusement . . . anyhow, as all argued, an awesome African army assembled and arduously advanced against an African anthill, assiduously annihilating ant after ant, and afterward, Alex astonishingly accuses Albert as also accepting Africa's antipodal ant annexation.
Alphabetical Africa, Walter Abish

· · · · ·

One summer afternoon Mrs. Oedipa Maas came home from a Tupperware party whose hostess had put perhaps too much kirsch in the fondue to find that she, Oedipa, had been named executor, or she supposed executrix, of the estate of one Pierce Inverarity, a California real estate mogul who had once lost two million dollars in his spare time but still had assets numerous and tangled enough to make the job of sorting it all out more than honorary.
The Crying of Lot 49, Thomas Pynchon

· · · · ·

I was born in the Year 1632, in the City of York, of a good Family, tho' not of that Country, my Father being a Foreigner of Bremen, who settled first at Hull; He got a good Estate by Merchandise, and leaving off his Trade, lived afterward at York, from whence he had

married my Mother, whose Relations were named Robinson, a very good Family in that Country, and from whom I was called Robinson Kreutznaer; but by the usual Corruption of Words in England, we are now called, nay we call our selves, and write our Name Crusoe, and so my Companions always call'd me.
Robinson Crusoe, Daniel Defoe

. . . . .

I, Tiberius Claudius Drusus Nero Germanicus This-that-and-the-other (for I shall not trouble you yet with all my titles) who was once, and not so long ago either, known to my friends and relatives and associates as "Claudius the Idiot," or "That Claudius," or "Claudius the Stammerer," or "Clau-Clau-Claudius" or at best as "Poor Uncle Claudius," am now about to write this strange history of my life; starting from my earliest childhood and continuing year by year until I reach the fateful point of change where, some eight years ago, at the age of fifty-one, I suddenly found myself caught in what I may call the "golden predicament" from which I have never since become disentangled.
I, Claudius, Robert Graves

. . . . .

I will tell you in a few words who I am: lover of the hummingbird that darts to the flower beyond the rotted sill where my feet are propped; lover of bright needlepoint and the bright stitching fingers of humorless old ladies bent to their sweet and infamous designs; lover of parasols made from the same puffy stuff as a young girl's underdrawers; still lover of that small naval boat which somehow survived the distressing years of my life between her decks or in her pilothouse; and also lover of poor dear black Sonny, my mess boy, fellow victim and confidant, and of my wife and child. But most of all, lover of my harmless and sanguine self.
Second Skin, John Hawkes

In the last years of the Seventeenth Century there was to be found among the fops and fools of the London coffee-houses one rangy, gangling flitch called Ebenezer Cooke, more ambitious than talented, and yet more talented than prudent, who, like his friends-in-folly, all of whom were supposed to be educating at Oxford or Cambridge, had found the sound of Mother English more fun to game with than her sense to labor over, and so rather than applying himself to the pains of scholarship, had learned the knack of versifying, and ground out quires of couplets after the fashion of the day, afroth with Joves and Jupiters, aclang with jarring rhymes, and string-taut with similes stretched to the snapping-point.

The Sot-Weed Factor, John Barth

· · · · ·

I wish either my father or my mother, or indeed both of them, as they were in duty both equally bound to it, had minded what they were about when they begot me; had they duly considered how much depended upon what they were then doing;—that not only the production of a rational Being was concerned in it, but that possibly the happy formation and temperature of his body, perhaps his genius and the very cast of his mind;—and, for aught they knew to the contrary, even the fortunes of his whole house might take their turn from the humours and dispositions which were then uppermost:—Had they duly weighed and considered all this, and proceeded accordingly,—I am verily persuaded I should have made a quite different figure in the world, from that, in which the reader is likely to see me.

Tristram Shandy, Laurence Sterne

· · · · ·

Mrs. Rachel Lynde lived just where the Avonlea main road dipped down into a little hollow, fringed with alders and ladies' eardrops and traversed by a brook that had its source away back in the woods of the old Cuthbert place; it was reputed to be an intricate, headlong brook in its earlier course through those woods, with dark secrets of pool and cascade; but by the time it reached Lynde's Hollow it was a quiet, well-conducted little stream, for not even a brook could run past Mrs. Rachel Lynde's door without due regard for decency and decorum; it probably was conscious that Mrs. Rachel was sitting at her window, keeping a sharp eye on everything that passed, from brooks and children up, and that if she noticed anything odd or out of place she would never rest until she had ferreted out the whys and wherefores thereof.

Anne of Green Gables, Lucy Maud Montgomery

· · · · ·

It was many years ago in that dark, chaotic, unfathomable pool of time before Germaine's birth (nearly twelve months before her birth), on a night in late September stirred by innumerable frenzied winds, like spirits contending with one another—mow plaintively, now angrily, now with a subtle cellolike delicacy capable of making the flesh rise on one's arms and neck—a night so sulfurous, so restless, so swollen with inarticulate longing that Leah and Gideon Bellefleur in their enormous bed quarreled once again, brought to tears because their love was too ravenous to be contained by their mere mortal bodies; and their groping, careless, anguished words were like strips or raw silk rubbed violently together (for each was convinced the other did not, could not, be equal to his love—Leah doubted that any man was capable of a love so profound it could be silent, like a forest pond; Gideon doubted that any woman was capable of comprehending the nature of a man's passion, which might tear through him, rendering him broken and exhausted, as vulnerable as a small child): it was on this tumultuous rain-lashed night that Mahalaleel came to Bellefleur Manor on the western shore of the great Lake Noir, where he was to stay for nearly five years.

Bellefleur, Joyce Carol Oates

Once upon a time two or three weeks ago, a rather stubborn and determined middle-aged man decided to record for posterity, exactly as it happened, word by word and step by step, the story of another man for indeed what is great in man is that he is a bridge and not a goal, a somewhat paranoiac fellow unmarried, unattached, and quite irresponsible, who had decided to lock himself in a room a furnished room with a private bath, cooking facilities, a bed, a table, and at least one chair, in New York City, for a year 365 days to be precise, to write the story of another person—a shy young man about of 19 years old—who, after the war the Second World War, had come to America the land of opportunities from France under the sponsorship of his uncle—a journalist, fluent in five languages—who himself had come to America from Europe Poland it seems, though this was not clearly established sometime during the war after a series of rather gruesome adventures, and who, at the end of the war, wrote to the father his cousin by marriage of the young man whom he considered as a nephew, curious to know if he the father and his family had survived the German occupation, and indeed was deeply saddened to learn, in a letter from the young man—a long and touching letter written in English, not by the young man, however, who did not know a damn word of English, but by a good friend of his who had studied English in school—that his parents both his father and mother and his two sisters one older and the other younger than he had been deported they were Jewish to a German concentration camp Auschwitz probably and never returned, no doubt having been exterminated deliberately X * X * X * X, and that, therefore, the young man who was now an orphan, a displaced person, who, during the war, had managed to escape deportation by working very hard on a farm in Southern France, would be happy and grateful to be given the opportunity to come to America that great country he had heard so much about and yet knew so little about to start a new life, possibly go to school, learn a trade, and become a good, loyal citizen. *Double or Nothing*, Raymond Federman

you wanna call it that?
titles authors later tossed

· ·

If you can't judge a book by its cover, you can certainly judge one by
its title. Some of these original titles might have left readers giving a
thumbs-down before they ever read the great stuff inside.

First Draft: *Incident at West Egg*
Why It Wouldn't Fly: Sounds like a bad omelet recipe.
Better Title: *The Great Gatsby,* F. Scott Fitzgerald

First Draft: *Paul Morel*
Why It Wouldn't Fly: Paul who?
Better Title: *Sons and Lovers,* D. H. Lawrence

First Draft: *First Impressions*
Why It Wouldn't Fly: My first impression is that that is a dull title.
Better Title: *Pride and Prejudice,* Jane Austen

First Draft: *The Sea-Cook*
Why It Wouldn't Fly: Oh sure, and then the sequel, *The Guy Who
Swabs the Deck.*
Better Title: *Treasure Island,* Robert Louis Stevenson

First Draft: *Mag's Diversions*
Why It Wouldn't Fly: Why would anyone name their daughter Mag?
Better Title: *David Copperfield,* Charles Dickens

First Draft: *Stephen Hero*
Why It Wouldn't Fly: Sounds like a comic book.
Better Title: *A Portrait of the Artist as a Young Man,* James Joyce

First Draft: *All's Well That Ends Well*
Why It Wouldn't Fly: Shakespeare had already used it.
Better Title: *War and Peace*, Leo Tolstoy

First Draft: *Ba! Ba! Black Sheep*
Why It Wouldn't Fly: I can hear it now: "Frankly my dear, I don't give a sheep."
Better Title: *Gone With the Wind*, Margaret Mitchell

First Draft: *Catch-18*
Why It Wouldn't Fly: Smells like Teen Spirit.
Better Title: *Catch-22*, Joseph Heller

First Draft: *A Jewish Patient Begins His Analysis*
Why It Wouldn't Fly: Sounds like the first line of a bad joke.
Better Title: *Portnoy's Complaint*, Philip Roth

First Draft: *Before This Anger*
Why It Wouldn't Fly: Before what anger? Whose anger? Huh?
Better Title: *Roots*, Alex Haley

First Draft: *They Don't Build Statues to Businessmen*
Why It Wouldn't Fly: Art history book? Dull business guide?
Better Title: *Valley of the Dolls*, Jacqueline Susann

First Draft: *At This Point in Time*
Why It Wouldn't Fly: At this point in time, I'd really rather read something else.
Better Title: *All the President's Men*, Carl Bernstein

across the ages through the pages:
brit lit 1

Literature is always a product of its time period and social context. That is, it is an expression of the private imagination, but it must also be understood within a particular political and cultural history. What it meant to write a sonnet in Renaissance England under Queen Elizabeth, for instance, would be very different from publishing a sonnet in the 21st century on the Internet. Simply put, literature arises out of and responds to the times.

It would take a lifetime to read all of the major literary works from *Beowulf* to Virginia Woolf. Instead, here is a thumbnail sketch of the periods of British Literature, in chronological order, and the least you need to know about a few representative works and writers along the way.

. . . . .

450–1066: The Old English (or Anglo-Saxon) Period

When Germanic tribes invaded Celtic England in the 5th century, Old English, or Anglo-Saxon, literature was born. During the Old English period, written prose and poetry began to develop from the oral tradition. The society invading the Anglo-Saxons was a warrior class ruled by a tribal chieftain; you can see the influence of this worldview in the most famous Old English work of literature, *Beowulf.*

Beowulf: The Least You Need to Know
- It is an early eighth-century epic of almost 3,200 lines of verse.
- It is the oldest surviving manuscript written in English.
- The story line is based on old Norse legends, combined with actual historical occurrences of early sixth-century Denmark.
- Having been brought to England by Danish invaders, the tale became further influenced by Christianity.

• The plot begins when Hrothgar, king of the Danes, builds a mead hall for his warriors, who soon become terrorized by the monster Grendel. Beowulf, nephew of King Hygelac of the Geats, arrives to save the day. In a fight with Grendel, he successfully rips the monster's arm off and mounts it like a prize. Grendel's mother, an even fiercer creature, avenges her son by attacking the mead hall. Beowulf fights her as well with a special sword made by giants. He kills both her and Grendel and is rewarded amply.

Literary Firsts

• *The first writer to submit a novel to a publisher that had been typed on a typewriter was Mark Twain.*

• *The first cloth binding of a book came from the British publisher William Pickering in 1822.*

• *The first book printed in Europe was the Gutenberg Bible in 1456.*

• *The Gutenberg Bible was also the first Bible to be printed from movable metal type.*

• *The first book printed in English was* The Recuyell of the Historyes of Troye *published in 1475 by William Caxton.*

laughing with the bard:
Shakespeare's comedies

While Shakespeare's comedies are, undoubtedly, humorous plays, they are only called by that name because of their light tone, their playful style, and their happy endings. Many of the comedies take place in pastoral settings, as if the natural world were a more appropriate place for ease and merriment. Other common features of the comedies include cross-dressing, mistaken identity, lovers struggling to end up together, clever servants, an inversion of the social order, multiple plots, singing, dancing, and, of course, laughter.

· · · · ·

As You Like It
Plot
The play begins with two pairs of brothers who treat each other badly. Oliver swore to his dying father that he would educate his brother, Orlando, but he reneges on the promise. Meanwhile, Duke Frederick seizes power from his brother, Duke Senior, and banishes him to the Forest of Arden. Senior's daughter, Rosalind, is allowed to remain in Frederick's court at least until he becomes angry and banishes her too. She disguises herself as a man named Ganymede and flees with Frederick's daughter, Celia, to the forest. A shepherdess falls in love with "Ganymede," but Ganymede has befriended Orlando, with whom she falls in love. Eventually the evil brothers repent, Celia marries Oliver, Rosalind married Orlando, and Duke Frederick gives his crown back to Duke Senior.

Themes
1. The course of true love never does run smoothly. Rosalind takes the condition of banishment and turns it into an opportunity to find love.
2. The forest/nature exerts a healing power. Once characters enter Arden, they seem to become more open and virtuous.

crying with the bard:
Shakespeare's tragedies
· ·

The genre of tragedy dates back to the ancient Greeks, but certain features almost always remain the same, even through Shakespeare's time. Strong emotions are produced in the audience and the protagonists generally take a fall. Usually the classic tragic hero was a person of admirable qualities who is undone by some tragic flaw, such as excessive pride. Most of the Bard's great tragedies were written between 1601–1608 in a brief flourish of creativity. In all of them, at least one, if not all, of the major characters dies. Brief moments of comedy alleviate the despair and sadness, but overall the tragedies point to the inevitability of death and the sheer force of suffering that often accompanies it because of the hero's fatal flaws.

· · · · ·

Timon of Athens
Plot
The title character of this tragedy begins the story as a lover of the arts, a gracious host, and a very generous friend. However, once he finds himself in financial straits, the cynical philosopher Apemantus rightly predicts that his "friends" will abandon him. Disillusioned and distraught, Timon becomes a recluse, leaving Athens and going to live in a cave, where, to his good fortune, he finds gold. He meets an Athenian general named Alcibiades, who, unjustly banished from Athens, has been gathering an army to march on Athens. With his newfound wealth, Timon agrees to provide funds for the venture. The Athenians hear that Timon has once again become wealthy, so they send a group of men to ask him to help them fight off Alcibiades. Timon refuses. In fact, he has grown so misanthropic that when robbers come to the cave to steal his gold, his bitterness is so strong that they almost repent of their crimes. By the end of the play, Alcibiades

reenters Athens to seek vengeance only on those who have hurt him and Timon. Timon, however, dies in his deep hatred of his fellow man, who turned on him early in the play.

Themes

1. You can't buy love. Timon's generosity comes as much from a desire to buy friends as it does from a sincere love of people. Thus, when he loses his money, he loses his so-called friends as well. True friendship has no price tag.
2. Misanthropy is deadly. The cause of Timon's death at the end of the drama remains unclear, but the play suggests that his unrelenting hatred most likely spurred his downfall.

Amazing Numbers

- *No surprise here. The best-selling children's books series of all time is the Harry Potter series, which has sold more than 250 million copies.*

- *In 2000, an original, four-volume subscription set of Audubon's* The Birds of America *sold at an auction for over $8 million.*

- *The most money ever paid for a single manuscript was $545,100 for an unfinished manuscript of* The Scarlet Letter.

learning with the bard:
Shakespeare's histories

We can laugh with the comedies and cry with the tragedies, but there is also much to learn from Shakespeare's histories, a group of plays most often based on the lives of British royalty. The source of most of the plays was *Holinshed's Chronicles* (1577), an ambitious work originally designed to chart the history of the world from the great flood until the reign of Queen Elizabeth. Shakespeare used the source for factual information, but he also felt free to use creative license whenever it helped flesh out the story. Living under the reign of a Tudor queen, Elizabeth I, Shakespeare slanted his work toward a praise of the Tudor dynasty, so that the medieval world often appears as one inevitable in its decline as the Tudors rose to ascendancy. The history plays were especially intriguing for the British audiences in the 16th century because they helped create a sense of a collective national memory, even if that memory sometimes had a particular bias. Regardless of political bias, the plays are an excellent way to examine past and to see it come alive in all the color and glory that only the Bard could bring.

To help you keep the history straight, here's a list of the rulers of England, many of whom appear as characters in Shakespeare's plays:

House of Plantagenet
Henry II, grandson of Henry I, 1154–89
Richard I (Cœur de Lion), third son of Henry II, 1189–99
John, youngest son of Henry II, 1199–1216
Henry III, son of John, 1216–72
Edward I, son of Henry III, 1272–1307
Edward II, son of Edward I, 1307–27
Edward III, son of Edward II, 1327–77
Richard II, grandson of Edward III, 1377–99

House of Lancaster
Henry IV, grandson of Edward III, 1399–1413
Henry V, son of Henry IV, 1413–22
Henry VI, son of Henry V, 1422–61, 1470–71

House of York
Edward IV, great-grandson of Edward III, 1461–70, 1471–83
Edward V, son of Edward IV, 1483
Richard III, brother of Edward IV, 1483–85

House of Tudor
Henry VII, descendant of Edward III, 1485–1509
Henry VIII, son of Henry VII, 1509–47
Edward VI, son of Henry VIII, 1547–53
Mary I, older daughter of Henry VIII, 1553–58
Elizabeth I, younger daughter of Henry VIII, 1558–1603

Really Old Stuff

• *The oldest bookstore in the United States is the Moravian Books Shop in Bethlehem, Pennsylvania. It was established in 1775.*

• *The oldest book fair in the United States is the New York Antiquarian Book Fair, which was established in 1961.*

• *The award for longest-running children's book series goes to* The Bobbsey Twins *(1904-72). There were 72 books in the series.*

---

learning with the bard

The First Part of Henry IV

Plot

Henry IV, also known as Henry Bolingbroke and Henry of Lancaster, was born in 1367 and died in 1413. He ruled as King of England from 1399 until his death. A year before his reign began, Richard II banished him from England, but in 1399, he invaded his homeland, forced Richard's abdication, and assumed the throne. Shakespeare's play portrays the early years of Henry's rule. It begins in 1401, when Hotspur (Henry Percy the Younger), the oldest son of the Earl of Northumberland, refuses to turn over prisoners to King Henry IV unless he ransoms Edmund Mortimer. The king refuses because Mortimer believes he has a claim to the throne. In their anger, Hotspur and his family switch allegiances, forming an alliance with the Welsh against the king. Not only does King Henry IV have troubles on the war front, but he also is facing problems on the home front. His son, Prince Hal, resists growing up. He spends most of his time drinking and carousing with one of Shakespeare's most famous comic creations, the fat, drunk, lecherous Falstaff. However, once Hal hears of Hotspur's rebellion, he takes sure and effective command of his father's troops, defeats the rebels at the battle of Shrewsbury on the Welsh-English border, and kills Hotspur. By the end of the play, it is clear that Prince Hal will serve as a worthy heir to the throne.

Themes

1. Courage on the battlefield is a hallmark of effective leadership. Until Hal goes to battle, it isn't entirely clear that he will be a serious, responsible leader, but once he is pressed into action, his valor marks him as a formidable future leader.
2. A misspent youth can be salvaged into a mature adulthood. Admittedly, Hal's revels with Falstaff and the gang allow him to continue his Peter Pan syndrome, but his association with the lower classes also affords the future king the opportunity to learn more about the people in his kingdom for an insider's perspective.

from dogs and frogs to cheshire cats #1:
animals in children's literature

In most children's literature, animals either appear as symbols or are given human characteristics. For instance, whereas the dog in *Where the Red Fern Grows* symbolizes the ultimate loyalty, the bear and the mouse in Beatrice Schenk de Regniers' book *How Joe the Bear and Sam the Mouse Got Together* interact with each other just as people do. Oh sure, they are a bear and a mouse, but they skate, eat ice cream, and bicker with each other just like any old human friends might do. From as far back as Greek mythology and Aesop's fables to the present day, animals reflect the best (and sometimes the worst) in human tendencies, filling the pages of juvenile fiction with four-legged excitement on every page. Just consider these creatures:

. . . . .

Aesop's Animals
Aesop's Fables, light, simple tales that speak to children as well as adults, use animals to represent human moral qualities, such as integrity or selfishness. They most likely appeared around 500 BC in Greece. Pre-Aesopic fables used animals to represent a particular person as when, for instance, Hesiod used a hawk to describe his brother and make a political criticism. But Aesop used animals more widely to speak about human nature in general.

. . . . .

Alice's Adventures in Wonderland
The Rev. Charles L. Dodgson penned the tale about Alice, the Cheshire Cat, the White Rabbit, and a host of other fantastical creatures in 1865, under the pseudonym Lewis Carroll. By trade, he was a mathematics professor at Oxford University. During a boat ride with a colleague's three daughters, he began making up a story whose protagonist he named Alice, after his favorite of the three daughters. When he had completed the book, he chose famous *Punch* illustrator John Tenniel

to animate it for publication. However, by then the real-life Alice had, to Carroll's chagrin, matured into a teenager, so she was transformed in the illustration to a blonde little girl. Alice's namesake grew up to celebrate the Lewis Carroll centenary in 1932 and to autograph a copy of the book for Queen Elizabeth. Though the story centers on Alice, its allure lies in the mysterious characters she encounters, including the Cheshire Cat, who, with his famous grin, appears and disappears at will. The White Rabbit, the first creature Alice meets, ushers her into Wonderland, where she meets a hookah-smoking Caterpillar, who teachers her how to shrink and grow. Carroll's collection of animals led to one unfortunate turn of events: *Alice in Wonderland* was banned in China in 1931, when officials deemed it inappropriate that animals use the same language as humans.

· · · · ·

Black Beauty

Anna Sewell wrote this beloved novel to "induce kindness, sympathy, and an understanding treatment of horses." Written in 1876, it became an immediate best-seller and the first animal story of major importance. The horse, Black Beauty, narrates a tale of cruelty to animals. He begins life on an English farm but finds himself over the years having to pull cabs in London and endure other hardships. The book is said to have led to the abolishment of the checkrein, a strap used to hold horses' heads upright in a painful manner.

Reading List:
pychological thrillers

Rebecca, Daphne du Maurier
Tension builds between main characters Maxim de Winter and his new wife as they attempt to live together underneath the shadow of de Winter's deceased first wife, Rebecca, and the domineering housekeeper, Mrs. Danver, one of literature's worst female villains. The book winds through dark tunnels to a shocking conclusion.

. . . . .

The Straw Men, Michael Marshall
Ward Hopkins, a former CIA agent, returns home for the funeral of his parents. When he finds a note from his father that reads, *"We're not dead,"* Hopkins begins a search for the truth. All the events in the book, culminating in the abduction of the Hopkins's daughter, create an unsettling truth.

. . . . .

The Ice Harvest, Scott Phillips
Lawyer Charlie Arglist spends Christmas Eve waiting for his partner in crime, an associate, to meet him and to escape Witchita, Kansas. Arglist is holding on to a large sum of embezzled money and winds up digging himself deeper and deeper into danger and trouble.

self-publishing hall of shame
[and fame]

Self-publishing has always been a touchy subject in the world of literature, as many tend to believe that a work is not truly "published" until picked up by an outside agent. Due to the bad name it has made for itself, the process is often done quietly. Therefore, it may be a shock to find out that some of the greatest literary minds actually self-published at one time in their career.

•••••

Caught: Robert Bly

Famous contemporary poet Robert Bly self-published many collections of his own poetry during the early 1970s through his own publishing company. Of course, throughout the 1980s, Bly won several major literary awards, including the National Book Award, and published over 20 books of prose, poetry, translation, and essays. The University of Minnesota purchased his archive of work in 2006, which contained over 80,000 pages of writing, for over $700,000.

•••••

Caught: Pat Conroy

The esteemed novelist and author of *Prince of Tides*, Pat Conroy, got his start by forking out thousands to self-publish and promote his first novel, *The Boo*. He later published over five more best-selling novels, all equipped with gigantic advances and print runs. His best-sellers include *The Water Is Wide*, *The Great Santini*, and *Beach Music*.

•••••

Caught: Amanda Brown

Author of the well-known novel-made-film *Legally Blonde*, Brown first published the title herself through the print-on-demand company

First Books. After the book was made into a movie starring Reese Witherspoon, Plume, a New York publishing company, decided to pick up the book and publish it with an extra chapter about the future of Elle Woods, the main character.

· · · · ·

Caught: E. E. Cummings

Internationally renowned poet E. E. Cummings self-published his first book of poetry, *No Thanks*, through funds from his mother. The poet listed all 13 publishers who had rejected the book on the title page, and the book later became one of his classics. Oops!

· · · · ·

Caught: William E. B. Du Bois

Author, civil rights leader, and cofounder of the NAACP, William E. B. Du Bois self-published his first book, *The Moon*, in 1906. He was the editor of *Crisis* until 1932, after which he wrote several other books that focused on the lives and struggles of African Americans.

Size Does Matter

- *Frankfurt is home to the largest book fair in the world, with over 9,500 exhibitions.*

- *The world's largest bookstore is Powell's Books of Portland, Oregon. The largest cyber-bookstore is Amazon.com*

- *The longest novel in English is* A Dance to the Music of Time, *a 12-volume work by Anthony Powell.*

---

laughing with the bard

. . . .

The Taming of the Shrew
Plot

Bianca is a lovely, sweet girl with whom many men are in love.
Unfortunately, her father will not allow her to wed until he can marry
off her violent, outspoken shrew of a sister, Katharina. It looks as
if Bianca will die a spinster, that is, until Petruchio, a strong-willed
gentleman of Verona, appears and promptly marries Katharina. He takes
Katharina to his house and proceeds to "tame" her to such an extent
that he wins a bet with two other men over whose wife is the most
obedient. However, many scholars argue that Katharina's final lecture
to the ladies about submitting to a husband's will is meant to be taken
ironically. In this case, she and Petruchio become well-matched spouses
who can spar with each other in mutual respect. Theirs is a much more
interesting relationship than the nice but boring marriage of Bianca
and Lucentio.

Themes

1. Gender inequality produces unhealthy relationships. Katharina's
   behavior as a shrew is guaranteed to render her unhappy in love, but
   so is Petruchio's overbearing patriarchal authority. They must strike a
   balance of power to be happy.
2. A battle of wits can win the heart. Flowers and love poems are a
   more typical route to romance, but so is verbal sparring and witty
   repartee.

learning with the bard

Richard III

Plot

Historically, this play picks up where *The Third Part of King Henry VI* leaves off. The hunchbacked Richard has always coveted the throne occupied by his brother, Edward IV. The play begins with Richard plotting against anyone who stands in his way to power. He convinces the king that their brother, George, Duke of Clarence, poses a threat to his authority. Clarence is imprisoned and dies. Richard marries Lady Anne, daughter-in-law of the late King Henry VI, who hates him. Once Edward IV dies, Richard immediately places Edward's two young sons in the Tower of London and assumes the throne. He has the boys killed, and he also has his wife, Lady Anne, killed so that he can marry the sister of the murdered boys, to strengthen his power. Elsewhere, the Earl of Richmond has invaded England, claiming the throne. He defeats the evil Richard's forces, and Richard, fighting on foot, proclaims the famous lines, "A horse! A horse! My kingdom for a horse!" He wins neither horse nor kingdom; instead, Richmond kills him and becomes Henry VII.

Themes

1. Ambition and evil often go hand in hand. Richard III has lusted for the throne throughout his entire life. Once he finally wins the crown, he continues to hurt everyone near him in order to solidify his power.
2. The outside mirrors the inside. Shakespeare depicts Richard as an ugly, grotesque hunchback, in part to emphasize that his evil heart within is mirrored by his foul features.

quick & easy shakespeare

The Tempest
Plot

The last play that Shakespeare wrote, *The Tempest,* is a meditation on power, love, and forgiveness. A magician named Prospero used to be the rightful Duke of Milan until he was usurped by his brother, Antonio. He now lives on an island with his daughter, Miranda, and two creatures, a spirit named Ariel and a beast named Caliban, whom he treats as a slave. With the help of his magic book, Prospero causes a terrible storm to wash ashore a ship that carries not only Antonio but also King Alonso of Naples and a group of unscrupulous noblemen. They quarrel among themselves as Alonso's son, Ferdinand, falls in love with Miranda. Prospero carefully orchestrates all that happens on the island. He lets Ferdinand woo his daughter, he persuades Ariel to torment Caliban and the evil shipwrecked men, and finally he offers forgiveness to his brother. By the end of the play, the young lovers are together, Ariel no longer has to serve as Prospero's servant, and only Caliban remains in captivity.

Themes

1. Forgiveness is the true path to wisdom. As wise and magical as Prospero is, his greatest achievement is in the forgiveness of Antonio.
2. Exploration often produces colonial exploitation. Many critics read Caliban sympathetically, viewing him as an example of indigenous cultures that are misunderstood and, therefore, abused by colonizing powers.

little-known literary info

- The proceeds from the sales of the book *Peter Pan* by James M. Barrie were donated in full to the Great Ormond Street Hospital for Children in London, England. The hospital owns the copyright, and the amount of money earned from the book is kept secret.

- Agatha Christie's *The Mouse Trap* is known for being the longest-running play ever, with more than 22,000 performances over a 55-year run.

- In John Milton's *Paradise Lost*, over 8,000 different words are used.

- Out of the 2,200 people quoted in the famous anthology *Bartlett's Quotations*, only 164 are female.

- *Uncle Tom's Cabin*, by Harriet Beecher Stowe, was the first novel in America to sell more than 1 million copies.

- It is rumored that Frank Baum, author of *The Wizard of Oz*, came up with the name for the Emerald City while gazing at his filing cabinet. One drawer was labeled "A to N" and another, "O to Z," which became *Oz*.

- Dr. Seuss' *Green Eggs and Ham* contains only 50 different words, 49 of which are monosyllabic (containing one syllable). It is rumored that Seuss' editor dared him to write a book using 50 words or less, which resulted in the long-treasured storybook.

- When Margaret Mitchell wrote *Gone With the Wind*, one of several working titles that she used was *Ba! Ba! Black Sheep*. Also considered were the titles *Tote the Weary Load*, *Tomorrow Is Another Day*, and *Not in Our Stars*.

- In 2000, Gao Xingjian became the first Chinese writer ever to be awarded the Nobel Prize for Literature. He is the author of the novels *Soul Mountain* and *The Other Shore*. Since 1986, all of his books and plays have been banned in China.

- In the 1922 novel *Aaron's Rod*, D. H. Lawrence uses the phrase both in the title and in the story to refer to the main character, Aaron, who leaves his family to become a traveling flute player. The actual phrase *Aaron's rod*, however, is an important symbol in the Bible.

Library Facts

- *No library is older than the Vatican Library, which was established in 1451.*

- *The oldest lending library in the United States is the Redwood Library and Atheneum, established in 1750 in Providence, Rhode Island.*

- *The first library in the United States was established in Peterborough, New Hampshire, in 1833.*

- *The first subscription library in the United States was the Library Company of Philadelphia, which was established in 1711.*

Children's Lit: the early years

The story of children's literature is a fascinating tale of a body of work that almost never got off the ground. Did you know:

- The printing press was invented in 1437, but the first books published were only for adults. William Caxton, the first English printer, published *Aesop's Fables*, which might be an early example of literature that crossed over from the adult world to young adult interests.

- In the 15th century, the hornbook was invented to help educate children. Not really a *book*, per se, the hornbook was more like a wooden paddle with lessons about the alphabet, simple mathematics, and the Lord's Prayer inscribed. Children not inclined to learning used their hornbooks to hit balls with, a sport that later led to cricket.

- Later in the 16th century, the chapbook came to replace hornbooks. Since they cost about one penny each, the chapbook derived its name from "cheap book." They were flimsy pamphlets under 20 pages long recounting stories of Robin Hood, King Arthur, and other popular legends.

- In the 1500s, the first English translation of the Bible was published, followed by the King James version in 1611. Puritan children were only allowed to read the Bible, and usually only on Sunday. By the 1670s, Puritan children were treated to such books as *A Token for Children: Being an Exact Account of the Conversion, Holy and Exemplary Lives,* and *Joyful Deaths of Several Young Children.* Titles such as this one scared kids away from sin by describing death and hell in lurid detail.

- John Bunyan's *Pilgrim's Progress* was read by children and adults alike. Published in 1678, it became so popular that it sold over 100,000 copies.

- In the 18th century, children became avid readers of two "adult" novels, *Robinson Crusoe* (1719) by Daniel Defoe and *Gulliver's Travels* (1726) by Jonathan Swift. Young readers were enthralled with the story of Robinson Crusoe's shipwreck and subsequent solitary existence on an uninhabited island for 24 years. Swift targeted the satire of *Gulliver's Travels* toward a critique of human reason, but readers old and young laughed at Gulliver's misadventures among the tiny people of Lilliput and the giants of Brobdingnag.

- The face of children's literature changed forever in the late 1690s with the publication of a small French book, *Contes de ma mere l'Oye*. Translated as *Tales of Mother Goose* in 1729, the eight fairy tales were vastly different from the hellfire and brimstone stories of the Puritans. *Mother Goose* was the first literature designed to entertain children instead of merely instruct. The original tales included "Sleeping Beauty," "Little Red Riding Hood," "Bluebeard," "Puss-in-Boots," "The Fairies," "Cinderella," and "Tom Thumb."

- Following the success of *Mother Goose*, John Newbery (1713–1767) became one of the first publishers of children's books. His motto was "Trade and Plumb-cake for ever. Huzza!" which was another way of expressing his interest in making money while having fun. Two of the ghostwriters he hired to write books would later go on to publish great works of their own: Oliver Goldsmith and Dr. Samuel Johnson. He published over 30 children's books and died a wealthy man. The Newbery Medal, established by Frederic Melcher in 1921 and awarded to the year's best American children's book, was named after him.

- In the early 1800s, Christian tract societies began warning parents about the dangers of reading for pleasure. Fiction was considered a breeding ground for crime because it fostered overly active imaginations. Such books as the 1825 *Glass of Whiskey* were published to warn youngsters about the dangers of drinking "demon Rum."

- Factual reference books, on the other hand, were considered proper reading for children of the 19th century. In 1827, Samuel Griswold Goodrich published *Tales of Peter Parley About America* which spawned 120 other informative books about America and sold over 7 million copies.

- Two German brothers, Jacob Ludwig Carl Grimm and Wilhelm Carl Grimm, collected German folktales that became known in the early 1800s as *Grimm's Fairy Tales*. They claimed to have gotten the material for the stories by interviewing peasants, though critics now dispute that claim.

- With the ascension of Queen Victoria to the English throne, children's literature became very popular. Hans Christian Anderson's *Fairy Tales* were translated into English at about the same time that the public library movement began, which helped distribute children's literature more widely. Series literature also became popular during Victoria's reign, both in England and America. Adventure, biography, and sports series became all the rage. Especially popular were Horatio Alger books about poor boys working hard and becoming successful. Alger wrote over 100 books, beginning with *Ragged Dick* in 1868.

- The domestic drama became another favorite category of Victorian children's literature. Louisa May Alcott published *Little Women* in 1868 and its sequel, *Little Men*, in 1871. Alcott also made money writing what she called "rubbishy novels," such as *Perilous Play*, a story about lovers who meet at a hashish party. It probably wasn't a big seller on the children's literature lists!

- In the 20th century, children's literature continued to thrive, especially because of the contributions of one writer, Theodor Geisel, also known as Dr. Seuss. Consider this: in 1940, Random House had no separate children's department, but 30 years later, their juvenile budget exceeded $13 million. They had numerous warehouses covering acres of land to store Dr. Seuss' books alone.

Literary Associations

- *The first writer's conference in America was the Bread Loaf Writer's Conference, established in 1926.*

- *The Authors Guild, founded in 1919, is the oldest professional society of published authors.*

- *The Book-of-the-Month-Club was established in 1926. The first book selected was* Lolly Willowes *by Sylvia Townsend Warner..*

a raunchy *start*

It is well known that many novelists and authors get their start by publishing short pieces in widely circulating magazines. It might be surprising to find, however, that many writers got their start by publishing short stories in the one and only *Playboy* magazine.

Author: Woody Allen
Story: "Match Wits with Inspector Ford," 1975

Author: Steven Barr
Story: "The Mirror of Gigantic Shadows," September 1963

Author: Ray Bradbury
Story: "Fahrenheit 451," parts 1–3, 1954

Author: John Cheever
Stories: "The Yellow Room," January 1968

Author: Robert Coover
Story: "Lucky Pierre in the Doctor's Office," December 1989

Author: Phillip K. Dick
Story: "Frozen Journey," September 1975

Author: Ian Fleming
Story: "The Property of a Lady," January 1964

Author: Shirley Jackson
Story: "A Great Voice Stilled," March 1960

Author: Stephen King
Story: "The Word Processor," January 1983

Author: Ursula K. Le Guin
Story: "Nine Lives," November 1969

Author: Vladimir Nabakov
Story: "The Dashing Fellow," December 1971

Author: Joyce Carol Oates
Story: "Saul Bird Says: Relate! Communicate! Liberate!," October 1970

Author: John Updike
Story: "I am Dying, Egypt, Dying," September 1969

Author: Kurt Vonnegut Jr.
Story: "Welcome to the Monkey House," January 1968

The Scoop on Paperbacks

- *City Lights Book Shop in San Francisco was the first bookstore to sell paperbacks exclusively.*

- *The first paperback to sell a million copies was* How to Win Friends and Influence People *by Dale Carnegie.*

The Power of the Pen:
the all-time top 10 must-reads in world lit

OK, we admit it's pretty difficult to boil the classics of world literature down to a top-ten list, but these global giants have made their mark on the world, and on the world of literature.

1. ***Tao Te Ching*** by Lao Tzu
   The *Tao Te Ching*, composed during the Chinese "Spring and Autumn Classical Period" (700–480 BC), is one of the oldest and most influential works of poetry ever written. Its 5,000 ancient Chinese characters are a mystical composition from the philosophical mystical base of Taoism. It is still widely read today as a universal book of wisdom for how to live.

2. ***The Mathnawi of Jalaluddin Rumi***
   Rumi was a 13th-century Persian Sufi mystic whose poetry is as transporting and beautiful today as it was centuries ago. *The Mathnawi* is a collection of fables, parables, and tales that encompasses everything from saints in the Jewish, Christian, and Muslim traditions to meditations on the divine. Rumi's range encompasses all humans experience from the most humorous highs to the most grief-stricken lows. His premier translator, Coleman Barks, delights in noting that this 13th-century writer is the best-selling poet in the United States today.

3. ***The Divine Comedy*** by Dante Alighieri
   Completed in 1321, this epic poem describes Dante's journey through hell, purgatory, and finally paradise, led along the way by Roman poet Virgil. The philosophy and theology of the poem come from St. Thomas Aquinas, but the literary genius is all Dante's own. The poem's 100 cantos, written in terza rima, are filled with heretics, history's villains, and, in the beautiful culmination, the lovely symbol of divine revelation, Dante's beloved Beatrice.

4. ***The Book of the City of Ladies*** by Christine de Pizan
In 1405, Pizan became Europe's first professional female writer with
this allegorical story designed as a rebuttal to popular misogynist
arguments of the day. Three allegorical goddesses, Lady Reason,
Lady Rectitude, and Lady Justice, provide a wealth of examples
from history, literature, and myth to prove that women have been as
influential and signficant in history as men.

5. ***Don Quixote*** by Miguel de Cervantes
Cervantes brought to life one of the most enduring symbols of
heroic idealism in 1605. *Don Quixote* is the most famous of all of the
literary works of Spain's golden age as it describes the adventures of
a country gentleman who refuses to believe that chivalry is dead. As
a literary masterpiece, it combines satire, romance, and irony in ways
that still feel modern. In fact, in 2002, a survey of 100 of the world's
leading authors voted it the best book of all time.

6. ***Faust*** by Johann Wolfgang von Goethe
The legendary story of a man who sells his soul to the devil has been
told since the 15th century, but it became immortalized by Goethe in
his 1808 tragic drama, *Faust.* The play has inspired countless operas,
paintings, and stories as it recounts the story of an old scholar whose
hunger for knowledge exceeds the bounds of morality. The work
still resonates with modern readers as a warning against excesses in
scientific exploration and human passion.

7. ***Eugene Onegin*** by Aleksander Pushkin
Pushkin is to the Russians what Shakespeare is to England. The
Russian poet, playwright, and fiction writer created almost an entire
literary heritage all on his own. *Eugene Onegin* (1833) describes a
Byronic hero who loses his joie de vivre, turning his back on luxury
and love. Pushkin's ironic portrayal became copied by many Russian
writers.

8. *A Doll's House* by Henrik Ibsen
From Norway comes this major work of drama that tells the story
of Nora Helmer, a protofeminist heroine who leaves her controlling
husband and children in order to find an authentic life of her own.
Produced in 1879, the play so scandalized Victorian society that
many husbands would not let their wives see it, and many theaters
refused to stage it. As a playwright concerned with intellectual and
social issues, Ibsen heavily influenced such writers as diverse as
Anton Chekhov and James Joyce.

9. **"The Metamorphosis"** by Franz Kafka
Austrian fiction writer Franz Kafka is one of the few authors whose
name has become an adjective. To describe a work as "Kafkaesque"
is to suggest that it has an absurd, almost grotesque unreality. The
most famous of Kafka's works is his 1937 story, *The Metamorphosis,*
which tells the tale of a man waking one morning to find he has
turned into a giant insect. Critics read the bizarre story as everything
from a case study in psychoanalysis to a Marxist commentary on the
alienation of labor. Whatever it is, it is, undeniably, Kafkaesque.

10. *The Satanic Verses* by Salman Rushdie
No sooner did Indian novelist Rushdie publish this book in 1989
than the Ayatollah Khomeini published a *hukm* against Rushdie,
accusing him of blasphemy and calling for his death. Rushdie
went into hiding for several years as a result. The plot of the novel
involves two men, a Bollywood star and an Indian expatriate, falling
out of a hijacked plane. They land, unharmed, on a beach, and the
story moves on from there through magical dream visions and an
imaginative retelling of the life of the prophet Muhammad. Critics
hail the book as an outstanding example not only of postmodern
literature, but of the necessity for artistic license.

Nobel Prize Winners *1901–1925*

Since the very first Nobel Prize in Literature award in 1901, writers worldwide have competed for this most coveted prize, given annually to an author who produces what Alfred Nobel called "the most outstanding work of an idealistic tendency." Folks have debated what exactly he meant by this, however. "Work" can mean a single work or a writer's entire career; "idealistic" can mean ideal/excellent or idealistic. Either way, the upshot is that someone gets a prize for some really fine writing. Here's a list of all of the winners to 1925 and what the Swedish Academy has had to say about them.

1901: Sully Prudhomme (pen name of René François Armand), whose poetry combines the heart and the mind in bold originality.

1902: Christian Matthias Theodor Mommsen, for being one of the best historical writers, especially in consideration of his work, *A History of Rome.*

1903: Bjørnstjerne Martinus Bjørnson, as a tribute to his "noble, magnificent and versatile poetry."

1904: The prize was divided equally between:
Frédéric Mistral, for original poetry and for his work as a Provençal philologist.
José Echegaray y Eizaguirre, for reviving the traditions of Spanish drama.

Close But No Nobel Cigar

These heavy hitters never received a Nobel Prize.

W. H. Auden	W. Somerset Maugham
Bertolt Brecht	Sean O'Casey
Anton Chekhov	Ezra Pound
Joseph Conrad	Marcel Proust
F. Scott Fitzgerald	Stevie Smith
Graham Greene	Dylan Thomas
Thomas Hardy	Leo Tolstoy
Henrik Ibsen	Mark Twain
Henry James	H. G. Wells
Jack London	Virginia Woolf

1905: Henryk Sienkiewicz, for his immense strengths as an epic writer.

1906: Giosuè Carducci, for his research, creativity, and poetic strength.

1907: Rudyard Kipling, who embodies all that is observant, imaginative, and virile in an author.

1908: Rudolf Christoph Eucken for his commitment to truth and his idealistic life philosophy.

1909: Selma Ottilia Lovisa Lagerlöf for her idealistic imagination and spiritual perceptions.

1910: Paul Johann Ludwig Heyse, a jack of all trades—"lyric poet, dramatist, novelist and writer of world-renowned short stories."

1911: Count Maurice (Mooris) Polidore Marie Bernhard Maeterlinck in appreciation of his multifaceted literary activities and especially his dramatic works.

1912: Gerhart Johann Robert Hauptmann, who is a chief practitioner of dramatic arts.

Most Awarded Languages	
Language	*Number of Laureates*
English	26
French	13
German	12
Spanish	10
Italian	6
Swedish	6

1913: Rabindranath Tagore for his gorgeous Indian poetry written in English verse.

1915: Romain Rolland for being a writer filled with "sympathy and love" for mankind.

1916: Carl Gustaf Verner von Heidenstam, who is "leading a representative of a new era in our literature."

1917: The prize was divided equally between:
  Karl Adolph Gjellerup for rich, lofty poetry.
  Henrik Pontoppidan for his depiction of contemporary Danish life.

1919: Carl Friedrich Georg Spitteler for his epic *Olympian Spring.*

1920: Knut Pedersen Hamsun for his significant work *Growth of the Soil.*

1921: Anatole France (pen name of Jacques Anatole Thibault) for embodying Gallic temperament.

1922: Jacinto Benavente for the "happy manner" in which he has continued traditions of the Spanish drama.

1923: William Butler Yeats for his strong, lyrical poetry, which expresses Irish spirit and the longings of the human heart.

1924: Wladyslaw Stanislaw Reymont (pen name of Reyment) for his important Polish epic *The Peasants.*

1925: George Bernard Shaw, whose writing is idealistic, satirical, and poetical.

Nobel *trivia*

· ·

While there is nothing trivial about the Nobel Prize for Literature, here's a list of interesting facts associated with the prize.

- Theodor Mommsen, age 85, was the oldest person to win the Nobel Prize in Literature.
- Rudyard Kipling became the youngest when he won it at age 42.
- Mommsen was born over 134 years before the most recently born laureate, Orhan Pamuk.
- Bertrand Russell, who died at 97, lived longer than any other prizewinner.
- The oldest living laureate is Aleksandr Solzhenitsyn, who was born in 1918.
- The laureate who lived the shortest life was Albert Camus, who died three years after receiving the award at age 46.
- TV and radio personality Gert Fylking began the tradition of shouting *"Äntligen!"* (Swedish for "At last!") when the award winner was announced.
- The first Asian laureate was Rabindranath Tagore.

it's GRÉÉK to me

From Euripides' *Medea* to James Joyce's *Ulysses*, tales of Greek myth lay the foundation for some great reads. Here's a guide to the gods.

. . . . .

Name: Zeus (Roman name Jupiter)
Superpower: The Big Cheese. King of Olympus, god of the sky. Best known for hurling thunderbolts when angry. When not busy ruling the universe, he committed adultery. Lots of it.

. . . . .

Name: Hera (Roman name Juno)
Superpower: Put up with philandering husband. Wife and sister of Big Cheese, Zeus. Queen of Olympus, goddess of marriage and childbirth. In her spare time, she punished all the women Zeus fell in love with. This kept her quite busy.

. . . . .

Name: Poseidon (Roman name Neptune)
Superpower: Brother of Zeus, god of the sea, and namesake of a cinematic cruise ship that turned upside down. Carried a really big fork called a trident, which he would wave before sinking entire islands in a fit of his famous anger. Although most often associated with water, Poseidon was also the god of horses. This came in handy when he wanted to disguise himself, literally, as a stud and find a girlfriend.

. . . . .

Name: Hades (Roman name Pluto)
Superpower: Other brother of Zeus, god of the underworld, the dead, and, on a lighter note, wealth. No amount of money, however, could persuade Persephone to marry him, so he kidnapped her on her wedding day. Nice.

Name: Hestia (Roman name Vesta)
Superpower: Sister of Zeus, goddess of the hearth. Unlike her brothers, Hestia lacked a flair for the dramatic. Her job was to protect stability, family, and the home. As a virgin-goddess, she showed no interest when Apollo and Poseidon flirted with her.

• • • • •

Name: Athena (Roman name Minerva)
Superpower: Smart and good with crops. Daughter of Zeus alone. She didn't have a mother. In fact, she just sprang from Zeus's head. This made her his favorite child. Goddess of wisdom and of the city and the protector of agriculture, she could be tough like her father. He let her carry his special shield, the aegis. Anyone who looked at it turned into stone.

• • • • •

Name: Hephaestus (Roman name Vulcan)
Superpower: Really ugly but good with tools. He was the child of Hera. She gave birth to him for revenge on Zeus for giving birth to Athena. Her vengeance was short-lived, however. Hephaestus was lame and considered so ugly that Hera threw him out of heaven. Despite his dysfunctional childhood, he grew up to be the god of the forge and fire and husband of Aphrodite.

• • • • •

Name: Ares (Roman name Mars)
Superpower: Big bad god of war. Well, sort of big and bad. He was the son of Zeus and Hera, both of whom hated him, and he was famous among the Greeks for being a coward. Whenever he was wounded in battle, he would run away. The Romans, on the other hand, saw him as brave and heroic, which might explain how such an angry god could come to be the lover of Aphrodite, goddess of love.

Name: Apollo (No separate Roman name)
Superpower: Son of Zeus and the Titan Leto. God of light, arts, medicine, and music, but he couldn't get a date. When the mortal Cassandra wouldn't return his affections, he cursed her with the gift of foretelling the future. She would always prophesy accurately, but no one would ever believe her.

• • • • •

Name: Artemis (Roman name Diana)
Superpower: Twin sister of Apollo. Goddess of hunting. In her chastity, she protected young girls. Like most of the gods, she had a fiery temper. When a hunter, Actaeon, spied her bathing naked, she turned him into a stag who was torn to pieces by his own dogs. That showed him. In the temple at Ephesus, a statue depicts her with numerous breasts, symbolizing her as a goddess of childbirth.

• • • • •

Name: Aphrodite (Roman name Venus)
Superpower: More seductive than Barry White. Daughter of Zeus and Dione, but in some stories is said to have emerged from the foam of the sea. Goddess of love, made famous by Italian artist Botticelli and 80s pop band, Bananarama. Like her father, she found it difficult to be a faithful spouse. Renowned for her beauty, she cheated on Hephaestus with the likes of Ares, Hermes, Dionysus, and the handsome mortal Adonis.

• • • • •

Name: Hermes (Roman name Mercury)
Superpower: One clever dude. Son of Zeus and the nymph Maia. Messenger of the gods. Of all the gods, he was the most cunning. He was famous for lying and stealing, which might explain why he became known as the god of commerce and the marketplace.

holding out for a *hero*

Mythological heroes form the basis of many of the world's great stories. From Jason and the Argonauts to Oedipus and his mom, stories of daring deeds inform much of what we read today.

• • • • •

The Hero: Jason (and his fellow Argonauts)
Daring Deed: Fetches the legendary Golden Fleece. Jason and his men built the largest ship in the world, the *Argo*, and set sail in search of the fleece. After a lot of sex and violence, they came to Colchis, where the fleece was kept. Before he could snatch it, Jason had to harness fire-breathing cattle, sow a field with dragon teeth, and slay a fierce dragon. He got by with a little help from his friends and from his future wife, Medea, the sorceress. After his fleecy adventures, he married Medea, but the darkest adventure he would endure was the loss of his children. After Jason left Medea for another woman, she killed their children. His story ends with him weeping next to *Argo*. In a final blow, a beam from the ship fell on his head and killed him.

• • • • •

The Hero: Gilgamesh
Daring Deed: Long before Jason, the epic of Gilgamesh, laid the foundation for courage and action. Gilgamesh might be a strange name for a hero, but his actions foreshadowed everyone from Jason to Superman to the X-Men. The intrepid Gil fights a fire-breathing monster, Humbaba, defends his town against rampaging warriors, and takes a long journey across "the waters of death" to fight scorpion-men. You might call him the first action hero.

The Hero: Prometheus
Daring Deed: Stole fire from the gods so that we humans wouldn't freeze our butts off. Born a Titan, Prometheus tricked Zeus into choosing only the bones and fat as the gods' portion of a sacrifice so the humans could feast on meat. Zeus wasn't amused. In his godlike anger, he withheld fire from men, but Prometheus wasn't about to let the poor humans freeze. He stole the fire in a fennel stalk. Now Zeus was really mad. He nailed the hero to a mountain where, every day an eagle tore out his liver. Each night Prometheus' liver regenerated, only to be pecked by the eagle again. Eventually fellow hero Hercules rescued poor Prometheus.

· · · · ·

The Hero: Hercules
Daring Deed: Where do we start? Besides rescuing Prometheus, Greek strongman Hercules managed to kill the Nemean lion; kill the snake-headed Hydra; capture the Erymanthian Boar and the Hind of Artemis; kill the man-eating Stymphalian birds; clean out the really nasty Augean stables; seize the Cretan bull, the horses of Diomedes, and the girdle of Hippolyta; kill the monster Geryon; capture the three-headed dog Cerberus; and steal the dragon-guarded apples of the Hesperides. He had lots of other adventures, but you get the point. This was one busy hero.

pop quiz #1

. . . .

1. How many pages of 8.5 x 11 inch, 20-pound paper does the typical tree make?

2. Which city was the first to establish printing presses in the New World: Cambridge, Massachusetts, or Mexico City?

3. The word *literature* derives from the Latin *littera*, meaning what?

4. What is the Dewey Decimal number for literature?

5. Name the four writers so far who have won a Pen/Nabokov Award.

6. What is the world's richest literary prize for a single work of fiction?

7. Which type of poem would you read at a wedding, an amphigory or an epithalamium?

8. Which type of poem typically has 14 lines, a sonnet or an elegy?

9. Who was the first detective to appear in a British novel?

10. What novel ends with the line, "Matter of fact, I think this the youngest us ever felt. Amen."

. . . . .

Answers
1. 11,500
2. Mexico City in 1533. Cambridge had one established in 1638.
3. Letter
4. 800–899
5. William Gass (2000); Mario Vargas Llosa (2002); Mavis Gallant (2004); Philip Roth (2006)
6. The International IMPAC Dublin Literary Award, valued at 100,000 Irish pounds
7. An epithalamium (wedding poem). An amphigory is a nonsense poem.
8. A sonnet. Elegies can have as many lines as the poet chooses.
9. Inspector Bucket in Charles Dickens' *Bleak House*
10. *The Color Purple*

The Booker Prize

The Brits were not about to be shown up by the Yanks and their Pulitzer Prize. In 1968, the Man Booker Prize for Fiction was founded for the best full-length novel written in English and published in the United Kingdom by a citizen of the Commonwealth or Republic of Ireland.

1969: Percy Howard Newby, *Something to Answer For*
1970: Bernice Rubens, *The Elected Member*
1971: V. S. Naipaul, *In a Free State*
1972: John Berger, *G.*
1973: James Gordon Farrell, *The Siege of Krishnapur*
1974: Nadine Gordimer, *The Conservationist, and Stanley Middleton, Holiday*
1975: Ruth Prawer Jhabvala, *Heat and Dust*
1976: David Storey, *Saville*
1977: Paul Scott, *Staying On*
1978: Iris Murdoch, *The Sea, the Sea*
1979: Penelope Fitzgerald, *Offshore*
1980: William Golding, *Rites of Passage*
1981: Salman Rushdie, *Midnight's Children*
1982: Thomas Keneally, *Schindler's Ark*
1983: J. M. Coetzee, *Life & Times of Michael K*
1984: Anita Brookner, *Hotel du Lac*
1985: Keri Hulme, *The Bone People*
1986: Kingsley Amis, *The Old Devils*
1987: Penelope Lively, *Moon Tiger*
1988: Peter Carey, *Oscar and Lucinda*
1989: Kazuo Ishiguro, *The Remains of the Day*
1990: A.S. Byatt, *Possession: A Romance*
1991: Ben Okri, *The Famished Road*

1992: Michael Ondaatje, *The English Patient,* and Barry Unsworth, *Sacred Hunger*
1993: Roddy Doyle, *Paddy Clarke Ha Ha Ha*
1994: James Kelman, *How Late It Was, How Late*
1995: Pat Barker, *The Ghost Road*
1996: Graham Swift, *Last Orders*
1997: Arundhati Roy, *The God of Small Things*
1998: Ian McEwan, *Amsterdam*
1999: J. M. Coetzee, *Disgrace*
2000: Margaret Atwood, *The Blind Assassin*
2001: Peter Carey, *True History of the Kelly Gang*
2002: Yann Martel, *Life of Pi*
2003: D. B. C. Pierre, *Vernon God Little*
2004: Alan Hollinghurst, *The Line of Beauty*
2005: John Banville, *The Sea*
2006: Kiran Desai, *The Inheritance of Loss*
2007: Ann Enright, *The Gathering*

Wacky Writers

- *Anne Brontë, Stephen Crane, Percy Bysshe Shelley, and Novalis all died when they were 29 years old.*

- *Zane Grey, Yu Hua, and Faye Kellerman all hold the D.D.S. degree.*

- *Barbara Cartland is the most prolific romance writer, with over 600 million copies of her novels in print.*

The basic plot *A–C*

Just as there are all kinds of books, there are all kinds of readers. Some folks love a good mystery. Others want to lose themselves in a sweeping romance. Before digging into a book, sometimes it is nice to know what the basic plot line is. That way you'll know if whether it's a rainy day book, a beach read, or a classic that demands your full and immediate attention. Throughout the *Reader's Bathroom Reader,* we'll introduce you to a world of great plots. Take your pick and jump right in!

$\cdots$

The Aeneid

Virgil's great epic poem, written in Latin in the first century BC, recounts the legendary exploits of Aeneas, the Trojan heartbreaker who became a founding ancestor of the Roman people. The story is divided into twelve books. The first six focus on Aeneas' voyage to Italy. The last six are a romping war story.

In the first half of the epic, Aeneas and his Trojan cohorts find themselves on the shores of Carthage, where beautiful Dido welcomes them with open arms. Aeneas tells her all about the Trojan horse and his flight from Troy. His wife died and, eventually, so did his dad. By Book IV, Aeneas' exciting, sad tales have won over Dido, and she falls for him hard. Nevertheless, he has a larger fate to pursue, so he leaves Dido to go to Sicily. She kills herself in grief. Aeneas goes to Hades and sees the future generations of Romans.

In the second half, Aeneas has another chance at love. King Latinus promises his daughter, Lavinia, to Aeneas. However, Prince Turnus has a prior claim on the maiden, and he is not about to have her stolen away. Turnus assaults the Trojan camp. Lots of battle scenes follow. Ultimately, as the title of the epic suggests, Aeneas kills Turnus. A nice wedding scene between Aeneas and Lavinia should have followed, but you'll have to imagine that for yourself, because Virgil died before he could finish the work.

The Blithedale Romance

Sounds like a Harlequin Romance, but this classic is one of Nathaniel Hawthorne's best. Blithedale is a Utopian community modeled on one in which Hawthorne actually participated in Massachusetts years before writing the novel. The voyeuristic narrator, Miles Coverdale, watches everyone like a hawk. Zenobia, a feminist, falls in love with the misogynist Hollingsworth, a zealous reformer who has the fun idea of converting Blithedale into a place where criminals can be reformed. Zenobia turns out to have a half-sister named Priscilla who falls under the dark influence of Westervelt, a mesmerist. When Hollingsworth falls in love with her, the love-sick Zenobia abandons her feminist ideals and, instead of leaving the jerk for her own independence, goes off and drowns herself. Hollingsworth blows off his prison-reforming plans in the wake of Zenobia's death, and by the end of the story both he and the narrator pine for the lovely Priscilla.

· · · · ·

Crime and Punishment

This is the first of Fyodor Dostoevsky's large works, and in it we already see his gift for acute psychological insight. An impoverished student, Raskolnikov, despairs over his plight. He, his mother, and his young sister struggle daily just to get by, so he hatches a brilliant scheme. He will kill an elderly pawnbroker. As bad luck would have it, he ends up having to kill the pawnbroker's sister too. Guilt slowly eats away at him as all of his rationalizations for the murders dissolve. He feels so disgusted with himself that he can't spend the stolen money. He turns to lovely Sonya Marmeladovna, a hooker with a heart of gold. She persuades Raskolnikov to confess his crime. He gets shipped off to Siberia, but Sonya follows him, and there in the middle of nowhere, he finally finds humility and peace.

Wilde at heart

Leave it to notorious wit Oscar Wilde to put his own unique spin on love and romance. You can't help but laugh at his honest assessment of matters of the heart.

There is nothing so difficult to marry as a large nose.

A man can be happy with any woman, as long as he does not love her.

Always forgive your enemies—nothing annoys them so much.

Between men and women there is no friendship possible. There is passion, enmity, worship, love, but no friendship.

Do you really think it is weakness that yields to temptation? I tell you that there are terrible temptations which it requires strength, strength and courage to yield to.

Hatred is blind, as well as love.

Men always want to be a woman's first love—women like to be a man's last romance.

One should always be in love. That is the reason one should never marry.

The only way to get rid of temptation is to yield to it.... I can resist everything but temptation.

A true friend stabs you in the front.

Bigamy is having one wife too many. Monogamy is the same.

He must have a truly romantic nature, for he weeps when there is nothing at all to weep about.

How can a woman be expected to be happy with a man who insists on treating her as if she were a perfectly normal human being.

How marriage ruins a man! It is as demoralizing as cigarettes, and far more expensive.

I see when men love women. They give them but a little of their lives. But women when they love give everything.

Keep love in your heart. A life without it is like a sunless garden when the flowers are dead.

Men marry because they are tired; women, because they are curious; both are disappointed.

One's past is what one is. It is the only way by which people should be judged.

There is nothing in the world like the devotion of a married woman. It is a thing no married man knows anything about.

Romance should never begin with sentiment. It should begin with science and end with a settlement.

When a man has once loved a woman he will do anything for her except continue to love her.

To love oneself is the beginning of a lifelong romance.

the write stuff:
a glossary of literary terms from A to C

. . . .

Literary terms send your head spinning? Fear not! This list gives you the lowdown on every word you need to sound smart in your book club.

Act – Plays are divided into these, and the curtain usually lowers between them. Shakespeare's plays are composed of five acts. Within those acts are different scenes.

Allegory – A story that means one thing on a literal level but something else on a symbolic level. For example, Hawthorne's story, "Young Goodman Brown" describes a wife named Faith. On the surface, she's just a wife, but she is also symbolic of anyone's religious faith. Allegories often have characters named after concepts, such as Hope or Envy or Love.

Alliteration – A technique typically found in poetry in which the same consonant sound is repeated over and over, usually at the beginning of a word. Such phrases as "long, lush lashes" or "fine furry friends" are examples. Note that it is the sound that gets repeated, not the letter, so the words "cut" and "kitchen" alliterate, even though they begin with different letters.

Allusion – A brief reference to something else, such as a famous person, a historical event, or a specific location, either real or fictional. Allusions require reading and cultural knowledge shared by the author and the reader, so if a story makes an allusion to George Washington and the reader doesn't know who he is, then the allusion doesn't work. Allusions lend authority to texts.

Ambiguity – A literary phrase for "vagueness" or "having more than one meaning." The meaning of a work is ambiguous when different interpretations can equally apply. The meaning of a work is just weak if no one can figure it out.

Antagonist – Officially, the character or force that produces conflict by opposing the main character. Unofficially, the bad guy.

Ballad – Either a song that tells a story and has been passed down through the generations, or a type of poem that imitates a ballad song. Keats's "La Belle Dame sans Merci" would qualify as a ballad.

Blank verse – Unrhymed iambic pentameter. Found often in Shakespeare's plays, this rhythm goes: du-Duh, du-Duh, du-Duh, du-Duh, du-Duh.

Cacophony – Language that sounds harsh and difficult to pronounce, such as this line from John Updike's "Player Piano": "never my numb plunker fumbles." When used intentionally, cacophony mirrors the meaning of the phrase.

Caesura – A pause within a line of poetry. Usually they show up in the middle of the line, sometimes after a comma, sometimes not.

Canon – The "masterpieces." *Moby Dick* would qualify.

Carpe diem – The Latin phrase meaning "seize the day." A common theme in poetry when the writer is concerned about how fast time is passing, or when he wants to persuade a woman to sleep with him because they're both getting older and time is passing.

Catharsis – A fancy word meaning "purgation," as in getting rid of all your emotions at the end of a tragedy. Aristotle first discussed the importance of releasing emotions after a tragedy. He said they teach us something about ourselves.

Cliché – At the end of the day, when it's all said and done, these words or phrases are ugly as sin because they are trite and overused.

Climax – The moment of greatest intensity in a story. Usually there's some kind of decision or confrontation, and things begin to resolve after that.

Closet drama – A play that is written to be read rather than performed onstage.

Colloquial – Conversational or slang words.

Connotation – The meaning of a word is suggested as opposed to its literal, dictionary definition.

proceed with CAUTION

Epigraphs are short quotations that precede a work of literature. They are the stuff you read before you read the stuff (and not to be confused with epitaphs, which are words written on a tombstone). An epigraph is like the opening band before the major act takes the stage.

Did I request thee, Maker, from my Clay
To mould me Man, did I solicit thee
From darkness to promote me?
　Frankenstein, Mary Shelley (comes from Milton's *Paradise Lost*)

Vengeance is mine; I will repay.
　Anna Karenina, Leo Tolstoy (comes from Romans 12:19)

Optima dies…prima fugit
　My Antonia, Willa Cather (comes from Virgil and translates as "in the lives of mortals, the best days are the first to flee")

"Only connect"
　Howard's End, E. M. Forster

Persons attempting to find a motive in this narrative will be prosecuted; persons attempting to find a moral in it will be banished; persons attempting to find a plot in it will be shot.
　The Adventures of Huckleberry Finn, Mark Twain

You are all a lost generation.
　The Sun Also Rises, Ernest Hemingway

For Ezra Pound
il miglior fabbro
　The Waste Land, T. S. Eliot (the phrase translates as "the better craftsman" and comes from Dante)

Already with thee! tender is the night…
But here there is no light,
Save what from heaven is with the breezes blown
Through verdurous glooms and winding mossy ways.
    Tender Is the Night, F. Scott Fitzgerald (comes from John Keats)

When a true genius appears in the world, you may know him by this sign, that the dunces are all in confederacy against him.
    A Confederacy of Dunces, John Kennedy Toole (comes from
    Jonathan Swift)

If the radiance of a thousands suns
were to burst into the sky,
that would be
the splendor of the Mighty One—
    Brighter Than a Thousand Suns, Robert Junck (comes from the
    Bhagavad Gita)

More Famous Firsts

- *The first book printed in the United States was a special translation of the Psalms. In 1640,* The Bay Psalm Book, *named after the Massachusetts Bay Colony, translated the Psalms into metrical rhythm.*

- *The first book entered for copyright was* The Philadelphia Spelling Book *on June 9, 1790.*

- *The first railway bookstall was opened in London in 1848.*

---

no thanks: best-selling books
rejected by at least ten publishers

If at first you don't succeed, try, try again. This old piece of advice worked well for the following writers, who stuck with their manuscripts even when the publishing world told them to hit the road. Look who's laughing now.

. . . . .

Harry Potter and the Sorcerer's Stone, J. K. Rowling
Around a dozen publishers just didn't see the magic in the story of a young wizard studying to vanquish evil, but now they're seeing red as J. K. Rowling rolls in the dough. Her fortune is estimated at over $1 billion. Forbes named her the second wealthiest female entertainer in the world, just behind Oprah Winfrey. The book was originally titled *Harry Potter and the Philosopher's Stone,* but Scholastic, which bought the US rights, thought Americans would be put off by the word "philosopher," so they changed it to something less, um, intimidating. After all, mystical sorcerers are much less off-putting than pesky philosophers.

. . . . .

Dubliners, James Joyce
At one point, Joyce was so upset with the hassle of trying to publish *Dubliners* that he exclaimed, "I regret to see that my book has turned out *un fiasco solenne.*" Publishers wanted him to cut out all of the curse words, to change real place names, and to cut some of the 15 stories they weren't too keen on, but he was having none of it. While they wanted a more tourist-friendly depiction of Dublin, Joyce wanted to portray it as both "dear" and "dirty." After 22 publishers passed on the project, it was finally accepted in 1914 by Grant Richards. Then, to make matters worse, one person bought all of the first editions and burned them because they seemed heretical.

Heaven Knows, Mr. Allison, **Charles Shaw**
Who wouldn't want to publish a funny novel about a Marine corporal shipwrecked on an island with no other companion than a nun? Nevertheless, Shaw was rejected by most Australian and British publishers for three years. Leave it to the Yanks to see a diamond in the rough. An American agent got it printed, and director John Huston adapted it to the screen in 1957. The film version received several Academy Award nominations, including Best Actress, Best Writing, and Best Screenplay Based on Another Medium.

• • • • •

Jonathan Livingston Seagull, **Richard Bach**
Eighteen publishers passed on this "gull in a million" tale of tenacity and nonconformity. But it finally came to print in 1970. From a humble 7,500 copies, the uplifting fable soon sold over 7 million in the US alone by 1975.

• • • • •

Dune, **Frank Herbert**
This 608-page science-fiction winner of the Hugo and Nebula Award was rejected by 13 publishers. They thought it was "too slow," "confusing and irritating," "too long," and, strangest of all, "old-fashioned." Well, this slow, long, old-fashioned megahit went on to sell over 10 million copies.

• • • • •

Lust for Life, **Irving Stone**
The tempestuous life of Vincent van Gogh just didn't appeal to 17 publishers, at least in Irving Stone's version. However, it was finally published in 1934, and in 1956, a film version starring Kirk Douglas won the Oscar for Best Actor in a Supporting Role (Anthony Quinn).

M*A*S*H, Richard Hooker

Can you imagine 1970s television or Robert Altman's career without this book? Hooker's cast of characters we all now know and love—Hawkeye Pierce, Hot Lips Houlihan, Trapper John, and Radar O'Reilly—almost never came to life. Over 20 publishers rejected the novel, but it was finally picked up in 1968.

More Wacky Writers

- *The best-selling German author of all time is Karl May.*

- *V. I. Lenin is the world's most-translated author.*

- *John Creasy is the most prolific mystery writer with 562 books published under 29 pen names.*

- *Marcel Proust, Alexander Pope, and Charles Dickens all suffered from insomnia.*

- *Percy Bysshe Shelley wrote under the following pseudonyms: Mr. Jones, Jeremiah Stukeley, the Hermit of Marlow, John Fitzvictor, and Victor.*

- *Edgar Allan Poe had a cat who used to sit on his shoulder when he wrote. When he was away on a trip, he used to write to her.*

The Pulitzer Prize *1918–1947*

The Pulitzer Prize for Fiction (from 1917-1948, the award was given as the Pulitzer Prize for the Novel) is awarded almost every year "for distinguished fiction by an American author." Each winner receives a gold medal and monetary compensation.

1918: *His Family* by Ernest Poole
1919: *The Magnificent Ambersons* by Booth Arrington
1921: *The Age of Innocence* by Edith Wharton
1922: *Alice Adams* by Booth Tarkington
1923: *One of Ours* by Willa Cather
1924: *The Able McLaughlin* by Margaret Wilson
1925: *So Big* by Edna Ferber
1926: *Arrowsmith* by Sinclair Lewis
1927: *Early Autumn* by Louis Bromfield
1928: *The Bridge of San Luis Rey* by Thornton Wilder
1929: *Scarlet Sister Mary* by Julia Peterkin
1930: *Laughing Boy* by Oliver Lafarge
1931: *Years of Grace* by Margaret Ayer Barnes
1932: *The Good Earth* by Pearl S. Buck
1933: *The Store* by T. S. Stribling
1934: *Lamb in His Bosom* by Caroline Miller
1935: *Now in November* by Josephine Winslow Johnson
1936: *Honey in the Horn* by Harold L. Davis
1937: *Gone With the Wind* by Margaret Mitchell
1938: *The Late George Apley* by John Phillips Marquand
1939: *The Yearling* by Marjorie Kinnan Rawlings
1940: *The Grapes of Wrath* by John Steinbeck
1942: *In This Our Life* by Ellen Glasgow
1943: *Dragon's Teeth* by Upton Sinclair
1944: *Journey in the Dark* by Martin Flavin
1945: *A Bell for Adano* by John Hersey
1947: *All the King's Men* by Robert Penn Warren

burn, baby, burn!

Fahrenheit 451 describes it. So does Heinrich Heine in his play *Almansor* when he writes, "When they have burned books, they will end in burning human beings." Sometimes books are burned for political reason, but sometimes it's just a case of...oops!

• • • • •

King Charles II was not amused by John Milton. Copies of Milton's books were burned publicly in 1660 because he was critical of ol' Charles.

• • • • •

In 1933, Hitler's right-hand man, Dr. Joseph Goebbels, lit a huge bonfire in Berlin, charring "un-German" works by authors such as Einstein, Freud, Gorky, Lenin, Hemingway, and Marx. More than 2,000 books were burned in all. In his usual creepy way, Goebbels said at the rally, "The old lies in the flames, but the new will arise from the flame of our own hearts."

• • • • •

Thomas Carlyle was proud of his *History of the French Revolution,* and sent it to John Stuart Mill to read. Making her daily rounds, however, Mill's maid burned it for wastepaper. Oh, to have a backup file! There was no copy, of course, but Carlyle rewrote it in six months. Feeling guilty, Mill offered him £200 to compensate for his efforts.
Imprisoned and despondent, Sir Walter Raleigh burned a volume of his *History of the World.* He had seen a man killed outside his cell window. When he realized that what he saw differed widely from what two other eyewitnesses reported, he thought to himself, "What chance have I of giving a true picture of the world's history when three eyewitnesses to something that took place just five minutes ago can't agree!"

After the death of British explorer Sir Richard Burton in 1890, his wife, Isabel, burned his 1,282-page translation of *The Perfumed Garden* because she was outraged by the eroticism. On a roll, she went on to destroy 26 of his other books as well, including all his journals and diaries.

· · · · ·

A case of whodunit: Gore Vidal's house burned to the ground when he was writing his third detective novel under the pseudonym Edgar Box. When he tried to rewrite the book, he couldn't remember who the murderer was.

Notes on Novels

- *The first American novel to be adapted to the stage was* The Spy *by James Fenimore Cooper. It premiered in 1821.*

- *The first dime novel, published by Beadle's Dime Novels series, was* Malaeska, the Indian Wife of the White Hunter *by Ann S. Stephens. It sold 200,000 copies its first year.*

- *The first novel published in the United States was William Hill Brown's 1789 book* The Power of Sympathy.

- *The first novel published by an African-American writer was* Clotelle, *published in 1853 by William Wells Brown.*

literary *quips* & quotations

Great authors often have great things to say about literature. So do the rest of us. Whether it's someone as serious as Albert Camus, or someone as hilarious as Groucho Marx, quips and quotations about writing remind us what is so important, and often so funny, about this business called literature.

Outside of a dog, a book is man's best friend. Inside of a dog, it's too dark to read.
— Groucho Marx

I was going to buy a copy of The Power of Positive Thinking, and then I thought: What the hell good would that do?"
— Ronnie Shakes

I often quote myself. It adds spice to the conversation.
— George Bernard Shaw

Someone's boring me. I think it's me.
— Dylan Thomas

I felt like poisoning a monk.
— Umberto Eco, on why he wrote *The Name of the Rose*

Where do I find the time for not reading so many books?
— Karl Kraus

The man who does not read good books is at no advantage over the man that can't read them.
— Mark Twain

The most essential gift for a good writer is a built-in shock-proof shit-detector.
— Ernest Hemingway

I can't understand why a person will take a year or two to write a novel when he can easily buy one for a few dollars.
— Fred Allen

Your borrowers of books—those mutilators of collections, spoilers of the symmetry, and creators of odd volumes.
— Charles Lamb

Books are hindrances to persisting stupidity.
— Spanish Proverb

When I get a little money, I buy books, and if any is left, I buy food and clothes.
— Erasmus

A book is a mirror; if an ass peers into it, you can't expect an apostle to peer out.
— Georg Lichtenberg

Books must be read as deliberately and reservedly as they were written.
— Henry David Thoreau

The reading of all good books is like a conversation with the finest men of past centuries...
— René Descartes

It took me fifteen years to discover I had no talent for writing, but I couldn't give it up because by that time I was too famous.
— Robert Benchley

I think there is a blossom about me of something more distinguished than the generality of mankind.
— James Boswell

I conceived at least one great love in my life, of which I was always the object.
— Albert Camus

I'm an alcoholic. I'm a drug addict. I'm homosexual. I'm a genius.
— Truman Capote

I am, really, a great writer; my only difficulty is in finding great readers.
—Frank Harris

Perfection is such a nuisance that I often regret having cured myself of using tobacco.
— Émile Zola

Books are for nothing but to inspire.
— Ralph Waldo Emerson

Read in order to live.
— Gustave Flaubert

I cannot live without books.
— Thomas Jefferson

All good books are alike in that they are truer than if they really happened and after you finished reading one you will feel that it all happened to you, and afterwards it all belongs to you.
— Ernest Hemingway

Literature is my utopia.
— Helen Keller

Reading is to the mind what exercise is to the body.
—Richard Steele

Books are good enough in their own way, but they are a mighty bloodless substitute for real life.
— Robert Louis Stevenson

"Classic." A book which people praise and don't read.
— Mark Twain

There is no such thing as a moral or an immoral book. Books are well written, or badly written.
— Oscar Wilde

More Wacky Writers

- *Percy Bysshe Shelley disliked cats so much that he tied one to a kite in a storm, hoping it would get electrocuted.*

- *Victor Hugo was only 14 years old when he wrote his first play.*

- *Jack Kerouac was 11 years old when he wrote his first novel.*

- *William Wordsworth wallpapered an entire room with newspapers.*

across the ages through the pages:
brit lit 2

1066–1500: **The Middle English Period**

The Middle English period consists of the literature produced between the Norman Conquest of 1066 and the early 16th century, when what we would recognize as modern English first began to emerge—though from reading such authors as Chaucer, it would still seem mostly like a foreign language. Most of the early works during this time were religious writings, but by the late 1300s, secular literature was becoming more and more common. At least two works you might recognize from the Middle English period are Geoffrey Chaucer's *Canterbury Tales* and the unattributed poem *Sir Gawain and the Green Knight.*

The Canterbury Tales: **The Least You Need to Know**

- Chaucer's original plan was to write 120 tales, according to the General Prologue, the framework for the tales. The plot centers around a poet who has joined 29 other pilgrims on their way to make their annual pilgrimage to visit the shrine of Saint Thomas Becket at Canterbury Cathedral. Their host at the Tabard Inn, Harry Bailly, comes up with the idea of a storytelling contest. Each person on the journey will tell four stories, two on the way to the shrine and two back. The winner will receive a free dinner.

- The tales are important in literary history because they popularized the literary use of English vernacular as opposed to Latin or French. Chaucer's innovations also include the use of the frame narrative, the inclusion of characters from a wide range of social classes, and the diversity of his writing styles, from romances to folktales to sermons to fables.

- Chaucer began the work in the 1380s but stopped working on it ten years later, completing only 24 of the proposed 120 pieces. Nevertheless, the tales that remain include the following:
  - The General Prologue
  - The Knight's Tale
  - The Miller's Prologue and Tale
  - The Reeve's Prologue and Tale
  - The Cook's Prologue and Tale
  - The Man of Law's Prologue and Tale
  - The Wife of Bath's Prologue and Tale
  - The Friar's Prologue and Tale
  - The Summoner's Prologue and Tale
  - The Clerk's Prologue and Tale (also known as The Oxford Cleric)
  - The Merchant's Prologue and Tale
  - The Squire's Prologue and Tale
  - The Franklin's Prologue and Tale
  - The Physician's Tale
  - The Pardoner's Prologue and Tale
  - The Shipman's Tale
  - The Prioress' Prologue and Tale
  - Chaucer's Tale of Sir Topas
  - The Tale of Melibee
  - The Monk's Prologue and Tale
  - The Nun's Priest's Prologue and Tale
  - The Second Nun's Prologue and Tale
  - The Canon's Yeoman's Prologue and Tale
  - The Manciple's Prologue and Tale
  - The Parson's Prologue and Tale
  - Chaucer's Retraction

Sir Gawain and the Green Knight: The Least You Need to Know

- It was written around 1370, but the author is unknown, though usually attributed to the Pearl Poet, someone who is known to have written three other poems, including one called "The Pearl."
- Considered one of the greatest Arthurian tales in English, it has been interpreted as a poem about Christian faith, as a verse about feminine power, and also as an excellent example of the romance, a genre outlining the adventures of a chivalrous knight who must go on a quest, defeat monsters, and win the favor of his lady fair.
- The plot begins in the middle of New Year celebrations at King Arthur's court at Camelot. A green knight arrives out of nowhere and challenges any knight to strike a blow at him with an axe on the condition that, within one year, he gets to return the blow. Sir Gawain, Arthur's nephew, takes him up on the offer and cuts off his head. The Green Knight takes his head and politely leaves. One year later, Sir Gawain searches for the Green Chapel to complete his agreement with the knight. He meets Lord Bertilak and his lovely wife. Like the Green Knight, Bertilak presents an unusual offer: every day he will bring Gawain whatever he kills in his hunting, in exchange for anything Gawain might win at his castle. While Bertilak hunts, Gawain is tempted by his wife. He exchanges the kisses of the lady for hunted boar. On the third day, the lady gives Gawain a green sash that will supposedly protect him from the Green Knight, but Gawain keeps it secret from Bertilak. As a result, when Gawain meets the Green Knight, he gets cut by the knight's blade to represent his dishonesty in not revealing his ownership of the sash. The Green Knight turns out to be Bertilak, who was testing him all along. Gawain returns to Arthur's court wearing the sash as a daily reminder of his sin of dishonesty.

laughing with the bard

. . . .

All's Well That Ends Well

Plot

The King of France has fallen seriously ill. Helena, the daughter of a famous doctor, uses a special potion to heal him. To show his gratitude, he offers her as a bride to Bertram, a young count with whom she is in love. Bertram, however, doesn't love Helena because he considers her socially inferior. The king orders their marriage anyway, but as Bertram writes to his mother as he sends Helena away, "I have sent you a daughter-in-law: she hath recovered the king and undone me. I have wedded her, not bedded her; and sworn to make the NOT eternal."
In fact, he so desperately wants to get away from Helena that he joins other French soldiers in a battle against Florence, claiming that he will not return until Helena manages to do two things: obtain a ring from his finger and bear his child. Helena remains undeterred. She disguises herself and goes to Florence, swaps places with Bertram's Florentine girlfriend, takes his ring, and becomes pregnant. Bertram hears that Helena has died, so he returns to France, only to discover that she is alive and pregnant. He realizes that he does love her and, as the title puts it, that all is well that ends well.

Themes

1. Judge people on their inner worth, not on their social standing. Bertram was wrong to assume Helena was an unworthy mate simply because she lacked his wealth.
2. Even if events unfold terribly, a happy ending makes everything all right. Helena suffers greatly for love, but once she finally wins her man, the world feels restored.

crying with the bard

. . . .

Antony and Cleopatra

Plot

Shakespeare assumes that the audience is familiar with the story of the assassination of Julius Caesar, and the formation of the triumvirate of rulers: Mark Antony, Octavius Caesar, and Marcus Aemilius Lepidus. During ensuing political struggle, Antony calls Queen Cleopatra of Egypt to Tarsus to explain Egypt's position. Instead of discussing politics, they fall in love, and he returns with her to Alexandria. The play begins at this point, with Antony having given up the life of the warrior for the life of hedonism. When he hears that Italy has been attacked and that his wife has died, he returns to Rome. He weds the sister of Octavius, which helps reunite the original triumvirate. However, Antony cannot stay away from Cleopatra for long. He returns to her in Egypt, and in retaliation for the insult to his sister, Octavius attacks his ally. Antony, failing to negotiate the peace and defeated in battle, wrongly believes Cleopatra is dead. In despair, he falls on his sword in an attempt to commit suicide. When he hears that Cleopatra is, in fact, still alive, he survives just long enough to kiss her good-bye. After his death, Cleopatra chooses to kill herself rather than live as Octavius' captive.

Themes

1. Reckless passion leads to disaster. Antony and Cleopatra cannot live without each other. As a result, they suffer military defeat and, ultimately, death.
2. Pride goes before a fall. Cleopatra's suicide is only partly motivated by her broken heart. She also refuses to allow Octavius to parade her in Rome as a captive, for she would rather die than suffer such humiliation.

learning with the bard

The Second part of King Henry IV
Plot

As the adventures of Prince Hal continue in this "sequel," his father, King Henry IV, suffers from insomnia when his guilt over usurping the throne from Richard II does not allow him to sleep. He is aging and growing ill. Prince Hal, having defeated Hotspur, returns to Falstaff and his friends at the pub. Meanwhile, the rebellion against the king continues to thrive. Prince Hal's brother, John of Lancaster, meets with the rebels and vows to hear their complaints if they will disperse. They agree only to have John go back on his word, arrest their leaders, and execute them. As the king lies dying, he hears this news and advises Prince Hal to rectify the situation. When Henry IV dies, Hal is named king, much to Falstaff's delight. He sees this as an opportunity to party with a higher class of friends, but Hal is having none of it. As the new King Henry V, he promptly turns his back on his reckless youth and tells Falstaff that he must stay away from him now.

Themes

1. One must keep good company. Although Falstaff has proven a festive friend, he is unfit company for the new King Henry V. Loyalty is a virtue, though, and to that end Hal is willing to maintain his friendship with Falstaff, but only if he agrees not only to grow up but also to sober up.
2. The necessity of atonement. King Henry IV wishes all of his life to travel to the Holy Land to atone for his sins against Richard II. Unable to do so, his son, Henry V will have to take up the mantel of battle to fight off the insurrections that prevented Henry IV from making peace. Likewise, as Prince Hal becomes Henry V, he must atone for his checkered past and learn to become a responsible, worthy king.

rhyme time 1: *poetry for children*

Isaac Watts

The first book of poetry written especially for children did not appear until 1715. *Divine Songs for Children*, by Isaac Watts, was a collection of verses designed to teach Christian lessons. Here was a typical poem:

"Praise to God for Learning to Read"

1 The praises of my tongue
I offer to the Lord,
That I was taught, and learnt so young
To read his holy Word.

2 That I am taught to know
The danger I was in,
By nature and by practice too
A wretched slave to sin.

3 That I am led to see
I can do nothing well;
And whither shall a sinner flee,
To save himself from hell?

Soon thereafter, children's verse developed from moral instruction to, well, this verse from the 1744 volume *Tommy Thumb's Pretty Song Book*:

Little Robin redbreast
Sitting on a pole,
Niddle, Noddle,
Went his head,
And Poop went in his Hole.

William Blake

A major romantic poet, William Blake made a substantial contribution
to children's poetry as well. In 1789, his book *Songs of Innocence*
featured poems about God and love, which he targeted to children as
well as adults. "The Lamb" and "Infant Joy" are two famous examples.
His next book, *Songs of Experience* (1794), while also a collection of
poetry, was definitely geared to a more mature audience, as Blake
explored such themes as evil and death.

· · · · ·

Clement C. Moore

The special holiday magic Clement C. Moore tapped into continues
to shape our ideas about Christmas in the modern era. On Christmas
Eve in 1822, Moore, a teacher at an Episcopal seminary in New York,
retired to his study for a few hours. When he came out, he read aloud
to his family a little poem he had written called "'Twas the Night Before
Christmas." He published it the next year in the newspaper, and it has
been famous ever since.

> *"Like any good writer, I write to amuse myself, not some*
> *imaginary audience, and I rather suspect that it is a great help*
> *if one has managed never really to grow up. Some writers,*
> *I have noticed, have a tendency to write down to children.*
> *That way lies disaster."*
>
> — E. B. White, author of *Charlotte's Web*

The Carnegie Medal in Literature: *1936-1975*

In 1936, this award was established in the United Kingdom for the outstanding book for children and young adult readers. It was named in honor of Scottish philanthropist Andrew Carnegie and is given annually to a book written in English and published in Britain within the previous year. The winner receives not only a gold medal but £500 worth of books that he or she can donate to a school or public library. Here is a list of winners since 1936:

1936: Arthur Ransome, *Pigeon Post*
1937: Eve Garnett, *The Family from One End Street*
1938: Noel Streatfeild, *The Circus Is Coming*
1939: Eleanor Doorly, *Radium Woman*
1940: Kitty Barne, *Visitors from London*
1941: Mary Treadgold, *We Couldn't Leave Dinah*
1942: "B. B." (D. J. Watkins-Pitchford), *The Little Grey Men*
1943: No award given
1944: Eric Linklater, *The Wind on the Moon*
1945: No award given
1946: Elizabeth Goudge, *The Little White Horse*
1947: Walter De La Mare, *Collected Stories for Children*
1948: Richard Armstrong, *Sea Change*
1949: Agnes Allen, *The Story of Your Home*
1950: Elfrida Vipont Foulds, *The Lark on the Wing*
1951: Cynthia Harnett, *The Wool-Pack*
1952: Mary Norton, *The Borrowers*
1953: Edward Osmond, *A Valley Grows Up*
1954: Ronald Welch (Felton Ronald Oliver), *Knight Crusader*
1955: Eleanor Farjeon, *The Little Bookroom*
1956: C. S. Lewis, *The Last Battle*
1957: William Mayne, *A Grass Rope*

1958: Philippa Pearce, *Tom's Midnight Garden*
1959: Rosemary Sutcliff, *The Lantern Bearers*
1960: Dr. I. W. Cornwall, *The Making of Man*
1961: Lucy M. Boston, *A Stranger at Green Knowe*
1962: Pauline Clarke, *The Twelve and the Genii*
1963: Hester Burton, *Time of Trial*
1964: Sheena Porter, *Nordy Bank*
1965: Philip Turner, *The Grange at High Force*
1966: No award given
1967: Alan Garner, *The Owl Service*
1968: Rosemary Harris, *The Moon in the Cloud*
1969: K. M. Peyton, *The Edge of the Cloud*
1970: Leon Garfield and Edward Blishen, *The God Beneath the Sea* (illustrated by Charles Keeping)
1971: Ivan Southall, *Josh*
1972: Richard Adams, *Watership Down*
1973: Penelope Lively, *The Ghost of Thomas Kempe*
1974: Mollie Hunter, *The Stronghold*
1975: Robert Westall, *The Machine Gunners*

Shakespearean Trivia

- *The only Shakespearean play that doesn't have a song in it is* The Comedy of Errors.

- *More than 400 films have been made from Shakespeare's plays.*

Young Adult Lit

Literature for young adults differs from children's fiction and juvenile fiction in a few important ways. Young adult (YA to your librarian) fiction focuses on the awkward adolescent years, when the protagonist of the story is too old for childish things, but not yet ready for the adult world. As such, the plots often revolve around coming-of-age narratives in which young men or women first begin to develop character and learn who they really are.

In 1802, British author and publisher Sarah Trimmer helped define the genre of YA literature in her journal, *The Guardian of Education*. For her, young adulthood spanned the ages of 14 to 21, and although the Victorians at the time did not recognize a separate youth culture, Trimmer noted that many works would be best suited for this unique audience. Major titles from the Victorian era include:

The Swiss Family Robinson (1812)

Oliver Twist (1838)

The Count of Monte Cristo (1844)

Tom Brown's Schooldays (1857)

Great Expectations (1860)

Alice's Adventures in Wonderland (1865)

Little Women (1868)

Tom Sawyer (1876)

Heidi (1880)

Treasure Island (1883)

Huckleberry Finn (1884)

Kidnapped (1886)

The Jungle Book (1894)

As YA literature moved into the 20th century, such books as *Rebecca of Sunnybrook Farm* (1903), *Anne of Green Gables* (1908), and *Johnny Tremain* (1943) captivated young readers. Since then, an explosion of talent has catapulted the genre into the literary mainstream.

Quotes on Children's Lit

All children's books are on a strict judgment poor books. Books written entirely for children are poor even as children's books.

—J. R. R. Tolkien, author of The Hobbit

One talks about writing for children—this is all piffle. There's no such thing as writing for children.

—Richard Adams, author of Watership Down.

I am trying to write for my readers the best story, the truest story of which I am capable.… We know that those of us who write for children are called, not to do something to a child, but to be someone for a child."

— Katherine Paterson, author of Bridge to Terabithia

ya lit: adventure/survival

··

The True Confessions of Charlotte Doyle, Avi
Thirteen-year-old Charlotte Doyle leaves England in 1832 to be
reunited with her parents. As the only female aboard *The Seahawk,*
Charlotte leaves her pampered life behind and learns to become a
resourceful young lady.

·····

Overboard, Elizabeth Fama
Emily had always felt like an outsider on the island of Sumatra, so she
runs away to meet her uncle on a nearby island. Disaster strikes when
the ferry she takes sinks, leaving her to try to swim ashore. She survives
with the help an Indonesian boy and his strong faith.

·····

Julie of the Wolves, Jean Craighead George
Thirteen-year-old Julie, an Eskimo, has been promised in marriage to
someone she doesn't love, so she runs away from home and survives in
Alaska by joining a wolf pack.

·····

Holes, Louis Sachar
Stanley Yelnats is sent to a correctional camp for a crime he didn't
commit. He is sentenced to a term digging holes in a dry lake bed, but
eventually he breaks the family curse of bad luck when he discovers
friendship, treasure, and more.

·····

Tomorrow When the War Began, John Marsden
Seven Australian teenagers come home after a week camping in the
bush to discover their animals have been killed, their families have

been taken prisoner, and their country occupied by invading foreign troops. The group of friends must decide whether they should fight back or surrender.

• • • • •

How I Live Now, Meg Rosoff
Winner of the Guardian Children's Fiction Prize 2004, *How I Live Now* tells the story of 15-year-old Daisy, who moves to England to live with her cousins. War breaks out and England becomes occupied. How will Daisy and her cousins fare during hostile times?

More Wacky Writers

• *Hans Christian Anderson had a terrible fear of being burned to death. He used to carry a piece of rope with him to slide out a window whenever he spent the night away from home.*

• *Samuel Johnson once shaved off all of his arm and chest hair just to see how long it would take for it to grow back.*

• *T. E. Lawrence liked to be spanked with a birch rod.*

• *Nathaniel Hawthorne was such a good friend to Herman Melville that he dedicated* Moby Dick *to him.*

"from books to movies for 100, please, alex."

It might be surprising to find that some major films were actually adaptations from short stories or novels. Below is a list of the lesser known book-to-film progressions.

Category: Action Films

Die Hard (from book titled *Nothing Lasts Forever*), Richard Thorp
Get Carter, Ted Lewis
Man on Fire, A. J. Quinnell
Mercury Rising (from book titled *Simple Simon*), Ryne Douglas Pearson
Rabbit-Proof Fence, Doris Pilkington
Gangs of New York, Herbert Asbury

Category: Comedies

Adaptation (from book titled *The Orchid Thief*), Susan Orlean
Big Bounce, Elmore Leonard
Cheaper by the Dozen, Frank B. Gilbreth Jr.
About a Boy, Nick Hornby
Chocolat, Joanne Harris
Forrest Gump, Winston Groom
Fried Green Tomatoes, Fannie Flagg
High Fidelity, Nick Hornby
Shopgirl, Steve Martin
Thank You for Smoking, Christopher Buckley
The Witches of Eastwick, John Updike
Thumbsucker, Walter Kirn

Common Phrases and Their Origins

Phrase: A bird in hand is worth two in the bush.
Meaning: It's better for one to have an assured small advantage or victory than the slight chance at a bigger one.
Origin: In the Bible (Ecclesiastes 9 to be exact) one can find the following adage: "A living dog is better than a dead lion." Later, in 1530, Hugh Rodes' *The Boke of Nurture or Schoole of Good Maners* quotes, "A byrd in hand – is worth ten flye at large." Clearly, the adage has evolved over time, and now there are even many pubs across Western society named the Bird in Hand.

· · · · ·

Phrase: The apple of my eye
Meaning: Literally, the central region of the eye; figuratively, something cherished above all other things.
Origin: The phrase first appeared in a work by King Aelfred of Wessex titled *Gregory's Pastoral Care*. In modern English, its first use is noted in *Old Mortality* by Sir Walter Scott: "Poor Richard was to me as an eldest son, the apple of my eye." The adage also appears in Deuteronomy 32:10.

· · · · ·

Phrase: Baker's dozen
Meaning: Thirteen, rather than the normal dozen.
Origin: It is believed that in medieval times, English bakers would often give out an extra loaf of bread when selling one dozen to avoid being accused of short-selling a customer. The practice seems to have begun centuries before the phrase was coined.

pen names of *famous pen holders* #1

Author: George Eliot
Famous Works: *Silas Marner, Middlemarch*
Real Name: Mary Ann Evans

Author: Mark Twain
Famous Works: *The Adventures of Tom Sawyer, Adventures of Huckleberry Finn, The Prince and the Pauper*
Real Name: Samuel Langhorne Clemens

Author: Lewis Carroll
Famous Works: *Alice's Adventures in Wonderland, Through the Looking Glass*
Real Name: Charles Lutwidge Dodgson

Author: Voltaire
Famous Works: *Candide, La Princesse de Babylone*
Real Name: François-Marie Arouet

Author: O. Henry
Famous Works: "The Furnished Room," "The Gift of the Magi"
Real Name: William Sydney Porter

the 411 *on a few short stories*
• •

"A Good Man Is Hard to Find" – Flannery O'Conner

This famous piece of short fiction by Catholic writer Flannery O'Conner appears in the esteemed collection of short fiction of the same title, *A Good Man Is Hard to Find.* In the story, a family is in the car on a trip with their pestering and old-fashioned grandmother when they have an accident, flipping the car in a ditch on the side of the road. On the scene of the accident appears a man with two accomplices, and the family soon realizes that the man is a serial killer known as the Misfit. The grandmother continues to plead with the Misfit as her family members are taken, one by one, into the woods and shot. Even though she insists that the Misfit is, indeed, a good man, he still shoots her three times in the chest, ending the story but not the decades of interpretations, criticism, and praise the piece has garnered.

• • • • •

"A Rose for Emily" – William Faulkner

This story, one of Faulkner's most famous, was first published in 1930 and takes place in a fictional city called Jefferson, Mississippi. The story follows an eccentric woman named Emily Grierson, who has become somewhat of an enigma in the town. After her father's death, Emily refused to enter the town, pay her taxes, or bother with the upkeep of her home. She is seen often with a man named Homer, rumored to be her lover, however peculiar. When Homer disappears, the townspeople assume that he, a transient worker, has simply left Emily. Many years later, when Emily is old and frail, she finally passed away. When townspeople enter her home, they find, astonishingly, the corpse of Homer, lying in her bed next to an impression in the mattress that suggests that Emily has, in fact, been sleeping with his corpse for decades.

A Timeline of the Greatest
in World Lit

· ·

Literature of the Ancients
- 2575 BC – Earliest fragments of Egyptian poetry composed
- 2000 BC – Legends about King Gilgamesh appear
- 1500 BC – Egyptian *Book of the Dead*
- 1300 BC – The epic of *Gilgamesh* written down
- 1000 BC – The Torah assembled
    - David and his son, Solomon, reign in Israel
    - Composition of Psalms
- Ca. 550 BC – Aesop, *Fables*
- Ca. 500 BC – Heraclitus, *On Nature*
- Ca. 450 BC – Herodotus, *The Histories*
- 397 BC – Plato, *The Apology*

Beginnings of Western Thought
- Ca. 700 BC – Homer, the *Iliad,* the *Odyssey*
- 600 BC – Sappho, poems
- Ca. 450–411 BC – Greek tragedies including Aeschylus, *The Oresteia;* Sophocles, *Antigone,* and Euripides, *Medea*

Earliest Works from the East
- Ca. 1400 BC – The Sanskrit *Rig Veda*
- Ca. 1000 BC – *I Ching*
- Ca. 900 BC – The Sanskrit *Upanishads*
- 550 BC – Confucius, the *Analects*
- Ca. 400 BC – The Sanskrit Indian war epic, *The Mahabharata*
- 100–200 BC – The beginning of 5-character-line Chinese poetry
- 1st century AD – *The Bhagavad-Gita*
- AD 750 – *The Man'yoshu,* Japanese poems
- 1001 – Murasaki Shikibu, *The Tale of Genji*
- 1375 – *Epic of Son-Jara*

- 1399 – Hindu epic *The Ramayana*
- 1573–1620 – Poetry of Yuan Hongdao
- 1627 – Wen Zhengen, "Treatise on Superfluous Things"
- 1716–1797 – Poetry of Yüan Mei
- 1791 – Cao Zhan, *Dream of the Red Chamber*

The Spread of the Roman Empire
- Ca. 83–53 BC – The poetry of Gaius Valerius Catullus
- Ca. 30 BC – Virgil, *The Aeneid*
- 87–54 BC – Catullus, poems
- 43 BC–AD 17 – Ovid, *Metamorphosis*
- AD 51 – Cicero, *De re publica*
- Ca. AD 86 – Plutarch, *Parallel Lives*
- Ca. AD 60 – Pliny the Elder, *Natural History*
- Ca. AD 69 – Tacitus, *Historiae*
- AD 96 – Quintilian, *On the Training of an Orator*

The Rise of Christianity
- AD 100 – Completion of Matthew, Mark, Luke, and John
- AD 367 – New Testament canon established
- Ca. AD 393–405 – Jerome translates the Bible into Latin
- AD 397 – Augustine, *Confessions*

The Rise of Islam
- AD 510–622 – Arabic oral heroic poetry
- AD 622–750 – Ghazals (love lyrics) invented
- AD 610–632 – The Qu'ran
- AD 813–833 – *The Thousand and One Nights*
- 1177 – Attar, *The Conference of the Birds*

The Beginnings of Western Literature
- 9th century – *Beowulf*
- 12th century – The *Lais* of Marie de France

- 1301–1321 – Dante, *The Divine Comedy*
- 1335 – Petrarch, sonnets
- 1353 – Boccaccio, *The Decameron*
- 1381 – *Sir Gawain and the Green Knight*
- 1390–1400 – Chaucer, *The Canterbury Tales*
- 1405 – Christine de Pizan, *The Book of the City of Ladies*

European Renaissance

- 1511 – Erasmus, *The Praise of Folly*
- 1517 – Luther, 95 Theses
- 1528 – Castiglione, *Book of the Courtier*
- 1532 – Machiavelli, *The Prince*
- 1551 – Sir Thomas More, *Utopia*
- 1597–1604 – Cervantes, *Don Quixote*
- 1611 – Shakespeare, *Hamlet*
- 1626 – Francisco Gómez de Quevedo, *Historia de la vida del Buscón*
- 1655 – Milton, *Paradise Lost*

European Enlightenment

- 1664 – Jean-Baptiste Poquelin Moliere, *Tartuffe*
- 1677 – Jean Racine, *Phaedra*
- 1717 – Alexander Pope, *The Rape of the Lock*
- 1719 – Daniel Defoe, *Robinson Crusoe*
- 1726 – Jonathan Swift, *Gulliver's Travels*
- 1751 – Denis Diderot, *Encyclopédia*
- 1759 – Voltaire, *Candide*
- 1766 – Jean-Jacques Rousseau, *Confessions*
- 1792 – Mary Wollstonecraft, *Vindication of the Rights of Woman*

European Romanticism

- 1781–1788 – Jean-Jacques Rousseau, *Confessions*
- 1798 – William Wordsworth and Samuel Taylor Coleridge, *Lyrical Ballads*

- 1808 – Johann Wolfgang von Goethe, *Faust, Part I*
- 1827 – Heinrich Heine, *Book of Songs*
- 1834 – Alexander Sergeyevich Pushkin, *The Queen of Spades*
- 1837 – Honoré de Balzac, *César Birotteau*
- 1845 – Frederick Douglass, *Narrative of the Life of Frederick Douglass, an American Slave*
- 1847 – Charlotte Bronte, *Jane Eyre*
- 1867 – Karl Marx, *Das Capital*
- 1871–1893 – Émile Zola, *Les Rougon-Macquart*
- 1882 – Arne Garborg, *Peasant Students*
- 1890 – Emily Dickinson, *Poems*
- 1891 – André Gide, *The Notebooks of Andre Walter*

Late 19th-Century Europe
- 1856 – Gustave Flaubert, *Madame Bovary*
- 1857 – Charles Baudelaire, *The Flowers of Evil*
- 1866 – Fyodor Dostoevsky, *Crime and Punishment*
- 1869 – Leo Tolstoy, *War and Peace*
- 1871 – George Eliot, *Middlemarch*
- 1871 – Arthur Rimbaud, *The Drunken Boat*
- 1890 – Henrik Ibsen, *Hedda Gabler*
- 1896 – Anton Chekhov, *The Seagull*

The Modern World
- 1908 – Anatole France, *Penguin Island*
- 1912–1922 – Rainer Maria Rilke, *The Duino Elegies*
- 1913 – Rabindranath Tagore, *The Crescent Moon*
- 1914 – Kotaro Takamura, *Dotei (Journey)*
- 1922 – James Joyce, *Ulysses*
- 1927 – Virginia Woolf, *To the Lighthouse*
- 1929 – Gabriel Garcia Lorca, *Poet in New York*
- 1935 – Kawabata Yasunari, *Snow Country*
- 1938 – Bertolt Brecht, *The Good Woman of Setzuan*

- 1940 – Richard Wright, *Native Son*
- 1944 – Jorge Luis Borges, *The Garden of Forking Paths*
- 1948 – Ezra Pound, *Pisan Cantos*
- 1954 – Kojima Nobuo, *The American School*
- 1956–1957 – Naguib Mahfouz, *The Cairo Trilogy*
- 1958 – Chinua Achebe, *Things Fall Apart*
- 1959 – Eugène Ionesco, *Rhinoceros*
- 1960 – Marguerite Duras, *Hiroshima mon amour*
- 1963 – Anna Akhmatova, *Requiem*
- 1967 – Gabriel García Márquez, *One Hundred Years of Solitude*
- 1972 – Sawako Ariyoshi, *The Twilight Years*
- 1975 – Wole Soyinka, *Death and the King's Horseman*
- 1976 – Maxine Hong Kingston, *The Woman Warrior*
- 1980 – Anita Desai, *Clear Light of Day*
- 1982 – Isabel Allende, *The House of Spirits*
- 1988 – Salman Rushdie, *The Satanic Verses*
- 1981 – Leslie Marmon Silko, *Ceremony*
- 2004 – Orhan Pamuk, *Snow*

Forbidden books have been around for a long time. The first Index of Forbidden Books *came out in 1559, published by the Sacred Congregation of the Roman Inquisition. It was revised up until 1948.*

---

flying blind:
authors with vision trouble

What worse fate could befall a writer than to lose one's vision? Nevertheless, many authors have had to contend with poor or no eyesight and yet have managed to produce works that still blind us with their brilliance.

• • • • •

Jean-Paul Sartre
Perhaps it isn't surprising that the existentialist Sartre, with such dark titles as *Being and Nothingness,* would become virtually blind toward the end of his life. He was able to continue writing by dictation. The words he wrote were so powerful that over 50,000 people attended his funeral.

• • • • •

William Wordsworth
The romantic poet of such lines as "But breath and eye-sight fail, and, one by one / The dogs are stretch'd among the mountain fern" found that his own eyesight was failing in his later years. Eventually he could only read for 15 minutes at a time.

• • • • •

Carson McCullers
Author of *The Member of the Wedding* and *Reflections in a Golden Eye,* McCullers suffered a series of strokes in her 20s from a childhood case of rheumatic fever. She lost sight in her right eye and suffered partial paralysis, so rarely could she write more than a page a day.

• • • • •

Ernest Hemingway
Hemingway's poor eyesight prevented him from joining the army in World War I, so he drove an ambulance near the Italian front. Later

in life, he read up to three books a week, in addition to indulging his passions for hunting and fishing, so the fear of losing his vision haunted him and contributed to his depression.

• • • • •

Fyodor Dostoevsky

Epilepsy was a recurring theme in Dostoevsky's life and writing. In his notebooks, he documented 102 seizures. During one of the seizures, he injured his right eye, which caused it to be permanently distended.

• • • • •

James Joyce

Many photographs of Joyce show him wearing an eye patch. No, he wasn't imitating a pirate. Instead, he underwent numerous eye operations stemming from an early bout of glaucoma. His great work *Ulysses* was written when his vision was severely blurred by recurring iritis. He had to use a magnifying glass to see words. In fact, some literary scholars theorize that his unusual use of language owes, in part, to his difficulty with seeing words on the page.

• • • • •

John Milton

Like the paradise of which he wrote, Milton's vision too was lost by the time he was 46 years old. He was able to finish *Paradise Lost* by composing verses in his head each night and dictating them the next day to his three daughters or to Andrew Marvell. "He sacrificed his sight, and then he remembered his first desire, that of being a poet," Jorge Luis Borges wrote.

• • • • •

Jorge Luis Borges

Perhaps Borges was so interested in Milton's blindness because he too lost his vision. "I knew I would go blind, because my father, my paternal grandmother, my great-grandfather, they had all gone blind," he once said. Before going blind, however, he used his eyes tirelessly, writing numerous stories and essays, cataloging books in the Buenos Aires Municipal Library, and directing the National Library in Argentina. "I speak of God's splendid irony in granting me at once 800,000 books and darkness," he said, as he took the library position with his vision failing.

• • • • •

Aldous Huxley
The author of *Brave New World* originally wanted to become a doctor. However, as a student at Eton, he developed a streptococcal infection in his eyes. He was blind for an entire year. Although he eventually recovered his sight, his vision was never very good after that.

• • • • •

James Thurber
In "The Secret Life of Walter Mitty," James Thurber describes a henpecked husband who escapes into a rich fantasy life of daydreams. Thurber's own imagination was heightened as his vision decreased. When he was seven years old, he lost sight in one eye after an accident involving a bow and arrow. What was left of his vision slowly decreased until the 1950s, when he became legally blind.

drama queens:
Pulitzer Prize for drama 1918–1950

It's high drama for the winner of the Pulitzer. The cash prize of $7,500 for the playwright plus a world premiere for a theater production equals enough to earn applause all around. Here's a list of winners (for years not listed, no award was given).

1918: *Why Marry?*, Jesse Lynch Williams
1920: *Beyond the Horizon*, Eugene O'Neill
1921: *Miss Lulu Bett*, Zona Gale
1922: *Anna Christie*, Eugene O'Neill
1923: *Icebound*, Owen Davis
1924: *Hell-Bent Fer Heaven*, Hatcher Hughes
1925: *They Knew What They Wanted*, Sidney Howard
1926: *Craig's Wife*, George Kelly
1927: *In Abraham's Bosom*, Paul Green
1928: *Strange Interlude*, Eugene O'Neill
1929: *Street Scene*, Elmer L. Rice
1930: *The Green Pastures*, Marc Connelly
1931: *Alison's House*, Susan Glaspell
1932: *Of Thee I Sing*, George S. Kaufman, Morrie Ryskind, and Ira Gershwin
1933: *Both Your Houses*, Maxwell Anderson
1934: *Men in White*, Sidney Kingsley
1935: *The Old Maid*, Zöe Akins
1936: *Idiot's Delight*, Robert E. Sherwood
1937: *You Can't Take It with You*, Moss Hart and George S. Kaufman
1938: *Our Town*, Thornton Wilder
1939: *Abe Lincoln in Illinois*, Robert E. Sherwood
1940: *The Time of Your Life*, William Saroyan

1941: *There Shall Be No Night,* Robert E. Sherwood
1943: *The Skin of Our Teeth,* Thornton Wilder
1945: *Harvey,* Mary Chase
1946: *State of the Union,* Russel Crouse and Howard Lindsay
1948: *A Streetcar Named Desire,* Tennessee Williams
1949: *Death of a Salesman,* Arthur Miller
1950: *South Pacific,* Richard Rodgers, Oscar Hammerstein II, and
     Joshua Logan

Pleonasm

*Pleo-*what? *Pleonasm! A pleonasm occurs when a person
uses more words or word-parts to express an idea than are
necessary. Some examples are:*

- *Null and void*
- *Terms and conditions*
- *Tuna fish sandwich*
- *Down south*
- *Future plans*
- *First began*

- *Protest against*
- *Reason why*
- *Blend together*
- *Face up to the facts*
- *Safe haven*
- *Free gift*

The basic plot *D–F*

The plots thicken. Check out these great reads.

• • • • •

A Doll's House

If this 1879 Ibsen play were written in the 1970s, it could have been called "I Am Woman, Hear Me Roar." *A Doll's House* tells the story of Nora, the pampered, sheltered wife of the patronizing Torvald. His pet names for her include "songbird" and "little squirrel," which tells you all you need to know about him. He fell ill early in their marriage, and in order to get the money to pay for his medical bills, Nora forged some papers. His pride would have been wounded if he had known that she had squirreled away the cash necessary to save him, so Nora never tells. Unfortunately, her secret is discovered by Krogstad, a disgruntled employee of Torvald's bank. He threatens to blackmail Nora. Eventually Torvald discovers the truth about her "crime." Never mind the fact that she saved his life. He berates her so harshly that by the time he tries to apologize for his cruel words, she is outta there. The play ends with her slamming the door, leaving Torvald in the dust.

• • • • •

Eugene Onegin

What makes this Russian novel so interesting is that it is written entirely in verse. Aleksandr Pushkin portrays the life of troubled hero Eugene. The social scene in St. Petersburg has bored poor Eugene to tears, so he heads out to a country estate, where he meets Tatyana, who, like many women, falls in love with him. He passes on her charms, preferring, instead, to pick a fight with the romantic poet Lensky. They duel. Eugene wins. Lensky dies. Eugene returns to the St. Petersburg social scene, not quite as bored as before. Tatyana follows him home and comes to an important realization. Browsing through his book collection, it dawns on her what a shallow putz Eugene is. She bids him farewell, goes off and marries a prince, and becomes the toast of St. Petersburg. Of course, now Eugene is interested in her, but Tatyana, though still in love with him for some odd reason, resists his affections out of duty to her husband.

· · · · · ·

For Whom the Bell Tolls

If you like Hemingway, then ask not for whom the bell tolls. It tolls for thee, dear reader. Grab a copy of this 1940 tale set against the backdrop of the Spanish civil war. Robert Jordan opens the story as an idealistic American who has come to Spain to enlist in the Republican army. He gets assigned to a band of guerrillas who are to blow up a bridge. Amidst the excitement of war, Robert falls in love with Maria, the beautiful, tragic girl who has been raped by Fascists— all the more reason for Robert to continue on with his guerrilla tactics. He blows up the bridge, despite his fears that he will die in the process. He is wounded and left on the hillside to die.

Henrik Ibsen's Crazy Habits

• *Henrik Ibsen began writing everyday at 4:00 a.m.*

• *He wrote with a pet scorpion on his desk.*

• *He had an affair with a 27-year-old when he was 63.*

---

some nice alliteration:
Pulitzer Prize for Poetry 1918–1940

It's hard to make a living as a poet, but winning the Pulitzer Prize for Poetry at least gets you a tasty $10,000, plus your name among some really impressive company.

1918: "Love Songs," Sara Teasdale
1919: "Old Road to Paradise," Margaret Widdemer; "Corn Huskers," Carl Sandburg
1922: *Collected Poems,* Edwin Arlington Robinson
1923: "The Ballad of the Harp-Weaver," Edna St. Vincent Millay
1924: "New Hampshire: A Poem with Notes and Grace Notes," Robert Frost
1925: "The Man Who Died Twice," Edwin Arlington Robinson
1926: "What's O'Clock," Amy Lowell
1927: "Fiddler's Farewell," Leonora Speyer
1928: "Tristram," Edwin Arlington Robinson
1929: "John Brown's Body," Stephen Vincent Benét
1930: *Selected Poems,* Conrad Aiken
1931: *Collected Poems,* Robert Frost
1932: "The Flowering Stone," George Dillon
1933: "Conquistador," Archibald MacLeish
1934: *Collected Verse,* Robert Hillyer
1935: "Bright Ambush," Audrey Wurdemann
1936: "Strange Holiness," Robert P. T. Coffin
1937: "A Further Range," Robert Frost
1938: "Cold Morning Sky," Marya Zaturenska
1939: *Selected Poems,* John Gould Fletcher
1940: *Collected Poems,* Mark Van Doren

Papa knows best

When it comes to writing, who knows more than Ernest Hemingway? Master of minimalist prose, he has more than just a few words to share about the craft of fiction. Here's a sampling of some of his wit and wisdom about writing.

In stating as fully as I could how things really were, it was often very difficult and I wrote awkwardly and the awkwardness is what they called my style. All mistakes and awkwardness are easy to see, and they called it style.

They can't yank a novelist like they can a pitcher. A novelist has to go the full nine, even if it kills him.

When I am working on a book or a story I write every morning as soon after the first light as possible. There is no one to disturb you and it is cool or cold and you come to your work and warm as you write.

A writer's problem does not change. He himself changes and the world he lives in changes, but his problem remains the same. It is always how to write truly and, having found out what is true, to project it in such a way that it becomes a part of the experience of the person who reads it.

When people talk, listen completely. Most people never listen.

A serious writer is not to be confounded with a solemn writer. A serious writer may be a hawk or a buzzard or even a popinjay, but a solemn writer is always a bloody owl.

All good books are alike in that they are truer than if they had really happened.

All modern American literature comes from one book by Mark Twain called Huckleberry Finn.

All my life I've looked at words as though I were seeing them for the first time.

Ezra [Pound] was right half the time, and when he was wrong, he was so wrong you were never in any doubt about it.

For a long time now I have tried simply to write the best I can. Sometimes I have good luck and write better than I can.

I don't like to write like God. It is only because you never do it, though, that the critics think you can't do it.

If a writer knows enough about what he is writing about, he may omit things that he knows. The dignity of movement of an iceberg is due to only one ninth of it being above water.

It's none of their business that you have to learn how to write. Let them think you were born that way.

Madame, all stories, if continued far enough, end in death, and he is no true story-teller who would keep that from you.

My aim is to put down on paper what I see and what I feel in the best and simplest way.

Pound's crazy. All poets are. They have to be. You don't put a poet like Pound in the loony bin.

Prose is architecture, not interior decoration, and the Baroque is over.

That is what we are supposed to do when we are at our best—make it all up—but make it up so truly that later it will happen that way.

The good parts of a book may be only something a writer is lucky enough to overhear or it may be the wreck of his whole damn life and one is as good as the other.

There are events which are so great that if a writer has participated in them his obligation is to write truly rather than assume the presumption of altering them with invention.

There is no friend as loyal as a book.

There is no rule on how to write. Sometimes it comes easily and perfectly; sometimes it's like drilling rock and then blasting it out with charges.

There is nothing to writing. All you do is sit down at a typewriter and bleed.

When writing a novel a writer should create living people; people not characters. A character is a caricature.

Writing and travel broaden your ass if not your mind and I like to write standing up.

~~banned~~!

Nothing makes you want to read a book more than to know that at one time it was banned. Such classics as *Ulysses, Slaughterhouse Five,* and *The Great Gatsby* have all been challenged in the past as books that should be removed from libraries, if they should have even been printed at all. What would the literary landscape look like without the following banner banned books?

· · · · ·

Bad Book: *The Great Gatsby,* F. Scott Fitzgerald
Rap Sheet: Baptist College in Charleston, South Carolina (1987), challenged the teaching of Fitzgerald's classic because of "language and sexual references in the book."

· · · · ·

Bad Book: *The Sun Also Rises,* Ernest Hemingway
Rap Sheet: Hemingway was no rising star when his book was banned in Boston, Massachusetts (1930), Ireland (1953), and in Riverside, California (1960). Not to be outdone, however, the Nazis burned it in bonfires in 1933.

· · · · ·

Bad Book: *The Lord of the Flies,* William Golding
Rap Sheet: Golding's harrowing tale was challenged at the Owen, North Carolina, High School (1981) because the book was "demoralizing inasmuch as it implies that man is little more than an animal."

Bad Book: *Of Mice and Men,* John Steinbeck
Rap Sheet: Perhaps if Steinbeck had titled his classic *Of Mice and Businessmen* things wouldn't have gotten too heated. His novel was challenged as a reading assignment for summer school kids in Chattanooga, Tennessee, in 1989 because "Steinbeck is known to have had an anti-business attitude." To add insult to injury, "he was very questionable as to his patriotism."

• • • • •

Bad Book: *Ulysses,* James Joyce
Rap Sheet: Oh sure, the Modern Library chose this book as the best novel of the 20th century, but what do they know? The good folks at the New York Post Office found *Ulysses* so shocking that in 1922 they burned all copies of it. Joyce was used to fanning the flames of controversy, however. Recalling how his book *Dubliners* had been burned years before, he said, "This is the second time I have had the pleasure of being burned while on Earth. I hope it means I shall pass through the fires of purgatory unscathed." The lifting of the US ban in 1933 came only after advocates fought for the right to publish the book. It was burned in the United States (1918), Ireland (1922), Canada (1922), and England (1923) and later banned in England in 1929.

• • • • •

Bad Book: *One Flew Over The Cuckoo's Nest,* Ken Kesey
Rap Sheet: In 1974, five people in Strongsville, Ohio, sued the board of education to remove Kesey's book. They claimed it was "pornographic," and they listed its offences. It supposedly "glorifies criminal activity, has a tendency to corrupt juveniles and contains descriptions of bestiality, bizarre violence, torture, dismemberment, death," and, perhaps most heinous of all, "human elimination."

Bad Book: *The Lord of the Rings,* J. R. R. Tolkien
Rap Sheet: As recently as 2001, folks in Alamagordo, New Mexico, burned this novel outside Christ Community Church along with other Tolkien novels, claiming they were satanic. The question remains: What did they think of the movies?

· · · · ·

Bad Book: *The Catcher in the Rye,* J. D. Salinger
Rap Sheet: In 1960, an English teacher in Tulsa, Oklahoma, was fired for assigning Salinger's novel to her 11th-grade class. (She was later reinstated, but the book was taken out of the school library.) In 1963, a group of Ohio parents asked the school board to ban the novel because they considered it "obscene" and "anti-white." (The school board refused their request.) School boards in the following cities have been challenged for allowing *The Catcher in the Rye* in the classroom:

Pittsgrove, New Jersey (1977)
Issaquah, Washington (1978)
Middleville, Michigan (1979)
North Jackson, Ohio (1980)
Anniston, Alabama (1982)
Morris, Manitoba (1982)
New Richmond, Wisconsin (1994)
De Funiak Springs, Florida (1985)
Medicine Bow, Wyoming (1986)
Napoleon, North Dakota (1987)
Linton Stockton, Indiana (1988)
Boron, California (1989)
Waterloo, Iowa (1992)
Duval County, Florida (1992)
Carlisle, Pennsylvania (1992)
New Richmond, Wisconsin (1994)
Corona Norco, California (1993)
Goffstown, New Hampshire (1994)

St. Augustine, Florida (1995)
Paris, Maine (1996)
Brunswick, Georgia (1997)
Marysville, California (1997)
Limestone County, Alabama (2000)
Savannah, Georgia (2000)
Summerville, South Carolina (2001)
Glynn County, Georgia (2001)

• • • • •

Bad Book: *The Grapes of Wrath,* John Steinbeck
Rap Sheet: Steinbeck's novel has faced all kinds of wrath from folks
as far away as Turkey for its language and mature content. In 1939,
the East St. Louis, Illinois, Public Library burned it. In the same year,
the Buffalo, New York, public library banned it because of its "vulgar
words." In 1973, several Turkish book publishers went on trial for
"spreading propaganda" with it. More recently, it was challenged in
1991 in the Greenville, South Carolina, schools because the book uses
the names of God and Jesus in a "vain and profane manner along with
inappropriate sexual references."

• • • • •

Bad Book: *To Kill a Mockingbird,* Harper Lee
Rap Sheet: The racial themes and language in Lee's portrayal of
southern life have caused many to want to "kill" this 1961 Pulitzer
Prize winner. In 1977, the book was temporarily banned because the
words "damn" and "whore lady" appear in the novel. In 1980, the
Vernon Verona Sherill (New York) school district deemed it a "filthy,
trashy novel." In the following year, the Warren, Indiana, township
schools ruled that the book does "psychological damage to the
positive integration process" and "represents institutionalized racism
under the guise of good literature." In 1985, the book was kept on
an eighth-grade reading list in the Casa Grande, Arizona, elementary

school district despite protests by the National Association for the Advancement of Colored People, who argued that the book was not appropriate for junior high readers. As recently as 2004, the Stanford Middle School in Durham, North Carolina, was challenged for allowing the book to be taught because of the use of the word "nigger."

• • • • •

Bad Book: *The Color Purple,* Alice Walker
Rap Sheet: It may have become a film and a musical, but Walker's novel received heaps of criticism prior to its cinematic and Broadway debuts. In 1984, it was challenged as appropriate reading in an Oakland, California, high school honors class because of its "sexual and social explicitness" and its "troubling ideas about race relations, man's relationship to God, African history and human sexuality." Nine argumentative months later, the weary Oakland Board of Education allowed its use. In 1986, in Newport News, Virginia, only students 18 and older, or with permission notes from their parents, were allowed to check out the book. The word "smut" was used to describe the book after it was banned in the Souderton, Pennsylvania, area school district in 1992. Finally, a group who called themselves Parents Against Bad Books in Schools challenged the novel in the Fairfax County, Virginia, school libraries in 2002. No one, however, seems to have challenged the name "Parents Against Bad Books in Schools."

poet laureate:
the big poetic cheese *1937–1974*

The Library of Congress has penned a wordy job description to the role of poet laureate: "The Poet Laureate Consultant in Poetry to the Library of Congress serves as the nation's official lightning rod for the poetic impulse of Americans. During his or her term, the Poet Laureate seeks to raise the national consciousness to a greater appreciation of the reading and writing of poetry." Here's a list of "lightning rods." See how many you recognize.

. . . . .

1937–1941: Joseph Auslander
  Vital Stats: Born in Philadelphia in 1897. Died in 1965.
  Best Known For: War poetry. Wrote "The Unconquerables" in 1943.
  Fun Facts: Married to Audrey Wurdemann, who won a Pulitzer Prize for Poetry. She came by it naturally—she was the great-great-granddaughter of Percy Bysshe Shelley.

. . . . .

1943–1944: Allen Tate
  Vital Stats: Born in Kentucky in 1899. Died in 1979.
  Best Known For: A founding member of the Fugitives, which sounds like a rock group but actually was a group of southern poets, including Robert Penn Warren, John Crowe Ransom, and Donald Davidson.
  Fun Facts: Won the Bollingen Prize in 1956. Was a professor of English at the University of Minnesota until his death.

. . . . .

1944–1945: Robert Penn Warren
  Vital Stats: Born in Kentucky in 1905. Died in 1989.

Best Known For: Poetry, yes, but also his novel *All the King's Men*, which won the Pulitzer Prize in 1947.

Fun Facts: OK, he also won two Pulitzers for poetry—one for his volume *Promises* in 1958 and "Now and Then" in 1979.

• • • • •

1945–1946: Louise Bogan

Vital Stats: Born in Maine in 1897. Died in 1970.

Best Known For: Formal poetry. Her *Collected Poems 1923-1953* won a Bollingen Prize in 1954.

Fun Facts: She reviewed poetry for 38 years for *The New Yorker* magazine. She didn't like confessional poetry, so many a confessional poet probably received rejection letters from her.

• • • • •

1946–1947: Karl Shapiro

Vital Stats: Born in Baltimore in 1913. Died in 2000.

Best Known For: His Pulitzer Prize-winning collection *V-Letter and Other Poems.*

Fun Facts: He can thank his fiancée for his early publications. While he was serving in World War II, he sent poems to her and she had them printed for him.

• • • • •

1947–1948: Robert Lowell

Vital Stats: Born in Massachusetts in 1917. Died in 1977.

Best Known For: He is considered the father of confessional poetry. For his efforts, he received the Pulitzer Prize in 1947 for "Lord Weary's Castle."

Fun Facts: His volume *Life Studies* represented a major turning point in American poetry. His confessional verse drew from his own unique life, including dropping out of Harvard, converting to Catholicism, being imprisoned during World War II as a conscientious objector, and suffering numerous episodes of manic depression.

• • • • •

1948–1949: Leonie Adams
Vital Stats: Born in New York in 1899. Died in 1988.
Best Known For: Her collection of poetry *Poems: A Selection* won the Bollingen Prize in 1954.
Fun Facts: Wrote poems in secret at Barnard College. Became friends with Hart Crane, with whom she shares a birthday.

• • • • •

1949–1950: Elizabeth Bishop
Vital Stats: Born in Massachusetts in 1911. Died in 1979.
Best Known For: Won the Pulitzer Prize, the National Book Award, and a National Book Critics Circle Award for her poetry, which often focuses on geography.
Fun Facts: OK, not such a fun fact: Her father died when she was only eight months old, and her mother was committed to a mental institution when she was five. Lived in Brazil for 15 years. She once said to fellow poet Robert Lowell, "When you write my epitaph, you must say I was the loneliest person who ever lived."

• • • • •

1950–1952: Conrad Aiken
Vital Stats: Born in Georgia in 1889. Died in 1973.
Best Known For: Poetry which delves into psychological themes. Won the Pulitzer in 1930 for *Selected Poems,* the National Book Award in 1954 for *Collected Poems,* and the Bollingen Prize.
Fun Facts: Again, not such a fun fact. His father killed his mother and then committed suicide.

1952: William Carlos Williams
Vital Stats: Born in New Jersey in 1883. Died in 1963.
Best Known For: One of the major American modernists. Most famous for the poem about the red wheelbarrow.
Fun Facts: When he wasn't writing poetry, he spent most of his time as a pediatrician.

· · · · ·

1956–1958: Randall Jarrell
Vital Stats: Born in Tennessee in 1914. Died in 1965.
Best Known For: World War II poetry, including "The Death of the Ball Turret Gunner."
Fun Facts: Was well known as a poetry critic too. Compared W. H. Auden to "someone who keeps showing how well he can hold his liquor until he becomes a drunkard."

· · · · ·

1958–1959: Robert Frost
Vital Stats: Born in San Francisco in 1874. Died in 1963.
Best Known For: The epitome of the New England poet. Wrote one of the most famous American poems, "The Road Not Taken." Won 4 Pulitzers and 44 honorary degrees.
Fun Facts: He read at John F. Kennedy's inauguration. Because the sunlight was so bright, he couldn't read from his prepared poem, so he just recited "The Gift Outright" from memory.

· · · · ·

1959–1961: Richard Eberhart
Vital Stats: Born in Minnesota in 1904. Died in 2005.
Best Known For: He received the Pulitzer Prize in 1966 for *Selected Poems 1930–1965*, and a 1977 National Book Award for *Collected Poems 1930–1976*.
Fun Facts: Do the math. He died at the ripe old age of 101.

1961–1963: Louis Untermeyer
Vital Stats: Born in New York City in 1885. Died in 1977.
Best Known For: Anthologizing poetry in such collections as *Modern American Poetry* and *Modern British Poetry* (1969).
Fun Facts: Was also well known for his amusing conversations. He became a panelist on the TV show *What's My Line?* in 1950.

· · · · ·

1963–1964: Howard Nemerov
Vital Stats: Born in New York City in 1920. Died in 1991.
Best Known For: His *Collected Poems* won both the National Book Award and the Pulitzer Prize.
Fun Facts: Served as a pilot for the Royal Canadian unit of the US Army Air Corps over the North Sea during World War II.

· · · · ·

1964–1965: Reed Whittemore
Vital Stats: Born in Connecticut in 1919.
Best Known For: Witty, ironic poetry and for founding *Furioso*, a Yale literary magazine.
Fun Facts: Served in the US Army Air Corps during World War II, but then traded in his uniform for professorial robes as he taught English at the University of Maryland for 17 years.

· · · · ·

1965–1966: Stephen Spender
Vital Stats: Born in London in 1909. Died in 1995.
Best Known For: Social protest poetry. Hung out with fellow poets W. H. Auden and Christopher Isherwood.
Fun Facts: Was knighted in 1983.

1966–1968: James Dickey
Vital Stats: Born in Georgia in 1923. Died in 1997.
Best Known For: His volume *Buckdancer's Choice* (1965), which won
the National Book Award in 1966, but he might be best known for
his novel *Deliverance.*
Fun Facts: He was a guitar-pickin', heavy-drinkin', animal-huntin' poet
who read at Jimmy Carter's inauguration.

• • • • •

1968–1970: William Jay Smith
Vital Stats: Born in Louisiana in 1918.
Best Known For: Ten collections of his own poetry and translations
of French, Hungarian, Dutch, and Brazilian poetry.
Fun Facts: Studied at Oxford University as a Rhodes Scholar.

• • • • •

1970–1971: William Stafford
Vital Stats: Born in Kansas in 1914. Died in 1993.
Best Known For: The poem "Traveling Through the Dark." He also
published more than 65 books of poetry and prose.
Fun Facts: His first volume of poetry was published when he was 46
years old. He wrote every day before the sun came up.

• • • • •

1971–1973: Josephine Jacobsen
Vital Stats: Born in Canada in 1908. Died in 2003.
Best Known For: Nine volumes of poetry for which she won the
Robert Frost Medal for Lifetime Achievement in Poetry in 1997.
Fun Facts: Her first poem appeared in print when she was only ten
years old.

1973–1974: Daniel Hoffman
Vital Stats: Born in New York City in 1923.
Best Known For: His volume *An Armada of Thirty Whales* (1954), was selected by W. H. Auden for the Yale Series of Younger Poets. Since then he won the Paterson Poetry Prize and was named a finalist for the National Book Award in 1985.
Fun Facts: He has lived over 40 years in Swarthmore, Pennsylvania, with his wife. Swarthmore College awarded him an honorary Doctor of Humane Letters degree.

More Wacky Writers

- *Joseph Conrad had a serious gambling problem. In 1878, his debts were so bad that he tried to shoot himself but survived.*

- *When he was feeling depressed, Graham Greene used to play Russian roulette.*

- *Vladimir Nabokov was an avid butterfly collector.*

- *Marcel Proust was so germ-phobic that if he dropped a pen on the floor, he refused to pick it up again.*

- *Wilkie Collins never married, but he had three illegitimate children with one woman, all the while living with another.*

- *Lord Byron fathered a child with his half-sister Augusta Leigh.*

poetry survival manual 1

Sometimes poetry is downright difficult. Here are some simple tricks to allow anyone to read like a professor.

Paradise Lost
The Trick: Read for enjambment.
Directions: Simply put, a line of poetry is "enjambed" if it carries over to the next line. In other words, it isn't end-stopped. Here's an example of some lines of poetry that are not enjambed:

> Roses are red.
> Violets are blue.
> Sugar is sweet.
> So are you.

Each line is a full, complete sentence on its own—it is end-stopped. The poet is telling the reader to stop at the end of the line (big clue: where there is a period) and pause for a second.

Sometimes, though, poets carry a thought over to the next line, thereby "enjambing" it. Here's an example:

> Roses are
> red. Violets are
> blue. Sugar
> is sweet. So are
> you.

The words are the same, but they are arranged on the lines differently and produce a different meaning. There is a natural, brief pause after the first line. A moment of suspense is built in when a line enjambs. Not only that, but enjambing a line produces, temporarily, a meaning all its own. Line one says "Roses are," which invites the reader to just sit with that phrase a while, pondering what roses are. They may be red, they may be fragrant, etc. Regardless, though, first and foremost they just simply are and therein lies some of their value.

A great poet, such as John Milton, will use enjambment to allow multiple interpretations of a single line. Here's the first two lines of his masterpiece *Paradise Lost:*

> Of Man's First Disobedience, and the Fruit
> Of that Forbidden Tree, whose mortal taste

This first sentence of the poem actually goes on for ten lines and basically says "Hey, Muse, sing about the fall of mankind in the Garden of Eden." That, however, wouldn't be very poetic, so Milton starts the whole entire epic with an enjambed line that emphasizes two things: sin and fruit, which is to say, bad stuff and good stuff. Man is on the left side, fruit on the right. The temptation is built into the architecture of the line. The fruit looks pleasing. There it is, just dangling there on the end of line one with no comma or period to anchor it, making the reader want to grab it and take a little bite.

But line one enjambs into line two, where Milton offers a little more information about that tasty fruit. Turns out it comes from a "Forbidden" tree, and just one taste will (as line three will tell) bring death into the world. The words fruit and taste tempt us to keep reading at the end of each line. They swirl over into the next line, luring the reader along, in the same way that Satan lured Eve many years ago.

Since the basic plot of *Paradise Lost* is the story of Adam and Eve, the poem can be appreciated for its enjambments, and the reader can discover how Milton deepens the tale simply by where he chooses to end a line.

weird book titles
· ·

Oh sure, there are a million Chicken Soup for the Soul titles out there, but how many times do you come across books with such strange titles as these?

The Unconscious Significance of Hair —George Berg, 1951

Truncheons: Their Romance and Reality —Erland Clark, 1935

The Inheritance of Hairy Ear Rims —Reginald Gates & P. N. Bhaduri

Why People Move —Jorge Balan (Ed.), 1981

A Toddler's Guide to the Rubber Industry —D. Lowe, 1947

Violence as Communication —Alex Schmid & Janny De Graaf, 1982

The Pleasures of the Torture Chamber —John Swain, 1931

I Knew 3000 Lunatics —Victor Small, 1935

How to Boil Water in a Paper Bag —Anon., 1891

Let's Make Some Undies —Marion Hall, 1954

Teach Yourself Alcoholism —Meier Glatt, 1975

Build Your Own Hindenburg —Alan Rose, 1983

Tosser, Gunman —Frank Carr, 1939

Grow Your Own Hair —Ron MacLaren, 1947

The Magic of Telephone Evangelism —Harold Metcalf, 1967

The Bright Side of Prison Life —Captain S. A. Swiggert, 1897

Old Age: Its Cause and Prevention —Sanford Bennett, 1912

Would Christ Belong to a Labor Union? —Rev. Cortland Myers, 1900

The Rubaiyat of a Scotch Terrier —Sewell Collins, 1926

ain't misbehavin' 1

Oh yes, they were! As these details reveal, some authors stir up quite a ruckus once they step away from the typewriter.

· · · · ·

While Charles Dickens was working on his novel *Our Mutual Friend,* he was in the middle of a love affair with a "friend," the actress Ellen Ternan. Returning from France with Ellen and her mother, the three were in a serious train wreck. Theirs was the only car not to fall into a stream when the train jumped the tracks. Dickens heroically helped rescue fellow passengers, but when he feared that others would see him with Ellen, he fled the scene.

· · · · ·

When not penning *The Communist Manifesto,* Karl Marx could be quite the fun guy to hang out with. One night in London, he went with two friends on a pub crawl with the goal of drinking something in every bar from Oxford Street to Hampstead Road. Considering how many watering holes there were, this was no mean feat, but they pulled off their "beer trip" without incident until some British men taunted the group of Germans, making fun of their politics and culture. Marx and his buddies defended Germany, but words almost turned to violence, so they hightailed it out of the bar. Remembering their schoolboy pranks, they grabbed rocks and hurled them at gaslights, breaking four or five. The wild night ended with their outrunning the police.

· · · · ·

Children's author Shel Silverstein was best friends with, of all people, *Playboy* founder Hugh Hefner. He wrote cartoons, little poems, and travelogues for the magazine and lived in the Playboy mansion for a while. Women were always hitting on him. In fact, one Playmate of the Year made him a needlepoint, which he framed and put on his wall. It said, "Shel Silverstein made me make this for him."

· · · · ·

Theodore Geisel (Dr. Seuss) was a bit of a wild child during his undergraduate days at Dartmouth College. Disappointed over not receiving any offers to pledge a fraternity, he became the editor of *Jack-O-Lantern*, Dartmouth's humor magazine. When Ted and his friends got caught throwing a wild party, however, the only way he could continue to write for the *Jack-O-Lantern* was under a pseudonym, Seuss. Later he was voted by fellow classmates as "least likely to succeed."

· · · · ·

Who can forget Jack Nicholson's portrayal of evil writer Jack Torrance in *The Shining*? What many viewers of the film and readers of the novel may not realize is that Stephen King based the character of Torrance on himself. For years he abused alcohol and drugs until the late 1980s, when his friends and family asked him to seek treatment.

· · · · ·

Best known for his novels *The Moonstone* and *The Woman in White*, Victorian writer Wilkie Collins was anything but a typical Victorian prude. He lived with Caroline Graves and her daughter but began an affair with Martha Rudd, who bore him three children. Graves left him to marry someone else but divorced and returned to Collins two years later. From then on, he divided his time between his two families, all the while battling a serious opium addiction.

· · · · ·

James Dickey was well respected by critics, but his remarks about fellow writers could hit below the belt. He called Edmund Wilson a "tiresome kind of old literary hack," and he chose the decidedly anti-poetic slur "super-jerk" to describe beloved American poet Robert Frost.

. . . . .

Like Dickey, Vladimir Nabokov could be quite insulting about fellow writers. In discussing Joseph Conrad's work he once said, "I cannot abide his souvenir-shop style, bottled ships, and shell necklaces of romantic clichés."

Frost Medal for Distinguished Achievement

The Poetry Society of America awards the Frost Medal each year to recognize the lifetime achievements of a poet. Past winners include:

1998: Stanley Kunitz	*2003: Lawrence Ferlinghetti*
1999: Barbara Guest	*2004: Richard Howard*
2000: Anthony Hecht	*2005: Marie Ponjot*
2001: Sonia Sanchez	*2006: Maxine Kumin*
2002: Galway Kinnell	

---

across the ages through the pages:
brit lit 3

1500–1660: The Renaissance

While the Renaissance, as we commonly use the term, began in Italy in the 14th century, it flourished in England with the ascent of King Henry VII of the House of Tudor to the English throne in 1485. More emphasis was placed on "humanism," that is, on humankind's artistic and intellectual capabilities instead of religious devotion. Universities arose and more writers began writing in the vernacular (the local language) in addition to Greek and Latin. Renaissance literature usually encompasses the Elizabethan Age, the Jacobean Age, the Caroline Age, and the Commonwealth or Puritan period.

· · · · ·

1558–1603: The Elizabethan Age

Not surprisingly, the Elizabethan Age of British literature begins with the reign of Elizabeth I from 1558 to 1603, a period in which Renaissance optimism and vitality began to overtake medieval tradition. Poetry, particularly the sonnet, and drama were the major styles of literature that poured from the pens of such heavy hitters as William Shakespeare and Christopher Marlowe.

Christopher Marlowe: The Least You Need to Know

- He is considered the father of English tragedy and the greatest Elizabethan dramatist writing before Shakespeare.
- His plays include *Tamburlaine the Great* (1587), *Dr. Faustus* (1601), *The Jew of Malta* 1589), and *Edward II* (1594), although some scholars believe he helped write some of Shakespeare's plays, including *Henry IV* and *Richard II*. Some even believe he was Shakespeare and just used the name as a pseudonym.
- His life is the stuff of legend. Although we don't know many historical facts, it is widely believed that he was a homosexual, a

spy, and a heretic. Despite the fact that he studied the Bible and theology at Cambridge, he abandoned his studies to carry out some sort of secret mission for the government. Most likely he was employed by the secretary of state of Queen Elizabeth to find out Catholic plots against her. In 1589, he was accused of murder and spent two weeks in prison, and he was later charged with counterfeit and deported from the Netherlands. Ultimately, at the age of 29, he was stabbed above the eye and killed in a brawl over who was supposed to pay a bar bill. However, some historians maintain that he was murdered for political reasons.

· · · · ·

1603–1625: The Jacobean Age

During the Jacobean Age, covering the time of the reign of James I, from 1603 to 1625, literature became more serious and political, but it also gave rise to such metaphysical poets as John Donne and Andrew Marvell.

Metaphysical Poetry: The Least You Need to Know

- The metaphysical poets were a group of 17th-century writers that included John Donne, Andrew Marvell, George Herbert, Henry Vaughan, and Thomas Traherne.
- The name "metaphysical" refers to the fact that the poets attempt to transcend reality, so that their poetry often reflects on beauty as a symbol of something more perfect in the divine realm. Often written about beautiful women and sexual relationships, their poetry is marked by its wit and complicated metaphors.
- The poetry of John Donne, one of the most famous of the metaphysical poets, moved from erotic works to religious poems. In the metaphysical tradition, he found ways to talk about love that were highly sophisticated yet very funny. For instance, in one of his most famous poems, "The Flea," the speaker attempts to seduce a woman by arguing that since a flea has bitten both him and her,

> *In his own personal life, Donne secretly married the love of his life, the 17-year-old Anne More, who bore him 11 children.*

and their blood is mixed in the insect's body, then they are practically married already. So what's wrong, he asks, with a little more mixing of bodily fluids?

• Donne was ordained in the Church of England, received a doctor of divinity degree from Cambridge, and then was made dean of St. Paul's in 1621. Naturally his poetry followed his religious leanings, most notably his Holy Sonnets. His "Meditation XVII" was the source of Hemingway's title *For Whom the Bell Tolls.*

• Andrew Marvell, another metaphysical poet, wrote one of the most famous poems of the 17th century, "To His Coy Mistress." Like Donne's poem "The Flea," it serves as a seduction poem. His method of persuasion is to invoke the idea of carpe diem, literally, "seize the day." The speaker tells the reluctant lady, "Had we but world enough and time / This coyness, Lady, were no crime." However, he argues, since they aren't getting any younger, they should go ahead and sexually consummate their relationship: "Now let us sport while we may," he says.

. . . . .

1625–1649: The Caroline Age

The beginning of the reign of Charles I, who ruled from 1625 to 1649, inaugurates the elegant Caroline Age. Emerging during this time, were the writers known as the "Cavalier Poets," most notably Robert Herrick, Richard Lovelace, Edmund Waller, and Thomas Carew. They were Royalists during the Civil Wars; their opponents, supporters of Parliament, were given the unfortunate name of "Roundheads." The work of the Cavalier Poets embodied the life of wealthy, pre-Commonwealth England.

Cavalier Poetry: The Least You Need to Know
- Also known as "sons of Ben," the cavalier poets claimed playwright and poet Ben Jonson as their literary father because they aspired to his urbane and witty sophistication.
- Robert Herrick lived the life of a country vicar, but at the same time, he wrote such erotic poems as "To the Virgins, to Make Much of Time," whose carpe diem argument for trying to seduce a young woman became one of the most popular songs of the age. His work fell out of fashion until the end of the 18th century, when critics rediscovered his simple pastoral images and playful rhymes. Victorian writer Charles Swinburne called Herrick "the greatest song writer...ever born of English race."
- Richard Lovelace penned the famous lines: "Stone walls do not a prison make / Nor iron bars a cage."   He knew what he was talking about. In 1646, after the capture of King Charles, Lovelace fought unsuccessfully for the king. He was soon captured and imprisoned in Peterhouse Prison in Aldersgate, where he wrote many poems.
- A courtier of Charles I, Thomas Carew was a libertine whose poem "A Rapture" was regarded as the most notorious erotic poem of the 17th century, probably because of such lines as the following: "There, my enfranchised hand, on every side / Shall o'er thy naked polish'd Ivory slide."

· · · · ·

1649–1660: The Commonwealth (or Puritan) Period
Puritan leader Oliver Cromwell exerted the strongest influence over this period of literature, and the dramatic arts were hit the hardest. In 1642, the Puritans closed the theaters claiming that they were immoral, and they remained closed until 1660. In the interim, writers such as John Milton were forced to turn their attentions to political or religious themes.

John Milton: The Least You Need to Know

- Milton is widely regarded as one of the most important writers in English literature, not only for his epic poem *Paradise Lost* but also for such prose works as *Areopagitica*, his famous argument against censorship.

- Before the English Civil War, Milton supported the Puritans by writing pamphlets and serving as Latin secretary to Oliver Cromwell. The vast amount of writing the job required, in addition to the creative writing he was doing on his own, eventually cost him his eyesight. He was assisted in his work by poet Andrew Marvell. In 1660, following the Restoration of Charles II, Milton was arrested as a defender of the Commonwealth, but Marvell intervened to help him avoid prison. Blind, old, and politically disillusioned, he turned to the comfort of his writing and published his masterpiece, *Paradise Lost.* Because he could not see, the poem was only able to be written with the help of his three daughters, who served as secretaries.

- Milton chose an epic style for *Paradise Lost* to tell the story of Adam and Eve and the fall from the Garden of Eden. He wanted the style to compete with the ancients such as Homer and Virgil, whose epics he had studied. Milton was a child when Shakespeare died, so he had always felt the playwright's powerful influence as well. It took him six years to complete the poem, and it was finally published in 1667, one year after the Great Fire of London. Milton sold the copyright to his publisher for a mere £10.

- *Paradise Lost* features Satan as a hero who wrestles with his own ambitions and doubts as he comes to terms with the creation of humankind. His evil ultimately undoes him, but nevertheless he is a fascinating character who famously proclaims that it is "better to reign in Hell than serve in Heaven."

laughing with the bard

The Comedy of Errors

Plot

A case of mistaken identity is unavoidable in a play that begins like
this: Aegeon and his wife, Aemilia, have twin sons, both of whom are
named Antipholus. After a shipwreck, one is carried to Ephesus and
the other to Syracuse. Each brother has a slave named Dromio, who are
also twins. The plot primarily revolves around Antipholus of Syracuse
searching for his brother, who marries a woman named Adriana.
Adriana mistakes the brother from Syracuse for her husband and later
has her actual spouse arrested. A kitchen maid falls in love with Dromio
from Syracuse. After much confusion, everyone ends up in court, where
one Antipholus recognizes the other. Romantic alliances are restored
as their mother is reunited with their father, who had come to Ephesus
looking for his lost son. Antipholus of Ephesus is reconciled with his
wife, and Antipholus of Syracuse becomes engaged to her sister.

Themes

1. Reckless family loyalty will bring everyone together in the end.
   Aegeon searches for his lost son, risking everything to find him.
2. Never give up, even in the face of bewildering confusion. Both pairs
   of men named Antipholus and Dromio could dissolve into frustration
   at their lots in life, but instead they roll with the punches until they
   are rightfully matched with proper mates, brothers, or masters.

crying with the bard

Coriolanus

Plot

The play is set in Italy in the 5th century BC. Here the proud yet honorable Coriolanus defeats an Italian tribe known as the Volscians, who had planned to attack Rome. When Coriolanus returns to Rome, his wife and his overbearing, controlling mother, Volumnia, greet him, proud that he has proven himself in battle. His mother is even more proud that Coriolanus has been nominated by the Senate to be a consul. However, two jealous tribunes, Brutus and Sicinius, turn the people against Coriolanus, who, in turn, criticizes the people for foolishness. As a result, he is driven out of the city. Furious, Coriolanus teams up with Aufidius, who is planning to attack Rome. When Volumnia tries to persuade her son to stop his mad revenge and to spare Rome, he relents and withdraws his troops. The citizens hail Volumnia as the savior of the city, praise which she has always longed for. Envious of Coriolanus's newfound popularity, Aufidius has him murdered.

Themes

1. Effective leadership requires understanding one's culture. Coriolanus is hopelessly out of step with the people's desire to move beyond the old aristocratic ways. Ultimately this costs him their loyalty.
2. Envy divides friends. Only after he has denounced Coriolanus as a traitor does Aufidius realize that, in fact, Coriolanus has been an honorable and true friend. However, the realization comes too late.

learning with the bard

The Life of King Henry V

Plot

Prince Hal is now King Henry V, and his first political decision is whether to invade France or not. Doing so would win back lands that England had lost and would also unite the rebel forces under his rule. In 1415, he leads an army into France. At Agincourt, where he faces a much larger army (approximately 6,000 British soldiers fighting 20,000 to 30,000 French soldiers), Henry proves to be a gifted speaker and is able to rally his troops to ultimate and unprecedented victory. Over the next five years, he consolidates English rule over France, even forging a peace treaty with King Charles VI of France. The treaty ensured that Henry V would be heir to the French throne and also accorded him the king's daughter, Katherine of Valois, as his queen. At first, she is a reluctant bride, fearing an alliance with "an enemy of France," but Henry assures her, in his broken French, that he is a friend to her people. They wed in 1420 and had a son, King Henry VI. King Charles' son, however, refused to acknowledge the validity of the treaty, so the stage is set for more battle in future years and in future Shakespearean plays.

Themes

1. Politics makes strange bedfellows. It is clear that Henry V has the wherewithal to rally a field of troops in battle, but can he win the heart of an enemy princess?
2. A noble cause can outweigh odds. The French outnumber the English at the Battle of Agincourt, but because the English so strongly believe in the righteousness of their cause, they are able to fight valiantly enough to win the day.

The Coretta Scott King Award: *1970–1988*

Since 1969, the American Library Association has given the Coretta Scott King Award to honor the work of Dr. Martin Luther King Jr. and his wife, in their "determination in continuing to work for peace and world brotherhood." It is awarded each year to an African-American author and, since 1979, illustrator for outstanding inspirational and educational contributions. Here is a list of winning titles:

1970: Lillie Patterson, *Martin Luther King, Jr.: Man of Peace*
1971: Charlemae H. Rollins, *Black Troubador: Langston Hughes*
1972: Elton C. Fax, *Seventeen Black Artists*
1973: Jackie Robinson, as told to Alfred Duckett, *I Never Had It Made: The Autobiography of Jackie Robinson*
1974: Sharon Bell Mathis, *Ray Charles* (illustration by George Ford)
1975: Dorothy Robinson, *The Legend of Africania* (illustration by Herbert Temple)
1976: Pearl Baily, *Duey's Tale*
1977: James Haskins, *The Story of Stevie Wonder*
1978: Eloise Greenfield, *Africa Dream* (illustration by Carol Byard)
1979: Text - Ossie Davis, *Escape to Freedom: A Play about Young Frederick Douglass*
Illustration - Tom Feelings, *Something on My Mind*
1980: Text - Walter Dean Myers, *The Young Landlords*
Illustration - Carole Byard, *Cornrows*
1981: Text - Sidney Poitier, *This Life*
Illustration - Ashley Bryan, *Beat the Story-Drum, Pum-Pum*
1982: Text - Mildred D. Taylor, *Let the Circle Be Unbroken*
Illustration - John Steptoe, *Mother Crocodile: An Uncle Amadou Tale from Senegal*
1983: Text - Virginia Hamilton, *Sweet Whispers, Brother Rush*
Illustration - Peter Magubane, *Black Child*

1984: Text - Lucille Clifton, *Everett Anderson's Goodbye*
    Illustration - Pat Cummings, *My Mama Needs Me*
1985: Text - Walter Dean Myers, *Motown and Didi*
    Illustration - No award given
1986: Text - Virginia Hamilton, *The People Could Fly: American Black Folktales*
    Illustration - Jerry Pinkney, *The Patchwork Quilt*
1987: Text - Mildred Pitts Walter, *Justin and the Best Biscuits in the World*
    Illustration - Jerry Pinkney, *Half a Moon and One Whole Star*
1988: Text - Mildred D. Taylor, *The Friendship*
    Illustration - John Steptoe, *Mufaro's Beautiful Daughters: An African Tale*

More Wacky Writers

- *Agatha Christie once claimed that some of her best ideas for fiction came when she was washing the dishes.*

- *Heinrich Heine kept a picture of August Strindberg on his desk to inspire him.*

- *Virginia Woolf once called James Joyce "a queasy undergraduate scratching his pimples."*

- *Miguel Cervantes wrote* Don Quixote *in Seville Prison after being incarcerated for his debts.*

What Is a WHAT?

. . . .

What is a roman à clef?

Roman à clef (pronounced "clay") translates loosely as "novel with a key." It describes a novel that is published as fiction but that contains things suggesting facts, such as secrets about the author's life. That is, a novel presents information and opinions from a real life, which may or may not be the author's, but the truth hides behind the mask of fiction. For instance, the roman à clef *Tender Is the Night* by F. Scott Fitzgerald is said to have been based on the lives of Gerald and Sara Murphy. Another example is George Orwell's *Animal Farm*, which uses satire to express opinions about the structure and bureaucracy of government. The following well-known romans à clef draw heavily on autobiographical material:

> *Heart of Darkness*, Joseph Conrad
>
> *The Bell Jar*, Sylvia Plath
>
> *The Things They Carried*, Tim O'Brien
>
> *Fear and Loathing in Las Vegas*, Hunter S. Thompson
>
> *Primary Colors*, Joe Klein

. . . . .

What is a literary canon?

A literary canon is a group of literary works that is considered to be the most important of a movement or time period. The canonization of literature, which can be comprised for an era, a country, a literary period, or all three, is a subjective process that usually involves the opinions of scholars, historians, and literary critics. Once a piece is canonized, it is typically widely respected and popularized by being associated with other esteemed works.

Examples of Literary Canons:

The Harvard Classics – a 51-volume anthology of international literary works deemed to be the most important texts pertinent to a liberal education.

Great Books of the Western World – a 54-volume collection begun by the University of Chicago to chronicle the most important books and literary pieces of Western society.

Amy Lowell Poetry Traveling Scholarship

This award, given each year to an outstanding American poet, provides the funds for the poet to spend a year in another country outside of North America. The writer is given the opportunity to pick the country that will most benefit his or her creative work. Past winners include:

1995: Mary Jo Salter   *2000: Richard Roerster*

1996: Craig Arnold   *2001: Nick Flynn*

1997: Caroline Finkelstein   *2002: Rick Hilles*

1998: Elizabeth Macklin   *2003: Mark Wunderlich*

1999: Phillip Levin

---

literary magazines:
popular hangouts for cutting-edge writing

Perusing the aisles of a major bookstore can sometimes be daunting for someone looking for a good reading list. Since thousands of books are published each week and new authors pop up from places all over the world, literary magazines can be an excellent resource for an introduction to a new author. Consider a few of the big guys.

・・・・・

Poetry

Perhaps the most well-endowed literary enterprise today, *Poetry* is a monthly magazine funded by a $200 million grant to the Poetry Foundation from philanthropist Ruth Lily. *Poetry* was founded in 1912 by writer Harriet Monroe with an infamous open-door policy, a vision that makes the magazine unique still today. That mission is to present the finest work from all over the world, no matter its origin. Therefore, *Poetry* claims to accept submissions from any walk of life at any stage in the writing career, and from any school or theory of literature. Writers such as John Ashbery and T. S. Eliot were first discovered, professionally, in *Poetry*.

・・・・・

Glimmertrain

A quarterly publication of international short fiction is *Glimmertrain*, sold in most major book chains. The journal archives some of the best fiction by established and new authors alike, devoting specific issues each year to emerging writers who have not yet published. The magazine also publishes a quarterly 16-page mini-mag called *Writers Ask*, which displays the techniques, tips, and craft lessons of writers from Ernest Gaines to Peter Carey.

Ploughshares

Regarded as one of the elite literary magazines in the United States, *Ploughshares* offers a wide range of fiction, essays, and poetry from all over the world. *Ploughshares*, published three times a year by Emerson College, is usually guest-edited by a reputable writer, including over the years such authors as Ann Beattie, Alice Hoffman, Charles Simic, and Tim O'Brien.

Theoretically Speaking

Literary theorists rush in where readers fear to tread. While most of us read a book simply for the pleasure of it, lit theory asks the hard questions: Does that darn light at the end of the pier symbolize something in The Great Gatsby, *or is Gatsby just obsessed with outdoor illumination? Why is Anna Karenina's suicide so important, or is it just a dramatic way to end a novel?*

New Criticism

Actually, it's not all that new anymore. New Criticism, aka Formalism, was all the rage between the 1940s and the 1960s. New Critics are like the detectives of the reading world. They want just the facts, ma'am. For New Critics, a close study of language reveals the hidden meanings in a work of literature. If "old" criticism concerned itself with historical influences and authorial intentions, then "new" criticism would strictly scrutinize the text itself. Formalists read closely for symbols, metaphors, irony, rhyme, and rhythm.

---

quick & easy shakespeare

Pericles, Prince of Tyre

Plot

In this play, which takes place in ancient Turkey and Tyre, on the coast of Lebanon, Prince Pericles is a young nobleman who discovers that King Antiochus is having an incestuous relationship with his own daughter. Pericles is forced into exile and shipwrecked at Pentapolis. There he marries Thaisa, the daughter of King Simonides. Once he learns that King Antiochus has died, he plans to take his pregnant wife back home to Tyre. However, a storm erupts as they are setting sail, and Thaisa gives birth to a daughter but is so exhausted that everyone believes she died in childbirth. Her body is placed in a chest along with a note proclaiming her royalty and asking anyone who finds her to bury her properly. She is then thrown overboard and eventually washes ashore at Ephesus. Miraculously, she survives and becomes a votaress in the temple of Diana. Pericles leaves Marina, his daughter, to be raised by Cleon, the governor of Tarsus, and his wife, Dionyza. Once Marina becomes a teenager, Dionyza tries to kill her, but she is taken in by pirates and placed in a brothel in Mytilene. The governor of Mytilene finds Marina so beautiful that he rescues her from a life of sexual slavery. Eventually Pericles finds his long-lost daughter and blesses her marriage to the governor. Then, in a dream vision, he learns that his wife, Thaisa, is still alive. He finds her in Ephesus, and they are happily reunited.

Themes

1. The good often suffer like Job. Pericles loses his wife and daughter but, after much suffering, is able to reconnect with both of them.
2. Severe family dysfunction affects more than just the family. The incestuous relationship between King Antiochus and his daughter serves as the catalyst for the difficulties Pericles will have to face for the rest of his life.

around the world in **80 days**

It might be difficult to travel the world in a mere 80 days, but this brief survey of modern writers from Africa, Asia, the Middle East, and Latin America can give you a real flavor of all the wide world has to offer.

AFRICA:

Chinua Achebe

Born in Ogidi, Nigeria, in 1930, Achebe is one of the best-known contemporary African writers. He earned a B.A. from the University College of Ibadan and worked for the Nigerian Broadcasting Corporation and the Institute of African Studies at Nsukka before starting his career as a writer. As president of the Association of Nigerian Authors, Achebe has received the Margaret Wrong Memorial Prize and a Rockefeller Fellowship, and he was a finalist for the 1987 Booker Prize in England.

His first and best-known work, *Things Fall Apart*, has been translated into more than 45 languages. It tells the story of Okonkwo who lives in the Nigerian village of Umuofia at the end of the 19th century before European colonization. As a successful family man and yam farmer, Okonkwo is the revered leader of the Ibo tribe. However, one day he accidentally shoots a fellow tribesman and must be punished. He is banned from the clan for a few years, so he goes to live with his mother's kinsmen in a nearby village. In his absence, the British begin colonizing, encountering violent opposition. By the end, an effort to arrive at peace results in the tragic suicide of Okonkwo.

Nadine Gordimer

Born near Johannesburg, South Africa, in 1923, Gordimer is a 1991 recipient of the Nobel Prize for Literature. Her books include such masterpieces as *The Lying Days, The Guest of Honor, The Conservationist,*

July's People, and *Crimes of Conscience.* Her novel, *A Sport of Nature* (1987), displays her brilliant postmodern writing style. The main character, a young Jewish woman named Hillela, is a kind of "sport of nature," which is to say, a type of variation or departure from the "parent stock." Her mother abandons her at a young age, so she is raised by two of her aunts, Olga and Pauline. From one she learns bourgeois values of fine manners. From the other, she learns political activism and social conscience. Ultimately, Hillela refuses to conform to her aunts' expectations. She marries a black revolutionary, has a daughter, and travels the world in a search for personal freedom and authenticity.

· · · · ·

CHINA and JAPAN:

Su Tong

Born in 1963 in Suzhou in Mainland China, Su Tong is best know for his 1990 book *Wives and Concubines,* which was made into the highly acclaimed film *Raise the Red Lantern.* Although his work is admired by critics, Tong lamented in a recent interview that "my books don't sell." A big fan of Ernest Hemingway, Tong creates memorable characters who jump to life off the page. However, he says problems with literary "piracy" and a general lack of interest in reading in China have contributed to poor book sales. This hasn't stopped the prolific Tong, though. His other works include *Blush, Rice,* and *My Life as Emperor.*

Kobo Abe

Born in 1924 in Tokyo, Japan, Abe grew up in the Manchurian city of Mukden, which was occupied by Japan. Feeling alienated from the Japanese, he changed his name from Kimfusa to the Chinese Kobo. He returned to Japan in 1941 and graduated from Tokyo University with a medical degree in 1948. However, his real passion was writing. He began by writing poetry, publishing *Poems of an Unknown Poet* in

1947. In 1948, his first novel, *The Road Sign at the End of the Street,* was published. Other novels include *The Face of Another, The Ruined Map, Inter Ice Age Four, The Box Man, Secret Rendezvous,* and *The Ark Sakura.* Critics compare his surrealistic writing to Franz Kafka and Eugène Ionesco.

In 1962, *The Woman at the Dunes* garnered him international attention. It was made into a film in 1964. An existential work, the novel portrays the experience of an entomologist who finds himself imprisoned along with a widow in a house in the bottom of a sand pit. His job is to shovel sand that will later be sold to nearby cities. Although he later has a chance to escape, he chooses to stay with the widow and their unborn child.

· · · · ·

AFRICA and the MIDDLE EAST:

Naguib Mahfouz

Born in 1911 in Cairo, Egypt, Mahfouz was the first Arab to win the Nobel Prize for Literature. He graduated with a degree in philosophy in 1934 from Cairo University and has since been Cairo's most prolific recorder of daily life. His novels, numbering over 30 in all, are filled with inhabitants from every social class in Cairo. Although he believed that art should be generous and liberating, Mahfouz himself suffered violence from fundamentalist attacks. He was placed on a death list by Islamic fundamentalists, and in 1994, he suffered a near-fatal stab wound.

The *Cairo Trilogy* consists of *Palace Walk* (1956), *Palace of Desire* (1957), and *Sugar Street* (1957). Totaling over 1,500 pages, the stories portray the family life of al-Sayyid Ahmad Abd al-Jawad in the early part of the 20th century. The vast panorama of characters and situations has led critics to compare the trilogy to works by Dickens or Tolstoy.

Orhan Pamuk

Born in 1952 in Istanbul, Turkey, Pamuk became the first Turkish writer to win the Nobel Prize. Initially he grew up wanting to study architecture, but then he turned his attention toward writing. With a degree from the University of Istanbul, he began writing his first novel, *Darkness and Light*, and went on to teach at Columbia University. *Istanbul: Memories of a City* was the book that helped earn him the Nobel Prize. He admitted that the book was difficult to write because he was suffering such personal difficulties as divorce and his father's death.

Many of his books capture tensions between the West and the East. His 2004 novel, *Snow*, tells the story of a poet named Ka who returns to Istanbul from Germany after years of exile. The city has lost much of its former grandeur and is now host to a series of unusual events like young womens' suicides and military crackdowns on extremists. Ka becomes involved in the intrigues as he rediscovers his gift for poetry.

· · · · ·

LATIN AMERICA:

Carlos Fuentes

Born in 1928 in Mexico City, Fuentes studied at the National University of Mexico and in Switzerland. Because his parents were diplomats, he has lived all over the world including Quito, Santiago, Rio de Janeiro, and Washington, DC. His publications include novels, plays, short stories, and works of criticism. He is also active in politics, having served as administrator at the Ministry of Foreign Affairs, as assistant director of the cultural department of the National University of Mexico, and as Mexico's ambassador to France. As an author, he argues that Latin American writers have to "assimilate the enormous weight of our past so that we will not forget what gives us life." His works include *Where the Air Is Clear* (1960), *The Death of Artemio Cruz* (1964), *Terra Nostra* (1976), and *Distant Relations* (1982).

In 1986, his novel, *Old Gringo*, became the first American best seller written by a Mexican author. In 1989, it was made into a film starring Gregory Peck. The story was inspired by the disappearance of writer Ambrose Bierce during the Mexico Revolution. Fuentes makes the main character a journalist and widower who meets the army of Pancho Villa. As the plot develops, the "old Gringo" works for the revolution and inspires a woman from Washington, DC, to join the cause as well.

Gabriel García Márquez

Born in 1928 in Aracataca, Columbia, Márquez was awarded the Nobel Prize for literature in 1982. His writing career began in journalism as he worked as a foreign correspondent for a Colombian paper. He began publishing short stories as early as 1955, but he achieved international recognition in 1967 for *One Hundred Years of Solitude*, a book that was eventually translated into more than 30 languages. It typifies his style of magical realism as he contrasts objective reality and poetic fantasy in a story that spans 100 years of the Buendia family.

Another best-selling novel, *Love in the Time of Cholera* (1985) was made into a film in 2007. It is a passionate story of unrequited love as the passions of three characters intertwine. Fermina Daza had a childhood romance with Florentino Aziza but chooses, instead, to marry the respectable Juvenal Urbino. Aziza swears eternal allegiance to Fermina, and eventually, once she is widowed, they are able to rekindle their passion from years before.

Russia 101

Before you dig into *War and Peace* or *Crime and Punishment*, here's a guide to help you with those Russian names, places, and titles.

Nicknames

If the character is named...	then they will often be called...
Aleksander/Aleksandra	Sasha
Andrei	Andryusha
Anna	Anya
Boris	Borya
Dmitri	Dimi
Fyodor	Dedya
Galina	Galya
Ivan	Vanya
Mikhail	Misha
Nikolai	Kolya
Serge	Seryozha
Tatiyana	Tanya
Yelena	Lena

Places

Balka	Archaic term for valley
Bereg	Riverbank
Dolina	Valley or plain
Gora	Mountain
Guba	Gulf
Ostrov	Island
Pole	Field

Titles

Count/Countess
Duke/Duchess

Baron/Baroness
Tsar/Tsarina
Emperor/Empress
Prince/Princess

Book Titles You Should Know
War and Peace by Leo Tolstoy
Anna Karenina by Leo Tolstoy
Crime and Punishment by Fyodor Dostoevsky
The Brothers Karamazov by Fyodor Dostoevsky
The Nose by Nikolai Gogol
Eugene Onegin by Aleksandr Pushkin
The Bronze Horseman by Aleksandr Pushkin
Poems by Anna Akhmatova
Doctor Zhivago by Boris Pasternak

More Wacky Writers

- *Before becoming a full-time writer, Honoré De Balzac studied law at the Sorbonne and clerked for three years.*

- *Philip Larkin was not only a poet but also a librarian. He worked at the Brynmor Jones Library at the University of Hull from 1955 to 1985.*

- *William Carlos Williams was a practicing poet and a pediatrician.*

The basic plot *G–I*

More great plots as we work our way through the alphabet.

. . . . .

The Great Gatsby

They don't call this book great for nothin'. F. Scott Fitzgerald paints a memorable portrait of the Jazz Age in this uncompromising examination of the American Dream. Handsome man of mystery Jay Gatsby lives in a splendid mansion on the north shore of Long Island. Despite his lavish parties and the free-flowing champagne, he is largely reclusive and unhappy. He has achieved fame and fortune but has not won the heart of his lady love, Daisy. The book begins with Daisy's cousin Nick telling the story. He has moved into a small house next door to Gatsby, and he is instantly intrigued by the man. Gatsby begins to open up to Nick, telling him that years ago he and Daisy had had an affair, but he had been too poor to marry her. She had married the philandering, boorish Tom Buchanan instead, and, like Gatsby, she is rich and unhappy. Gatsby persuades Nick to help reunite him with Daisy now that he's wealthy enough for her. They rekindle their romance, but soon Daisy accidentally runs over her husband's mistress, Myrtle. Myrtle's husband blames Gatsby for his wife's death and shoots him. Daisy, shallow to the end, stays with her husband, Tom, and their comfy lifestyle.

. . . . .

Hamlet

Even if you've never read this play, everyone has quoted its best-known line, "To be or not to be." So who says that and why? Here's the story. Prince Hamlet is upset because his father has died. Dad's brother, Claudius, wasted no time in marrying Mom. Dad's ghost appears to Hamlet and gives him the scoop. Claudius actually killed him and now Hamlet should exact revenge. Not sure how to go about killing Claudius, Hamlet hangs around the castle acting crazy until a better plan comes along. All this craziness (Is he pretending? Is he really going mad?) causes him to break up with his girlfriend, Ophelia, who later drowns herself. At this point, Hamlet wonders if he would be better off dead, hence the whole "To be or not to be" question. Finally he quits waxing philosophical long enough to hatch a plan. He gets some traveling actors to stage the murder of his father as if it were a play. Claudius gets so nervous during the performance that Hamlet is convinced he is guilty and stabs him behind a curtain. Oops. That wasn't Claudius Hamlet stabbed. It was Ophelia's father. With Ophelia and her dad dead, her brother, Laertes, comes to Denmark to duel Hamlet. To stack the odds in Laertes' favor, Claudius places a poisoned drink near Hamlet, so that even if Laertes doesn't stab him, the poison will kill him. Hamlet's mom accidentally drinks the poison. Hamlet kills Claudius and Laertes. Laertes kills Hamlet. At the end of the play, as you can imagine, there's a bunch of dead bodies on the ground. Quintessential Shakespearean tragedy.

· · · · ·

The Importance of Being Earnest

Oscar Wilde is at his most clever in this satire of the British upper class. Identities get confusing, so we'll try to keep this simple. Lady Bracknell has a lovely daughter, Gwendolyn. She would like Gwendolyn to marry someone with a prestigious family line. Along comes Jack Worthing, whose prestige is limited to the fact that he was found as a baby in a handbag in Victoria Station. Not such a good match in Lady Bracknell's opinion. Love wins the day once it is discovered that Jack is actually Lady Bracknell's nephew who was raised outside of the family simply because a governess lost him at Victoria Station. His real name is Ernest Moncrieff, which proves he is the brother of his best friend, Algernon Moncrieff. In order to skip out on his job as a tutor to his student, Cecily, so that he could go visit Gwendolyn, Jack used to pretend he had a brother named Ernest who needed his help. By the end, Cecily marries Algernon, Jack ends up with Gwendolyn, and "Ernest" is no longer needed. Sounds complicated, but it's actually really funny to see how "earnest" everyone is in discovering the identity of "Ernest."

Theoretically Speaking

Biographical Criticism

Unlike New Criticism, biographical theory says the life of the author tells us a lot about the literary work. If you know that Ezra Pound has fascist sympathies, it makes interpreting the Cantos *a lot easier. If you consider the fact that Jane Austen never married, you might better understand her skepticism about marital bliss in* Pride and Prejudice.

Initial here

Some writers go by their full name, but others like to keep it short and sweet. Here's a list of folks you might only know by their initials, with the full name that lurks beneath the letters.

A. A. Milne – Alan Alexander Milne
A. E. Housman – Alfred Edward Housman
C. S. Lewis – Clive Staples Lewis
E. B. White – Elwyn Brooks White
E. E. Cummings – Edward Estlin Cummings
G. B. Shaw – George Bernard Shaw
G. K. Chesterton – Gilbert Keith Chesterton
H. G. Wells – Herbert George Wells
H. H. Munro – Hector Hugh Munro (pen name: Saki)
H. L. Mencken – Henry Louis Mencken
J. D. Salinger – Jerome David Salinger
J. K. Rowling – Joanne Kathleen Rowling
J. R. R. Tolkien – John Ronald Reuel Tolkien
P. B. Shelley – Percy Bysshe Shelley
P. D. James – Phyllis Dorothy James
P. G. Wodehouse – Pelham Grenville Wodehouse
P. J. O'Rourke – Patrick Jake O'Rourke
T. S. Eliot – Thomas Stearns Eliot
W. B. Yeats – William Butler Yeats
W. E. B. DuBois – William Edward Burghardt DuBois
W. H. Auden – Wystan Hugh Auden

jack of all trades

Jack London ranks right up there with Ernest Hemingway as a writer who lived an adventurous life. He marched cross-country to protest unemployment. He sailed on a schooner to Japan. He got caught up in the frenzy of the Klondike gold rush. Oh, and he wrote such great works as *The Call of the Wild* and *The Sea Wolf.* What most people don't know is that London also maintained literary friendships with a number of prominent authors. Even his letters reveal the spirit of an adventurer.

· · · · ·

June 4, 1915, to Joseph Conrad
Jack London and Joseph Conrad wrote many letters to each other as part of a mutual admiration society. In an early exchange, London confessed to Conrad, "I never wrote you. I never dreamed to write you. But VICTORY has swept me off my feet." To beef up the praise, London included in his letter a copy of something he had written to his friend, Cloudesley Johns, the day before: "First of all, whatever you do, read Conrad's latest—Victory. Read it, if you have to pawn your watch to buy it. Conrad has exceeded himself…. In brief, I am glad that I am alive, if, for no other reason, because of the joy of reading this book."

Conrad responds:
Conrad wrote London three months later: "My Dear Sir, I am intensely touched by the kindness of your letter—that apart from the intense satisfaction given me by the approval of an accomplished fellow craftsman and a true brother in letters of whose personality and art I have been intensely aware of for many years."

London, Johns, and the Possum:
While sailing on the Sacramento River with his buddy Cloudesley
Johns, London read *Victory* aloud to pass the time. Johns took notes
in the book as they went, and on one special day, they discovered that
they weren't the only ones interested in Conrad's novel. According to
Johns' annotations: "Possum, without warning, leaped into my lap as I
was reading this page. His feet were not clean."

• • • • •

London, Greek, and Wolf
Another good friend of Jack London's was bohemian Californian poet
George Sterling. He and his wife, Carrie, often visited the Londons at
their ranch. Perhaps all that exposure to the great outdoors prompted
their nicknames: Sterling called London "Greek," and London referred
to Sterling as "Wolf."

• • • • •

A Friend in Need Is a Friend Indeed
Sometimes London had trouble coming up with ideas for new stories.
He confessed to Johns, "Well, I can't construct plots worth a damn, but
I can everlastingly elaborate." He became friends with and purchased
story plots from Sinclair Lewis, a good choice since Lewis was the
first American to win the Nobel Prize. London would write up formal
invoices for the purchase, as if to indicate the seriousness of the
business at hand. In one letter, Lewis responded, "I hope to gawd that
you will feel like taking a considerable part of [the plots], because, if
you do, it will probably finally give me the chance to get back to free
lancing—nothing but writing—which I haven't done for over a year; can
the job and really get at decent work."

Nobel Prize Winners *1926–1955*

Here's another list of some Nobel Prize winners and what the Swedish Academy has had to say about them.

1926: Grazia Deledda (pen name of Grazia Madesani née Deledda) for transforming Sardinia into mythic proportions.

1927: Henri Bergson in recognition of his bold ideas about the spirit of energy and life that infused his philosophy.

1928: Sigrid Undset for making life during the Middle Ages a real page-turner.

1929: Thomas Mann principally for his important novel *Buddenbrooks.*

1930: Sinclair Lewis for his strong descriptive capabilities and his sharp wit.

1931: Erik Axel Karlfeldt for an intentionally archaic style of Swedish poetry.

1932: John Galsworthy for his unique art of narration as seen in *The Forsythe Saga.*

1933: Ivan Alekseyevich Bunin for continuing the strong classical Russian traditions in the short story and the novel.

1934: Luigi Pirandello for wildly original drama.

1936: Eugene Gladstone O'Neill for a new spin on tragic drama.

1937: Roger Martin du Gard for his novel cycle *Les Thibault.*

1938: Pearl Buck (pen name of Pearl Walsh née Sydenstricker), who makes Chinese peasant life fascinating.

1939: Frans Eemil Sillanpää for putting Finland on the literary map.

1944: Johannes Vilhelm Jensen for a sweeping poetic imagination and a new, creative style.

1945: Gabriela Mistral (pen name of Lucila Godoy y Alca-Yaga) for her emotional poetry, which aligned her with the idealistic aspirations of the entire Latin American world.

1946: Hermann Hesse for writings which are bold, idealistic, and stylish.

1947: André Paul Guillaume Gide for his commitment to truth and for his sharp psychological perceptions.

1948: Thomas Stearns Eliot for being one of the major Modernist poets. He gave a voice to the terror and sense of displacement felt everywhere in early 20th-century life.

1949: William Faulkner for his inimitable contribution to southern writing, in particular, and to the modern American novel, in general.

1950: Earl Bertrand Arthur William Russell, who extols humanitarian ideals and freedom of thought.

1951: Pär Fabian Lagerkvist for poetry that seeks to answer our most enduring questions.

1952: François Mauriac for deep spiritual insight and intensity.

1953: Sir Winston Leonard Spencer Churchill for mastering history, biography, and oratory.

1954: Ernest Miller Hemingway for influencing contemporary narrative style with his strong, spare prose.

1955: Halladorór Kiljan Laxness for putting Iceland on the 20th-century literary map.

Theoretically Speaking

New Historicism

Like New Criticism, New Historicism isn't all that new anymore, but it is still a handy literary theory. Since the 1980s, New Historicists have tried to describe the culture of a period by reading many different kinds of texts. Likewise, they describe a text by looking closely at its historical moment. So, for instance, to gain a clearer understanding of Taming of the Shrew, *they might read scripts from 17th-century Punch and Judy puppet shows that made fun of wife beating.*

---

pop quiz #2

1. Which author's last words were "Either the wallpaper goes, or I do"?

2. Which author's last words were "Does nobody understand"?

3. Which author's last words were "I've had 18 straight whiskies. I think that's a record"?

4. Who said, "We die only once, and for such a long time"?

5. From which Shakespeare play comes the phrase "chronicle small beer"?

6. From which Shakespeare play comes the phrase "a charmed life"?

7. From which Shakespeare play comes the phrase "murder most foul"?

8. From which Shakespeare play comes the phrase "lean and hungry look"?

9. From which Shakespeare play comes the phrase "the world's a stage"?

10. Who said, "The golden rule is that there are no golden rules"?

Answers

1. Oscar Wilde
2. James Joyce
3. Dylan Thomas
4. Molière
5. *Othello*
6. *Macbeth*
7. *Hamlet*
8. *Julius Caesar*
9. *As You Like It*
10. George Bernard Shaw

[consumed]

· ·

Before the advent of antibiotics, tuberculosis claimed the lives of many famous writers. Here's a list of just a few who died too soon.

Jane Austen at 43

Aubrey Beardsley at 25

Anne Brontë at 29

Charlotte Brontë at 39

Emily Brontë at 30

Stephen Crane at 28

Franz Kafka at 40

John Keats at 25

D. H. Lawrence at 44

Katherine Mansfield at 35

George Orwell at 46

something borrowed, *something blue*

· ·

The authors of these books may not have been planning weddings necessarily, but they were certainly wedded to previous sources for their great titles.

· · · · ·

For Whom the Bell Tolls
Although some might think this title originated with Ernest Hemingway's 1940 novel, the phrase "for whom the bell tolls" actually comes from John Donne's poem "Meditation XVII," written in 1624:

> Any man's death diminishes me, because I am
> involved in mankind, and therefore never send to
> know for whom the bell tolls; it tolls for thee.

In 17th-century England, when someone died, the church rang funeral bells, one ring for every year he or she was alive. The ominous sound of tolling bells reminded people of their own mortality.

· · · · ·

The Sun Also Rises
Hemingway strikes again. This time he borrowed his novel's title from the Bible—Ecclesiastes 1:5 to be exact: "The sun rises and the sun sets, and hurries back to where it rises." Originally, he planned to call the novel *Fiesta*, but that title only ended up on the Spanish and UK editions of the book. It may have seemed too festive, ultimately, for a novel about the Lost Generation after World War I. The Ecclesiastes reference lets Hemingway allude to Solomon's biblical lament that life is vain and meaningless.

East of Eden

The Bible inspired not only Hemingway but also John Steinbeck in his 1952 Cain and Abel story set in California. He borrowed the title from Genesis 4:16, "So Cain went out from the Lord's presence and lived in the land of Nod, east of Eden." The biblical allusion worked better than some of his original ideas: *The Salinas Valley, My Valley,* and *Cain Sign.* The good Lord must have been pleased—the book became an immediate best seller, and ten years later Steinbeck won the Nobel Prize.

· · · · ·

Of Mice and Men

East of Eden wasn't the first time Steinbeck had borrowed a title. In 1937, he published *Of Mice and Men,* a novella about two migrant workers in the Great Depression. Oversize simpleton Lennie Small accidentally kills a mouse while trying to pet it and, later on, accidentally kills a young woman. Steinbeck originally wanted to call the book *Something That Happened,* but how boring is that? Fortunately he stumbled upon Robert Burns' 1785 poem, "To a Mouse," which has the lines:

> The best laid schemes of mice and men
> Go often askew…

Like Steinbeck, Burns used a simple little mouse to show how even the biggest human dreams can fail.

· · · · ·

The Grapes of Wrath

Two years later, Steinbeck was stumped once again. He was struggling to come up with a good title for a story about a poor family in the Great Depression. His wife, Carol, recommended the words from "The Battle Hymn of the Republic":

Mine eyes have seen the glory of the coming of the Lord:
He is trampling out the vintage where the grapes of wrath are
stored...

The song refers to Revelation 14:19–20:

And the angel thrust in his sickle into the earth, and gathered the
vine of the earth, and cast it into the great winepress of the wrath
of God. And the winepress was trodden without the city, and blood
came out of the winepress, even unto the horse bridles, by the space
of a thousand and six hundred furlongs.

Something about all that divine anger appealed to Steinbeck as he
scripted the plight of the Joads.

· · · · ·

Brave New World

Huxley borrowed the phrase "brave new world" from Shakespeare's
The Tempest, Act V, scene 1:

O wonder!
How many goodly creatures are there here!
How beauteous mankind is!
O brave new world
That has such people in't!

In these lines, Prospero's dim-witted daughter, Miranda, lays eyes for
the first time on a man other than her father. Understandably, she's
quite enthusiastic. She doesn't realize, however, that humankind is
far from "goodly" and "beauteous." The irony in her exclamation fits
perfectly for Huxley, who wanted to warn his fellow man about the
dangers of the "brave" new world of technology.

The Sound and the Fury

Heck, if you're going to borrow from someone, Shakespeare is a great choice. Aldous Huxley knew it. So did William Faulkner. He took the title of his most famous southern novel from *Macbeth*, Act V, scene 5. Macbeth has become king and, overcome with corruption and fear, learns that his wife has committed suicide. In a famous soliloquy he says:

> To-morrow, and to-morrow, and to-morrow,
> Creeps in this petty pace from day to day
> To the last syllable of recorded time,
> And all our yesterdays have lighted fools
> The way to dusty death. Out, out, brief candle!
> Life's but a walking shadow, a poor player
> That struts and frets his hour upon the stage
> And then is heard no more: it is a tale
> Told by an idiot, full of sound and fury,
> Signifying nothing...

Faulkner found lots in these lines to use in his book—the first chapter is narrated by the mentally impaired Benjy and the rest of the book, like the soliloquy, is concerned with despair and the fall from greatness.

The Pulitzer Prize *1948–1975*

. . . .

1948: *Tales of the South Pacific* by James A. Michener

1949: *Guard of Honor* by James Gould Cozzens

1950: *The Way West* by A. B. Guthrie Jr.

1951: *The Town* by Conrad Richter

1952: *The Caine Mutiny* by Herman Wouk

1953: *The Old Man and the Sea* by Ernest Hemingway

1955: *A Fable* by William Faulkner

1956: *Andersonville* by MacKinlay Kantor

1958: *A Death in the Family* by James Agee (posthumously)

1959: *The Travels of Jaimie McPheeters* by Robert Lewis Taylor

1960: *Advise and Consent* by Allen Drury

1961: *To Kill a Mockingbird* by Harper Lee

1962: *The Edge of Sadness* by Edwin O'Connor

1963: *The Reivers* by William Faulkner

1965: *The Keepers of the House* by Shirley Ann Grau

1966: *Collected Stories* by Katherine Anne Porter

1967: *The Fixer* by Bernard Malamud

1968: *The Confessions of Nat Turner* by William Styron

1969: *House Made of Dawn* by N. Scott Momaday

1970: *Collected Stories* by Jean Stafford

1972: *Angle of Repose* by Wallace Stegner

1973: *The Optimist's Daughter* by Eudora Welty

1975: *The Killer Angels* by Michael Shaara

of *course* he wrote that

Consider these book titles and the names of the people who wrote them. What else could they have written with names like these?

Motorcycling for Beginners — Geoff Carless, 1980

The Inner Flame — Clara Louise Burnham, 1912

A Botanic Guide to Health — Albert Isaiah Coffin, 1845

The Able Coincidence — J. N. Chance, 1969

Anatomy of the Brain — William W. Looney, 1932

Crocheting Novelty Pot-holders — L. Macho, 1982

Spices from the Lord's Garden — Rev. E. I. D Pepper, 1895

Causes of Crime — A. Fink, 1938

Diseases of the Nervous System — Walter Brain, 1933

Common Truths from Queer Texts — Revd Joseph Gay, 1908

Riches and Poverty — L. G. Chiozza Money, 1905

Grace of God— A. Lord, 1859

The Imperial Animal — Lionel Tiger & Robin Fox, 1972

Art of Editing — Floyd Baskette and Jack Z. Sissors

Oppositions of Religious Doctrines — William A. Christian, 1972

The High Rise — Leo Heaps, 1972

The Boy's Own Aquarium — Frank Finn, 1922

Sewerage Treatment and Disposal — G. M. Flood, 1926

Alpine Plants of Distinction — A. Bloom, 1968

Electronics for Schools — R. A. Sparkes, 1972

The Lord's Supper — William Gilbert Ovens, 1940

Operation Earth — B. Trench, 1969

The World of My Books — I. M. Wise, 1954

Fuel Oil Viscosity — G. B. Vroom, 1926

The Professionals: Prostitutes & Their Clients — I. Scarlet, 1972

Writing with Power — Peter Elbow, 1981

Your Teeth — John Chipping, 1967

Violence Against Wives — Emerson and Russell Dobash, 1980

By Reef and Shoal — William Sinker, 1904

war of the words

· ·

When the literati engage in a battle of the wits, watch out! As tongue lashings go, these are vicious…and sometimes wickedly funny.

· · · · ·

Ivan Turgenev and Leo Tolstoy

Tolstoy got so angry at his neighbor, Turgenev, that he threatened to shoot him. The argument stemmed not from a literary disagreement, but a parenting one. Turgenev boasted that his daughter was learning to be more charitable by giving money to the poor and mending their clothes. Tolstoy said that a well-dressed girl handling poor people's laundry was hardly a genuine act of charity. Turgenev threatened to box Tolstoy's ears. In response, Tolstoy sent him a letter challenging him to a pistol duel. Turgenev wrote back apologizing for his temper but refusing to fight.

· · · · ·

Ivan Turgenev and Fyodor Dostoevsky

Leo Tolstoy wasn't the only writer Turgenev couldn't get along with. Dostoevsky annoyed members of his literary circle with his arrogance and irritability, which prompted Turgenev to taunt him at every opportunity. He spread a rumor that the haughty Dostoevsky insisted on having one of his books printed with gold edgings. Dostoevsky made fun of Turgenev in print. So Turgenev, in turn, wrote a satirical poem, which said, "Dostoevsky, you dear blow-hard, you redden the nose of literature like a new pimple."

James Joyce and Samuel Beckett
At first it must have seemed like destiny to Beckett. His plan was to be an accountant, but he discovered a love of languages in school in Dublin, and this led him to the École Normale Superieure in Paris. In the City of Lights, he met James Joyce and became one of his assistants. He could have no better friend or tutor, that is, until his friend's schizophrenic daughter developed a crush on him. Beckett wasn't interested in Lucia Joyce romantically, but he still desperately wanted to retain Joyce's friendship. The situation proved too awkward for Joyce. When Beckett came over one day and said curtly to poor Lucia, "I'm here to see your father, not you," Lucia's feelings were hurt and Joyce, the protective father, never forgave Beckett.

· · · · ·

Norman Mailer and Gore Vidal
In 2003, both Mailer and Vidal published critiques of the war in Iraq, but this doesn't mean they see eye to eye on most things. One famous incident involves a party to which both were invited. The inebriated Mailer challenged Vidal to a fight, but Vidal ignored him. This prompted Mailer to toss a drink in Vidal's face. Unflappable, Vidal quipped, "Once again, words have failed Norman."

· · · · ·

Ernest Hemingway and William Faulkner
Alcohol fueled the feud not only between Mailer and Vidal but also between earlier literary giants Hemingway and Faulkner. The latter claimed that Hemingway "had no courage." Later, when Faulkner said, "Hemingway has never been known to use a word that might send a reader to the dictionary," Papa retaliated: "Poor Faulkner. Does he really think big emotions come from big words? He thinks I don't know the ten dollar words. I know them all right. But there are older and simpler and better words, and those are the ones I use." Perhaps some of those "older and simpler words" included "Old Corndrinking Mellifluous," a pet name Hemingway devised for Faulkner.

Dorothy Parker and Clare Booth Luce
The caustic Dorothy Parker might be the last woman with whom you'd want to battle wits, as playwright Clare Boothe discovered. As the two women were going through a door, Luce motioned for Parker to go first, sniping, "Age before beauty." Without hesitation, Parker shot back, "And pearls before swine," as she left Luce in the dust.

More Wacky Writers

- *Gerard Manley Hopkins was a priest as well as a poet.*

- *Jorge Luis Borges was director of the National Library of Argentina for 20 years.*

- *W. Somerset Maugham was 84 when he wrote* Points of View.

- *Johann Goethe completed* Faust *when he was 81.*

- *Winston Churchill was 82 when he wrote* A History of the English Speaking People.

- *Leo Tolstoy was 82 when he wrote* I Cannot Be Silent.

---

some nice alliteration:
Pulitzer Prize for poetry 1941–1965

1941: "Sunderland Capture," Leonard Bacon

1942: "The Dust Which Is God," William Rose Benét

1943: "A Witness Tree," Robert Frost

1944: "Western Star," Stephen Vincent Benét

1945: *V-Letter and Other Poems*, Karl Shapiro

1947: "Lord Weary's Castle," Robert Lowell

1948: "The Age of Anxiety," W. H. Auden

1949: "Terror and Decorum," Peter Viereck

1950: "Annie Allen," Gwendolyn Brooks

1951: *Complete Poems*, Carl Sandburg

1952: *Collected Poems*, Marianne Moore

1953: *Collected Poems, 1917–1952*, Archibald MacLeish

1954: "The Waking," Theodore Roethke

1955: *Collected Poems*, Wallace Stevens

1956: *Poems—North & South*, Elizabeth Bishop

1957: "Things of This World," Richard Wilbur

1958: *Promises: Poems, 1954–1956*, Robert Penn Warren

1959: *Selected Poems, 1928–1958*, Stanley Kunitz

1960: "Heart's Needle," William Snodgrass

1961: *Times Three: Selected Verse from Three Decades*,
        Phyllis McGinley

1962: *Poems*, Alan Dugan

1963: "Pictures from Breather," William Carlos Williams

1964: "At the End of the Open Road," Louis Simpson

1965: *77 Dream Songs*, John Berryman

wolves at the door

From Tobias Wolff to Virginia Woolf, when these "wolves" come howling at the door, it's best to listen. Here are a few great thoughts about writing from literary "wolves."

Tobias Wolff (author of *This Boy's Life*)

But a lot of writers—and I'm one of them—do tend to feel dissatisfied. It makes you a little hard to live with, but it's a goad and does keep you alert and restless.

Everything has to be pulling weight in a short story for it to be really of the first order.

I believe that the short story is as different a form from the novel as poetry is, and the best stories seem to me to be perhaps closer in spirit to poetry than to novels.

I try to help people become the best possible editors of their own work, to help them become conscious of the things they do well, of the things they need to look at again, of the wells of material they have not even begun to dip their buckets into.

Most of us don't live lives that lend themselves to novelistic expression, because our lives are so fragmented.

There are very few professions in which people just sit down and think hard for five or six hours a day all by themselves.

Tom Wolfe (author of *Bonfire of the Vanities*)

What they [the amateurs] are really saying is "I have a story and I want it told." This compulsion is what enables the journalist to get his information. It's the writer's job to flesh out the stories he hears.

Not even the most powerful organs of the press, including *Time*, *Newsweek*, and *The New York Times*, can discover a new artist or certify his work and make it stick…They can only bring you the scores.

Thomas Wolfe (author of *Look Homeward, Angel*):

What I had to face, the very bitter lesson that everyone who wants to write has got to learn, was that a thing may in itself be the finest piece of writing one has ever done, and yet have absolutely no place in the manuscript one hopes to publish.

A young man is so strong, so mad, so certain, and so lost. He has everything and he is able to use nothing.

If a man has a talent and cannot use it, he has failed. If he has a talent and uses only half of it, he has partly failed. If he has a talent and learns somehow to use the whole of it, he has gloriously succeeded, and won a satisfaction and a triumph few men ever know.

Gene Wolfe (sci-fi author of *The Book of the New Sun*)

Ambiguity is necessary in some of my stories, not in all. In those, it certainly contributes to the richness of the story. I doubt that thematic closure is never attainable.

I met a nice little boy named Nick. (He's not quite so little now.) He was very, very bright, and crazy about knights and the whole medieval scene. I tried to figure out what attracted him to it so much, and began to write a book.

My whole life experience feeds into my writing. I think that must be true for every writer. Clearly the Army and combat were major influences; just the same, you need to understand that many of the writers we have now couldn't load a revolver.

Online publication is fine with me, in part because I hope to collect those stories later.

Virginia Woolf (author of *To the Lighthouse*)

A good essay must have this permanent quality about it; it must draw its curtain round us, but it must be a curtain that shuts us in not out.

A masterpiece is something said once and for all, stated, finished, so that it's there complete in the mind, if only at the back.

A woman must have money and a room of her own if she is to write fiction.

Every secret of a writer's soul, every experience of his life, every quality of his mind is written large in his works.

Indeed, I would venture to guess that Anon, who wrote so many poems without signing them, was often a woman.

Literature is strewn with the wreckage of men who have minded beyond reason the opinions of others.

Masterpieces are not single and solitary births; they are the outcome of many years of thinking in common, of thinking by the body of the people, so that the experience of the mass is behind the single voice.

Really I don't like human nature unless all candied over with art.

The poet gives us his essence, but prose takes the mold of the body and mind.

the write stuff:
a glossary of literary terms from D to G

Here are some more literary terms to keep you in the know.

Dénouement – A French word that means "unraveling." It is used to describe the action following a climax.

Dramatic monologue – A type of lyric poem in which a character speaks to someone imagined in the poem in such a way that we find out something about the speaker's personality. Robert Browning's poem "My Last Duchess" is a dramatic monologue that slowly reveals the speaker to be a murderous nut job.

Elegy – A sad poem that mourns someone who has died or that meditates on a melancholy theme. Thomas Gray's "Elegy Written in a Country Churchyard" would be a good example, as the title of the poem suggests.

Epic – A long narrative poem, told in an elevated style, which focuses on the adventures of someone legendary. Homer's *Iliad*, Virgil's *Aeneid*, and Milton's *Paradise Lost* are all examples.

Epigram – A brief, witty poem that usually makes a satiric or funny point.

Epigraph –Not to be confused with "epigram." An epigraph is a short quotation at the beginning of a story or poem that clues you in to some of the major themes.

Epiphany – The big aha! moment in a work of fiction. A character figures something out (finally), a truth is revealed, that sort of thing.

Euphony – The opposite of cacophony, euphony refers to language that actually sounds good to the ear. Tennyson's line "the moan of doves in immemorial elms" would be a good example. "The moan of screeching little doves up there in those dang trees" would not be a good example.

Farce – A type of comedy with exaggerated characters in ridiculous situations. There are usually quick shifts in emotion and action and even a little slapstick. Some Shakespeare comedies are farcical.

Figures of speech – Words that deviate from the literal, denotative meaning. To call someone "dumber than a bag of hammers" would be a good example, although it might get you punched in the nose.

Fixed form – A poem that has to play by the rules. Sonnets have to have 14 lines. Other fixed forms include limerick and sestina. You can't just write a haiku and call it a limerick because you want to. A limerick has certain rules.

Flashback – A scene relived in someone's memory. A classic example is hearing the choppers whirring in a Vietnam flashback.

Foil – A character whose behavior contrasts with (usually) that of the protagonist. In *Hamlet*, Laertes acts as a foil to Hamlet, because his willingness to act proves the protagonist's passivity.

Free verse – Poetry without the rules. It doesn't have to have a certain rhythm or rhyme. Robert Frost compared writing free verse to "playing tennis without a net."

Genre – A fancy French word meaning "type." Some genres in literature are poetry, fiction, drama, and essays. Comic books might count as a literary genre too. Depends on who you ask.

across the ages through the pages:
brit lit 4

1660–1785: The Neoclassical Period

The neoclassical period was heavily influenced by contemporary French literature, which was flourishing at the time. As a result, wit, elegance, refinement, and a healthy dose of skepticism shaped the language. It was such a complex time creatively that scholars divide the period into three parts: the Restoration, the Augustan Age, and the Age of Sensibility. As we have seen, during the Restoration, from 1660 to 1700, John Milton wrote *Paradise Lost.* The Augustan Age, from 1700 to 1745, refers to an elegant yet satirical period of literature with such writers as Jonathan Swift leading the way. Moreover, during this time, the first modern novel in English was written, *Pamela* by Samuel Richardson (1740). From 1745 to 1785, the Age of Sensibility reflected an interest in medieval ballads and folk literature. Its emphasis on emotion and sensitivity helped produce such important works Henry Fielding's *Tom Jones* (1749). The Age of Sensibility is also known as the Age of Johnson because of the strong influence of Samuel Johnson.

Jonathan Swift: The Least You Need to Know

- Swift is one of the first major Irish writers of literature. He was born in Dublin, but his parents were English. In 1689, he went to England to serve as secretary to Sir William Temple. His exposure to political and religious arguments there led him to write his first important works: *A Tale of a Tub,* a satire mocking religious extremism, and *The Battle of the Books,* a satire lambasting literary arguments about whether classical writing was superior to contemporary writing.

- *Gulliver's Travels* (1726) is his best-known work. It is a satire that can be read as an amusing story for children or, on a deeper level, as a condemnation of human nature. The book takes the form of Lemuel Gulliver's journal. As a ship's doctor, he travels to Lilliput, where he meets people only six inches tall. From there he goes to Brobdingnag, a land of giants, and then to Laputa, a floating island. Finally he ends up in Houyhnhnmland, where horses rule over Yahoos, hideous, irrational creatures who turn out to be humans. The fantastic landscapes and creatures in the book serve to highlight the foolishness of religious dispute, the depth of man's corruption, and the need for a wider use of reason in human affairs.

Pamela: The Least You Need To Know

- Subtitled "Virtue Rewarded," *Pamela* by Samuel Richardson became a best seller. It was read aloud in early book groups and used in sermons to illustrate virtuous principles.
- Initially Samuel Richardson did not set out to write a novel. He imagined *Pamela* to be more like the popular 18th-century "conduct book," an early example of self-help manuals. However, as he kept drafting, the story took shape and grew organically into an epistolary novel, that is, a novel written in the form of letters and documents. Nevertheless, his hope was that the book, even though it was highly entertaining, would instruct people in proper conduct.
- The plot revolves around an unsophisticated, 15-year-old servant girl named Pamela Andrews. The wealthy woman who employs her, Lady B., dies. Her son, Mr. B., spends much of the book trying to seduce the unwilling Pamela. Finally she convinces him that they should get married so that she can embark on a program to reform his licentious ways. After they are wed, the community admires Pamela for her virtue and goodness.

Tom Jones: The Least You Need to Know

- Henry Fielding wrote *Tom Jones* in 1749, and it is widely considered to be a masterpiece for its widely inclusive portrait of British society and for the way it holds together under Fielding's authorial vision and ironic tone.

- In the beginning of the story, Squire Allworthy finds an infant in his house, names him Tom Jones, and raises him along with the child of his sister, a boy named Blifil. Tom is mischievous yet amiable, but Blifil is a naughty child who constantly tries to get Tom into trouble. The boys fight over the neighbor girl, Sophia, and eventually Tom is kicked out of the house. He embarks on several adventures on his way to London, where Sophia also flees to escape a forced marriage to Blifil. In the end, Blifil is exposed for his evil crimes, and Tom marries Sophia and becomes the rightful heir of Squire Allworthy.

Samuel Johnson: The Least You Need to Know

- Holding the LL.D. and M.A degrees, the very learned Samuel Johnson is best known as Dr. Johnson. Writer Tobias Smollett gave him the nickname the Great Cham (Khan) of Literature.
- Johnson was highly respected as an essayist, lexicographer, poet, and moralist. From 1750 to 1752, he wrote *The Rambler*, a series of periodical essays about literature, morality, and culture. He wrote the philosophical romance *Rasselas* (1759) in one week to help pay for his mother's funeral expenses. Often compared to Voltaire's novel *Candide* it is one of Johnson's most highly respected works.
- Another of his highly respected works is none other than *The Dictionary of the English Language*, which he published in 1755. It served as the standard until Noah Webster's dictionary appeared in 1828. In the preface to his dictionary, Johnson admits that it might not be perfectly inclusive of every word ever written, but at least he tried to compile something that no one else had ever attempted.
- Johnson is one of the most quoted writers of all time, with such sayings as "In order that all men may be taught to speak the truth, it is necessary that all likewise should learn to hear it" and "Love is the wisdom of the fool and the folly of the wise."

across the ages through the pages:
american lit 1

Naturally enough, American literature is charted slightly differently than British because of historical differences. Technically, one could argue that early American literature begins with Native American tales. Consider the richness, for example, of the Native American creation myths, which feature characters such as Spider Woman, a typical female creator among indigenous tribes. Likewise, their ritual poetry, as opposed to the private lyric voice, allowed tribes a communal expression of faith, healing, or other ceremonial concerns. A poem like "Sayatasha's Night Chant," for instance, would have been chanted with priests as it told the story of visiting sacred shrines in order to meet communal needs.

Once pilgrims and explorers from England came to the New World, new types of literature emerged, reflecting the excitement of discovery, the loss of home and traditions, the dictates of different religious beliefs, and the clash of native and colonial cultures. Most scholars chart American literature as beginning with the colonial period and working through to our contemporary era.

. . . . . .

1607–1776: The Colonial Period

The colonial period of literature spans the time between the founding of the first settlement at Jamestown to the outbreak of the American Revolution. Many of the writers were Puritans who based their work on literal interpretations of the Bible. They believed in ideas of original sin, limited atonement, and predestination. Major writers of the colonial period include Cotton Mather, Benjamin Franklin, and Anne Bradstreet.

Cotton Mather: The Least You Need to Know

- Born in 1663, Mather, the son of well-known minister Increase Mather, was so bright that he enrolled at Harvard when he was only 12 years old. He became a pastor and historian who wrote on topics as varied as smallpox and witchcraft.
- Mather is often placed in literary history as a last-ditch effort of Puritan hysteria before the rationality of the Enlightenment took hold. He believed in witchcraft to such a degree that in 1688 he blamed an Irish washerwoman for the afflictions of four children in her care. "An Army of Devils is horribly broke in upon the place which is our center," he proclaimed. Active in the Salem witch trials, Mather wrote *The Wonders of the Invisible World* in 1693, which betrayed his fundamentalist enthusiasm for trials and executions.

Benjamin Franklin: The Least You Need to Know

- Best known as an early American statesman, printer, inventor, and scientist, Ben Franklin could add author to his list of accomplishments as well. His literary career began at the age of 12 when he worked for a printer and contributed newspaper essays, works eventually collected as *The Dogood Papers* (1722). Inspired to establish his own newspaper, he ran away to Philadelphia when he was 17 years old and published *Poor Richard's Almanack*, under the pen name Richard Saunders. Many of his most famous sayings appeared here, including "Early to bed and early to rise makes a man healthy, wealthy, and wise," and "God helps those who help themselves."
- Undoubtedly Franklin's writing seems most influential in his help with drafting the Declaration of Independence. However, he is also very well known for his *Autobiography*, which he began writing in 1771 and worked on until his death. The depiction of his amazing range of interests from politics and religion to science and philosophy made it a classic in the autobiographical genre. In a famous passage, Franklin reveals the key to his success:

It was about this time I conceiv'd the bold and arduous project of arriving at moral perfection. I wish'd to live without committing any fault at any time; I would conquer all that either natural inclination, custom, or company might lead me into. As I knew, or thought I knew, what was right and wrong, I did not see why I might not always do the one and avoid the other. But I soon found I had undertaken a task of more difficulty than I bad imagined. While my care was employ'd in guarding against one fault, I was often surprised by another; habit took the advantage of inattention; inclination was sometimes too strong for reason. I concluded, at length, that the mere speculative conviction that it was our interest to be completely virtuous, was not sufficient to prevent our slipping; and that the contrary habits must be broken, and good ones acquired and established, before we can have any dependence on a steady, uniform rectitude of conduct. For this purpose I therefore contrived the following method.

Here Franklin made a list of virtues, which he would check off every day to make sure that he always kept in mind the important qualities of a good life. Which 13 qualities did he consider most important?

1. **Temperance**. Eat not to dullness; drink not to elevation.
2. **Silence**. Speak not but what may benefit others or yourself; avoid trifling conversation.
3. **Order**. Let all your things have their places; let each part of your business have its time.
4. **Resolution**. Resolve to perform what you ought; perform without fail what you resolve.
5. **Frugality**. Make no expense but to do good to others or yourself; i.e., waste nothing.
6. **Industry**. Lose no time; be always employ'd in something useful; cut off all unnecessary actions.
7. **Sincerity**. Use no hurtful deceit; think innocently and justly, and, if you speak, speak accordingly.

8. **Justice**. Wrong none by doing injuries, or omitting the benefits that are your duty.
9. **Moderation**. Avoid extremes; forbear resenting injuries so much as you think they deserve.
10. **Cleanliness**. Tolerate no uncleanliness in body, clothes, or habitation.
11. **Tranquility**. Be not disturbed at trifles, or at accidents common or unavoidable.
12. **Chastity**. Rarely use venery but for health or offspring, never to dullness, weakness, or the injury of your own or another's peace or reputation.
13. **Humility**. Imitate Jesus and Socrates.

Anne Bradstreet: The Least You Need to Know

- One of the earliest American women writers, Bradstreet was born in England but emigrated to America with her husband in 1630 when she was only 16 years old. She had received an excellent education, especially for a young girl, so she was able to infuse in her writing two layers of meaning—a surface layer in which she appears to adhere to the conventional standards of femininity at the time, but also a subversive layer in which she addresses religious doubt, sexual desire, and other "taboo" topics of the day. For instance, in 1666, her house burned down, prompting her to write the poem, "Upon the Burning of Our House, July 1666," in which she calls on God for comfort even as the poem, implicitly, blames God for her suffering.
- Her best-known poem, "The Author to Her Book," displays early feminist thought, as she lays claim to the same rights and privileges afforded any male author. By positioning herself as a mother and her book as her child, Bradstreet can appear to conform to social standards for women even as she praises her own writing gifts. She humbly calls her writing an "ill-formed offspring of my feeble brain," but clearly she does not believe her self-deprecating comment as the text of the poem proves:

Thou ill-form'd offspring of my feeble brain,
Who after birth did'st by my side remain,
Till snatcht from thence by friends, less wise than true,
Who thee abroad expos'd to public view,
Made thee in rags, halting to th' press to trudge,
Where errors were not lessened (all may judge).
At thy return my blushing was not small,
My rambling brat (in print) should mother call.
I cast thee by as one unfit for light,
Thy Visage was so irksome in my sight,
Yet being mine own, at length affection would
Thy blemishes amend, if so I could.
I wash'd thy face, but more defects I saw,
And rubbing off a spot, still made a flaw.
I stretcht thy joints to make thee even feet,
Yet still thou run'st more hobbling than is meet.
In better dress to trim thee was my mind,
But nought save home-spun Cloth, i' th' house I find.
In this array, 'mongst Vulgars mayst thou roam.
In Critics' hands, beware thou dost not come,
And take thy way where yet thou art not known.
If for thy Father askt, say, thou hadst none;
And for thy Mother, she alas is poor,
Which caus'd her thus to send thee out of door.

laughing with the bard

Love's Labour's Lost

Plot

In order to become famous scholars, King Ferdinand of Navarre and three of his lords, Biron, Longaville, and Dumain, take a vow to avoid women and give up worldly pleasures. No sooner do they make such a promise than the Princess of France arrives on business of the state and brings with her three beautiful ladies, Maria, Rosaline, and Katherine. Because the men want to avoid sexual temptation, they house the women in the park of the king's estate. Of course, the men fall in love, King Ferdinand with the princess, Longaville with Marie, Biron with Rosaline, and Dumain with Katherine. Along the way, the lovers disguise themselves to fool each other, and for a while everyone ends up with the wrong love interest. At one point, the princess learns that her father has died and that she must return to France. The men all ask for the ladies' hands in marriage, but the women refuse. After all, they wouldn't want the men to break their vows of renunciation. The ladies agree they will consider marriage only after the four suitors complete various tasks: Ferdinand must spend a year in a hermitage, Biron must work in a hospital, and Dumain and Longaville must mature more. The lighthearted plot would have been recognizable in Shakespeare's day as representative of court life.

Themes

1. Knowledge should not be separated from love. The men make a mistake in pursuing learning at the cost of romance. The two do not have to be mutually exclusive.
2. Spain is not the global power it thought it was. In 1588, King Philip II attacked England and was soundly defeated. Shakespeare based one of the pompous, comical characters in the play on Philip to criticize the king's pride.

crying with the bard
. . . .

Julius Caesar
Plot

The play begins in Rome on February 15, 44 BC. It is the day of the
annual Feast of Lupercalia. Cassius, an envious and clever senator,
forms a conspiracy against Julius Caesar. Even a man as noble
as Brutus joins in on the plot, once he is convinced that Caesar's
power is detrimental to the republic. Caesar's wife has dreams of his
assassination, but he ignores her warnings and goes to the Senate
on March 15, the Ides of March. His wife was right; he is stabbed
repeatedly by the conspirators. The cruelest blow, however, comes
when he realizes that his good friend Brutus is among them: "Et tu,
Brute?" he asks in disbelief (the Latin phrase translating as "And you,
Brutus?"). When Marc Antony learns of his leader's death, he pretends
to be sympathetic to the conspirators' cause and merely requests that he
can speak at the funeral. When they agree, he seizes the opportunity, in
a brilliant rhetorical move, to turn the people against the conspirators.
When Antony, Lepidus, and Octavius battle the assassins, Cassius and
Brutus kill themselves. In the closing words of the play, Antony praises
Brutus as the only noble conspirator, the only one who thought he was
helping Rome by killing Caesar.

Themes

1. Lofty ambition often brings ruin. Cassius' envy starts a chain of
   events that leads to the deaths of many senators and soldiers.
   Caesar's ambition and pride, likewise, prevent him from heeding the
   warning about the Ides of March.
2. Idealism may lead to death. Brutus so honors his ideas of political
   freedom that he is willing to risk everything to defend them,
   including his own life and the life of his good friend Caesar.

learning with the bard

··

The First Part of King Henry VI

Plot

Three plays make up the trilogy that dramatizes the early years of King
Henry VI's reign. The first part of *Henry VI* also has three story lines,
so it is like a miniature trilogy-within-a-trilogy. The play begins in
1422 with England mourning the death of King Henry V, who fought
so bravely against the French: "England never lost a king of so much
worth," laments the Duke of Bedford. Henry VI was only eight months
old when he ascended the English throne, and shortly thereafter
he also became the King of France when his maternal grandfather,
Charles VI, died. Under those circumstances, John, Duke of Bedford,
was appointed Regent of France and Humphrey, Duke of Gloucester,
became Regent of England. The vying for power on the part of Henry's
two uncles constitutes the first plotline in the play. About this same
time, Joan of Arc is beginning to wage her campaign to expel the
English from France, so the political situation is touchy to say the least.
In addition to this second plotline, a third one revolves around Richard
Plantagenet, who becomes the Duke of York. He begins to argue with
the Beaufort family in the house of Lancaster because he believes his
family has been cheated out of the throne over the years. Out of this
quarrel, the Wars of the Roses will evolve. In the play, the Yorks and
Lancasters manage to reconcile briefly. It is decided that Henry will
marry the daughter of the French earl of Armagnac to help solidify the
peace between England and France. However, one of the members of
the Lancaster faction, the Earl of Suffolk, convinces the 24-year-old
Henry to marry Margaret of Anjou instead, believing that Margaret
will exert her influence over Henry and, in turn, the earl can influence
Margaret.

Themes

1. Beware enemies within as well as enemies without. England wages war against France, but the discord between the Yorks and Lancasters threatens to unravel English solidarity.
2. Women are as powerful as men. Joan of Arc's legend has endured valiantly through the ages, but in this play, Shakespeare paints her as evil.

Theoretically Speaking

Cultural Criticism

This approach to interpretation looks at the history, politics, economics, and social forces that affect a literary work. You might laugh to read an article by a cultural critic because they often incorporate pop culture in their studies. Cultural critics get the fun job of delivering papers at conferences on such topics as "Parallels Between Rambo and Ahab in Moby Dick*" or "A Study of Symbolism in* The Sopranos*."*

Gay and Lesbian Criticism

As you might guess by the title, gay and lesbian literary theory focuses on homosexual authors, how homosexuals are represented in literature, and whether sexuality is something we are born with or something society defines. Gay and lesbian critics might discuss homoeroticism in Billy Budd *or how Virginia Woolf's affair with Vita Sackville-West influenced her novel* Orlando.

The Newbery Medal: *1922–1965*

Established in 1922, the John Newbery Medal is awarded annually to the author of the outstanding American book for children. Winners include:

1922: Hendrik Van Loon, *The Story of Mankind*
1923: Hugh Lofting, *The Voyages of Dr. Dolittle*
1924: Charles Hawes, *The Dark Frigate*
1925: Charles Finger, *Tales from Silver Lands*
1926: Arthur Chrisman, *Shen of the Sea*
1927: Will James, *Smoky, the Cow Horse*
1928: Dhan Mukerji, *Gay-Neck, the Story of a Pigeon*
1929: Eric P Kelly, *The Trumpeter of Krakow: A Tale of the Fifteenth Century*
1930: Rachel Field, *Hitty, Her First Hundred Years*
1931: Elizabeth Coatsworth, *The Cat Who Went to Heaven*
1932: Laura Adams Armer, *Waterless Mountain*
1933: Elizabeth Lewis, *Young Fu of the Upper Yangtze*
1934: Cornelia Meigs, *Invincible Louisa: The Story of the Author of* Little Women
1935: Monica Shannon, *Dobry*
1936: Carol Ryrie Brink, *Caddie Woodlawn*
1937: Ruth Sawyer, *Roller Skates*
1938: Kate Seredy, *The White Stag*
1939: Elizabeth Enright, *Thimble Summer*
1940: James Daugherty, *Daniel Boone*
1941: Armstrong Sperry, *Call It Courage*
1942: Walter D. Edmonds, *The Matchlock Gun*
1943: Elizabeth Janet Gray, *Adam of the Road*
1944: Esther Forbes, *Johnny Tremain*
1945: Robert Lawson, *Rabbit Hill*
1946: Lois Lenski, *Strawberry Girl*

1947: Carolyn S. Bailey, *Miss Hickory*
1948: William Pène du Bois, *The Twenty-One Balloons*
1949: Marguerite Henry, *King of the Wind*
1950: Marguerite de Angeli, *The Door in the Wall*
1951: Elizabeth Yates, *Amos Fortune, Free Man*
1952: Eleanor Estes, *Ginger Pye*
1953: Ann Nolan Clark, *Secret of the Andes*
1954: John Krumgold, *...And Now Miguel*
1955: Meindert DeJong, *The Wheel on the School*
1956: Jean Lee Latham, *Carry On, Mr. Bowditch*
1957: Virginia Sorensen, *Miracles on Maple Hill*
1958: Harold V. Keith, *Rifles for Watie*
1959: Elizabeth George Speare, *The Witch of Blackbird Pond*
1960: John Krumgold, *Onion John*
1961: Scott O'Dell, *Island of the Blue Dolphins*
1962: Elizabeth George Speare, *The Bronze Bow*
1963: Madeleine L'Engle, *A Wrinkle in Time*
1964: Emily C. Neville, *It's Like This, Cat*
1965: Maia Wojciechowska, *Shadow of a Bull*

More Wacky Writers

- *After Andrew Marvell died, his housekeeper posed as his widow in order to inherit his money.*

- *William Faulkner was prevented from enlisting in the army during World War I because he was only 5'5".*

- *Arthur Conan Doyle served as an army doctor during the Boer War.*

- *Samuel Beckett fought in the French Resistance during World War II.*

Literary Gossip

. . . .

Harper Lee and Truman Capote

Rumor: Harper Lee's classic *To Kill a Mockingbird* was actually written by fellow novelist Truman Capote. According to certain conspiracy theorists, Capote either cowrote or ghost-wrote the novel. The rumor comes from a glowing blurb written by Capote in the dust jacket of a first edition, as well as a newspaper reporter's insistence that Capote's father, Archulus Persons, had told him that Capote had written most of the book himself.

The truth: Capote was a childhood neighbor and friend of Harper Lee's growing up and was the inspiration for the young character Dill. In a letter to a relative penned in 1959, Capote addresses the idea that he wrote the book, stating that "I did not see Nelle last winter, but the previous year, she showed me as much of the book as she'd written, and I liked it very much." Lee's sister Alice has referred to the rumor as the "biggest lie ever told," and since 2006, the rumor has been laid to rest.

. . . . .

J. K. Rowling and a Gay Headmaster

In October 2007, author J. K. Rowling stated to a crowd at Carnegie Hall that a character from *Harry Potter*, Albus Dumbledore, was homosexual. The comment stirred controversy and many questions, and many fans and readers were angered by the statement. Rowling commented on the furor later, stating, "He is my character...and I have the right to say what I say about him."

the 411 *on a few more short stories*

"Hills Like White Elephants" – Ernest Hemingway
Unfolded nearly entirely with dialogue, this famous Hemingway story details a couple's important decision. In a train station in Spain, the two main characters, an American and a woman named Jig, sit and talk over beers. As their conversation becomes more and more serious, the man tries to convince Jig that she ought to have an operation. Though it is never said what the operation is, it is implied in the dialogue that the two are discussing an abortion. First published in 1927 in a collection of fiction, "Hills Like White Elephants" has become a famous and highly debated piece of literary fiction. Many critics consider it to be a groundbreaking piece in its use not only dialogue but also setting to reveal the overarching and controversial themes of the piece.

. . . . .

"The Gift of the Magi" – O. Henry
This story, one of O. Henry's most famous, tells the tale of a very poor couple at Christmastime trying to buy the perfect gifts for one another. Jim and Della Dillingham each scrounge the money they can find but soon realize that they cannot afford the gifts they most want for one another. Della decides that she must buy Jim a chain for his cherished pocket watch, a possession handed down to him by his father. To afford the chain, Della cuts off her long, beautiful hair to sell it to a wigmaker. Meanwhile, Jim decides to buy Della a set of combs for her hair, her most prized possession, but realizes that he cannot afford them. He sells the pocket watch to afford the combs for Della. In the end, both Jim and Della realize that the value of their love for one another is much higher than the value of their tangible possessions. The story was first published in 1906 and has since been referenced in popular culture in motion pictures, television shows, and many adaptations of Christmas stories and songs.

Parlez-vous Français:
french writers everyone should know

Marie de France

Twelfth-century poet born in France. *The Lais of Marie de France* are a collection of short Anglo-Norman romances, which solidified the tradition of courtly love that would become so popular during the Middle Ages.

. . . . .

Pierre de Ronsard

Sixteenth-century poet and leader of a group known as the Pléiade, whose writing helped to revitalize French literature by imitating ancient Greeks and Romans. Ronsard's *Odes* were modeled on the odes of Pindar, and his later *Sonnets pour Hélène* are well known for their melancholy lyricism.

. . . . .

François Rabelais

Sixteenth-century French humanist, scholar, and physician. He left the monastic life to study medicine and eventually began to publish outrageously satirical works, such as *Gargantua and Pantagruel,* an adventure about two giants.

. . . . .

Molière

Molière is the pen name for 17th-century comic dramatist Jean Baptiste Poquelin. He cofounded the Illustre Théatre in 1643 and began writing such masterpieces as *Le Tartuffe,* a witty comedy about religious hypocrisy that was, at one time, suppressed from the stage for its scandalous subject matter.

Honoré de Balzac
Seventeenth-century French novelist who is considered to be the founder of the realistic school. Like Dickens, his works are filled with scrupulous attention to the details of social life, yet he also incorporates melodramatic plots in such works as *La Comédie humaine.* Later, Oscar Wilde quipped that Balzac invented the 19th century!

· · · · ·

Savinien Cyrano de Bergerac
Seventeenth-century author and playwright who might be best remembered for his long nose. Cyrano wrote fantastical works imagining trips to the moon in addition to scathing satires of French life in such comedies as *The Pedant Tricked* (1654) and *The Death of Agrippina* (1653)

· · · · ·

Madame de La Fayette
Her 1678 novel *La Princesse de Clèves* is important in literary history because it is one of the earliest known novels. The plot revolves around a princess who struggles to remain faithful to her husband although she is in love with another man. The book's focus on psychological states makes it a precursor for modern fiction.

· · · · ·

Voltaire
Seventeenth-century French satirist and philosopher Voltaire is best known for his Enlightenment masterpiece, *Candide,* which satirizes the ideals of humanism and progress.

· · · · ·

Denis Diderot
Most famous for compiling the 18th-century masterwork *Encyclopédia,* which spans 28 volumes and helps mark the Enlightenment commitment to asserting facts over and against the superstitious beliefs of the Middle Ages.

Jean-Jacques Rousseau
Swiss-born 18th-century French philosopher and political theorist.
He became instantly famous with the publication of his 1750 work
Discourses on the Sciences and Arts in which he argued that scientific and
artistic progress actually have a negative effect on mankind. *The Social
Contract* (1762) asserts that people in society have no natural authority
over each other, so we should enter into rational, reciprocal relationships
with the individual relinquishing his or her rights to the state.

• • • • •

Victor Hugo
As the leader of French Romanticism, Hugo thought of the writer's
role as public and prophetic. Famous works like *The Hunchback of Notre
Dame* and *Les Misérables* certainly foretold an enduring fascination with
panoramic melodrama, as contemporary Broadway versions attest.

• • • • •

Stendhal
French novelist and critic whose 1830 novel *The Red and the Black*
bridged the romantic and realistic schools of writing as it portrays a
psychological study of Julien Sorel and the French social order.

• • • • •

Gustave Flaubert
The history of the novel would not be the same without Flaubert's
significant contribution, *Madame Bovary* (1856), which focuses on the
inner life of an ordinary woman and, in so doing, catapults fiction into
a new "art for art's sake" direction.

• • • • •

Émile Zola
Leader of the naturalist school, 19th-century author Zola made his
mark on literary history by writing works that focused with intense
precision on issues of reform and justice. More than half of his novels
were part of a 20-volume work titled *Les Rougon-Macquart*.

Arthur Rimbaud

French symbolist poet whose work became an early precursor to surrealist writing. His 1871 collection of poems *The Drunken Boat* exemplifies his commitment to free-verse and extravagant metaphor.

•••••

Marcel Proust

Arguably the most significant novelist ever, Proust immortalized the stream-of-consciousness technique. His monumental work, *Remembrance of Things Past*, is a semi-autobiographical exploration of consciousness. The book portrays the life of the neurotic, sensitive narrator Marcel, who discovers his love of writing as he reflects on his childhood and tries to navigate his way through fashionable French society.

•••••

André Gide

French novelist and moralist Gide produced works encompassing symbolist influences and questions of politics. He won the Nobel Prize in 1947 for such works as *Travels in the Congo*, in which he exposes the horror of French treatment of native inhabitants.

•••••

Albert Camus

Algerian-born existentialist whose 1942 novel *The Stranger* and essay *The Myth of Sisyphus* outlined his allegiance to human freedom amid absurdity. He won the Nobel Prize in 1957, presumably for his writings against capital punishment.

•••••

Jacques Derrida

French philosopher and literary critic Derrida is most famous for inventing deconstruction, a complex and difficult approach to reading texts, which suggests that texts always mean what they say *and* their opposite. He outlines this precursor to postmodernism in such works as *Speech and Phenomena* (1973) and *Of Grammatology* (1976).

poetry survival manual 2

Shakespeare's Sonnets

The Trick: Divide a sonnet into four chunks.

Directions: The good thing about Shakespeare's sonnets is that they are composed of 14 lines, no more, no less. There's a reason for this number. Structurally speaking, the sonnet is built out of three big chunks and one smaller one. In literary speak, we call the big chunks quatrains because each chunk has four lines. The final couple of lines are known as a couplet.

So, basically, Shakespearean sonnets look like this:

Lines 1–4

Lines 5–8

Lines 9–12

and then the final couplet:

Lines 13–14

To make things easier, and to sound better, these chunks rhyme in the following way:

abab

cdcd

efef

gg

Here's how those rhymes translate in Sonnet 18

Chunk (aka Quatrain) 1:

day (a)

temperate (b)

May (a)

date (b)

Chunk 2:
   shines (c)
   dimmed (d)
   declines (c)
   untrimmed (d)
Chunk 3:
   fade (e)
   ow'st (f)
   shade (e)
   grow'st (f)
Final Couplet:
   see (g)
   thee (g)

So, every other line rhymes in each chunk. This is a clue. The first three quatrains form the beginning of an argument. The poet has a point to make: first A, then B, then C; consider this, then this, then this. What is his point? The answer to that question is found in the final couplet, that is, A + B + C = the couplet.

In Sonnet 18 ("Shall I compare thee to a summer's day?"), Shakespeare basically addresses his lover and says:

Quatrain 1: You're prettier than a summer day, because in May the wind blows too hard, and anyway, summer doesn't last that long.

Quatrain 2: Furthermore, you're better than a summer day because it gets dang hot outside.

Quatrain 3: Moreover, although summer doesn't last long, you will live forever. Why?

Couplet: Because I've written this sonnet about you, and as long as folks read it, you will be immortalized.

Each Shakespearean sonnet can be approached by watching how an argument develops in the first three quatrains and then gets resolved in the couplet.

drama queens:

Pulitzer Prize for drama 1952–1982

1952: *The Shrike,* Joseph Kramm

1953: *Picnic,* William Inge

1954: *The Teahouse of the August Moon,* John Patrick

1955: *Cat on a Hot Tin Roof,* Tennessee Williams

1956: *The Diary of Anne Frank,* Frances Goodrich and Albert Hackett

1957: *Long Day's Journey into Night,* Eugene O'Neill

1958: *Look Homeward, Angel,* Ketti Frings

1959: *J. B.,* Archibald MacLeish

1960: *Fiorello!,* George Abbott, Jerome Weidman, Jerry Bock,
and Sheldon Harnick

1961: *All the Way Home,* Tad Mosel

1962: *How to Succeed in Business Without Really Trying,* Frank Loesser
and Abe Burrows

1965: *The Subject Was Roses,* Frank D. Gilroy

1967: *A Delicate Balance,* Edward Albee

1969: *The Great White Hope,* Howard Sackler

1970: *No Place to Be Somebody,* Charles Gordone

1971: *The Effect of Gamma Rays on Man-in-the-Moon Marigolds,*
Paul Zindel

1973: *That Championship Season,* Jason Miller

1975: *Seascape,* Edward Albee

1976: *A Chorus Line,* conceived by Michael Bennett

1977: *The Shadow Box,* Michael Cristofer

1978: *The Gin Game,* Donald L. Coburn

1979: *Buried Child,* Sam Shepard

1980: *Talley's Folly,* Lanford Wilson

1981: *Crimes of the Heart,* Beth Henley

1982: *A Soldier's Play,* Charles Fuller

writers on CENSORSHIP

· ·

If you can't annoy somebody with what you write, I think there's little point in writing.
—Kingsley Amis

...There is more than one way to burn a book. And the world is full of people running about with lit matches. Every minority, be it Baptist/Unitarian, Irish/Italian, Octogenarian/Zen Buddhist, Zionist/Seventh-Day Adventist, Women's Lib/Republican, Mattachine/FourSquareGospel feels it has the will, the right, the duty to douse the kerosene, light the fuse. Every dimwit editor who sees himself as the source of all dreary blanc-mange plain porridge unleavened literature, licks his guillotine and eyes the neck of any author who dares to speak above a whisper or write above a nursery rhyme....
—Ray Bradbury

A free press can be good or bad, but, most certainly, without freedom a press will never be anything but bad.
—Albert Camus

Every human being has a right to hear what other wise human beings have spoken to him. It is one of the Rights of Men; a very cruel injustice if you deny it to a man!
—Thomas Carlyle

Every burned book enlightens the world.
—Ralph Waldo Emerson

Wherever they burn books they will also, in the end, burn human beings.
—Heinrich Heine, *Almansor*

inspired

. . . .

The ancient Greeks believed the nine Muses inspired human creativity.

The Nine Muses and Their Realms:

Calliope	epic poetry and eloquence
Euterpe	music or lyric poetry
Erato	love poetry
Polyhymnia	oratory or sacred poetry
Clio	history
Melpomene	tragedy
Thalia	comedy
Terpsichore	choral song and dance
Urania	astronomy

Nine Facts:

1. The early Greek poet Hesiod was the first to name the Muses in the *Theogony.*
2. Homer famously invoked the Muse in the *Iliad* and the *Odyssey.*
3. Like his epic predecessor, Virgil invoked the Muse at the beginning of the *Aeneid.*
4. In English poetry, one of the earliest invocations comes from Geoffrey Chaucer. In *The Canterbury Tales,* the Man of Law calls on the Muse of poetry to help him tell a moral story.
5. John Milton invokes the aid of a Muse at the first of *Paradise Lost.*
6. The earliest sites of the Muses' worship were Pieria, near Mount Olympus in Thessaly, and Mount Helicon in Boeotia.
7. Roman, Renaissance, and Neoclassical artists often distinguished Muses by certain props so viewers could recognize them:

   Calliope (epic poetry) carries a writing tablet.
   Clio (history) carries a scroll and books.
   Erato (love poetry) carries a lyre and a crown of roses.

Euterpe (music) carries a flute.
Melpomene (tragedy) wears or holds a tragic mask.
Thalia (comedy) wears or holds a comic mask.
Polyhymnia (sacred poetry) has a thoughtful look on her face.
Terpsichore (dance) carries a lyre.
Urania (astronomy) carries a staff, which she points at a globe.

8. Plato complimented the poet Sappho by calling her "the tenth muse." Since then, other female poets to earn that compliment have included Anne Bradstreet and Sor Juana Inés de la Cruz.

9. Muse comes from Latin *musa*, from Greek *mousa*. The name of Mnemosyne, the goddess of memory and mother of the Muses, comes from the Greek word *mnemosune*, "memory," which comes from the Greek and Indo-European root *men*, "to think." *Men* is the root word of amnesia, mental, and mind.

Theoretically Speaking

Structuralism

In a room of literary theorists, you can always spot the structuralist. He's the one who looks most like a scientist. He would also be the one least likely to be caught dead at a poetry slam. Structuralism grew out of linguistics and, as such, argues that literature can be analyzed by looking for opposites within a text. For instance, how does good vs. evil play out in Canterbury Tales*? Structuralists also look for commonly recurring structures or motifs that pop up in literature through the ages. Structuralists might notice, for example, that knights or knight figures always face some kind of sexual temptation, whether they appear in such works as* Sir Gawain and the Green Knight *or the Arthurian romances.*

gay? *not that there's anything wrong with that*

Maybe Jerry Seinfeld and George weren't gay, but rumors of same-sex love have circulated around the following writers.

• • • • •

William Shakespeare

For the Elizabethans, what we call bisexuality today was often considered merely a sexual act, as opposed to a commitment to a sexual orientation. Nevertheless, readers have speculated for centuries about the Bard's orientation. Although he was married to Anne Hathaway, Shakespeare's sonnets call his sexuality into question. Many of them appear to be love poems addressed to a married woman, the Dark Lady. (This is the same writer who bequeathed to his wife his "second-best bed" in his will). Another 126 sonnets are addressed to a beautiful young man known as the Fair Lord.

• • • • •

Virginia Woolf

Although she was married to Leonard Woolf, Virginia had an affair with Vita Sackville-West for five years. Vita's son described Woolf's novel *Orlando* as an elaborate and charming love letter from Woolf to his mother. Leonard Woolf knew about the affair, but promiscuity was common in the Bloomsbury group, so he didn't mind.

• • • • •

Bret Easton Ellis

When *Less Than Zero* catapulted this Generation X writer to fame, he was still in the closet. However, in August 2005, he confessed to the *New York Times* that his lover, Michael Kaplan, had died. Ellis said they never lived together, and that theirs was a "loose kind of partnership." Nevertheless, Ellis was so grief-stricken by his death that he couldn't even bring himself to leave his mother's house to attend Kaplan's funeral.

. . . . .

Carson McCullers

This southern novelist may have married, divorced, and remarried her husband, Reeves McCullers, but her passion for fellow writer Katherine Anne Porter was equally fiery. At the Yaddo writer's community, McCullers was so infatuated with Porter that she threw herself on the floor outside Porter's door. In a cool rebuff, Porter simply stepped over McCullers and went straight to dinner.

Theoretically Speaking

Deconstruction

D-con picks up where structuralism left off. Like structuralists, deconstructionists are also intrigued by oppositions; they begin, for instance, by looking at how goodness is defined by its opposite, evil. We can't understand happiness without knowing what sadness is. We can't comprehend Sonny without understanding Cher. You get the point. However, deconstructionists then go on to say that, if you think about it, oppositions are never really all that different. For example, there's always a little bit of good in even the most evil character—consider Raskolnikov in Crime and Punishment, *for example. In fact, opposites collapse so easily that often a statement means exactly what it is trying not to say. When Shakespeare writes, "My mistress's eyes are nothing like the sun," he is saying, on the one hand, her eyes are dull and lifeless. On the other hand, though, he is implicitly suggesting that her eyes are just like the sun, bright and full of fire. Keep reading the sonnet and you'll see just how hot she really is by the end.*

---

logophilia

· ·

A person who loves books is a bibliophile. Someone who loves words is a logophile. Are all bibliophiles logophiles? Are all logophiles bibliophiles? Leave it to the logicians to figure that out. In the meantime, here's the word on, well, words.

Words are slippery.
—Henry Adams

Slang is a language that rolls up its sleeves, spits on its hands, and goes to work.
—Carl Sandburg

A blow with a word strikes deeper than a blow with a sword.
—Robert Burton

What so wild as words are?
—Robert Browning

Fine words and an insinuating appearance are seldom associated with true virtue.
—Confucius

You can stroke people with words.
—F. Scott Fitzgerald

Fair words cost nothing.
—John Gay.

By thy words thou shalt be justified, and by thy words thou shalt be condemned.
—Matthew 12:37

A word said is a shot fired.
—Uzbek proverb

Language is the archives of history.
—Ralph Waldo Emerson

Every word is a preconceived judgment.
—Friedrich Nietzsche

The use of language is all we have to pit against the death of silence.
—Joyce Carol Oates

The great enemy of clear language is insincerity.
—George Orwell

Theoretically Speaking

Feminism

Why does the princess always have to lie around passively (or unconsciously) waiting for some prince to rescue her? Why did Victorian women writers have to publish under male pen names? Why were female authors considered "hysterical" while their male counterparts were merely "creative"? Was Ophelia simply insane, or would dating Hamlet make any woman want to kill herself? These are just a few of the thousands of questions that feminist theory brings to the table where, traditionally, only men have been seated.

The basic plot *J–L*

From *Jane Eyre* to *Lady Chatterley's Lover,* these plots are hot, hot, hot.

. . . . .

Jane Eyre

From orphan to lover, young Jane makes quite a journey in this romantic novel by Charlotte Brontë. Unlike typical Victorian heroines, Jane is a bit plain but really smart. She gets shipped off to boarding school, where she befriends the long-suffering Helen, who dies. From there, she becomes governess to the daughter of Edward Rochester of Thornfield Hall. She falls in love with the moody Rochester, but he has a secret. The reason he is so cold to Jane is because he has a crazy wife hidden in the attic. When Jane finds out, she flees and almost marries a clergyman. Turns out, she comes into a fortune from a long lost uncle. She leaves the odious clergyman, who only wanted to marry her so she could function as a servant to him during his missionary work. In a freaky, mystic way, she hears Rochester calling to her, so she returns to Thornfield, only to discover that his crazy wife has burned it to the ground and jumped off the roof. Rochester is blind and crippled. Jane is wealthy and free. With the power balanced out in the relationship, they happily marry.

. . . . .

"The Knight's Tale"

One of the *Canterbury Tales* by Geoffrey Chaucer, this story is told by a noble knight, but it is hardly a simple, heartwarming little tale. Theseus of Athens takes two Theban cousins, Palamon and Arcite, as prisoner. He locks them up in a tower where they spy the beautiful Emily, sister-in-law to Theseus. Arcite is released from prison on the condition that he is banished, but that won't stop him from courting Emily. He returns disguised as a servant. In the meantime, Palamon escapes from the tower so he too can woo Emily. The two cousins find each other and vow to fight it out, knight-style, with armor and all that. Theseus interrupts them and stages a much bigger battle. He tells them each to bring 100 knights to a tournament in one year. Behind the scenes, as it turns out, poor Emily doesn't want to marry either one of the guys. She prays that they will forget about her, but they don't. Palamon prays to the goddess of love to help him; Arcite prays to the god of war. Arcite wins the battle but gets thrown off his horse. In his last dying gasps, he says he hopes Palamon will wed Emily. Arcite dies. Emily gets over her aversion to Palamon and the two marry, living happily ever after.

• • • • •

Lady Chatterley's Lover

Mystic sex is at the heart of D. H. Lawrence's controversial 1928 novel which was banned in the United States and in England until 1959. Connie is married to emotionally stunted and sexually impotent British aristocrat Clifford Chatterley. No wonder, then, that she falls in love with her gamekeeper, Oliver Mellors. Lots of steamy sex and a pregnancy later, Lady Chatterley goes to Venice to figure out what to do about the baby. In her absence, Mellors's wife spreads rumors about him and Connie. She returns home and tells her husband that she is carrying Mellors's child. Clifford won't give her a divorce. Mellors gets fired. The story ends with them hoping that one day they will end up together.

frost *bites*

When it comes to sound bites about the writing life, America's most-beloved poet, Robert Frost, is the master.

I have never been good at revising. I always thought I made things worse by recasting and retouching. I never knew what was meant by choice of words. It was one word or none.

Writing a poem is discovering.

A poet never takes notes. You never take notes in a love affair.

All the fun is in how you say a thing.

People who read me seem to be divided into four groups: twenty-five percent like me for the right reasons; twenty-five percent for the wrong reason; twenty-five percent hate me for the right reasons. It's that last twenty-five percent that worries me.

Poets are like baseball pitchers. Both have their moments. The intervals are the tough things.

A poem is never a put-up job, so to speak. It begins as a lump in the throat, a sense of wrong, a homesickness, a love sickness. It is never a thought to begin with.

You can be a little ungrammatical if you come from the right part of the country.

Poets need not go to Niagara to write about the force of falling water.

No tears in the writer, no tears in the reader. No surprise for the writer, no surprise for the reader.

There are three things, after all, that a poem must reach: the eye, the ear, and what we may call the heart or the mind. It is most important of all to reach the heart of the reader.

The poet, as everyone knows, must strike his individual note sometime between the ages of fifteen and twenty-five. He may hold it a long time, or a short time, but it is then he must strike it or never.

Like a piece of ice on a hot stove the poem must ride on its own melting.

Theoretically Speaking

Marxism

If, on the most simple level, feminists divide the world into male and female, then Marxists, taking their cue from ol' Karl Marx himself, split the world into the haves and the have-nots. Marxist critics look at what they call the ideological content of a work, which means they examine the hidden values about class, politics, and power that literature reveals. A story like "The Garden Party" by Katherine Mansfield is fertile ground for Marxists. In it, a rich young girl named Laura begs her family to cancel their fancy garden party when she learns that a working-class man down the hill has died. Her wealthy mom could not care less about the sufferings of the poor, so Laura ventures to the "other side of the tracks" to learn first-hand about poverty.

I spy a symbol

One of the first things budding literary critics learn to do is to spot a symbol. They start off pretty easy—crosses allude to Christ, the rising sun promises hope.

• • • • •

An Optometrist's Billboard

Who can forget the eyes of Doctor T. J. Eckleburg staring out over the wasteland between New York and West Egg in *The Great Gatsby*? Disembodied and staring, the eyes form a parody of the eyes of God—they look, but they see nothing. No one great and wise is watching over this world of drunken flappers and wannabes.

• • • • •

The Green Light Across the Bay

Another enduring symbol from *The Great Gatsby*, the green light on the Buchanans' dock delivers the same "come hither" appeal that Daisy does. When Nick, the narrator, first sees Gatsby, he is staring at the light, recalling his love of Daisy and relishing his hope that once again he and his beloved can unite to live out the American Dream. Alas, the light should have been red, as in stop, as in no way. It just ain't meant to be.

• • • • •

Two Roads Diverging in the Woods

Robert Frost made forever famous the symbol of a forking path in "The Road Not Taken." "I took the [road] less traveled by," says the speaker, "And that has made all the difference." Most readers interpret the road that the speaker chooses as the one less traveled and, thus, more unique and individualistic. Folks love to quote this poem whenever they need an example of heroic iconoclasm. However, a more careful examination of the poem proves that both roads are the same ("both that morning equally lay in leaves no step had trodden black"). Ultimately, therefore, it makes no difference which road the speaker chooses. The road that isn't taken is the same as the one that is taken. The final line of the poem is another example of Frost's brilliant ability to pull the wool over our eyes. We want to look into nature to find something profound, but oftentimes what we find is as ordinary as we are.

•••••

A Madeleine

Proust's madeleine is the ultimate cliché confection. Only the cannoli of *The Godfather* can compete. In *Remembrance of Things Past*, one taste of the symbolic cookie reminds the narrator of his childhood and the Sunday mornings at Combray. Dipping the madeleine into tea is, you have to admit, a shade more poetic than dunking an Oreo into milk.

•••••

Eldorado

Yes, in some circles it symbolizes garish automotive wealth, but in the world of literature, Voltaire created the city of Eldorado for his satire *Candide*. Legend held that Eldorado was a city of gold, but for Voltaire it became an urban symbol of utopia and the power of human reason. Of course, poor Candide doesn't end up living here, but by the time he "cultivates his garden" at the end of the book, he realizes that life in Eldorado, while ideal, might ultimately get a bit boring.

•••••

Skylark/Squirrel/Songbird

All three of these words have something more in common than the fact that they are little creatures whose names begin with an S. They also happen to be some of the pet names Torvald bestows on his poor wife, Nora, in Henrik Ibsen's play *A Doll's House*. While Torvald intends them to be synonymous with such common pet names as "honey" and "sweetie pie," they come to symbolize the power imbalance between the two spouses. Nora is caged in Torvald's dollhouse and, like a skylark, squirrel, or songbird, eventually she has to fly the coop.

• • • • •

The Mississippi River
In *The Adventures of Huckleberry Finn*, Mark Twain chooses a strong symbol for freedom and the spirit of adventure—the mighty Mississippi. While land in the novel symbolizes the restrictions of both civilization and the institution of slavery, the wide, flowing river stands for unfettered independence. No wonder Jim and Huck grab a raft and head out.

• • • • •

The Glass Menagerie
The dominant symbol in Tennessee Williams' play, *The Glass Menagerie*, is (you guessed it!) the glass menagerie. Laura's collection of little glass animals clearly symbolizes her own delicacy and fragility. Of all the animals, she most identifies with the glass unicorn. Like the mythical creature, Laura just wasn't made for this world, as Jim comes to find out when he accidentally breaks off the unicorn's horn and, in turn, breaks Laura's heart as well.

• • • • •

The Rat
Native Son paints a racist world that preys upon and, ultimately, kills the main character, Bigger. In order to set this theme up at the very beginning of the book, Richard Wright uses a symbolic rodent. Bigger stalks and kills an ugly black rat, which foreshadows Bigger as a predator who will kill Bessie and Mary but which also symbolizes the brutal manhunt the police will enact as they stalk Bigger.

poet laureate:
the big poetic cheese *1974–*

· ·

Here are the rest of the poet laureates, from 1974 to the present.

· · · · ·

1974–1976: Stanley Kunitz
   Vital Stats: Born in Massachusetts in 1905. Died in 2006.
   Best Known For: Ten books of poetry, including *Selected Poems,
   1928-1958,* which won the 1959 Pulitzer Prize and *Passing Through:
   The Later Poems, New and Selected,* which won the 1995 National Book
   Award.
   Fun Facts: He also served as poet laureate in the year 2000 at the age
   of 95.

· · · · ·

1976–1978: Robert Hayden
   Vital Stats: Born in Michigan in 1913. Died in 1980.
   Best Known For: The poem "Those Winter Sundays."
   Fun Facts: He was the first African-American to be appointed
   consultant in poetry. His popularity grew worldwide; in 1966, he
   was awarded the grand prize for poetry at the First World Festival of
   Negro Arts in Dakar, Senegal, for his book *Ballad of Remembrance.*

· · · · ·

1978–1980: William Meredith
   Vital Stats: Born in New York City in 1919.
   Best Known For: Won the National Book Award in 1997 for *Effort
   at Speech.* His volume *Partial Accounts: New and Selected Poems* (1987)
   won both the Los Angeles Times Book Award and the Pulitzer Prize.

Fun Facts: His book *Effort at Speech* came about after suffering a stroke which produced expressive aphasia, a condition in which the patient knows what he wants to say but can't get the words out.

• • • • •

1981–1982: Maxine Kumin
Vital Stats: Born in Pennsylvania in 1925.
Best Known For: Keeping busy winning the Pulitzer Prize in 1973, raising three kids, teaching at Tufts University, and publishing 11 books of poetry.
Fun Facts: Raised horses on a farm in New Hampshire.

• • • • •

1982–1984: Anthony Hecht
Vital Stats: Born in New York City in 1923. Died in 2004.
Best Known For: Witnessed the liberation of the Flossenburg concentration camp, which produced a stoicism in all of his work, including "The Hard Hours," which won the Pulitzer Prize in 1968.
Fun Facts: On a lighter note, poets appreciate his invention of the "double dactyl," a metrical form similar to the limerick.

• • • • •

1984–1985: Robert Fitzgerald
Vital Stats: Born in Illinois in 1910. Died in 1985.
Best Known For: Translations of Greek and Latin poetry, as well as his own work
Fun Facts: Served as literary executor for Flannery O'Connor, who was a boarder in his house for two years.

• • • • •

1984–1985: Reed Whittemore
Vital Stats: Born in Connecticut in 1919.
Best Known For: Was also poet laureate from 1964–1965.
Fun Facts: Stepped in to help out Fitzgerald as his health failed.

1985–1986: Gwendolyn Brooks
Vital Stats: Born in Kansas in 1917. Died in 2000.
Best Known For: The poem "We Real Cool." She was also the first
African-American recipient of the Pulitzer Prize.
Fun Facts: "We Real Cool" was banned in West Virginia and
Mississippi schools because the word "jazz" supposedly had sexual
connotations.

• • • • •

1986–1987: Robert Penn Warren
Vital Stats: Born in Kentucky in 1905. Died in 1989.
Best Known For: He had been a consultant in poetry from 1944
to 1945, and then became the first to be designated poet laureate
consultant in poetry.

• • • • •

1987–1988: Richard Wilbur
Vital Stats: Born in New York City in 1921.
Best Known For: Won two Pulitzer Prizes, one for "Things of This
World" in 1957, and one for *New and Collected Poems* in 1989.
Fun Facts: He was a cryptographer in the US Army during World War
II.

• • • • •

1988–1990: Howard Nemerov
Vital Stats: Born in New York City in 1920. Died in 1991.
Best Known For: Was also poet laureate from 1963 to 1964.

• • • • •

1990–1991: Mark Strand
Vital Stats: Born in Canada in 1934.
Best Known For: Ten volumes of poetry. "Blizzard of One" won the
Pulitzer Prize in 1999

Fun Facts: Studied painting with Josef Albers at Yale. In his spare time he makes collages, prints, and etchings.

•••••

1991–1992: Joseph Brodsky
Vital Stats: Born in Leningrad in 1940. Died in 1996.
Best Known For: Winning the Nobel Prize in 1987.
Fun Facts: He started his poetry career at the tender age of 18. Prior to writing, he worked as a milling machine operator and as a geologist-prospector.

•••••

1992–1993: Mona Van Duyn
Vital Stats: Born in Iowa in 1921. Died in 2004.
Best Known For: Six women previously served with the title consultant in poetry, but Van Duyn was the first female to get the new name, poet laureate. Not only that, but she won a National Book Award in 1971 and a Pulitzer in 1991.
Fun Facts: Van Duyn received the strangest summation of her work when she was appointed poet laureate. Fellow writer Judith Hall described her poetry as: "narrative draped around a rumination; accentual stanzaic pattern with end rhymes, slanted and supported by internal assonance. Suburbia; a friend; a garden, but with dog's penises in it and wounds."

•••••

1993–1995: Rita Dove
Vital Stats: Born in Ohio in 1952.
Best Known For: "Thomas and Beulah," which won the 1987 Pulitzer Prize.
Fun Facts: The future poet laureate was already "most likely to succeed." During her senior year in high school, she was a Presidential Scholar, one of the top 100 best US graduates in 1970.

1995–1997: Robert Hass
Vital Stats: Born in California in 1941.
Best Known For: His first book, *Field Guide* (1973), was selected by
Stanley Kunitz for the Yale Series of Younger Poets Award. His essays
in *Twentieth Century Pleasures,* won the National Book Critics Award
in 1985.
Fun Facts: Not only does he write his own poetry, but for many
years he collaborated with noted Polish poet Czeslaw Milosz on
translations of his work.

· · · · ·

1997–2000: Robert Pinsky
Vital Stats: Born in New Jersey in 1940.
Best Known For: In 1994, his translation of Dante's *Inferno* became a
best seller.
Fun Facts: He must have been really good at his job. He was the
first poet laureate to serve three consecutive terms. During that time,
he started the Favorite Poem Project, an audio and video archive of
regular folks reading their favorite poems.

· · · · ·

2000–2001: Stanley Kunitz
Vital Stats: Born in Massachusetts in 1905. Died in 2006.
Best Known For: Also served from 1974 to 1976.

· · · · ·

2001–2003: Billy Collins
Vital Stats: Born in New York City in 1941.
Best Known For: Conversational, witty poems on the one hand.
Reading an occasional poem to mark the first anniversary of
September 11th on the other.
Fun Facts: He was the first recipient of the Poetry Foundation's Mark
Twain Award for humorous poetry in 2004.

2003–2004: Louise Glück
Vital Stats: Born in New York City in 1943.
Best Known For: Pulitzer Prize-winning volume *The Wild Iris*.
Fun Facts: Precocious at 18, Glück skipped college and went straight
to a poetry workshop at Columbia University, where she studied with
1948 poet laureate Leonie Adams.

• • • • •

2004–2006: Ted Kooser
Vital Stats: Born in Iowa in 1939.
Best Known For: 2005 Pulitzer Prize-winning volume, "Delights
& Shadows." Add to that two National Endowment for the Arts
fellowships, a Pushcart Prize, and the Stanley Kunitz Prize from
Columbia University.
Fun Facts: He's the tortoise, not the hare: "I feel that I'm really
fortunate if at the end of a year, after writing every day, I have a
dozen poems I care about," he told Melissa Block at NPR.

• • • • •

2006– : Donald Hall
Vital Stats: Born in Connecticut in 1928.
Best Known For: Winning the National Book Critics Circle Award
for his book *The One Day* (1988), and for serving as founding editor
of the Paris Review from 1953 to 1962, where he interviewed such
heavy hitters as T. S. Eliot and Ezra Pound.
Fun Facts: Whether teaching at the University of Michigan or writing
from his farm in New Hampshire, Hall rails against what he calls the
"McPoem," any poem cranked out in routine style from university
workshops.

with this *ring,* I thee dread

Most of the time, a marriage proposal is romantic fuel for a writer's imagination. However, occasionally popping the question is just a bad idea all around. Here are five potential grooms who never made it down the aisle with their lady loves.

. . . . .

Oscar Wilde

Oscar Wilde once said, "Men marry because they are tired; women because they are curious. Both are disappointed." Wilde learned first-hand that a lover can be disappointed even before approaching the altar. In 1879, his friend Leonard Montefiore died suddenly. Wilde grew close to Leonard's sister, Charlotte, and two years later he proposed. When she rejected him, Wilde was sure to get the last word. He wrote back to her and said, "I am so sorry about your decision. With your money and my brain, we could have gone so far."

. . . . .

W. B. Yeats

If at first you don't succeed, try, try again. This was Yeats' motto when it came to trying to marry the beautiful Irish Nationalist Maud Gonne. Yeats didn't share her activist passions, so his love remained unrequited. In 1888, he asked her to marry him. She said no, so he proposed again in 1899, in 1900, and in 1901. In 1903, she married John MacBride, but Yeats' was at least somewhat mollified five years later when Maud agreed to spend the night with him in Paris. A final proposal in 1916 earned him yet another rejection, so, being a man of great persistence, he asked Maud's daughter, Iseult, to marry him. Like her mother, she politely declined.

Lytton Strachey

Virginia Woolf was beautiful and talented, so no wonder men were attracted to her. However, Lytton Strachey was a most unlikely suitor to ask for her hand. He was openly gay, but this didn't stop him from popping the question. To his surprise, she said yes. He later wrote his brother, saying, "It was an awkward moment, as you may imagine, especially as I realised, the very minute it was happening, that the whole thing was repulsive to me. Her sense was amazing, and luckily it turned out that she's not in love. The result was that I was able to manage a fairly honorable retreat." No harm done. They remained friends despite her disappointment.

· · · · ·

Franz Kafka

And the award for worst proposal goes to...Franz Kafka. The same man who wrote in his diary that sex was the punishment for the happiness of married life wrote to Felice Bauer the following proposal: "Marry me and you will regret it. Marry me not and you will regret it. Marry me or marry me not and you will regret either." Surprise, surprise. She said no.

· · · · ·

Jonathan Swift

Esther Vanhomrigh was so in love with her witty tutor, Jonathan Swift, that she asked him to marry her. He turned her down, although he did her the honor of fictionalizing her in his poem "Cadenus and Vanessa." (The name Vanessa came from the first syllable of her last name and "Esse," a shorter version of Esther.) Swift wrote, "Each girl, when pleased with what is taught / Will have the teacher in her thought." Esther remained "hot for teacher" for years; in fact, some accused him of breaking her heart and causing her death. For his part, Swift remembered her not only in his poem, but also by keeping a lock of her hair for the rest of his life.

there's *no place like home*

. . . .

Some of the world's best writers had to leave home in order to let their imaginations run wild. Here's a list of expatriate writers on the move.

. . . . .

Ezra Pound

It's a long way from Idaho to a zoo cage in Italy, but modernist poet Pound managed to make the trek. Born in Hailey, he moved to Gibraltar in 1908 via cattle boat. During World War II, he ended up in Pisa, Italy, where he was imprisoned in an iron cage for treason.

. . . . .

Lord Byron

You can't be a major romantic poet without wandering the globe. Byron bid farewell to England in 1809 and spent two years traveling through the Mediterranean. He returned to England, where he was a popular member of London society until rumors of debts and incest forced him to leave in 1816, never to return. He traveled to Italy, Albania, and Turkey and died in Greece. His body was returned to England, but neither Westminster nor St. Paul's would permit his burial, so his coffin was laid to rest in the family vault in Nottinghamshire.

. . . . .

D. H. Lawrence

The coal mining town of D. H. Lawrence's birth, Eastwood, Nottinghamshire, just did not prove big enough for this major talent. In 1908, he moved to London. Then, in 1912, he met the love of his life, Frieda Weekley; despite the fact she was already married with three children, they ran off to Germany. They returned to England briefly, but her German family and his antimilitary stance made them objects of suspicion in 1914 London. They spent the rest of their lives on the move to such romantic locales as Italy, Sri Lanka, Australia, and Mexico. Lawrence died in France. Oddly enough, his remains ended up in Taos, New Mexico, of all places, after Frieda moved there with her third husband.

· · · · ·

T. S. Eliot

This *Waste Land* poet may have been born in Missouri, but the Show-Me state couldn't show him enough of the world. He spent three years studying at the Sorbonne in Paris and eventually settled in London. In 1927, he became a British citizen.

· · · · ·

W. Somerset Maugham

The novelist who one day would write *The Razor's Edge* straddled the edge of nationalities as early as his birth. Because his father worked for the British embassy in Paris, Maugham could be conscripted in the French army if he were to be born on French soil. So, to solve that problem, his mother made sure he was born at the British embassy, technically, therefore, on British soil. He grew up in England, but spent his adult years on the "razor's edge" of such places as China, Mexico, Italy, Africa, and India.

· · · · ·

Truman Capote

Such a colorful character as Capote might have been born in the equally colorful Big Easy, New Orleans, but he couldn't possibly stay there. On the one hand, he lived in such relatively dreary places as Monroeville, Alabama, where he was neighbors with Harper Lee, author of *To Kill a Mockingbird.* To research *In Cold Blood,* he traveled to Holcomb, Kansas. However, the flamboyant socialite eventually found himself in such exciting places as New York City, Greece, Switzerland, Africa, Russia, and the Far East. He died in Los Angeles.

Djuna Barnes

From a log cabin to the Left Bank, Djuna Barnes saw it all. Born in a cabin on Storm King Mountain in New York, Barnes moved to New York City in 1912. Then, in 1921, she moved to Paris, where she quickly became at home in the fashionable salons. In the 1930s, she lived in England, where she began drinking more heavily. In 1940, her family sent her to New York to seek help for her alcoholism in a sanatorium. She finally settled in Greenwich Village, dying a recluse in 1982.

To Sleep, Perchance to Dream

It is a common experience that a problem difficult at night is resolved in the morning after the committee of sleep has worked on it.

—John Steinbeck

All men whilst they are awake are in one common world: but each of them, when he is asleep, is in a world of his own.

—Plutarch

Sleeping is no mean art: for its sake one must stay awake all day.

—Friedrich Nietzsche

Dawn: When men of reason go to bed.

—Ambrose Bierce

The repose of the night does not belong to us. It is not the possession of our being. Sleep opens within us an inn for phantoms. In the morning, we must sweep out the shadows.

—Gaston Bachelard

Maugham's the word

W. Somerset Maugham was one of the best-loved, best-paid writers during the 1930s and 1940s. He is known not only for novels (*Of Human Bondage, The Razor's Edge*) but also for plays (*The Circle, The Constant Wife*) and short stories ("Miss Thompson," "Rain"). As effortless as he makes writing look, it wasn't always easy, as he was all too fond of explaining.

I often think how much easier life would have been for me and how much time I would have saved if I had known the alphabet. I can never tell where I and J stand without saying G, H to myself first. I don't know whether P comes before R or after, and where T comes in has to this day remained something that I have never been able to get into my head.

There are three rules for writing the novel. Unfortunately, no one knows what they are.

Writing is a whole time job; no professional writer can afford only to write when he feels like it.

I have never met an author who admitted that people did not buy his book because it was dull.

To write simply is as difficult as to be good.

We do not write because we want to. We write because we have to.

Art is merely the refuge which the ingenious have invented when they were supplied with food and women, to escape the tediousness of life.

It is cruel to discover one's mediocrity only when it is too late.

Anyone can tell the truth but only a few of us can make epigrams.

What has influenced my life more than any other single thing has been my stammer. Had I not stammered I would probably... have gone to Cambridge as my brothers did, perhaps have become a don and every now and then published a dreary book about French literature.

Theoretically Speaking

Postcolonialism

This theory focuses on literature and culture from previously colonized regions, such as writings from India under British rule. Postcolonialists might ask how British values affect Indian writing, or how Indian values changed British culture. Readers often reevaluate a work of literature after reading it through a postcolonial lens. The best-known example of this was in 1975, when Nigerian writer Chinua Achebe criticized Heart of Darkness *for its racism.*

Reader-Response Criticism

Instead of all this focus on the literary work, why not look at the reader himself or herself? This is just what reader-response critics do. They try to describe what goes on in readers' minds when they read something. This makes sense if you consider how differently a Holocaust survivor might interpret Primo Levi's memoir, Survival in Auschwitz, *compared to anyone else. Reader-response folks argue that there is no single definitive meaning of a work, because readers create different meanings depending on who they are, where they come from, and so on.*

around *the bend*

· ·

Maybe it was the stress. Maybe it was the syphilis. Whatever the reason, these writers ended up a few pages shy of a book, if you know what we mean.

· · · · ·

Ezra Pound

You might think Pound was crazy just by trying to wade through the *Cantos*, but actually his behavior was erratic even before he was institutionalized. Always eccentric, he left America to live in Italy, where he published his first book of poems on his own. His wide-ranging interests, from Chinese poetry to economics, led him to become a supporter of fascist dictator Mussolini. In radio broadcasts, he condemned the US government during the beginning of World War II. This type of "eccentricity" didn't go over well. He was tried for treason, declared insane, and institutionalized for 12 years.

· · · · ·

Paulo Coelho

Despite his literary talents, Brazilian author Coelho came from a family who didn't value the artistic life. His parents wanted him to become an engineer. When he refused, his father had him committed to an asylum three different times over the course of three years to receive electroconvulsive therapy. Ultimately, Coelho proved "crazy like a fox;" later in life, when he was tortured as a political prisoner, he was able to escape only by hurting himself in front of his captors.

· · · · ·

John Ruskin

He fell in love with a ten-year-old but didn't propose marriage to her until seven years later. She refused, and her death in 1875 prompted more of what had become a series of episodes of mental illness. Ruskin became convinced that her portrait had been painted centuries before by a Renaissance master. He tried to contact her ghost. At one point, he had an episode of madness during a lecture at Oxford and had to be dragged away kicking and screaming.

· · · · ·

Guy de Maupassant

During his late 30s, Maupassant became overwhelmed with fears of death. Despite his love of solitude, he had contracted syphilis years before. By the time he had died at the age of 42, the syphilis had led to his being declared insane in 1891 and institutionalized.

· · · · ·

Friedrich Nietzsche

A famous episode in Nietzsche's biography might lead one to see him merely as sympathetic. He was always intelligent and moody, but one day he saw a horse being beaten, and the sheer cruelty of it sent him over the edge. He ran to the horse, embracing it, and collapsed. From 1889 until his death, he was in an asylum. He had often suffered bouts of madness and lived a life on the edge, including having an incestuous relationship with his sister. Scholars debate whether his madness was a product of syphilis, his philosophy, or both.

· · · · ·

Charles Lamb

Madness seemed to run in the Lamb family. His sister, Mary, killed their mother. Lamb suffered from alcoholism and bouts of mania, and for six weeks between December 1795 and January 1796, he was treated at Hoxton House, an asylum. He wrote his good friend Coleridge with his typical sardonic wit, "My life has been somewhat diversified of late." He went on to explain: "your very humble servant [has been] very agreeably in a madhouse, at Hoxton. I am got somewhat rational now, and don't bite anyone. But mad I was." Hey, at least he was honest about it.

good things come in 4s

· ·

As these literary quartets show, sometimes good things come in 3s plus 1.

· · · · ·

The Rabbit Tetralogy

Most people simply refer to this John Updike series as the Rabbit books. No, they aren't about floppy-eared woodland creatures. Far from it. The first, *Rabbit, Run* (1960), features Harry "Rabbit" Angstrom, a former high-school basketball star who is now a disgruntled salesman with an alcoholic, pregnant wife. Middle-class life fills Angstrom with angst, and he spends much of the book running away from this troubled family. *Rabbit Redux* (1971) picks up where *Run* left off. Rabbit's wife, Janice, has left him, so he and his son set up housekeeping with a teenager named Jill, until she is killed in a house fire. Rabbit and Janice manage to reunite. The title of the third book, *Rabbit Is Rich* (1981), suggests that things should be looking up for Angstrom, but despite his wealth at midlife, he is still plagued by an overactive libido and spiritual malaise. The final book, *Rabbit at Rest* (1990), takes the reader from Rabbit and Janice's retirement in Florida to Rabbit's death. After a tumultuous life, finally he achieves some peace.

· · · · ·

The Alexandria Quartet

Lawrence Durrell set out to "complete a four-decker novel whose form is based on the relativity proposition." His goal translates into *Justine* (1957), *Balthazar* (1958), *Mountolive* (1958), and *Clea* (1960). Each of the four books gives a different point of view about the same characters. Justine and Darley have a tempestuous affair. Later he learns that she also loves the oddly named Pursewarden. Throw in some illegal political maneuverings, Palestinian gun-running, and a talented artist named Clea and you have an amazing tribute to the same exotic city that once housed the world's most famous library.

· · · · ·

The Time Quartet

If you were an avid reader in your youth, your first literary quartet may well have been Madeleine L'Engle's four books: *A Wrinkle in Time* (1962), *A Wind in the Door* (1973), *A Swiftly Tilting Planet* (1978), and *Many Waters* (1986). A powerful blend of science fiction, fantasy, and adventure, the four books tell the story of the Murry siblings, Meg, Charles Wallace, Sandy, and Dennys, and their buddy Calvin, as they try to rescue the world from evil. This is no small task, but they handle it with wisdom beyond their years. In *A Wrinkle in Time*, Meg and Charles Wallace get sent through time to rescue their father on a faraway planet. *A Wind in the Door* takes place the following year, as Meg gets to know her friend Calvin by traveling into his mitochondria to save him from a terrible illness. Next, in *A Swiftly Tilting Planet*, Charles Wallace manages to save the planet from certain nuclear catastrophe. Finally, in *Many Waters*, the twins, Sandy and Dennys, get time in the literary spotlight as they travel back in time to help the biblical Noah.

The basic plot *M–O*

From France to Germany to a road trip across the United States these plot summaries cover the world.

. . . . .

Madame Bovary

Bourgeois, bored housewife Emma Bovary learns a difficult life lesson in this 1856 classic by Gustave Flaubert. Married to nice but dumb village doctor Charles Bovary, the beautiful Emma feels unfulfilled by her romantic dreams. Not too bright herself, she falls for the unscrupulous Rodolphe Boulanger and begins a three-year love affair. He dumps her; she amasses debt and finally swallows arsenic. Her poor husband grieves for her, despite her foolishness, and dies a recluse.

. . . . .

The Nibelungenlied

It's not just anyone who can say they've read *The Nibelungenlied* (much less pronounce it!). The famous German epic poem was written around 1200 and inspired much of Wagner's opera *Der Ring des Nibelungen*. In a nutshell, the hero, Siegfried, travels to Worms to win the hand of the lovely Kriemhild. Her three brothers get the skinny on Siegfried—turns out he is a war hero; he owns a cape of darkness that makes him invisible; and he is thick-skinned, literally, because when he killed a dragon, its blood washed over him, making him a bit scaly and horny. Not the prettiest complexion, perhaps, but a darn useful one in battle. They approve of him as a spouse for their sister, but first one of them needs a favor.

Here's where things get weird. Brother Gunther is in love with Queen Brunhild of Iceland, but he needs help in winning her love. Siegfried agrees to help him in exchange for the hand of his sister, Kriemhild. Brunhild will be no easy catch for Gunther, however. She has sworn that she will only marry a man who can throw a spear farther than her. Siegfried, in his invisible cape, helps Gunther pull off the stunt. Gunther marries Brunhild; Siegfried married Kriemhild. However, Brunhild suspects that her darling Gunther really isn't as strong as she is. So, like so many brides, on their wedding night she ties little Gunther into a knot and hangs him on a wall like a picture. This was not Gunther's idea of fun. In a kinky display of heroism, Siegfried arrives in his invisible cloak and wrestles Brunhild into submission. He steals her girdle and ring and gives them to Kriemhild. Later, in a catfight between the two brides, Kriemhild shows Brunhild that she now has her girdle and ring, thus proving that Siegfried fooled the hefty Brunhild.

From this bizarre episode, the plot takes numerous turns. Kriemhild betrays Siegfried, and he gets killed by her brothers. She remarries and kills her brothers but then gets killed herself, proving the story is truly the stuff of opera...or at least soap opera.

· · · · ·

On the Road

Jack Kerouac's novel is considered by many to be the defining work of the Beat Generation, although it wasn't universally admired. Truman Capote once said of it, "This isn't writing; this is typing." Nevertheless, the autobiographical narrator, Sal Paradise, spins an adventurous tale of hitchhiking across America. He meets up with his buddy Dean Moriarty (a pseudonym for Neal Cassady) in Denver and then goes it alone to California. The next year, Dean signs Sal up for another wacky road trip through New Orleans to San Francisco. As you can imagine, the trip is anything but tame. The next year, they travel down to Mexico City. Over the course of three years, lover boy Dean will gain three wives and four kids, and the reclusive Sal will gain confidence and bravado. The thrill of the plot lies in the language, which Allen Ginsberg described as "bop prosody."

across the ages through the pages:
brit lit 5

1789–1830: The Romantic Period

Scholars date the beginning of the literary romantic period as 1789, with the publication of a watershed book: William Wordsworth and Samuel Taylor Coleridge's collection of poems *Lyrical Ballads.* The movement was greatly influenced by the events of the French Revolution. In general, the traits illustrated in romantic literature include its criticism of the past, its personal nature, its strong use of feeling and colorful imagery, and its exploration of nature and the supernatural. Romantics believed that literature, in general, should be what Wordsworth called a "spontaneous overflow of powerful feelings" and that poetry, in particular, should sound like the way people really spoke, not in carefully measured lines. The romantic period produced some of the world's greatest poets, including Wordsworth, Coleridge, and John Keats. Likewise, during the romantic period, Gothic literature became popular for its melodramatic, supernatural gloominess, best exemplified in the novel *Frankenstein* by Mary Shelley.

William Wordsworth: The Least You Need to Know

- Wordsworth is, in many ways, the father of British romantic literature. His *Preface to the Lyrical Ballads* outlined the key features of romantic poetry, including its spontaneity, its use of vernacular English, and its emphasis on the experiences of simple people interacting in and with nature.
- As a young man, Wordsworth was inspired by the ideas of freedom and equality arising from the French Revolution. He visited France in 1792 and had a love affair with Annette Vallon. Even though she gave birth to their daughter, because of political tensions between his country and France, he returned to England without his family. Thereafter his closest companion became his sister, Dorothy, whom he famously addresses at the end of his poem *Tintern Abbey.*

• One of Wordsworth's best-known poems illustrates the mind of the poet, how the poet can have a powerful emotional experience and later "recollect it in tranquility" to turn it into verse. The famous poem "I Wandered Lonely as a Cloud" forever made daffodils an important part of poetry:

I wandered lonely as a cloud
That floats on high o'er vales and hills,
When all at once I saw a crowd,
A host, of golden daffodils;
Beside the lake, beneath the trees,
Fluttering and dancing in the breeze.

Continuous as the stars that shine
And twinkle on the milky way,
They stretched in never-ending line
Along the margin of a bay:
Ten thousand saw I at a glance,
Tossing their heads in sprightly dance.

The waves beside them danced; but they
Out-did the sparkling waves in glee:
A poet could not but be gay,
In such a jocund company:
I gazed—and gazed—but little thought
What wealth the show to me had brought:

For oft, when on my couch I lie
In vacant or in pensive mood,
They flash upon that inward eye
Which is the bliss of solitude;
And then my heart with pleasure fills,
And dances with the daffodils.

Samuel Taylor Coleridge: The Least You Need to Know

- In 1797, Coleridge began his pivotal friendship with William Wordsworth, a collaboration which produced *The Lyrical Ballads* and some of Coleridge's finest poems, including "The Rime of the Ancient Mariner."
- He suffered from severe toothaches and ill effects of the Lake District climate. As a result, he became an opium addict. Under the influence, he produced the poem "Kubla Khan," saying it was written in an "opium dream" but remained unfinished because the writing was interrupted by the knock on a door by a person from Porlock. Poet Stevie Smith would later write a famous poem about this alleged "person" and how she wished that she too could be interrupted and not have to finish her work.
- "Kubla Khan" expresses the boundless creative and visionary power of the poet:

In Xanadu did Kubla Khan
A stately pleasure-dome decree:
Where Alph, the sacred river, ran
Through caverns measureless to man
Down to a sunless sea.

So twice five miles of fertile ground
With walls and towers were girdled round:
And there were gardens bright with sinuous rills,
Where blossomed many an incense-bearing tree;
And here were forests ancient as the hills,
Enfolding sunny spots of greenery.

But oh! that deep romantic chasm which slanted
Down the green hill athwart a cedarn cover!
A savage place! as holy and enchanted
As e'er beneath a waning moon was haunted
By woman wailing for her demon-lover!

And from this chasm, with ceaseless turmoil seething,
As if this earth in fast thick pants were breathing,
A mighty fountain momently was forced:
Amid whose swift half-intermitted burst
Huge fragments vaulted like rebounding hail,
Or chaffy grain beneath the thresher's flail:
And 'mid these dancing rocks at once and ever
It flung up momently the sacred river.
Five miles meandering with a mazy motion
Through wood and dale the sacred river ran,
Then reached the caverns measureless to man,
And sank in tumult to a lifeless ocean:
And 'mid this tumult Kubla heard from far
Ancestral voices prophesying war!

The shadow of the dome of pleasure
Floated midway on the waves;
Where was heard the mingled measure
From the fountain and the caves.
It was a miracle of rare device,
A sunny pleasure-dome with caves of ice!

A damsel with a dulcimer
In a vision once I saw:
It was an Abyssinian maid,
And on her dulcimer she played,
Singing of Mount Abora.
Could I revive within me
Her symphony and song,
To such a deep delight 'twould win me
That with music loud and long
I would build that dome in air,
That sunny dome! those caves of ice!
And all who heard should see them there,

And all should cry, Beware! Beware!
His flashing eyes, his floating hair!
Weave a circle round him thrice,
And close your eyes with holy dread,
For he on honey-dew hath fed
And drunk the milk of Paradise.

John Keats: The Least You Need to Know

- Keats is the name that springs to mind whenever you think of a beautiful, long-suffering poet dying young. He contracted tuberculosis when he was 23 years old, the same year he met the love of his life, Fanny Brawne. They got engaged at Christmas, and Keats began writing some of his best poetry in the following months, including "The Eve of St. Agnes" and "La Belle Dame Sans Merci." By 1820, however, his disease had progressed so much that his doctor told him he had to leave the British climate in order to survive. Though he went to Rome, he died the next year.

- Keats is best known for a series of odes he wrote around 1819, including "Ode on Melancholy," "Ode to Psyche," "Ode to a Nightingale," and "To Autumn." An ode is a type of poem that expresses an intense state of emotion. One of the most famous in all of English literature is Keats' "Ode on a Grecian Urn," in which he describes the timeless perfection of a work of art that, because of its permanence, never has to endure change. The poem is especially poignant because Keats knew he was about to die, so he was naturally drawn to topics of immortality. Since it was written, scholars have debated the meaning of the final two lines about truth and beauty:

Thou still unravished bride of quietness!
Thou foster-child of silence and slow time,
Sylvan historian, who canst thus express
A flow'ry tale more sweetly than our rhyme:
What leaf-fringed legend haunts about thy shape

Of deities or mortals, or of both,
In Tempe or the dales of Acidy?
What men or gods are these? What maidens loth?
What mad pursuit? What struggle to escape?
What pipes and timbrels? What wild ecstasy?

Heard melodies are sweet, but those unheard
Are sweeter; therefore, ye soft pipes, play on;
Not to the sensual ear, but, more endeared,
Pipe to the spirit ditties of no tone:
Fair youth, beneath the trees, thou canst not leave
Thy song, nor ever can those trees be bare;
Bold Lover, never, never canst thou kiss,
Though winning near the goal—yet, do not grieve;
She cannot fade, though thou hast not thy bliss,
For ever wilt thou love, and she be fair!

Ah, happy, happy boughs! that cannot shed
Your leaves, nor ever bid the Spring adieu;
And, happy melodist, unwearied,
For ever piping songs for ever new;
More happy love! more happy, happy love!
For ever warm and still to be enjoyed,
For ever panting and for ever young;
All breathing human passion far above,
That leaves a heart high-sorrowful and cloyed,
A burning forehead, and a parching tongue.

Who are these coming to the sacrifice?
To what green altar, O mysterious priest,
Lead'st thou that heifer lowing at the skies,
And all her silken flanks with garlands drest?
What little town by river or sea-shore,
Or mountain-built with peaceful citadel,

Is emptied of its folk, this pious morn?
And, little town, thy streets for evermore
Will silent be; and not a soul to tell
Why thou art desolate, can e'er return.

O Attic shape! Fair attitude! with brede
Of marble men and maidens overwrought,
With forest branches and the trodden weed;
Thou, silent form, dost tease us out of thought
As doth eternity: Cold pastoral!
When old age shall this generation waste,
Thou shalt remain, in midst of other woe
Than ours, a friend to man, to whom thou sayst,
"Beauty is truth, truth beauty,—that is all
Ye know on earth, and all ye need to know."

Frankenstein: The Least You Need to Know

- Mary Shelley, author of *Frankenstein*, was the daughter of British philosopher William Godwin and early feminist writer Mary Wollstonecraft, who died ten days after giving birth to her (a fact that recurs in the death of the main character's mother early in the novel). Shelley was only 21 when she published this novel in 1818.
- Shelley was the second wife of Percy Bysshe Shelley, another famous romantic poet who wrote such works as *Queen Mab*, "Hymn to Intellectual Beauty," and "Ozymandias." As the story goes, the couple went to Geneva to vacation near romantic poet Lord Byron, who had recently impregnated Mary's stepsister, Claire. One rainy night, the group decided to have a contest to see who could write the best ghost story. Recent news reports of a doctor reanimating a dead frog's legs with electricity inspired Mary to begin and then later to pursue her famous story.
- The title *Frankenstein* is frequently misunderstood as referring to the monster of the tale, but of course it refers to Dr. Victor

Frankenstein, who brings back to life a corpse he has sewn together from various body parts. The creature is actually a very sympathetic character in the book, shunned by society because of his disfigurement. He longs for an education and for companionship, but when his creator abandons him, he lashes out.

Thomas Hardy: The Least You Need to Know

- *The work of Thomas Hardy, who lived from 1840 to 1928, spans the romantic, Victoria, Edwardian, and modernist periods of British literature and, as such, reflects the bitter ironies of life.*

- *Hardy himself grouped his early writings into what he called "novels of character and environment," and these works include some of his best-known, such as* Tess of the D'Urbervilles *and* Jude the Obscure. *Both of these demonstrate the overarching theme of Hardy, that man struggles against an indifferent force of nature, which rules the world and inflicts suffering upon him.*

- *Although he denied that he was a pessimist, Hardy wrote poetry that seemed to take a stern, hard look at the worst. In his poem "Hap," that is, chance, he voices the frustration of life at the hand of uncaring gods:*

  > *...How arrives it joy lies slain,*
  > *And why unblooms the best hope ever sown?*
  > *—Crass Casualty obstructs the sun and rain,*
  > *And dicing Time for gladness casts a moan....*
  > *These purblind Doomsters had as readily strown*
  > *Blisses about my pilgrimage as pain.*

---

across the ages through the pages:
american lit 2

1765–1828: The Age of Revolution and Early Nationalism

Many of the great works of American history were written during the American Revolutionary period, most notably the Declaration of Independence, the Articles of Confederation, and *The Federalist Papers*. In 1789, the Constitution of the United States was ratified, so this was an important time for political writing. In correlation, though, it was also an exciting and influential time for literary composition, as writers began to find a truly American voice apart from that of their British ancestors. To that end, such writers as Washington Irving and James Fenimore Cooper began to define the American literary landscape in ways that still fascinate modern readers.

Washington Irving: The Least You Need to Know

- Irving originally wanted to become a lawyer, but his family encouraged his literary aspirations instead. The War of 1812 hurt his family's trade business, so he moved to Europe and began writing to help out financially. He would later accept a position in the US embassy in Madrid and continue his international travels.

- Despite his European interests, though, Irving's best-known works are set on the American East Coast. "The Legend of Sleepy Hollow," set in the Dutch settlement of Tarry Town, New York, recounts the harrowing tale of schoolmaster Ichabod Crane, who wants to win the hand of Katrina Van Tassel. However, his rival, Brom Bones, masquerades one night as the legendary Headless Horseman, the ghost of a decapitated soldier. Poor Ichabod runs for his life, and Brom and Katrina live happily ever after.

- "Rip Van Winkle," published in 1819, is set in the Catskill Mountains before the Revolutionary War. As Irving's most popular tale, it describes the adventures of a man who drinks from a dwarf's keg and falls asleep for 20 years. He returns to his hometown to discover that his shrewish wife has died and that George Washington has replaced King George III. In many ways, Rip's story is the first "American dream" in American literary history, and, as such, it reveals the baffled state of mind early colonists must have felt as they "awoke" to a new world and civilization vastly different from the British one they knew.

James Fenimore Cooper: The Least You Need to Know

- As the son of Judge William Cooper, who founded Cooperstown, New York, James F. Cooper developed an interest in uniquely American culture from an early age. At the age of 13, he enrolled at Yale but was expelled for committing schoolboy pranks. Eventually he matured to the point of becoming a farmer and a man of letters.

- In 1823, he published the first in a series of novels known collectively as *The Leatherstocking Tales*. They all revolve around the main character of Natty Bumppo, a frontiersman uncorrupted by "civilized" life. The most famous of *The Leatherstocking Tales* is *The Last of the Mohicans*, which describes two daughters trying to join their father, a British commander, during the French and Indian War. Their efforts are thwarted by Magua, a cruel leader of the Hurons. Natty Bumppo and Uncas, the last of the Mohicans, try to help the girls, but one of the daughters and Uncas die in the process.

laughing with the bard

. . . .

Measure for Measure

Plot

The kind and lenient Duke Vincentio has ruled Vienna too generously, and as a result, crime has flourished. Therefore, he decides to let his tough chief deputy, Angelo, rule the city while he pretends to leave. In reality, Vincentio disguises himself as a friar and hides in Vienna to see how Angelo fares. The first thing Angelo does is to reinstate an old law against sex before marriage. He sentences Claudio, a gentleman, to death for getting a young woman, Juliet, pregnant. Claudio's sister, Isabella, begs Angelo to spare her brother's life. In his hypocrisy, Angelo agrees, provided that Isabella will sleep with him. She refuses but Claudio asks her to do whatever it takes to keep him alive. Duke Vincentio overhears the siblings' conversation and comes up with a plan. He tells Isabella to agree to sleep with Angelo, but in her stead they will send Mariana, a woman who used to be engaged to Angelo before he left her. The duke's plan works, although Angelo tries to renege on his promise to free Claudio. At that point, Duke Vincentio abandons his friar disguise, chastises Angelo, and forces him to marry Mariana. Claudio and Juliet are reunited, and the duke asks Isabella to be his bride.

Themes

1. Absolute power corrupts absolutely. Once Angelo comes into power, he exerts a fierce control over Vienna, although he tries to remain above the law.
2. Effective leadership requires a balance of leniency and strictness. Duke Vincentio is not stern enough as a ruler, but Angelo rules too cruelly while the duke is supposedly gone.

crying with the bard

King Lear

Plot

Considered by many critics to be one of Shakespeare's greatest tragedies, *Lear* tells the tale of an aged king ready to hand over his kingdom to his three daughters, Goneril, Regan, and Cordelia. He devises an unusual method to determine which daughter should receive which portion of the kingdom. He asks each daughter to proclaim her love for him in a public show of affection. Goneril and Regan try to outdo each other, declaring a deep fidelity to their father in order to gain the largest amount of power. However, the youngest daughter, Cordelia, who is her father's favorite, refuses to play the game, despite her love for him. As a result, Lear, in anger and disappointment, banishes her from Britain. The King of France, recognizing Cordelia's integrity, marries her and takes her away. Immediately, Goneril and Regan, in their greed for power, conspire to disempower their father even more. Pushed to the brink of sanity, Lear goes out into a storm raving madly. When Cordelia learns of her father's encroaching madness, she raises an army. While she and her father reunite in a French camp, Goneril and Regan argue over the love of Edmund, the illegitimate son of Lear's friend. Goneril poisons Regan and kills herself. In the main plot, Lear and Cordelia are taken prisoner, Cordelia is hanged, and Lear, in his sorrow, dies.

Themes

1. With age comes wisdom, but sometimes it comes too late. Despite King Lear's advancing years, he foolishly forces his three daughters, to compete for his kingdom. As a result, he loses his power and all of his daughters as he learns, too late, about greed, lust, and how "sharper than a serpent's tooth it is to have a thankless child."
2. Suffering has a transformative power. Only once Lear has suffered at the hands of his daughters does he learn to pity the Fool, the poor of his kingdom, and the condition of his friend Gloucester, the father of Edmund.

learning with the bard

The Second Part of King Henry VI
Plot

The Earl of Suffolk was right at the end of the first part of the play.
Margaret of Anjou is able to dominate King Henry VI, in part because
she and the earl share a mutual attraction and conspire together against
the king. They plot to overthrow Henry's uncle Humphrey, Duke of
Gloucester, by convicting his wife, Eleanor Cobham of sorcery. The
duchess knows that if anything should happen to Henry, her husband,
the duke, would ascend to the throne, so she summons a witch to
her garden to foretell the possibility of her one day becoming queen.
Enemies of Gloucester find out, accuse her of dealing in the dark
arts, and banish her to the Isle of Man. When the Duke of Gloucester
becomes so ashamed and grief-stricken that he resigns his position,
Margaret is greatly pleased because she figures that she and Suffolk can
now rule behind the scenes. Suffolk kills Gloucester, but Henry begins
to realize that Suffolk is plotting against him. Suffolk is banished
and later captured by pirates, who are convinced that he is to blame
for England's political woes. They murder him and send his head to
the queen. In the meantime, Richard Plantagenet convinces fellow
noblemen of his right to the throne, as he was beginning to do in
the previous play. Before he goes to help quell a revolt in Ireland, he
persuades a rabble-rousing commoner, Jack Cade, to launch a rebellion
of his own. At the start of that rebellion, which would become the War
of the Roses between the House of Lancaster and the House of York,
Richard returns to England and defeats the king's troops at St. Albans.

Themes

1. What a wicked web we weave… The Houses of York and Lancaster
   manipulate King Henry VI through lies and deceit. Even his own
   queen, Margaret of Anjou, plots against him in her alliance with
   Suffolk. Elsewhere, Richard Plantagenet, the leader of the House of

York, incites commoners to rebel against the young king so that he can one day seize the throne. A kingdom so divided cannot stand.

2. Beware jealousy. This is a recurring theme in many Shakespeare plays, from *Othello* and *Macbeth* to *The Second Part of King Henry VI.* Queen Margaret envies most of the other characters in the play when, in her opinion, they stand in the way of her increasing power.

The 411 on Literary Prizes

- *The Pulitzer Prizes were first established in 1917, with nonfiction awards going to J. J. Jusserand, for history writing for* With Americans of Past and Present Days, *and to Laura E. Richards and Maude Howe Elliot, for their biography of Julia Ward Howe. The first Pulitzer for fiction was given in 1918 to Ernest Poole for the novel* His Family.

- *The National Book Awards were first awarded in 1950. The fiction award went to Nelson Algren for* The Man with the Golden Arm, *the nonfiction award went to Ralph L. Rusk for his biography of Ralph Waldo Emerson, and the poetry award went to William Carlos Williams.*

  Other noted awards for writers and their books include:
  - *The Edgar Award for best mystery novel*
  - *The Hugo Award for the best science fiction novel*
  - *The Nebula Award for science fiction/fantasy*

---

rhyme time 2: *poetry for children*

· ·

Christina Rossetti

When she wasn't modeling for pre-Raphaelite painters, Victorian poet Christina Rossetti wrote poems for adults and children alike. Her long narrative poem *Goblin Market* described a young girl who ate magical fruit that produced in her near-deadly cravings for more. Although contemporary literary critics read the poem as a Freudian depiction of sexuality or even bulimia, Victorian children were enthralled with the tale, despite its dark undertones. Her 1872 volume, *Sing Song*, was written more explicitly for young readers and contains a poem that serves as the basis for the modern "Patty cake, patty cake, bakers man...."

· · · · ·

Robert Louis Stevenson

The author of *The Strange Case of Dr. Jekyll and Mr. Hyde* (1866) had a bit of a split personality himself. As a child suffering from tuberculosis and often bedridden, he passed the time making up stories before he even learned to read. As an adult, he wrote, on the one hand, such books as *Dr. Jekyll* and the historical romance *Kidnapped* and, on the other hand, such books as *Treasure Island* and one of the most famous books of poetry for children ever, *A Child's Garden of Verses* (1885). In a self-deprecating letter to a friend, he said that the book proved that he had a total "incapacity to write verses," but the reading public disagreed. He is often considered the poet laureate of childhood.

· · · · ·

T. S. Eliot

Like Stevenson, Eliot is not a name one might immediately associate with children's verse. After all, he is the author of such poems as *The Waste Land* and "The Love Song of J. Alfred Prufrock." However, in 1939, he published *Old Possum's Book of Practical Cats*, the title of which came from his nickname, Old Possum. The delightful volume describes such cats as "Old Deuteronomy," "Skimbleshanks: The Railway Cat," "Bustopher Jones: The Cat About Town," and "The Rum Tum Tugger." The book is now best known as the inspiration for the Andrew Lloyd Webber musical *Cats*.

· · · · ·

Dr. Seuss

Advertising cartoonist and Hollywood screen artist Theodor Seuss Geisel is better known to millions of readers as the beloved Dr. Seuss. His pen name came from the fact that his father had always wanted him to grow up to be a doctor, so when he began writing children's books, he adopted the "Dr." His first book, *To Think That I Saw It on Mulberry Street*, was rejected 29 times before it finally saw publication.

The Cat in the Hat series began when he learned that many children were illiterate in part because there was nothing interesting and fun for them to read. Books focusing on only a small amount of vocabulary words were producing dull "Dick and Jane" type stories that left young readers cold. Dr. Seuss took up the challenge of writing a book with 223 required vocabulary terms, and *The Cat in the Hat* was the successful result. *Green Eggs and Ham*, another "limited vocabulary" book, was composed on a bet that he couldn't write a book using only 50 words. After that, his rhymes became full of hilarious, invented words that children love to pronounce out loud.

Dr. Seuss never had children of his own. In fact, his widow claimed that he was actually a bit afraid of them. His books have been translated into 15 languages and have sold over 220 million copies worldwide.

The Caldecott Medal *1938–1970*

Since 1938, the American Library Association each year has awarded the Caldecott Medal to the illustrator of the most distinguished American picture book for children. Readers young and old alike will marvel at the artistic range of expression in the following winning titles:

1938: Dorothy P. Lathrop, *Animals of the Bible*

1939: Thomas Handforth, *Mei Li*

1940: Ingri and Edgar Parin d'Aulaire, *Abraham Lincoln*

1941: Robert Lawson, *They Were Strong and Good*

1942: Robert McClosky, *Make Way for Ducklings*

1943: Virginia Lee Burton, *The Little House*

1944: Louis Slobodkin, *Many Moons* (text by James Thurber)

1945: Elizabeth Orton Jones, *Prayer for a Child* (text by Rachel Field)

1946: Maud and Miska Petersham, *The Rooster Crows*

1947: Leonard Weisgard, *The Little Island* (text by Golden MacDonald [Margaret Wise Brown])

1948: Roger Duvoisin, *White Snow, Bright Snow* (text by Alvin Tresselt)

1949: Berta and Elmer Hader, *The Big Snow*

1950: Leo Politi, *Song of the Swallows*

1951: Katherine Milhous, *The Egg Tree*

1952: Nicolas Mordvinoff, *Finders Keepers* (text by William Lipkind)

1953: Lynd K. Ward, *The Biggest Bear*

1954: Ludwig Bemelmans, *Madeline's Rescue*

1955: Marcia Brown, *Cinderella, or, The Little Glass Slipper* (text by Charles Perrault)

1956: Feodor Rojankovsky, *Frog Went A-Courtin'* (text by John Langstaff)

1957: Marc Simont, *A Tree Is Nice* (text by Janice May Udry)

1958: Robert McCloskey, *Time of Wonder*

1959: Barbara Cooney, *Chanticleer and the Fox* (text by adapted from Geoffrey Chaucer)

1960: Marie Hall Ets, *Nine Days to Christmas* (text by Marie Hall Ets and Aurora Labastida)

1961: Nicolas Sidjakov, *Baboushka and the Three Kings* (text by Ruth Robbins)

1962: Marcia Brown, *Once a Mouse*

1963: Ezra Jack Keats, *The Snowy Day*

1964: Maurice Sendak, *Where the Wild Things Are*

1965: Beni Montresor, *May I Bring a Friend?* (text by Beatrice Schenk de Regniers)

1966: Nonny Hogrogian, *Always Room for One More* (text by Sorche Nic Leodhas)

1967: Evaline Ness, *Sam, Bangs & Moonshine*

1968: Ed Emberley, *Drummer Hoff* (text by Barbara Emberley)

1969: Uri Shulevitz, *The Fool of the World and the Flying Ship* (text by Arthur Ransome)

1970: William Steig, *Sylvester and the Magic Pebble*

More Wacky Writers

- *George Sand wrote her novels at night.*

- *Katherine Anne Porter always wrote her last lines first.*

- *Charles Baudelaire kept a caged bat near his writing desk.*

What Is a WHAT?

What is a philologist?

Philology translates literally to "lover of words" and refers to a type of linguist that specializes in literature, rather than languages. In modern academia, philologists typically study the meaning of ancient literary texts. The modern idea of philology originated back in the early 19th century, when linguists began deciphering the meaning of the Rosetta Stone and later the signification of ancient hieroglyphics.

. . . . .

What is FanFic?

FanFic is the modern expression meaning Fan Fiction, a phenomenon in modern literature where readers desire more background story than popular novels or literary works provide. FanFic can become an extension of particular novels, in which readers actually craft backgrounds and side stories to accompany what has already been published. Sometimes sexually oriented, FanFic can be identified as slash fiction, in which fans create fictional sexual or romantic relationships between characters in a series of novels. A popular example is the FanFic that has risen from the *Lord of the Rings* trilogy, in which fans internationally have created sexual side stories between the characters in the popular books and films. FanFic has become so popular that some major publishing companies, such as Harper Collins, offer contests for FanFic or slash fiction, to introduce new authors to the publishing scene or to serve as a publicity move for many already published works.

"from books to movies for 200, please, alex."

Category: Drama

About Schmidt, Louis Begley
Atonement, Ian McEwan
Being There, Jerzy Kosinski
Children of Men, P. D. James
Crash, J. G. Ballard
Enduring Love, Ian McEwan
Field of Dreams (from book titled *Shoeless Joe*), W. P. Kinsella
Friday Night Lights, H. G. Bissinger
Last King of Scotland, Giles Foden
One Flew over the Cuckoo's Nest, Ken Kesey
Requiem for a Dream, Hubert Selby
Sleepers, Lorenzo Carcaterra
The 25th Hour, David Benioff
Waiting to Exhale, Terry McMillan
Trainspotting, Irvine Welsh
Secretary (from short story titled *Bad Behavior*), Mary Gaitskill
Jarhead, Anthony Swofford
The Pianist, Wladyslaw Szpilman

Category: Children's

The Wizard of Oz, Frank Baum
Jumanji, Chris Van Allsberg
The Incredible Journey, Sheila Burnford
The Secret Garden, Frances Hodgson Burnett
Stuart Little, E. B. White

Common Phrases and Their Origins

· ·

Phrase: Pass the buck
Meaning: To hand over responsibility to another person.
Origin: Certain card games use a marker known as a "buck" to distinguish the dealer from the other players. As players take turns as dealer, the buck is passed around to signify the current dealer. When the buck is passed on, so is the responsibility to deal.

Phrase: Pushing the envelope
Meaning: To challenge existing boundaries or borders.
Origin: The phrase originated in the mid-20th century in the US Air Force test pilot program. Pushing the envelope meant to fly beyond the plane's known or suggested limits.

Phrase: Bang for the buck
Meaning: Value for the price.
Origin: The phrase originates from the Cold War era when America was deliberating the idea of buying new weapons. The US Air Force claimed, at the time, that missiles such as ICBM's could do more damage to an enemy for the cost than a US Navy aircraft carrier; hence, it had more "bang" for the buck.

Phrase: Read between the lines
Meaning: To understand what is implied, not literally stated.
Origin: Long ago, in the days of hand delivered communication, writers would write in messages that could only be revealed using a reagent. For example, lemon juice is typically transparent but becomes discolored when heated. The author of a message would write a message in ink and then write the real message between the lines, using an invisible substance.

quick & easy shakespeare:

Cymbeline

Plot

Britain's King Cymbeline is most displeased. His sons had been kidnapped as infants, and his daughter, Imogen, has eloped with a man named Posthumus Leonatus, the son of one of the king's soldiers. Cymbeline wanted Imogen to marry Cloten, his obnoxious stepson, in order to please his new queen. Because Imogen defied his wished, the king banishes Posthumus, who goes to Rome. Then Posthumus meets a villain named Iachimo, who bets that he can seduce fair Imogen. When she refuses Iachimo's advances, he sneaks into her bedroom, steals a bracelet, and uses it as proof to Posthumus that he has slept with her. Furious, Posthumus orders a servant to kill Imogen, but instead the servant allows her to escape. She disguises herself as a boy and flees to Wales, where Cymbeline's abducted sons have been living. Eventually Imogen is reconciled with Posthumus, and Cymbeline is reunited with his long-lost boys, who are delighted to discover that the "boy" they met in Wales is really their sister.

Themes

1. Appearances can be deceiving. Posthumus believes Imogen was unfaithful based on faulty evidence.
2. Redemption is always possible. At one point, Posthumus plotted to kill Imogen, but he regrets his evil thoughts. Iachimo confesses his trickery and is forgiven.

biblio-tastic

Book lovers should know the following "biblio" terms for all things bookish.

Biblioclast: Someone who destroys a book, in other words, a really bad guy.

Bibliogony: The art of producing books. The more bibliogony out there, the better.

Biblioklept: Someone who steals books, that is, a kleptomaniac in the library.

Bibliomancy: Predicting the future by interpreting a passage chosen at random from a book, usually the Bible. Any book will do, but something like a refrigerator repair manual might yield odd results.

Bibliomaniac: Most likely, if you are reading this book, you are someone who is really fond of collecting and owning books.

Bibliopegy: The fine art of bookbinding. Very important for keeping those pages together.

Bibliophage: Someone who devours books. If you read at least a book a day, you can add this word to your resume.

Bibliophile: Oh, aren't we all? Someone who loves books.

Bibliophobia: A fear or dread of books. Kinda like arachnophobia, but less reasonable, because, let's face it, spiders are a lot scarier than books.

Bibliopole: No, it isn't a large pole that books are stacked near. It is someone who deals in rare books.

Bibliotheca: A bookseller's catalog or library. *Vamos a bibliotheca!*

literary funny bones

You know when you read Oscar Wilde or Tom Robbins that you are in for some zany humor, but numerous authors crack wise in ways that might just surprise you.

There is no happiness in love, except at the end of an English novel.
—Anthony Trollope, *Barchester Towers*

Discovering that priests were infinitely more attentive when she was in process of losing or regaining faith in Mother Church, she maintained an enchantingly wavering attitude.
—F. Scott Fitzgerald, *This Side of Paradise*

...for the stress of circumstances, Fred felt, was sharpening his acuteness and endowing him with all the constructive power of suspicion.
—George Eliot, *Middlemarch*

Shakespeare is the happy hunting ground of all minds that have lost their balance.
—James Joyce, *Ulysses*

Indeed, he seemed to approach the grave as a hyperbolic curve approaches a straight line—less directly as he got nearer, till it was doubtful if he would ever reach it at all.
—Thomas Hardy, *Far from the Maddening Crowd*

The advantage of doing one's praising for oneself is that one can lay it on so thick and exactly in the right places.
—Samuel Butler, *The Way of All Flesh*

Indeed, he would sometimes remark, when a man fell into his anecdotage, it was a sign for him to retire from the world.
—Benjamin Disraeli, *Lothair*

It has been the great fault of our politicians that they have all wanted to do something.
—Anthony Trollope, *Phineas Finn*

Babbitt spoke well—and often—at these orgies of commercial righteousness about the "realtor's function as a seer of the future development of the community, and as a prophetic engineer clearing the pathway for inevitable changes"—which meant that a real-estate broker could make money by guessing which way the town would grow. This guessing he called Vision.
—Sinclair Lewis, *Babbitt*

Exactly. She does not shine as a wife even in her own account of what occurred. I am not a whole-souled admirer of womankind, as you are aware, Watson, but my experience of life has taught me that there are few wives having any regard for their husbands who would let any man's spoken word stand between them and that husband's dead body. Should I ever marry, Watson, I should hope to inspire my wife with some feeling which would prevent her from being walked off by a housekeeper when my corpse was lying within a few yards of her.
—Sir Arthur Conan Doyle, *The Valley of Fear*

...an unalterable and unquestioned law of the musical world required that the German text of French operas sung by Swedish artists should be translated into Italian for the clearer understanding of English-speaking audiences.
—Edith Wharton, *The Age of Innocence*

...she would have despised the modern idea of women being equal to men. Equal, indeed! she knew they were superior.
—Elizabeth Gaskell, *Cranford*

I discovered early that crying makes my nose red, and the knowledge has helped me through several painful episodes.
—Edith Wharton, *The House of Mirth*

I try his head occasionally as housewives try eggs—give it an intellectual shake and hold it up to the light, so to speak, to see if it has life in it, actual or potential, or only contains lifeless albumen.
—Oliver Wendell Holmes Sr., *The Autocrat at the Breakfast Table*

Three Things You Never Knew About: Maya Angelou

- *She was born Marguerite Johnson.*

- *She was once kicked out of school for being afraid to speak in front of the class.*

- *She took a pilgrimage to Ghana in the 1960s so her son could attend the University of Ghanato and get in touch with his African roots.*

---

some nice alliteration:
Pulitzer Prize for poetry 1966–1990

1966: *Selected Poems,* Richard Eberhart

1967: "Live or Die," Anne Sexton

1968: "The Hard Hours," Anthony Hecht

1969: "Of Being Numerous," George Oppen

1970: "Untitled Subjects," Richard Howard

1971: "The Carrier of Ladders," William S. Merwin

1972: *Collected Poems,* James Wright

1973: "Up Country," Maxine Winokur Kumin

1974: "The Dolphin," Robert Lowell

1975: "Turtle Island," Gary Snyder

1976: "Self-Portrait in a Convex Mirror," John Ashbery

1977: "Divine Comedies," James Merrill

1978: *Collected Poems,* Howard Nemerov

1979: *Now and Then: Poems, 1976–1978,* Robert Penn Warren

1980: *Selected Poems,* Donald Rodney Justice

1981: "The Morning of the Poem," James Schuyler

1982: *The Collected Poems,* Sylvia Plath

1983: *Selected Poems,* Galway Kinnell

1984: "American Primitive," Mary Oliver

1985: "Yin," Carolyn Kisser

1986: "The Flying Change," Henry Taylor

1987: "Thomas and Beulah," Rita Dove

1988: *Partial Accounts: New and Selected Poems,* William Meredith

1989: *New and Collected Poems,* Richard Wilbur

1990: "The World Doesn't End," Charles Simic

holding out for a *hero* II

The Hero: Achilles

Daring Deed: Great hero of the Trojan War, with one weak spot. After King Agamemnon stole his girlfriend, he refused to fight, even though his fellow soldiers and friends were being trounced by the Trojans. Once Hector killed his best friend, Patroclus, Achilles flew into the fiercest rage recorded in myth. He single-handedly slaughtered Trojans by the hundreds. Eventually he found Hector and killed him without mercy. Still furious, he tied Hector's body behind his chariot and dragged it around the city to mutilate it completely. This led Hector's father to beg Achilles to return what was left of his son's body. Achilles gave in, knowing that he too was destined to die. Even though his mother had tried to make him invulnerable by dipping him into the River Styx, the part of the ankle she held him from was not protected by the river. In another battle, Paris, lover of Helen, managed to shoot an arrow into Achilles' heel and kill him.

· · · · ·

The Hero: Odysseus

Daring Deed: The most wily and clever of all Greek heroes, Odysseus was memorialized in everything from Homer's *Odyssey* to Tennyson's "Ulysses." During the Trojan War, a decade of battle had rendered the Greek forces weary and ready for home. It was Odysseus who turned the tide. He persuaded the Greeks to build a huge wooden horse and hide inside. When the Trojans led the horse into their city walls, the Greeks were able to infiltrate and kill them by the thousands.

In addition to the Trojan horse story, Odysseus kept busy in other ways. His journey home to Ithaca allowed for several heroic deeds. He killed Polyphemus, a Cyclops, by forging a giant spear and poking out his one eye. He resisted the witch Circe, who turned most of his men into swine. He descended into Hades to learn from a ghost how to get home, and he managed to sail past the alluring Sirens without crashing on the rocks. Once he finally got home, Odysseus, along with his son, Telemachus, killed all of the suitors who had been swarming like flies around his wife while he was away on business.

• • • • •

The Hero: Oedipus
Daring Deed: Killed the Sphinx. The story of Oedipus starts off happily but doesn't end that way. His father, King Laius of Thebes, was told by Apollo, the god of truth, that one day his son would kill him. Frightened by the prophecy, Laius poked a spike through baby Oedipus' heel and left him to die on Mount Cithaeron. Rescued by a shepherd, the young boy was raised by a neighboring king. As an adult, Oedipus was warned by the oracle at Delphi that he would kill his father and marry his mother. He avoided his adopted parents, trying to protect them. Unbeknownst to him, however, he met his biological father on a road and killed him in an argument. The oracle was right so far.

His life took a turn for the better when he returned home to find Thebes being terrorized by the Sphinx. When Oedipus was the only man who could answer the Sphinx's riddle, she killed herself. As a reward, Oedipus was given the king's widow, Queen Jocasta, as a wife. The oracle's prediction had come true. Neither of them knew that they were mother and son. When a plague fell on Thebes, the oracle at Delphi, whom Oedipus must have been sick of by now, said the city would be saved only if they drove out the murderer of King Laius. Oedipus pieced together that it was, indeed, the king whom he had killed on the road years ago. Horrified that the prophecy was fulfilled, Jocasta killed herself, and Oedipus poked out his eyes with her brooch.

• • • • •

The Hero: Aeneas
Daring Deed: Rome's answer to the Greek hero. The son of Aphrodite, Aeneas fought against the Greeks in the Trojan War. According to Virgil, Aeneas carried his father, Anchises, on his shoulders out of the

ruined city and fled to Carthage. There he fell in love with Dido, the queen. Since his destiny was to produce heirs who would eventually found the city of Rome, Mercury told Aeneas to leave Dido and get on about his heroic business. When he did, she killed herself. Aeneas, however, went on to Italy, where he founded the colony that would become Rome.

Ian McEwan: The Least You Need to Know

- *Though his work is less easily categorized than that of his many contemporaries, Ian McEwan nonetheless may be one of the most prizewinning authors of our time. Four of his novels have been shortlisted for Britain's most prestigious literary award, the Booker Prize for Fiction:* The Comfort of Strangers; Amsterdam, *which won the prize in 1998;* Atonement; *and* On Chesil Beach.

- *Early works were notorious for their dark, disquieting themes and violent subject matter, but his later books explore broader issues of how society and politics affect ordinary people who find themselves in unusual situations.*

- *Film adaptations of his novels include* The Comfort of Strangers, *for which Harold Pinter wrote the screenplay, and* Atonement, *which was nominated for an Academy Award for best picture.*

- *In other formats, he has written several librettos for operas, as well as plays for television, including the three works known collectively as* The Imitation Game, *specifically focusing on the position of women in our society.*

big ol' libraries

You can get lost in the stacks for hours in these ten largest libraries (according to the number of books, not square footage).

In the United States

1. Library of Congress
2. Harvard University Library
3. New York Public Library
4. Yale University Library
5. Queens Borough (New York City) Public Library
6. University of Illinois Library, Champaign/Urbana
7. University of California, Berkeley
8. The Public Library of Cincinnati and Hamilton County
9. Chicago Public Library
10. Free Library of Philadelphia

In the World

1. Library of Congress
2. National Library of China
3. National Library of Canada
4. Deutsche Bibliothek (Germany)
5. British Library
6. Harvard University Library
7. Vernadsky Central Scientific Library (Ukraine)
8. Russian State Library
9. New York Public Library
10. Bibliothèque Nationale de Paris

ain't misbehavin' 2

Another set of authors caught disturbing the peace.

· · · · ·

Paul Verlaine married Mathilde Mauté de Fleurville in 1870, but a year later he began an affair with Arthur Rimbaud. His marriage was marked by bouts of violence, including throwing his infant son against a wall. His love affair with Rimbaud was equally tumultuous. In 1873, he shot Rimbaud in the wrist during a drunken argument, so he spent the next 18 months in prison.

· · · · ·

Percy Bysshe Shelley led a life that was anything but ordinary. He was expelled from Oxford University for publishing a pamphlet called "The Necessity of Atheism." Four months later, he married a 16-year-old named Harriet Westbrook and promptly tried to convince her of the pleasures of an open marriage. She resisted, and soon he fell in love with 16-year-old Mary Godwin. He left the pregnant Harriet, married Mary, and later spent three years in a ménage à trois with Mary and her stepsister Claire.

· · · · ·

W. H. Auden married German divorcée Erika Mann, despite the fact that he was gay. His reasons for marrying had nothing to do with love. Erika wanted to become a British citizen, so Auden obliged. They had never met before their wedding day, and they never lived together after it.

· · · · ·

Oscar Wilde didn't think of marriage in exactly idealistic terms. He once quipped, "The one charm of marriage is that it makes a life of deception absolutely necessary to both parties."

T. E. Lawrence had masochistic tendencies throughout his life. He subjected himself to grueling exercise and diet programs. At one point, he hired a man to beat him because he enjoyed the pain.

• • • • •

Public readings are a great time for poets to misbehave. Stevie Smith disguised her serious poems on love and death in a childish, singsong style. To intensify the disparity between heavy subject and lighthearted style, she would dress in a pinafore and little rolled-down socks, stand on a table, and sing her poems. Anne Sexton was just the opposite. She would show up late to her readings, light up a cigarette, and tell the audience they could leave if they didn't like her.

• • • • •

When Sylvia Plath found out that her husband Ted Hughes was having an affair with Assia Wevill, she kicked him out of the house. A few months later, she killed herself. Hughes and Assia had a child together, but he was unfaithful to her as well. Six years after Plath's suicide, Assia killed herself and Hughes' daughter. The next years he married a nurse named Carol Orchard. She never left him, although his adulterous habits continued.

• • • • •

Few could understand William Faulkner's 1949 Nobel Prize speech, not because it was too literary or too deep, but because Faulkner was drunk when he delivered it. Between his thick southern accent, his inebriated mumbling, and his standing too far from the microphone to be heard, the Stockholm crowd was largely befuddled by his remarks.

the write stuff:
a glossary of literary terms from H to P

Here are some more literary terms to keep you sounding smart!.

Haiku–Japanese-inspired poem of three lines: five syllables in the first line, seven syllables in the second, and then five again. Packed into this tight structure is an image of nature, which leads to a spiritual insight of some sort.

Hamartia–Aristotle used this term to describe "some error or frailty" that brings about the downfall for a tragic hero such as greed, weakness, or the inability to coordinate one's belt and shoes.

Hubris–An ego the size of Texas. In Greek tragedy, this kind of pride leads humans to blow off the gods, which they never like. Hubris is the worst kind of hamartia.

Hyperbole–Really big exaggeration, as in "I'm hungry enough to eat a horse. No, make that a herd of horses."

Iambic pentameter–An iambic foot is one unstressed syllable followed by a stressed syllable, as in the word "regard." Iambic pentameter is metrical pattern in poetry, which consists of five iambic feet per line, so that the line sounds like this: du-Duh, du-Duh, du-Duh, du-Duh, du-Duh. Here's an example from John Keats: "when I have FEARS that I may CEASE to BE."

Irony–A literary device that uses contradiction to reveal a reality different from what appears on the surface. For instance, it would be ironic for a plumbing supplies warehouse to flood. There are different kinds of irony. Verbal irony is when someone means the opposite of what they say. Take, as a famous example, Jonathan Swift's suggestion in "A Modest Proposal" that the starving Irish should just eat their young. Sarcasm is a lot like verbal irony, but it's simpler and, well, often ruder. For instance, if Walter shows up at the bank meeting wearing a grease-stained tie, his boss might snip, "Nice tie. Planning on wearing that to the board meeting?" That would be an example of sarcasm. Not nice, but then again, sometimes necessary. Dramatic irony occurs when the audience knows something the characters don't. The best example of this is when Oedipus chooses a bride. We all know she is his mother, but he has no clue.

Lyric–A brief poem that expresses the thoughts and feelings of a speaker. The important thing to remember is that the speaker is not necessarily the poet. Just because you write a poem in the voice of a 19th-century firefighter doesn't mean that you have traveled back in time to battle blazes, and nor should your reader assume you have. When William Carlos Williams writes the lines "I have eaten the plums that were in the icebox," he may just be making that up. Sad poems don't necessarily come from sad poets. Same goes for angry or happy poems.

Melodrama–Basically, a literary soap opera, except usually ending happily.

Metaphor–A metaphor compares two things without using the word *like* or *as*. If you say "my love is a rose," you have created a metaphor, unless, in fact, you happen to be in love with a flower. An extended metaphor cranks the whole thing up a notch. A poet may develop a whole poem from a single metaphor, extending it line after line. For example, the Puritan poet Anne Bradstreet develops an extended metaphor of a book as a child in "The Author to Her Book."

Narrator–The speaker of a story. See the entry on lyric poetry about not assuming that a speaker (or narrator) is actually the author. An omniscient narrator is one who doesn't actually participate in the events of the story. Instead, he or she can move freely through the minds of any of the characters. An unreliable narrator is one who, accidentally or on purpose, tells events in a distorted or untruthful way. Narrators may be unreliable because they're young, stupid, drunk, or crazy–basically any of the reasons that anyone may be unreliable.

Ode–A type of lyric poem. Odes are usually serious and formal. Keats wrote "Ode on a Grecian Urn." You'd never see "Ode on My Collection of Tupperware."

Onomatopoeia–A word that sounds like what it means. Examples include *buzz, oink,* and *rattle.* As fun as they are, none is as fun as the word *onomatopoeia* itself.

Oxymoron–This sounds like a type of insult, but no, it's a paradoxical phrase in which two opposite words are used together, as in "original copy," or "jumbo shrimp."

Paraphrase–To restate the idea of something in your own words. Readers will often paraphrase a poem to help make sense of it, but the poem itself is always superior to the paraphrase, because the poem has a keener sense of language.

Parody–A comic imitation of another, usually serious, work. A good example, as you can see from the title, is Anthony Hecht's poem "Dover Bitch," which parodies Matthew Arnold's poem "Dover Beach."

Personification–A figure of speech in which human characteristics are given to nonhuman things. A writer might describe rain by saying that "the sky is crying." This makes readers identify with the situation all the more since they understand what crying is.

Plot–The particular selection and arrangement of incidents in a story that helps unfold the narrative. The plot isn't simply what happens. Instead, it is the way the author puts those events in order. A story may proceed chronologically–first A happens, then B, then C. However, an author might plot the events differently–first we learn about C and then we get the backstory of A and B.

Point of view–The perspective from which a story is told. A child's point of view will render a very different tale than an old man's, for instance. The point of view the author chooses affects how readers will respond to events. A first-person narrator says, "I saw this. I did that." The reader has to rely on that "I" to get the details. A third-person narrator, on the other hand, presents a more neutral point of view: "They saw this. They did that."

Problem play–A type of drama that became popular in the 19th century, in which a social issue was dramatized in order to inspire the audience to action. Prostitution, feminism, and economic injustice are common themes dealt with in problem plays. Despite their titles, problem plays can actually be very entertaining.

Other Common Oxymorons

- *Constant variable*
- *Exact estimate*
- *Only choice*
- *Act naturally*
- *Old news*
- *Same difference*
- *Alone together*

pop quiz #3

1. Which of the following authors did not renounce his US citizenship: T. S. Eliot, W. E. B. DuBois, or Ezra Pound?

2. Who said, "I never lecture... I detest the kind of people who go to lectures and don't want to meet them."

3. Which of the following authors graduated from Notre Dame: Nicholas Sparks, Barry Lopez, or Michael Collins?

4. Which of the following poets won the most Pulitzer Prizes: Robert Lowell, Edward Arlington Robinson, or Robert Frost?

5. Which of the following novelists won the most Pulitzer Prizes: William Faulkner, John Cheever, or John Updike?

6. Who was the first author to use the term "eyeball?"

7. Who said, "There is no agony like bearing an untold story inside of you."

8. Why was the Geneva Bible nicknamed the Breeches Bible?

9. Which contemporary writer is a distant cousin of Bill Clinton?

10. Which British playwright edited the script for *Indiana Jones and the Last Crusade?*

Answers
1. Ezra Pound
2. H. L. Mencken
3. All of them
4. Robert Frost (won four). Lowell and Robinson each won two.
5. John Updike (won three). Faulkner and Cheever each won two.
6. Shakespeare in *A Midsummer Night's Dream.*

7. Maya Angelou
8. Because it was the first Bible to depict Adam and Eve wearing pants instead of the usual translation, "aprons."
9. John Grisham
10. Tom Stoppard

More Wacky Writers

- *Bram Stoker married one of Oscar Wilde's ex-girlfriends in 1878.*

- *The first book Robert Browning every purchased was* Ossian.

- *In the late 1800s, Jack London worked making burlap in a jute mill for $1 per day and at an electrical company shoveling coal.*

- *In 1920, when Roald Dahl was only three years old, his older sister died of appendicitis and his father died of pneumonia.*

The basic plot *P–R*

Finding a plot for the letter P was no challenge—ya gotta go with *Paradise Lost*. The letter Q wasn't so easy, but you'll be delighted to see what we found. And as for the letter R, well, grab some tea and a madeleine. You're going to be here for awhile.

• • • • •

Paradise Lost

Almost everyone is familiar with the story of Adam and Eve, but John Milton tells the tale of the fall from paradise in such a unique way that the old story gains a fresh, if not slightly devilish, perspective. Milton wrote his 1667 epic poem in 12 books, giving the reader a panoramic sweep of heaven, hell, and the brief paradise in between. Surprisingly, some argue that the real hero of the book is the rebel with a (flawed) cause, Satan. Poet William Blake once said that Milton was "of the Devil's party without knowing it." Satan comes off as a Promethean hero battling against an unfair god, at least for the first half of the story, where he begins as a fallen angel curious about God's latest creation. He calls a council of fellow fallen angels, and they agree to send him on a fact-finding mission. As we all know, he eventually tempts Eve to eat the forbidden fruit, but again, Milton takes a slightly radical approach. He portrays Eve as the more intelligent of the two humans. She deliberates and reasons, and poor Adam just follows along. After the couple's expulsion from the garden, the angel Michael ends the story on a happy note, as he assures the pair that the Son of God has already offered himself as a ransom to pay for their misdeeds.

The Quiet Don

No, this isn't part of Mario Puzo's *Godfather* stories. *The Quiet Don*, written in four volumes between 1928 and 1940 by Mikhail Sholokhov, is considered by many to be the most significant work of early Soviet literature. The story describes the revolution moving into the Don Cossack region of Russia. Gregor Melekhov, a young Cossack hero, sits on the political fence. Initially, he sides with the Bolsheviks in the civil war, but later he takes up arms with the Whites in order to maintain Cossack freedom. Like Hamlet, he hesitates throughout the work, feeling torn between the Bolsheviks and the Whites. During the book's composition, Soviet officials most likely expected Melekhov eventually to become a strident Communist, but Sholokhov never delivered that little plot twist. By the publication of the fourth volume, the series was so popular that the Soviets could not condemn the work too harshly.

· · · · ·

Remembrance of Things Past

Writer Alain De Botton published a book called *How Proust Can Change Your Life*, which gives you some indication of the respect with which the author of *Remembrance of Things Past* is treated. This seven-volume meganovel is difficult to describe because so much of it is "in search of lost time." Proust relies heavily on memory and flashbacks to show the consciousness changes over the course of a lifetime. Volume 1, *Swann's Way*, recalls the narrator's childhood and his love for Swann's daughter, Gilberte, and for Odette. In *Within a Budding Grove* the narrator falls out of love with Gilberte and in love with Albertine. Volume 3, *The Guermantes Way*, finds the narrator climbing the social ladder. In *Cities of the Plain*, he discovers that one of the upper crust, Baron Charlus, is gay. The homosexual theme doesn't stop there, however. As it turns out, the narrator learns that Albertine may be a lesbian. He was about to break up with her, but this discovery makes her suddenly cool again. By volume 5, *The Captive*,

Albertine is living with the narrator, but she runs away amid various scandals. As one can tell from the title of the next volume, *The Sweet Cheat Gone*, Albertine dies. Gilberte has risen in the social ranks to become Mlle. de Forcheville. In the final volume, *The Past Recaptured*, World War I rages, as the narrator realizes that his fellow socialites are much less interesting than his own personal memories.

Ben Jonson: The Least You Need to Know

- *His work as a dramatist and poet bridged the reigns of Elizabeth I and James I, who granted him a pension and a position that was essentially that of England's first poet laureate.*

- Every Man in His Humour, *his first important play, was performed by the Lord Chamberlain's company in 1598 and featured William Shakespeare in the cast.*

- *In his younger years, he was imprisoned a number of times for work that he called satirical but that the government called seditious and slanderous.*

I ching, you ching, we all ching for the i ching

The I Ching (pronounced *EE-Ching*) is one of the oldest works of human literature. For centuries, people have consulted it to predict the future. We predict you'll understand its mysteries much better after reading this.

·····

Brief History:
I Ching translates as "The Book of Changes." The book is over 3,000 years old, but the philosophy behind it is even older. Chinese mystics developed keen sensitivities about the world around them through contemplative activities and meditation, and they recorded what they figured out. From one generation to the next, they passed down these "ancient Chinese secrets," and by 1200 BC, they had begun to be recorded. Eventually Confucius got in on the act, helping to codify some of the material. By the 17th century, Jesuit missionaries became interested in the I Ching, and in 1876, the first complete English language translation appeared.

·····

How to Consult the Oracle
The I Ching is some fun reading in and of itself, but most folks treat it as an oracle that provides answers (however enigmatic) to their questions. It reveals how the forces of the universe are working at any given time. While there are many ways to approach the I Ching, the easiest way is to use three coins or sticks and toss them six times. Afterward, instructions included in most editions show how to develop a six-line figure known as a hexagram. There are 64 possible hexagrams. Each one tells something different about a situation.

The Hexagrams

A hexagram is actually composed of two trigrams (3 lines + 3 lines = a 6-line hexagram). The trigrams are divided into eight natural elements: Heaven, Thunder, Water, Mountain, Earth, Wind, Fire, and Lake. So, in any given hexagram, you might have a combination of Fire + Water (you can imagine this produces conflict) or Mountain + Earth (two elements that go together more smoothly). The combination of the two trigrams gives you your answer.

The Art of War

General Sun Tzu was reported to have never lost a battle. He maintained that the best battle was the one that is won without being fought. His no-nonsense style led him to be called Sun the Warrior.

Sun Tzu's treatise is the first-known written strategy on how to fight and win a war. Though this ancient Chinese text was written more than 2,000 years ago, its principles are still applicable today.

Sun Tzu's insight and simple instructions make The Art of War *timeless. Many find that his strategies on war, such as these below, are also directly applicable to the business world, and to life in general.*

- *All warfare is based on deception.*
- *Hold out baits to entice the enemy. Feign disorder, and crush him.*
- *Attack him where he is unprepared; appear where they are not.*

cocktail banter

The next time you're at a cocktail party and feel the need to wax literary, drop these famous lines into your conversation, and you'll sound like someone who has read it all.

Call me Ishmael.

Don't use this line when being introduced to people, or for the rest of the night they'll never get your name right. Instead, just cite it as one of your favorite lines from *Moby Dick*. You can bet that most people haven't read much Melville, but if someone gets testy and challenges you, you can always bust out another Moby line, "from hell's heart I stab at thee; for hate's sake I spit my last breath at thee." That should send them back over to the cocktail weenies table.

Neither a borrower nor a lender be.

Admittedly, this famous *Hamlet* line comes from the blowhard Polonius, but it still sounds like good economic advice. If anyone seeks investment advice, just tell them you subscribe to that old wisdom from the Bard. If they disagree, ask them what the APR is on their credit card. That should do the trick.

Love is a great beautifier.

Should someone compliment you on your appearance, you can drop this little line from *Little Women*. If your spouse or significant other is within earshot, you are sure to score points.

I was much further out than you thought and not waving but drowning.

This line from Stevie Smith's great poem "Not Waving but Drowning" is a classic statement of miscommunication. The poem depicts a group of people bemoaning the loss of a friend, who, evidently, wasn't merely greeting them with a friendly wave from out in the middle of the ocean. If you need to escape a boring conversation at a party, you might give a hand signal to a good friend who can pull you away. If they refuse to come to your rescue, you can scold them later: "Hey, I wasn't waving! I was drowning over there!"

The Prince

Niccolo Machiavelli was one of the greatest political philosophers of the late Renaissance period. His originality led him to be called brilliant, devious, and cruel. Today, his practical methods would be summarized as the ends justifying the means.

His most famous work, The Prince, *outlines how to gain and maintain power. His goal was to create a better government for his people. In the book, he offers this advice:*

- *A wise man ought always to follow the paths beaten by great men, and to imitate those who have been supreme.*

- *He who is the cause of another becoming powerful is ruined.*

- *Two men working differently bring about the same effect, and of two working similarly, one attains his object and the other does not.*

Nobel Prize Winners *1956–1980*

1956: Juan Ramón Jiménez for Spanish language lyrical poetry.

1957: Albert Camus for pinpointing problems of the human conscience in contemporary society.

1958: Boris Leonidovich Pasternak, who embodies at once a great poet and a great epic writer. (Accepted first, later caused by the authorities of his country to decline the prize.)

1959: Salvatore Quasimodo for passionate Italian poetry depicting social conditions and frustrations.

1960: Saint-John Perse (pen name of Alexis Léger) for what the Academy calls "the soaring flight and the evocative imagery of his poetry." Lovely.

1961: Ivo Andric for the force with which he has drawn strong psychological portraits from the history of Yugoslavia.

1962: John Steinbeck for humorous and poignant social perception.

1963: Giorgos Seferis (pen name of Giorgos Seferiadis), who portrays the Hellenic world of culture with profound emotion.

1964: Jean-Paul Sartre for work that influenced existentialists everywhere. He declined the prize, saying that homage can weaken or undermine one's commitments.

1965: Michail Aleksandrovich Sholokhov for the literary power of *The Quiet Don*, a multivolume novel about the conflicts of the Don Cossack region of Russia.

1966: The prize was divided equally between:
Shmuel Yosef Agnon, the master of modern Hebrew fiction.
Nelly Sachs, who reads the fate of Israel with poignant strength.

1967: Miguel Angel Asturias for highlighting the traditions of Indian peoples of Latin America.

1968: Yasunari Kawabata, who expresses the essence of the Japanese imagination.

1969: Samuel Beckett for an unmistakable spare style that elevates humankind even as it depicts our destitution.

1970: Aleksandr Isaevich Solzhenitsyn for charging Russian literature with a powerful ethical force.

1971: Pablo Neruda for a poetry that, with the action of an elemental force, illuminates Chile's dreams as a nation. Plus, some of the best love poetry you will ever read.

1972: Heinrich Böll, whose gift for characterization renews German literature.

1973: Patrick White for putting Australia on the literary map.

1974: The prize was split equally between:
Eyvind Johnson, who emphasized themes of freedom.
Harry Martinson for writings that (how poetic is this?) "catch the dewdrop and reflect the cosmos."

1975: Eugenio Montale for unique verse that looks with clear eyes at the human condition.

1976: Saul Bellow, who can analyze contemporary culture as no one else can.

1977: Vicente Aleixandre, who renews literary traditions of Spanish writing in fresh ways.

1978: Isaac Bashevis Singer, who, with roots in a Polish-Jewish cultural heritage, illustrates enduring human themes.

1979: Odysseus Elytis (pen name of Odysseus Alepoudhelis), who uses Greek tradition to invigorate his poetry powerfully.

1980: Czeslaw Milosz, who lays it all out for you in poetry that isn't afraid to be political when it needs to.

Did You Know?

Did you know that many beloved writers attended Harvard University? Norman Mailer, James Agee, E. E. Cummings, W. E. B. DuBois, T. S. Eliot, Henry David Thoreau, and Thomas Wolfe all took classes at the Ivy League school.

Pig Latin *without the pig*

Many English words derive from Latin, as we all remember (and have now forgotten!) from high school. Here's a brief primer on the linguistic legacy of Latin.

Latin Abbreviations

Ca. (circa): About. Indicates an approximate date, as in "Chaucer wrote ca. 1370s."

Cf. (confer): Compare. Often found in literary annotations, as in "Auntie Em," cf. *The Wizard of Oz*.

Et al. (et alia) And others, as in "Modernist writers include Joyce, Woolf, Lawrence, et al."

E.g. (exempli gratis): For example, as in "Yeats wrote many great poems, e.g., 'The Second Coming.'"

N.b. (nota bene): Take note or note well. You might pencil n.b. in the margin of a book next to a great line.

Viz. (videlicet): Namely, as in "There are many great Victorian poets, viz., Robert Browning."

Latin Phrases

Ad nauseam: To the point of making you sick

Antebellum: Before the Civil War

Carpe diem: Seize the day

Ex libris: From the book collection of…

Finis: The end

In medias res: In the middle of things

In situ: In position

In toto: Completely or wholly

Juvenilia: Works written when young

Magnum opus: Masterpiece

Modus operandi: How someone works, or a method of working

Mutatis mutandis: With necessary changes
Non sequitur: It does not follow, as in something completely random
Post scriptum (p.s.): Written after
Tabula Rasa: Blank slate (usually refers to John Locke's theory of the mind)
Verbatim: Word for word, exactly

Three Things You Never Knew About: F. Scott Fitzgerald

- *He was named after Francis Scott Key, a distant relative famous for penning* The Star-Spangled Banner *in the early 1900s.*

- *His wife, Zelda, developed schizophrenia and was permanently hospitalized in 1932. She died when a fire broke out at the Highland Mental Institution in Asheville, North Carolina, in 1948.*

- *An avid drinker, Fitzgerald died of a heart attack while visiting a friend. He was only 44 years old.*

it's a mystery to me

Who better to comment on the mysteries of the universe than some of
the world's best mystery writers. Here they are in their own words.

. . . . .

Edgar Allan Poe

All that we see or seem is but a dream within a dream.

As an individual, I myself feel impelled to fancy a limitless succession
of Universes. Each exists, apart and independently, in the bosom of
its proper and particular God.

Men die nightly in their beds, wringing the hands of ghostly
confessors on account of the hideousness of mysteries which will not
suffer themselves to be revealed.

The boundaries which divide Life from Death are at best shadowy
and vague. Who shall say where the one ends, and where the other
begins?

. . . . .

Arthur Conan Doyle

Any truth is better than indefinite doubt.

For strange effects and extraordinary combinations we must go to
life itself, which is always far more daring than any effort of the
imagination.

It has long been an axiom of mine that the little things are infinitely
the most important.

There is nothing as deceptive as an obvious fact.

Our ideas must be as broad as Nature if they are to interpret Nature.

· · · · ·

Agatha Christie

Crime is terribly revealing. Try and vary your methods as you will, your tastes, your habits, your attitude of mind, and your soul [are] revealed by your actions.

There is nothing more thrilling in this world, I think, than having a child that is yours, and yet is mysteriously a stranger.

Very few of us are what we seem.

There's too much tendency to attribute to God the evils that man does of his own free will.

· · · · ·

Dorothy Sayers

Lawyers enjoy a little mystery, you know. Why, if everybody came forward and told the truth, the whole truth, and nothing but the truth straight out, we should all retire to the workhouse.

There certainly does seem a possibility that the detective story will come to an end, simply because the public will have learnt all the tricks.

While time lasts there will always be a future, and that future will hold both good and evil, since the world is made to that mingled pattern.

The great advantage about telling the truth is that nobody ever believes it.

war and *(not so much)* peace:
tempestuous tidbits about Tolstoy

One of the greatest of all novelists, Leo Tolstoy lived a life as large as the books he wrote. Here are some things you might not have known about this prolific Russian.

......

Merry Prankster

Little Leo came from a long line of nobility. Peter the Great had given one of his ancestors the title of Count, but this tony upbringing didn't prevent Tolstoy from pulling pranks. He purchased portraits of other people's ancestors and hung them in his house to fool his friends. He would make up stories about this aunt or that uncle to the delight of his visitors. Maybe this was his way of inventing characters he would later use in his books.

......

Not So Merry Honeymoon

Tolstoy's genius for writing didn't extend into all areas of his life, however. When it came to love, Leo was lacking in the charm department. Admittedly, he often smelled, he lost his teeth over time, and he contracted a venereal disease at least once. This didn't stop Sonya Andreyevna Behrs from marrying him, however. Had she known what her wedding night would be like, she might have reconsidered. Leo made her read his old diaries which recounted his past sexual experiences, drinking bouts, and gambling addiction. She was horrified by all of the details, including the discovery of an illegitimate son. Nevertheless, she went on to have 13 children with him.

War and Peasantry

Despite the success of *War and Peace* and *Anna Karenina,* Tolstoy longed for something more. He tried to reinvent himself from author to sage. In the 1880s, he would occasionally walk out on Sonya and the kids, trying to renounce his wealth and comfort to live as a peasant. His searching into new forms of spiritualism led him to be excommunicated by the Russian Orthodox Church. He left home for the last time in 1910. He wanted to wander as an ascetic and pretty much got his wish, at least for a few weeks, until he died of pneumonia in a remote railway station.

Hagakure

Drawn from a collection of commentaries by the samurai Yamamoto Tsunetomo, Hagakure *contains insight and instruction into what it truly means to be a warrior, including behavior, dress, philosophy, and warfare. The central premise of* Hagakure *is laid out in its opening pages: "The Way of the Samurai is death." Though it may seem archaic, it is as relevant today as it was when written in the early 1700s and covers many topics including loyalty, honor, and integrity.*

across the ages through the pages:
american lit 3

1828–1865: The American Renaissance

The period between 1828 and 1865 is called the American Renaissance because of the sheer quantity of masterpieces that were produced up to and during the Civil War. The era is also became known as the Age of Transcendentalism when such writers as Ralph Waldo Emerson and Henry David Thoreau reacted against rationalism in favor of an almost mystical sense of the unity of all things and the "divinity" of humankind. Other major writers of the period include poet Edgar Allan Poe, Nathaniel Hawthorn, Herman Melville, Walt Whitman, and Emily Dickinson.

Ralph Waldo Emerson: The Least You Need to Know

- A leading figure of transcendentalism, Emerson began his career as a minister in Boston but soon resigned his position and left for Europe, where he met such writers as Thomas Carlyle and Samuel Taylor Coleridge. Their influential friendships helped shape Emerson's new philosophical thought, which relied on intuition over reason and a belief in the supremacy of the individual. In 1835, he married and settled in Concord, Massachusetts, where he became the center of a literary circle that included such writers as Margaret Fuller and Henry Thoreau.

- In 1836, he published anonymously a book simply titled *Nature*. In it, he dissolves the barrier between the self and the natural world, so that humanity and nature become united in one grand spiritual vision. In a famous metaphor, he exclaims, "I become a transparent eyeball. I am nothing. I see all. The currents of Universal Being circulate through me; I am part or particle of God."

- In one of his famous essays, "Self-Reliance" (1841), he convinces the reader to discover a relationship with nature and God. We must learn to trust our own judgment, Emerson argues, and to avoid conformity at all costs. In a famous phrase, he says, "A foolish consistency is the hobgoblin of little minds."

Henry David Thoreau: The Least You Need to Know

- Like Emerson, his friend and neighbor, Thoreau was a naturalist, an essayist, and a transcendentalist. Educated at Harvard, he taught school in Massachusetts and, in 1843, helped Emerson edit the transcendentalist magazine, *The Dial.* In 1845, he retreated to Walden Pond where he built a cabin and lived as simply as he could for two years. He recorded the experience in his best-known work, *Walden.* His goal was to "front only the essential facts of life," so he reduced his dependency on material comfort, instead finding an almost religious experience in such menial daily chores as keeping warm or hunting for food. Ultimately, his pared-down existence enabled, for him, a much greater degree of self-expression and authenticity.

- Despite his periods of solitude, Thoreau was deeply committed to justice. His 1849 essay "Civil Disobedience" argues that the best government is "one which governs least." He opposed slavery and the Mexican-American War, and he even spent a night in jail for his resistance to paying poll taxes. He was a strong literary influence on such later leaders as Mahatma Gandhi and Martin Luther King Jr., who both avidly read his works.

Edgar Allan Poe: The Least You Need to Know

- Poe's life was as dramatic as the literature he wrote. His parents were actors, but both died when he was only two years old. He was adopted by a Virginia merchant, with whom he grew increasingly hostile before running away to join the army. His first book of poems was published in 1827, and he continued to write thereafter, despite such personal upheaval as his marriage to his 13-year-old cousin, her death a decade later, and his heavy drinking.

- In order to appeal to as many readers as possible, Poe filled his stories with bizarre characters—murderers, lunatics, and necrophiliacs. "The Fall of the House of Usher" (1839) tells the horrifying tale of Roderick Usher and his deceased sister who rises from the family vault. For "The Murders in the Rue Morgue" (1841), considered the first detective fiction story, Poe creates an amateur detective, C. Auguste Dupin, who solves the case of a brutal double murder. In the equally grim story, "The Tell-Tale Heart" (1843), a murderer buries his victim's body beneath a floor, only to hear what he thinks is the heart still beating. Driven mad with horror, he confesses his crime to the police.

- Poe was equally well known for his poetry. "Annabel Lee" (1849), written after the death of his young wife, revolves around what Poe called "the most poetical topic in the world"–the death of a beautiful woman. His most famous poem, "The Raven," describes a man tormented by the death of his beloved Lenore. A raven appears and torments him with the recurring phrase, "Nevermore!"

Nathaniel Hawthorne: The Least You Need to Know

- Descending from an old New England family active in the Salem witch trials, Hawthorne often wrote about Puritans and a sense of guilt. He worked as a writer and as a surveyor for the Customs House in Boston, until he moved to a commune, Brook Farm, in 1841. He based his novel *The Blithedale Romance*, in part, on the experience. He eventually returned to living in Salem and working for the Customs House, in addition to traveling throughout Europe.
- Puritan themes find their most dramatic expression in his 1850 novel *The Scarlet Letter*. In the story, a young, attractive woman named Hester Prynne is forced to wear a red letter A as punishment for the crime of adultery. She gives birth to a daughter out of wedlock but refuses to name the father, because, as it turns out, he is the respected minister, Arthur Dimmesdale. Tormented with guilt, Dimmesdale finally joins Hester and her daughter on the pillory as he reveals his own secret, a scarlet letter etched on his chest.

Herman Melville: The Least You Need to Know

- Born into a prominent family, Melville and his parents faced financial difficulty early in his life. After the death of his father, he pursued several occupations, including going to sea, a vocation that informed the writing of his masterpiece, *Moby Dick*. In addition to writing about whaling, though, Melville also pursued themes of civil disobedience in, "Bartleby the Scrivener," a story about a legal proofreader who makes a stand against meaningless work by repeating the phrase "I would prefer not to."

- *Moby Dick* is a whale of a book, if you'll pardon the pun. Incorporating a riveting adventure plot along with theology, philosophy, and a fascinating study in the psychology of obsession, the book is considered one of the truly great American novels. The title of the book refers to a great white whale who had once bitten off the leg of Captain Ahab. As a result, from aboard his ship, *The Pequod*, Ahab has relentlessly pursued the creature ever since. The story is told from the perspective of one of the hands on deck, Ishmael. As a narrator, he realizes that Ahab's greed and obsession are unhealthy, to say the least. After many pages reflecting on the whale as a symbol of ultimate evil, the book ends when Moby Dick sinks *The Pequod*, killing everyone on board except Ishmael.

Leaves of Grass: **The Least You Need to Know**

- When Ralph Waldo Emerson wrote his essay "The Poet" in 1843, little did he know that his desire for a uniquely American poet would be satisfied in the wide range of works by Walt Whitman, whose 1855 volume *Leaves of Grass* represented a watershed moment in American poetry. It introduced readers to Whitman's signature long lines, his musical effects, his colloquial speech, his frank sexuality, and his ideas on American destiny. He calls the United States itself "the greatest poem" of all and credits the American people as fellow geniuses. He sent the first edition of *Leaves of Grass* to Emerson, who called the book extraordinary. Numerous editions were to follow until 1892.

- The longest and best-known poem in the collection, "Song of Myself," consists of nearly 2,000 lines. There Whitman not only offers a portrait of American society at the time, but he also describes himself and his personal vision of the equality of all things, as the famous opening lines of the work declare:

I CELEBRATE myself, and sing myself,
And what I assume you shall assume,
For every atom belonging to me as good belongs to you.

I loafe and invite my soul,
I lean and loafe at my ease observing a spear of summer grass.

My tongue, every atom of my blood, form'd from this soil, this air,
Born here of parents born here from parents the same, and their parents the same,
I, now thirty-seven years old in perfect health begin,
Hoping to cease not till death.

Creeds and schools in abeyance,
Retiring back a while sufficed at what they are, but never forgotten,
I harbor for good or bad, I permit to speak at every hazard,
Nature without check with original energy.

Emily Dickinson: The Least You Need to Know

- Dickinson was one of the most famous recluses in American literature. She attended Mount Holyoke Female Seminary but primarily spent most of her time at her home in Amherst, a place she compared to "the definition of God."
- She wrote most of her poems in her bedroom, dividing them into packets that she tied up with needle and thread. In 1862, she sent some of them to T. W. Higginson, who gave advice to budding poets in the *Atlantic Monthly*. Although she wrote over 1,800 poems, only a few were ever published in her lifetime. Higginson

published an 1890 edition of her work, but he heavily edited their lack of capitalization, and their frequent use of dashes and slant rhyme.

- Despite the fact that most of her poems are very short, they encompass a full breadth of subject matter. Love, nature, time, and eternity were only a few of her themes. One of her most consistent themes, however, was death. She often personified Death as if it were just another character in her world and, therefore, less frightening. Noted poet and critic Allen Tate considers the following poem as one of the greatest in the English language. It is easy to see why:

Because I could not stop for Death,
He kindly stopped for me;
The carriage held but just ourselves
And Immortality.

We slowly drove, he knew no haste,
And I had put away
My labor, and my leisure too,
For his civility.

We passed the school, where children strove
At recess, in the ring;
We passed the fields of gazing grain,
We passed the setting sun.

Or rather, he passed us;
The dews grew quivering and chill,
For only gossamer my gown,
My tippet only tulle.

We paused before a house that seemed
A swelling of the ground;
The roof was scarcely visible,
The cornice but a mound.

Since then 'tis centuries, and yet each
Feels shorter than the day
I first surmised the horses' heads
Were toward eternity.

More Wacky Writers

- *Robert Louis Stevenson had a pet donkey.*

- *Charles Dickens was afraid of bats.*

- *Fyodor Dostoevsky was desperately afraid of being buried alive.*

- *Voltaire suffered from chronic constipation.*

- *William Wordsworth had no sense of smell.*

across the ages through the pages:
brit lit 6

1832–1901: The Victorian Period

Queen Victoria's accession to the throne in 1837 inaugurated the
Victorian period, which lasted throughout the century until her death
in 1901. While romantic literature focused inward on the imagination
or outward on the natural world, Victorian literature confronted social
issues of the day, such as the position of women in society, the effects
of the Industrial Revolution, growing class tensions, pressures toward
political reform, and the impact of Charles Darwin's theory of evolution
on religious thought. If Mary Shelley's comparison of Dr. Frankenstein
to the mythological figure Prometheus exemplifies romantic thinking
in all of its brazen heroism, then the figure who best typifies Victorian
literature would be Alfred, Lord Tennyson's version of the classical
mythology hero who, in a poem titled "Ulysses," seeks new worlds:

> Come, my friends.
> It is not too late to seek a newer world.
> Push off, and sitting well in order smite
> The sounding furrows; for my purpose holds
> To sail beyond the sunset, and the baths
> Of all the western stars, until I die.
> It may be that the gulfs will wash us down;
> It may be we shall touch the Happy Isles,
> And see the great Achilles, whom we knew.
> Tho' much is taken, much abides; and tho'
> We are not now that strength which in old days
> Moved earth and heaven, that which we are, we are,–
> One equal temper of heroic hearts,
> Made weak by time and fate, but strong in will
> To strive, to seek, to find, and not to yield.

Curiously, though, Victorians by and large did not see their age as heroic. They were facing new social and political changes, but overall they felt a crisis of faith, even as they witnessed the spirit of progress in the industrial world. As Victorian poet Matthew Arnold wrote in his famous work "Dover Beach":

> The Sea of Faith
> Was once, too, at the full, and round earth's shore
> Lay like the folds of a bright girdle furled.
> But now I only hear
> Its melancholy, long, withdrawing roar,
> Retreating, to the breath
> Of the night wind, down the vast edges drear
> And naked shingles of the world.

In addition to Alfred, Lord Tennyson and Matthew Arnold, other major Victorian writers include Elizabeth Barrett Browning, Charles Dickens, and Charlotte and Emily Brontë.

Elizabeth Barrett Browning: The Least You Need to Know
- As a child she suffered from tuberculosis and later a spinal injury. As a result, she was often bedridden, but her physical condition didn't keep her from learning Hebrew so that she could read the Old Testament. When she was only 20 years old, in 1826, she published *Essay on Mind, with Other Poems.* Two years later, her mother died, and she remained living with her increasingly tyrannical father.
- In 1844, she published a volume simply titled *Poems,* which caught the attention of fellow poet Robert Browning. He wrote her a letter praising the work; over the span of their romantic courtship, in fact, they exchanged over 500 letters. Because her father did not want her to marry, Elizabeth and Robert eloped and lived in Italy, where her health markedly improved.

- In 1850, she published the volume *Sonnets from the Portuguese*, a collection of love poems addressed to Robert. The most famous is Sonnet 43:

How do I love thee? Let me count the ways.
I love thee to the depth and breadth and height
My soul can reach, when feeling out of sight
For the ends of being and ideal grace.
I love thee to the level of every day's
Most quiet need, by sun and candle-light.
I love thee freely, as men strive for right.
I love thee purely, as they turn from praise.
I love thee with the passion put to use
In my old griefs, and with my childhood's faith.
I love thee with a love I seemed to lose
With my lost saints. I love thee with the breath,
Smiles, tears, of all my life; and, if God choose,
I shall but love thee better after death.

Charles Dickens: The Least You Need to Know

- Dickens is one of the most famous and most widely read Victorian novelists. Like many of his characters, he suffered a difficult childhood marked by his parents' debt and his lack of education. He worked in a law firm and as a reporter to sharpen his writing skills.
- None of his novels has ever gone out of print. They remain popular for their social criticism, their sympathy with children, their panoramic view of London, and their wide array of characters. Most of them were written in a serial fashion, so that episodes of them appeared weekly or monthly in literary journals.
- *Oliver Twist* was one of his first novels to shed light on Victorian social problems. Dickens wrote the book in reaction to the 1834 Poor Law, which ended welfare payments to the poor and required family members, including children, to pay out their

debts with workhouse labor. Oliver, the main character, is born in a workhouse and, in a famous scene, asks for more gruel. He is promptly punished and runs away, ending up with gang of thieves. Eventually he is rescued by the kind Mr. Brownlow who provides him with a home and an education.

- In 1843, Dickens published a classic, *A Christmas Carol.* The novella sold 6,000 copies in one week and is still read each holiday season by millions. The story centers on the miserly Ebenezer Scrooge, who meets the ghosts of Christmas past, present and future. From them he learns the values of generosity and charity, and thus he gives his employee Bob Cratchit a raise to help care for Bob's lame son, Tiny Tim.

Charlotte and Emily Brontë: The Least You Need to Know

- Charlotte and Emily were two of six children born to Reverend Patrick Brontë and his wife, who died when they were very young. Because it was unusual for women to publish during the Victorian era, they adopted male pseudonyms—Currer Bell (Charlotte) and Ellis Bell (Emily).
- When their mother died, the girls were sent to boarding school, a terrible experience from which Charlotte drew inspiration for her novel *Jane Eyre.* Two of their older sisters died there, so Charlotte and Emily were allowed to return home. They spent much of their childhood playing in the wild, isolated Yorkshire moors, which would become the setting for Emily's novel, *Wuthering Heights.*
- *Jane Eyre,* published by Charlotte in 1847, tells the story of one of the most heroic and beloved girls in Victorian literature. Orphaned and shy, Jane is raised by her cruel aunt, who sends her off to Lowood, a boarding school where she receives further mistreatment. She grows up to become a governess for Edward Rochester, a moody, wealthy man who secretly harbors an insane wife in his attic. Rochester falls in love with Jane's strength and intelligence, and after his wife dies, he and Jane wed.

- Emily Brontë's novel, *Wuthering Heights*, does not end on such a happy note, however. The story begins when Catherine Earnshaw's father adopts a homeless boy named Heathcliff, whose passionate, emotional nature matches Catherine's perfectly. When she foolishly remarks that it would be beneath her to marry Heathcliff one day, he runs away, leaving the bereft Catherine to wed the wealthy but boring Edgar Linton. Meanwhile, Heathcliff makes his own fortune and marries Edgar's sister in order to make Catherine jealous. Eventually Catherine and Heathcliff confess their love, but she dies while giving birth to Edgar's child. Heathcliff lives for many tormented years, inflicting his rage on Catherine's daughter and his own son, until he finally dies and is buried next to his beloved.

The Book of Five Rings

Miyamoto Musashi, known to the Japanese as Kensei or "sword saint," was born in 1584. A samurai, he won more than 60 battles by killing all of his opponents. Although his actions might convey that he was a malicious man, he pursued a pure ideal revealed in The Book of Five Rings. *Of his own work, Musashi said it is "a guide for men who want to learn strategy." The book offers an insightful look into the strategy of winning, and its practical applications extend far beyond martial artists to all who want to incorporate the mastery of conflict into their professional and personal lives.*

across the ages through the pages:
american lit 4

1865–1910: The Realist Period

Realist American literature responded to changes in postwar society by concentrating its efforts on detailing and interpreting the changing world. From expanding urban areas to declining rural regions, the cultural landscape led writers to emphasize common, everyday situations, ordinary characters, and the language of regular folk. New subjects such as factory life, the hopes of African Americans following Reconstruction, and a critical look at marriage and family expectations emerged as well. The major writers of the realist period include Mark Twain, Henry James, and Kate Chopin.

Mark Twain: The Least You Need to Know

- Born Samuel Langhorne Clemens, Twain took his pen name from a riverboating phrase meaning "two fathoms deep."
- Many of his stories are set along the Mississippi River, where he grew up along its banks in the town of Hannibal, which he fictionalized as St. Petersburg in *Tom Sawyer*. He became so interested in regional dialects that in the 1870s he worked hard at recording the speech patterns of a young African-American boy. Later he would mimic the dialect through the character of Jim in *Huckleberry Finn*.
- Despite his uniquely American voice and brand of humor, Twain also traveled widely. He made a trip around the world in 1895, which he wrote about in *Following the Equator*.
- In 1876, he wrote *The Adventures of Tom Sawyer* (1876), a novel about a clever young boy, Tom, and his adventurous friend, Huckleberry Finn. They witness a murder and run away to hide on Jackson's Island because they know that the wrong man has been convicted of the crime. Fearing that others had thought they were dead, the boys return home, identify the real murderer as Injun Joe, and discover his buried treasure.

- The sequel to *Tom Sawyer* was Twain's masterpiece, *The Adventures of Huckleberry Finn* (1884). Ernest Hemingway once said, "All modern American literature comes from [this] book." Through the voice of Huck Finn, Twain found an outlet to address such issues as the immorality of slavery. The novel is told in Huck's distinct vernacular style. Raised by a drunken father, Huck escapes his violent home by running away to the river. There he meets another runaway, the slave Jim. The story of their time together on the raft drifting down the Mississippi is filled with the cast of characters they meet, including con men, actors, thieves, and lynch mobs. Eventually Jim gains his freedom, and Huck, always resistant to the "civilizing" forces of urban culture, ends the novel by proclaiming that he will head out to Indian territory rather than let Tom Sawyer's family adopt him.

Henry James: The Least You Need to Know

- If Hemingway was right that modern American literature originated with Mark Twain, the American novel, in many ways, found its highest artistic expression in the work of Henry James, a master craftsman with a keen perception into human psychology and a gift for critical analysis of fiction.
- Born in New York City in 1843, James came from an aristocratic line. His grandfather was one of the first millionaires in America. As a result, many of his works focus on the leisure class and social distinctions.
- James wrote most clearly in the realist tradition in such works as *Daisy Miller* (1878), whose plot revolves around an unsophisticated girl from New York who travels to Europe and encounters snobbish, aristocratic expatriates who are offended by Daisy's independent, nonconforming ways.
- James' major theme of the clash of old European and new American cultures is further explored in his 1877 novel, *The American*. Wealthy Christopher Newman hopes to marry Claire, the daughter of an aristocratic French family. The family prevents the

marriage, and so Christopher contemplates revenge by exposing skeletons in the family closet. Finally, though, he comes to the realization that exacting revenge would compromise his principles, and he makes peace with Claire, who enters a convent.

- First published in *The Atlantic Monthly*, James' greatest novel, *The Portrait of a Lady* (1881), combines feminist themes with deep psychological insight into its main character, the independent and romantic Isabel Archer. Isabel inherits a fortune and marries American expatriate Gilbert Osmond. Only later does she discover that the marriage was set up by a disloyal friend who wanted to get a share of Isabel's money.

Kate Chopin: The Least You Need to Know

- Because she wrote about such questionable topics as divorce, miscegenation, alcoholism, and sexuality, Chopin remained a challenge to critics for years. Her first novel, *At Fault* (1890), boldly featured a strong female character contemplating divorce. The book received little critical attention, and so she began, for awhile, writing children's stories.
- Despite her nonconformist themes, Chopin's life was relatively traditional. She grew up in St. Louis in a Catholic family and got married when she was 19 years old to a Louisiana businessman. She bore six children in nine years and was widowed at the age of 32. She began writing to make money and published 95 short stories, two novels, and one play. Her early short stories established a theme she would pursue throughout her writing: the conflict a woman faces between serving as a traditional wife or developing a life and identity of her own.
- Chopin's focus on the confinements of marriage comes to light most clearly in one of her best works, *The Awakening*. The main character of the novel, Edna Pontellier, is a wife and mother of two children. On a family vacation, she meets and falls in love with Robert Lebrun, a charismatic young man. Edna realizes how her passions have been denied in her marriage, so when she

returns home from the vacation, she moves out of her house in the hopes of being able to continue her relationship with Robert. Unfortunately, Robert loses interest in Edna once she establishes a new freedom for herself, so, in the end of the novel, she goes alone on vacation and takes a long swim until she drowns in an apparent suicide.

Quotes on Children

There is always one moment in childhood when the door opens and lets the future in.

—Graham Greene, *The Power and the Glory*

In old days there were angels who came and took men by the hand and led them away from the city of destruction. We see no white-winged angels now. But yet men are led away from threatening destruction: a hand is put into theirs, which leads them forth gently towards a calm and bright land, so that they look no more backward; and the hand may be a little child's.

—George Eliot, *Silas Marner*

Children sweeten labours, but they make misfortunes more bitter.

—Francis Bacon, *Essays*

laughing with the bard

. . . .

The Merchant of Venice

Plot

Antonio, a wealthy Venetian merchant, wants to help his friend,
Bassanio, court the rich and beautiful Portia. Bassanio needs money, so
Antonio borrows money from Shylock, the Jew. He promises to repay
the loan within three months. If not, Shylock can have, in exchange,
a pound of his flesh. Time passes and as Bassanio is about to marry
Portia, he learns that Antonio will not be able to repay Shylock after
all. Fearing that his friend will, literally, have a pound of flesh cut
from his body, Bassanio returns to Venice to attend Antonio's trial.
His wife, Portia, comes to the trial as well, disguised as a lawyer. She
beats Shylock in court by arguing that if he is going to take a pound
of flesh, he must take flesh only, not a drop of blood or anything else.
At the end of the play, everyone is happy but Shylock. Portia reveals
her identity, and Antonio regains money he had lost, so that he is once
again a wealthy Venetian merchant.

Themes

1. Anti-Semitism results from Christian bigotry. Many critics argue
   that Shakespeare's portrayal of Shylock was intended to criticize his
   mistreatment.
2. Don't count your chickens before they hatch. Antonio agrees to loan
   Bassanio money because he is sure that ships at sea will bring in his
   cargo. When the ships wreck, he is forced to borrow money from
   Shylock, to potentially disastrous results.

crying with the bard

. . . .

Macbeth

Plot

Macbeth holds the distinction of being Shakespeare's shortest play, but it is still full of intrigue, weighty issues, and profound character development. The play opens eerily, as two Scottish generals, Macbeth and Banquo, meet three prophetic witches who greet Macbeth as thane (or lord) of Glamis, thane of Cawdor, and the future king of Scotland. They then predict that Banquo's sons will sit upon the throne. Macbeth already holds the title thane of Glamis, but once he learns that he is also to become thane of Cawdor, he begins to believe the witches. More importantly, so does his wife. She sees the possibility of her husband's becoming king, and she will do all she can to speed his empowerment. She convinces Macbeth to kill King Duncan. Once he does so, he fears Banquo and his potential right to the throne, according to the witches' prophecy. He hires assassins to kill Banquo and his son, but his son, Fleance, escapes. The murders continue when Macbeth hears that the thane Macduff has joined Duncan's son, Malcolm, to fight him. Macbeth has Lady Macduff and her children killed. Soon thereafter, Lady Macbeth herself commits suicide, after being plagued by her guilty conscience. Macduff returns to Scotland, kills Macbeth, and Malcolm is given the throne.

Themes

1. "Fair is foul and foul is fair." Sometimes what appears good, such as a prophecy of power, actually harbors evil, and sometimes what appears evil is actually good.
2. A guilty conscience outweighs criminal fortune. Lady Macbeth helps her husband seize power, but she cannot wash away the guilt of her sins.

learning with the bard

···

The Third Part of King Henry VI
Plot

The Third Part of King Henry VI concludes Shakespeare's trilogy about the infant king who rose to power amid the War of the Roses. We've watched him make a disastrous marriage to Margaret of Anjou. We've seen Richard Plantagenet (Duke of York) claim the throne. Now Part III opens with Henry asking Richard to be allowed to reign for his lifetime. Richard agrees provided that Henry confers the power of the crown to him after he dies. Henry agrees, but his queen, Margaret, is angry because this means that her son will never inherit the throne. In her rage, she sets out to destroy Richard any way she can. She raises an army and fights him at Wakefield, where she has him and his son Edmund killed. She then goes on to order Richard decapitated and to have his head displayed on the gates at York. However, Richard's remaining sons, Edward and Richard, defeat Margaret in another battle, and the older son becomes Edward IV. Henry, who had fled all of the violence, is captured in northern England and held prisoner in the Tower of London. In order to forge an alliance with the French, plans are made for Edward to marry Lady Bona, sister of Louis XI. Margaret opposes the marriage because she realizes that it would forever prevent Henry from reclaiming the crown. As it turns out, Edward has fallen in love with a widow, Lady Grey, and he marries her instead. This so angers the Earl of Warwick, who had been negotiating Edward's marriage to Bona, that he joins Margaret's cause to restore Henry as king. The French support them as well. Only Edward's brother, the hunchback Richard, supports his marriage, but he does so not out of filial loyalty, but because he wants to stay close to Edward in the hopes of one day usurping the throne. Several battles ensue between Edward and Margaret's forces. Eventually he defeats her, kills her son, and exiles her to France. Richard murders Henry in the Tower of London, telling him that he has killed his son as well. In the end, Edward maintains the crown as his brother lurks nearby, always waiting for his chance to become Richard III.

Themes

1. The lust for power ruins all involved. Margaret continues to wage wars in an effort to maintain her control of Henry. Warwick and the French make poor political choices in their desire for control. Finally, brother will eventually turn on brother as Richard III plots against Edward.

2. The wicked add insult to injury. Not only does Margaret arrange for York's son to be killed, but she allows him to be tortured too. Before killing York, she places a paper crown on his head and mocks him, saying, "Ay, marry, sir, now looks he like a king!" After he has already been killed, she stabs him again and has his head put on display. She is truly one of the most ruthless women in all of Shakespeare's canon.

Gray's Anatomy

Henry Gray, born in 1827 in England, was light-years ahead of his time. His book Gray's Anatomy *has changed the way the medical community studies the human body. Instantly acclaimed for its comprehensive text and superb illustrations, it has remained widely popular through numerous editions for 150 years. Illustrated with intricate detail, the text scrupulously explains the complex workings of human anatomy.*

---

from dogs and frogs to cheshire cats #2:
animals in children's literature

The Black Stallion

Walter Farley published a series of novels about a wild stallion
beginning in 1944, when he was only in high school. *The Black Stallion*
is the first in the series. It tells the story of young Alec Ramsey, who
is shipwrecked on a desert island with a horse. The boy and the horse
rely on each other to survive, even after they are rescued. The stallion
goes on to win horse races and, in sequels, survives kidnapping and
sires a fabulous colt.

· · · · ·

Charlotte's Web

Author E. B. White published this tale of a spider and a pig in 1952, an
unusual achievement considering that his earlier publications included
such books as *Is Sex Necessary?*, a satire he coauthored with James
Thurber. The story begins with the birth of a runt pig named Wilbur,
who is loved by a little girl named Fern. A spider named Charlotte
saves him from slaughter by spelling the phrase "Some Pig" in her
web, in order to impress the humans who would otherwise eat him.
Charlotte's Web has sold over three million hardback copies and ranks
78th on the all-time best-selling hardback book list.

· · · · ·

Mythology

Cerberus

Cerberus was a three-headed dog with a snake for a tail that was the
keeper of the entrance to Hades. His job was to make sure that the
spirits of the dead could enter, but that no one could escape. In Dante's
Inferno, which describes him with a human head so that he symbolizes
human rage and watchfulness, Cerberus punishes the gluttons in hell.
In other stories, the Greek hero Hercules manages to drag Cerberus to

earth by wrestling him into submission. Orpheus was able to lull him to sleep with the sound of his music, and Hermes put him to sleep with water from the river of forgetfulness.

Chiron

A centaur was a wild creature with the head, arms, and chest of a man, but the legs and body of a horse. Usually they were depicted as part of the hedonistic revels of Dionysus. They could become so violent that they came to symbolize dark, uncontrollable natural forces or even the darkest impulses in human nature. Chiron, however, was an unusual centaur. He was so well known for his intelligence and kindness that he became the teacher of music, hunting, and medicine to such heroes as Achilles, Jason, and Aeneas. Although he was immortal, he was wounded accidentally by one of Hercules' poisonous arrows. He gave up his immortality in order to be allowed to die rather than suffer in pain the rest of his life. Some stories claim that Zeus transformed Chiron into the constellation Sagittarius.

The Minotaur

In Greek myth, the Minotaur was a monster with a human body and a bull's head. It seems that King Minos needed validation of his right to rule, so Poseidon sent a bull to show his approval. But when Minos failed to sacrifice the bull to Poseidon, the angry god caused Minos' wife to fall in love with the animal. From their union, the Minotaur was born. Minos promptly imprisoned the beast in a labyrinth, though every ninth year it was given a human sacrifice to appease it. Finally Theseus killed it, with the help of Ariadne, Minos' daughter, who gave him a ball of thread to unravel as he wound his way deeper into the labyrinth. Once he had slayed the Minotaur, he could easily find his way out.

Pegasus

Pegasus was an extraordinary winged horse with an unusual family tree. His father was Poseidon, god of the sea, and his mother was Medusa, the gorgon who had snakes for hair. When Persues decapitated

Medusa, Pegasus sprang forth from her pregnant body. Far from being a frightening creature, the winged Pegasus was strong and brave. One day, Bellerophon, a grandson of Sisyphus, decided he wanted Pegasus for himself. Armed with a golden bridle given to him by Athena, he caught the winged horse, and they flew far and wide, killing evil creatures and delighting onlookers Filled with pride, Bellerophon attempted to fly to heaven, but Zeus, furious because of the attempt, sent a gadfly to sting Pegasus, who promptly tossed Bellerophon off his back. Pegasus was protected in the sacred stalls of Olympus, getting Zeus' thunderbolts for him, but poor Bellerophon spent the rest of his life in exile.

The Sphinx

In Egypt, the Sphinx is usually depicted as a lion with a human head and chest. He was meant to symbolize Ra, the sun god. In Greece, the Sphinx takes on feminine traits, with the face of a woman, the wings of a bird, and the body of a lion. According to Greek myth, the Sphinx arrived in Thebes and plagued the city's inhabitants. She would ask a particular riddle, and if anyone answered it incorrectly, she would eat him. The riddle she posed was: What walks on four legs in the morning, on two legs at midday, and on three legs in the evening. The answer, a man, was given correctly by Oedipus: as an infant, man crawls on four legs, he walks upright as an adult, and he uses a cane in old age. After Oedipus successfully solved the riddle, the Sphinx threw herself off a cliff and died.

The Carnegie Medal in Literature: *1976-2007*
. . . .

1976: Jan Mark, *Thunder and Lightnings*

1977: Gene Kemp, *The Turbulent Term of Tyke Tiler*

1978: David Rees, *The Exeter Blitz*

1979: Peter Dickinson, *Tulku*

1980: Peter Dickinson, *City of Gold*

1981: Robert Westall, *The Scarecrows*

1982: Margaret Mahy, *The Haunting*

1983: Jan Mark, *Handles*

1984: Margaret Mahy, *The Changeover*

1985: Kevin Crossley-Holland, *Storm*

1986: Berlie Doherty, *Granny Was a Buffer Girl*

1987: Susan Price, *The Ghost Drum*

1988: Geraldine McCaughrean, *A Pack of Lies*

1989: Anne Fine, *Goggle-Eyes*

1990: Gillian Cross, *Wolf*

1991: Berlie Doherty, *Dear Nobody*

1992: Anne Fine, *Flour Babies*

1993: Robert Swindells, *Stone Cold*

1994: Theresa Breslin, *Whispers in the Graveyard*

1995: Philip Pullman, *His Dark Materials: Book 1, Northern Lights*

1996: Melvin Burgess, *Junk*

1997: Tim Bowler, *River Boy*

1998: David Almond, *Skellig*

1999: Aidan Chambers, *Postcards from No Man's Land*

2000: Beverley Naidoo, *The Other Side of Truth*

2001: Terry Pratchett, *The Amazing Maurice and His Educated Rodents*

2002: Sharon Creech, *Ruby Holler*

2003: Jennifer Donnelly, *A Gathering Light*

2004: Frank Cottrell Boyce, *Millions*

2005: Mal Peet, *Tamar*

2007: Meg Rosoff, *Just in Case*

ya lit: fantasy

· ·

Artemis Fowl, Eoin Colfer
The author describes this book as *"Die Hard* with fairies." Brilliant
12-year-old criminal mastermind Artemis Fowl resolves to replenish
the family fortune by kidnapping and holding a fairy for ransom.
However, LEPRecon (Lower Elements Police Reconnaissance) will stop
at nothing to rescue fairy Holly Short, even if that means using clever
gadgets, technology, and magic.

· · · · ·

So You Want to Be a Wizard, Diane Duane
When Nita and Kit take the sacred Wizard's Oath, they learn that they
have sworn to save the universe from Starsnuffer. This is the first in an
eight-part series, and it won the Quick Pick for Reluctant Young Adult
Readers award from the American Library Association.

· · · · ·

The Lion, the Witch, and the Wardrobe, C. S. Lewis
This classic novel, written in 1950, tells the adventures of four children
who find, through the back of a wardrobe, a portal that leads into
Narnia, a land torn by war, where the good Lion Aslan, an allegorical
figure for Christ, fights the evil White Witch. It is the first of the seven-
volume *Chronicles of Narnia.*

· · · · ·

The Amazing Maurice and His Educated Rodents, Terry Pratchett
This book is part of a much larger comedic fantasy book series. It
retells the "The Pied Piper of Hamelin" story in a very funny way as
Maurice, a street-smart tomcat, leads a group of intelligent rats to fight
evil in the streets of the town of Bad Blintz.

Harry Potter and the Sorcerer's Stone, J. K. Rowling

The best-selling young adult series of all time opens with a young boy named Harry Potter, an orphan among "muggles," who learns that he is a wizard. School never became so fascinating as when he enrolls at Hogwarts School for Wizards and Witches. Harry's further adventures are recounted in *Harry Potter and the Chamber of Secrets, Harry Potter and the Prisoner of Azkaban, Harry Potter and the Goblet of Fire, Harry Potter and the Order of the Phoenix, Harry Potter and the Half-Blood Prince*, and, finally, *Harry Potter and the Deathly Hallows*.

· · · · ·

The Hobbit, J. R. R. Tolkien

Tolkien wrote this story in the late 1920s and it has become a classic ever since. The life of kind hobbit Bilbo Baggins changes drastically after he is chosen to go on a quest to recover treasure from the dragon Smaug. The tale is filled with amazing characters, from Gandalf, the wizard, to dwarfs, elves, and trolls.

· · · · ·

The Lord of the Rings: The Fellowship of the Ring, The Two Towers, The Return of the King, J. R. R. Tolkien

Following the success of *The Hobbit*, Tolkien wrote this trilogy between 1937 and 1949. The small hobbit, Frodo Baggins, and his faithful servant, Samwise, go on a quest to destroy the One Ring of Power, a ring that the Dark Sauron needs to destroy their world. Gandalf the wizard, plus a host of dwarfs, elves, and other magical creatures help the hobbits, while goblins, hobgoblins, and orcs plot against them. Ultimately good triumphs against evil in this series, which has become one of the most popular and highly acclaimed in the world.

Reading List:
short & *sweet* must-reads

● ●

The Catcher in the Rye, J. D. Salinger
Salinger's famous novel covers a mere 48 hours in the life of prep
school teen Holden Caulfield, who is considered a somewhat unreliable
narrator because of his heavy criticism of others and highly opinionated
personality. Caulfield decides to leave school, but upon meeting his
younger sister and realizing that he has influenced her to leave school
as well and follow him, Caulfield changes his mind. He recognizes a
certain responsibility, which comes as a surprise and turning point in
the end of the novel. The book sells nearly 250,000 copies each year,
and was chosen by *Time* magazine as one of the 100 best English
language novels since 1923.

● ● ● ● ●

Pobby and Dingan, Ben Rice
Set in Australia, this story focuses on a pair of two small children,
Ashmol and Kellyanne, who attempt to deal with the alleged death
of Kellyanne's two imaginary friends, Pobby and Dingan. Kellyanne
offers the friends to her father one day, who plays along and agrees
to take them with him to his mining job. When he returns home, he
has forgotten about the game, and Kellyanne becomes confinced that
Pobby and Dingan are, in fact, lost or dead. The witty and imaginative
novella was written in 2000 and is a highly regarded first novel.

● ● ● ● ●

Candide, Voltaire
This French satire tells the story of a young man who struggles
to maintain optimism even while coming across extraordinarily
exaggerated hardships and bad luck. Written in 1759, the witty
novella pokes fun at government, religion, philosophy, and many great
philosophers and theologians.

a few more major literary hubs

The Paris Review

Founded in 1953 by writers George Plimpton, Harold L. Humes, and Peter Matthiessen, *The Paris Review* was created in a mission to present more literature and less criticism. This mission came from a period where most major literary publications focused on scholarly criticism of well-known texts, not actual new writing. The magazine also focuses on the craft of famous writers, such as how they write their prose or novels. One issue, for example, explained to readers how Richard Powers wrote novels on a remote keyboard so as not to view the writing until it was already finished.

·····

The Kenyon Review

Published by Kenyon College, *The Kenyon Review* was founded in 1939 as a journal that represented some of the most revered and internationally known writers of its time. The first editor, John Ransom, published writers such as Robert Penn Warren, Allan Tate, and William Empson, while also introducing young writers such as Flannery O'Connor and Robert Lowell. In the late 1960s, the magazine was forced to shut down because of financial burdens, but it reopened in 1979, when the magazine hired an internationally known poet, Marilyn Hacker, as a full-time editor. Hacker began to widen its scope to include minority viewpoints, at which time it became more widespread and better known. The magazine is now one of the most esteemed and most award-winning publications in international literature.

·····

The Southern Review

Published by Louisiana State University on a quarterly schedule, *The Southern Review* is one of the most revered journals of the literary world. Founded in the late 1930s with Charles Pipkin as the first editor and Robert Penn Warren as a managing editor, the journal has published the likes of Aldous Huxley, T. S. Eliot, Mark Van Doren, Wallace Stevens, and Nelson Algren. In 1942, the journal was shut down because of World War II and the university's feeling of priority. The unfulfilled subscriptions to the magazine were replaced by the still-operating *Kenyon Review* of Kenyon College. But the magazine is now operating again and is distributed worldwide, showcasing writers both nationally and internationally. Work from *The Southern Review* is regularly selected for the Pushcart Prize, the O. Henry Prize, and many major anthologies, including the annual *Best American Short Stories*.

Heteronyms A–C

Heteronyms are words that are spelled the same but mean different things depending on how they are pronounced.

August *AUgust* - month; *auGUST* - important

The month of August was named after the august Roman Emperor Augustus.

Bass *BASE* - a string instrument; *(rhymes with mass)* - a spiny-finned fish, often with a large mouth

The best way to catch bass is to play a bass on the riverbank. Barring that, just use a hook and some really good bait.

Convict *kunVIKT* - to find guilty; *KAHNvikt* - a person in jail

When you convict a convict, you send him to prison, unless prison is against your convictions. In that case, you can just let him go free and hope he changes his ways.

---

self-publishing hall of shame
[and fame]

. . . .

Caught: Irma Rombauer

After her husband's death, Irma Rombauer used several thousand dollars from his estate to self-publish the popular cookbook *The Joy of Cooking* in 1931. It has sold more than 18 million copies and is known as one of the best-selling cookbooks of the United States.

. . . . .

Caught: Mark Twain

Fed up with publishers, Mark Twain paid for the publication and distribution of *The Adventures of Huckleberry Finn* himself. His book was a success, and from the money it produced, he invested in developing a typewriter. In fact, Twain spent most of the money from his publishing success investing in inventions, some of which were failures that left him with empty pockets. His ability to lecture and write, however, always afforded him the ability to recover financially and pay his debts.

. . . . .

Caught: Virginia Woolf

Author of such famous titles as *Mrs. Dalloway* and *To the Lighthouse*, Virginia Woolf got her start by self-publishing her first few works. Her first novel, *The Voyage Out*, was published by her half-brother, who controlled an imprint. Much of her other work was self-published through Hogarth Press, a company started by Woolf and her husband, Leonard Woolf.

the 411 *on a few more short stories*

. . . .

"The Lottery Ticket" – Anton Chekhov

In this short story, a couple gets the idea that they have a winning
lottery ticket. The two get carried away with fantasizing about what to
do with the winnings, going so far as to become lost in daydreams of
the life they would live with the $75,000 prize. The husband dreams
of eating hot soup and dozing in the sun, never worrying about going
to work. He then drifts into dreaming about traveling abroad, and
upon mentioning this idea to his wife, he sours at her response that
she would like to come too. He soon remembers that it is, in fact, his
wife's lottery ticket, not his own, and grows angry at the idea that
she would begrudge him his dreams. His wife grows angry as well,
imagining him as the first of many who would steal her winnings. The
two are abruptly interrupted from their thoughts when they realize that
the last two numbers do not match the ticket and that they have not
won a single dime. The two fall ill and weary, no longer satisfied with
anything around them, after filling their minds with possibility and the
idea of one another as an obstacle to their own happiness.

. . . . .

"The Lottery" – Shirley Jackson

The story takes place in a small town with a population of around 300
people. The townspeople are jovial and excited on this particular day,
the day of the lottery, when each family steps forward to draw a slip of
paper from a large black box. The Hutchinson family "wins" and steps
forward again to draw and find out which family member is the chosen
one. Tessie Hutchinson, the mother, is selected as the winner. The
townspeople, including the women, children, and elderly, crowd around
her with rocks and proceed to stone her to death. Even her own family
takes part in the stoning. The story was first published in *The New
Yorker* in 1948. Seemingly for the purpose of highlighting the story's

inherent commentary on American society, *The New Yorker* changed the date in the story to make it one day before the date of the publication of the issue. The story inspired controversy and angered many readers, hundreds of whom cancelled their subscriptions to *The New Yorker* in protest. The famous story has been adapted for radio, television, opera, and theatre, and has been reprinted in many magazines and textbooks.

The Sword and the Mind

The Sword and the Mind *is the legendary samurai Yagyu Munenori's treatise on Japanese swordsmanship and wisdom. One of the most definitive books on military strategy ever written, Munenori's text draws on his achievement as one of his country's top swordsmen and the insight gained from many years of service and battle under the powerful reign of the Tokagawa shogunate. Written in 1632, his work is a blend of swordmenship and mental strategy based in Zen mind-thought with the latter often taking precedent.* The Sword and the Mind *has sold millions of copies in several different languages.*

little-known literary info

· ·

- Crafted in 11th-century Japan, *The Tale of Genji* is the oldest complete novel ever to be written.

- Housing over 130 million items, including photographs, maps, books, and recordings, the Library of Congress in Washington, DC, is the largest library in the world. It was destroyed by the British during the War of 1812 but was restored by Thomas Jefferson, who sold his personal library and used the funds to help rebuild the damaged building.

- *Remembrance of Things Past,* by French author Marcel Proust, is the longest novel ever written, containing approximately 9,609,000 characters.

- *The Guinness Book of World Records* is the world's best-selling copyrighted book. Since it was first published in 1955, more than 100 million copies of the book have sold, and it has been translated into 37 languages.

- Agatha Christie is the world's best-selling fiction author. Her 78 mystery novels have been translated into 44 languages and have sold more than 2 billion copies.

- The father of Scientology, L. Ron Hubbard, is the most translated author in the history of literature. His books have been translated into more 65 different languages.

- In 1945 at Nag Hammnodi, Egypt, several texts were discovered, including Gnostic gospels or secret books (apocryphal) ascribed to Thomas, James, John, Peter, and Paul. They were apparently buried in AD 350, but the originals are thought to have been written during the first century after the death of Jesus.

- With 6 billion copies sold in more than 2,000 languages and dialects, the Bible is the world's best-selling book.

Miguel de Cervantes Prize

. . . .

The Miguel de Cervantes Prize is considered to be similar to the Nobel Prize for Spanish language literature. The sum of 90,000 euros is given each year by the Ministry of Culture of Spain to honor the lifetime achievement of a writer in the Spanish language. Here is a list of winners:

1976: Jorge Guillén (Spain)
1977: Alejo Carpentier (Cuba)
1978: Dámaso Alonso (Spain)
1979: Jorge Luis Borges (Argentina) and Gerardo Diego (Spain)
1980: Juan Carlos Onetti (Uruguay)
1981: Octavio Paz (Mexico)
1982: Luis Rosales (Spain)
1983: Rafael Alberti (Spain)
1984: Ernésto Sábato (Argentina)
1985: Gonzalo Torrente Ballester (Spain)
1986: Antonio Buero Vallejo (Spain)
1987: Carlos Fuentes (Mexico, born in Panama)
1988: María Zambrano (Spain)
1989: Augusto Roa Bastos (Paraguay)
1990: Adolfo Bioy Casares (Argentina)
1991: Francisco Ayala (Spain)
1992: Dulce María Loynaz (Cuba)
1993: Miguel Delibes (Spain)
1994: Mario Vargas Llosa (Peru)
1995: Camilo José Cela (Spain)
1996: José García Nieto (Spain)
1997: Guillermo Cabrera Infante (Cuba)
1998: José Hierro (Spain)
1999: Jorge Edwards (Chile)
2000: Francisco Umbral (Spain)

2001: Álvaro Mutis (Colombia)
2002: José Jiménez Lozano (Spain)
2003: Gonzalo Rojas (Chile)
2004: Rafael Sánchez Ferlosio (Spain)
2005: Sergio Pitol (Mexico)
2006: Antonio Gamoneda (Spain)
2007: Juan Gelman (Argentina)

Lord of the Flies: The Least You Need to Know

The novel opens with a group of British schoolboys stranded on a deserted island without any adults. You later learn that nuclear war is raging in the skies overhead. The boys must learn to fend for themselves and begin to hunt. Eventually, their innocent hunting trips turn into tribal ceremonies centered on sacrifices. Typically the offerings are make-believe, but one takes a fatal turn as Simon gets trapped in the circle and is beaten to death. Jack, the antagonist and lead hunter, is symbolic of evil, which becomes evident upon the descriptions of his black clothing and red hair. He gradually begins to corrupt the other boys, and his mission is nearly complete when a naval officer rescues them.

Ralph and Jack engage in a power struggle throughout most of the novel, but as the only boy to survive Jack's demonic reign on the island, Ralph triumphs and emerges as the true leader of the pack. Upon Simon's tragic death, Ralph begins to feel guilty for taking part in the killing, which helps him become stronger and more willing to fight the regression of the other boys.

The Lord of the Flies, what the boys call the Beast, is merely a pig's head on a stick.

---

give the devil his due

From John Milton's *Paradise Lost* to Dan Brown's *Angels and Demons*, literature has been bedeviled by harmful sprites and spirits. Here's the rundown on some of the folks from low down.

. . . . .

Mephistopheles

Centuries before blues players met at the crossroads and cut a deal with the devil, the Faust legend was told in plays, poems, and operas. Dr. Johann Faust has learned all there is to know but is thirsty for more. He turns to the dark arts and learns to conjure spirits, including one particularly wily one, Mephistopheles. He promised Dr. Faust all the power and worldly pleasures he could want in exchange for Faust's soul. Faust foolishly agreed and lived high on the hog for 24 years. Then it was time to pay. Goethe allowed Faust salvation, but other versions of the story conclude with his joining Mephistopheles in hell.

. . . . .

Xipe Totec

Despite the festive-sounding name, Xipe Totec was a demon of the Mexican underworld who appeared whenever there was bloodshed. He was known as "night drinker" because he would drink the blood of any dead souls who weren't diligent in doing their penance in hell. To Mexican peasants, he was a vampire. To Aztec enemies, he was worshipped.

. . . . .

Itzpapalotl

Speaking of Aztecs, the most feared of ancient female Aztec demons was Itzpapalotl, whose name means "the obsidian knife butterfly." She combined beauty and terror in one scary costume. Butterfly wings edged in knives grew from her shoulders. Her tongue was also a knife. She had jaguar claws and eagle toes but spruced herself up a bit with makeup. She was the patron of witches and human sacrifices. On unlucky days, she would fly through town on her butterfly wings leading an army of dead witches also shaped like butterflies.

• • • • •

Leviathan

Before mean old Moby Dick, Leviathan, demon whale of the ocean, swam through Hebrew stories. In the book of Jonah, he swallowed God's prophet and held him in his belly for three days before spitting him out on the land. In *Paradise Lost*, Milton called him "the Arch-Fiend." Leviathan would let sailors think his large, dark back was an island. They would anchor their boats on him, and he would drag them to the bottom of the sea. In many mythic tales, he ruled over all the beasts of sea and land.

• • • • •

Beelzebub

This bad guy is right up there with Satan as far as demons go. Pharisees accused Jesus of casting demons out in the name of Beelzebub. Medieval texts describe him as a giant with a band of fire on his head and, of course, horns. Some texts claimed he had duck feet, but that kind of detracts from the fear factor. Even the British Museum houses a manuscript with a spell designed to speak to him.

• • • • •

Cerberus

Greek mythology has its fair share of demons, including this three-headed beast. At the center was a lion's head. Flanking either side was the head of a dog and the head of a wolf. He comes from fine stock. His dad, Typhon, was a dragon, and his mom, Echidna, sported the head and torso of a lovely maiden and the body of a snake. Her favorite pastime was eating men alive. Cerberus was the watchdog of Hades. His job was to eat anyone trying to escape hell. He and his mother had strange culinary habits indeed.

what's in a name?
the stories behind the pseudonyms

Sometimes writers are at their most creative when it comes to changing their own names. For various reasons, they often adopt pseudonyms under which they publish their work. Why all the secrecy? Here's a little information on the name game.

• • • • •

Gabriela Mistral

She was the first Latin American author to win the Nobel Prize, but before the world knew her as Gabriela Mistral, she was Lucila Godoy y Alcayaga. She made her living teaching in rural schools in Chile. As a young teacher, she worried that she would lose her job if people read her emotional, passionate verse. To protect her anonymity, she chose her first name based on the archangel Gabriel. Her last name, Mistral, is the word for a sea wind.

• • • • •

Oscar Wilde

Oscar Fingal O'Flahertie Wills Wilde (mercifully!) wrote simply under his first and last name most of his life. However, after he was sentenced to two years of hard labor in prison for his homosexuality, his name and reputation were ruined. After his release, he adopted the name Sebastian Melmoth. However, when he wrote a poem about the death penalty, "The Ballad of Reading Gaol," he chose to publish it under the name C.3.3, which stood for his prison address: building C, floor 3, cell 3.

• • • • •

Stevie Smith

British poet Stevie Smith was born Florence Margaret Smith in 1902. Although her family called her Peggy, she acquired the masculine nickname Stevie quite by accident. She was riding a horse by a group of young boys one day. They shouted, "Go, Steve!" in reference to the jockey Steve Donaghue. As was often the case with Stevie, she took what was meant to be mockery and made it her own. She liked the sound of the name and feminized it to Stevie. The name stuck with everyone except her stuffy aunt, who refused to call her anything but Peg. When she published her first book, *Novel on Yellow Paper*, critics had no idea who Stevie Smith was, so, given her writing style, they thought she might be Virginia Woolf.

• • • • •

Mark Twain

Although the name Samuel Clemens is almost as well known, everyone has heard the pseudonym Mark Twain. It was a more poetic choice for Clemens than an earlier pen name he used, Thomas Jefferson Snodgrass. From 1857 to 1961, Twain earned a living as a riverboat pilot on the Mississippi. He would often hear the cry "Mark twain!" meaning "by the mark of two fathoms." He liked the sound of it, and who can blame him? Sounds better than Snodgrass.

• • • • •

Charlotte, Emily, and Anne Brontë

In the Victorian era, writing books was not, traditionally, considered an appropriate activity for young ladies. Jane Austen, for instance, would hide her writing under her needlework whenever someone walked in the room. The talented Brontë sisters, therefore, had to find a way to keep their gender hidden in order to get published. Enter the male pseudonym to the rescue. Charlotte became Currer Bell. Emily wrote under Ellis Bell, and Anne took the name Acton Bell.

• • • • •

William Makepeace Thackeray

For a long time, Thackeray loved to write under various pen names as he worked on everything from magazine articles to novels. For his humorous pieces, he chose such names as Our Fat Contributor, Michael Angelo Titmarsh, Miss Tickletoby, Launcelot Wagstaff, Policeman X, and Ikey Solomon. When it came time to get serious and publish his magnum opus, *Vanity Fair,* he abandoned his hilarious pseudonyms and stuck with his given name.

. . . . .

Yukio Mishima

Despite the fact that many critics consider Mishima one of the most significant Japanese novelists, his family was not impressed with his literary leanings. He was born Kimitake Hiraoka, but his father, a stern government official, considered literature too effeminate for his son. In order to conceal his writing from his dad, he changed his name to Yukio Mishima, which translates as "mysterious devil bewitched with death." One wonders if his anti-literary father would have liked such a name!

. . . . .

Anne Rice/Anne Rampling /A. N. Roquelaure

The story of Anne Rice's various names is as intriguing as the Vampire Chronicles. She was given the name Howard Allen at birth because her mother wanted to name her after her father, regardless of the fact that she was a girl. She changed her name to Anne on her first day of school so other kids wouldn't make fun of her. After the success of the vampire series, she published adult-oriented fiction under the name Anne Rampling. From there, she moved on to sado-masochistic erotica, so she chose yet another name, A. N. Roquelaure. A roquelaure was a type of 18th-century cloak, so the name worked well to "cloak" her true identity. Perhaps unsurprisingly, when she wrote *Christ the Lord: Out of Egypt* in 2005, she returned to plain old Anne Rice.

Rebecca West

Her given name was Cicely Isabel Fairfield. She later changed the spelling of her first name to Cicily. Considering that this same woman had worked in the women's suffrage movement, had an affair with H. G. Wells that produced an illegitimate child, and had attended the Nuremberg trials, it is clear that she could do anything she wanted, including changing the spelling of her name, or changing her name altogether. As an actress, she greatly admired the play *Rosmersholm* by Henrik Ibsen. The heroine, Rebecca West, is a strong, freethinking woman. Cicily loved the name and took it as her own. Who's gonna argue? After all, this is the same woman who once said, "I myself have never been able to find out what feminism is; I only know that people call me a feminist whenever I express sentiments that differentiate me from a doormat."

monster *knows best*

Oh sure, we expect Plato or Shakespeare to deliver wisdom when we need it, but were you aware of how many literary monsters have smart things to say too? Ponder these quotations from the pages of monstrosity and you just might learn something.

• • • • •

From *Dracula* by Bram Stoker

No man knows till he has suffered from the night how sweet and dear to his heart and eye the morning can be.

I have learned not to think little of any one's belief, no matter how strange it may be. I have tried to keep an open mind, and it is not the ordinary things of life that could close it, but the strange things, the extraordinary things, the things that make one doubt if they be mad or sane.

Despair has its own calms.

• • • • •

From *Frankenstein* by Mary Shelley

...nothing contributes so much to tranquilize the mind as a steady purpose.

The companions of our childhood always possess a certain power over our minds which hardly any later friend can obtain.

From *The Hound of the Baskervilles* by Sir Arthur Conan Doyle

The world is full of obvious things which nobody by any chance ever observes.

The past and the present are within the field of my inquiry, but what a man may do in the future is a hard question to answer.

• • • • •

From *Moby Dick* by Herman Melville

All men live enveloped in whale-lines. All are born with halters round their necks; but it is only when caught in the swift, sudden turn of death, that mortals realize the silent, subtle, ever present perils of life.

...because truly to enjoy bodily warmth, some small part of you must be cold, for there is no quality in this world that is not what it is merely by contrast. Nothing exists in itself.

By this, he seemed to mean, not only that the most reliable and useful courage was that which arises from the fair estimation of the encountered peril, but that an utterly fearless man is a far more dangerous comrade than a coward.

Ignorance is the parent of fear...

what I really want to do is direct...
I mean, write

How many times do you hear an actor or actress say, "I love acting, but what I really want to do is direct"? If actors want to be directors, what do directors want to be? Writers, of course!

• • • • •

Oliver Stone: Vietnam from Film to Fiction

Stone may be respected as the director of such films as *Platoon* and *Born on the Fourth of July,* but his foray into fiction left the critics feeling some battle fatigue. When he was only 19 years old, Stone began a novel that was roundly rejected by publishers. In despair, he enlisted for Vietnam. Over 30 years later, he pieced the book back together in his memory and published it under the title *A Child's Night Dream: A Novel.* Largely autobiographical, it tells the story of young Oliver, whose adventures include teaching in a Catholic school, sailing with the merchant marines, and fighting Charlie in the jungle. *The Library Journal* took the role of critical sniper in its assessment of the book: "This debut novel is mostly hogwash."

• • • • •

Woody Allen: Existential Angst on Page and Screen

As movies such as *Love and Death* show, Woody Allen is up on many things literary, from Russian novelists to existential philosophy. Before making his mark as an auteur, he crafted hilarious comedy sketches. *Getting Even, Without Feathers,* and *Side Effects* feature such one-liners as "Eternal Nothingness is OK if you're dressed for it." His movies may not suit everyone's taste, but his writing tickles the funny bone every time.

Alan Parker: San Fran Through the Eyes of a British Filmmaker

He don't need no education... From directing *Pink Floyd: The Wall* to writing his 2004 debut novel, *The Sucker's Kiss*, Alan Parker is a self-taught master. Actually, he has had plenty of education in writing. He wrote advertising copy and television commercials before directing such films as *Midnight Express, Shoot the Moon,* and *Mississippi Burning*. *The Sucker's Kiss* received much critical acclaim, including this comment from Frank McCourt, author of *Angela's Ashes:* "Memo to Writers Guild of America and the Screen Actors Guild: Please go on strike more often. Why? Well, while you were picketing and protesting, a director and writer, Alan Parker, decided to write a hell of a novel."

· · · · ·

Barry Levinson: More, More Baltimore

Director Barry Levinson revived the Baltimore of his youth in the writing and directing of such films as *Diner, Avalon, Tin Men,* and *Liberty Heights*. His screenwriting talents eventually led to his first novel, *Sixty-Six*, which imagines similar characters as the ones in *Diner*, only seven years later. They wonder about women, sports, and their futures with the funny, bittersweet style that characterizes all of Levinson's Baltimore work.

out of Africa

Many readers have heard of Nigerian author Chinua Achebe's book *Things Fall Apart*, but his is only one of many excellent novels to come out of Africa.

From Nigeria

The Concubine by Elechi Amadi
The Bride Price by Buchi Emecheta
I Saw the Sky Catch Fire by T. Obinkaram Echewa
Jagua Nana by Cyprian Ekwensi
The Famished Road by Ben Okri
The Interpreters by Wole Soyinka
The Palm Wine Drinkard by Amos Tutuola
Efuru by Flora Nwapa

From Ghana

Our Sister Killjoy by Ama Ata Aidoo
The Beautyful Ones Are Not Yet Born by Ayi Kwei Armah
This Earth, My Brother by Kofi Awoonor

From South Africa

Mine Boy by Peter Abrahams
Maru by Bessie Head
In the Fog of the Season's End by Alex LaGuma
Chaka by Thomas Mofolo

From Senegal

God's Bits of Wood by Sembene Ousmane
Scarlet Song by Mariama Bâ
Tales of Amadou Koumba by Birago Diop
Ambiguous Adventure by Cheikh Hamidou Kane
The Beggars' Strike by Aminata Sow Fall

mapquest: *literature*

Literary locales often become as famous as the books that describe them. From the idealistic Camelot to the doomed Gomorrah, the landscapes of literature have a globe of their own.

Atlantis: A legendary island inhabited by noble people who, once corrupted by power and greed, were destroyed when Zeus allowed the island to be swallowed by the Atlantic Ocean.

Avalon: The legendary island where King Arthur was buried.

Azkaban: Fictional wizard prison in Harry Potter series.

Brobdingnag: Fictional land in Jonathan Swift's *Gulliver's Travels*, where giants live.

Camelot: The fictional capital of King Arthur's realm.

Forest of Arden: Setting of Shakespeare's play *As You Like It*.

Garden of Eden: Paradisial garden from which Adam and Eve are expelled.

Hodmimir's Forest: In Norse mythology, the only humans who survive the battle at the end of the world will emerge from here.

Hogwarts: School of Witchcraft and Wizardry that Harry Potter attends.

Island of Dr. Moreau: Titular location of H. G. Wells' sci-fi novel, where mad scientist Moreau has created creatures that are half-human, half-animal.

Lake Wobegon: Fictional town in Minnesota where Garrison Keillor's stories from *A Prairie Home Companion* take place.

Lilliput: Fictional land in Jonathan Swift's *Gulliver's Travels*, where the inhabitants were only six inches tall.

Mount Olympus: Mythological home of the Greek gods.

Mudville: Fictional town where the poetic character Casey comes up to bat.

Neverland: Fictional island in *Peter Pan*, where no one ever grows up.

Parnassus: Mythological home of the Greek Muses.

Peyton Place: Fictional New Hampshire setting of Grace Metalious's novel by the same name.

Sherwood Forest: A real forest in Nottinghamshire, England, where the legendary Robin Hood lived.

Sleepy Hollow: A private glen in New York, where the Headless Horseman pursued Ichabod Crane.

Smallville: Fictional hometown of Clark Kent.

Sodom and Gomorrah: Biblical towns destroyed by God for their sinfulness.

Tara: Fictional plantation setting of *Gone With the Wind*.

Valhalla: Mythological heaven for Norse warriors.

Yoknapatawpha County: Fictional county in Mississippi, where William Faulkner based many of his stories.

Heteronyms D–F

Desert *dihZURT* - to leave or abandon; *DEZert* - a barren, hot, dry region

If you desert your camel and your caravan in the desert, you will probably receive your just desserts. Be smart. Stay with the group.

Excuse *EKskyooz* - to pardon; *EKskyoos* - an explanation

Excuuuuuse me, but I just don't buy your excuse. Oh sure, the dog ate your homework. Yeah. Right.

Forte *FOERT* - the strongest part of a blade; *forTAY* - something at which a person does well.

I have many gifts and fortes, but finding the forte on this dull butter knife is definitely not one of my talents. Bring me a steak knife, please.

---

all about *books*

From the clay tablets of the very first books to the signed first editions we covet today, books have long held our fascination. Despite the threats of an entirely paperless society, our love affair with bound pages is sure to endure forever. Here are some fun facts about the things that fill our bookshelves...and we don't mean knickknacks!

Don't Know Much About History

First came clay tablets. Then came papyrus scrolls. By AD 400, parchment, manufactured from animal skins, made scrolls all but obsolete. From the 7th to the 13th centuries, religious manuscripts were made by hand. The making of them, in fact, constituted a kind of religious practice. For the next 200 years, book subjects became more secular because of the rise of universities and the discoveries, during the Crusades, of ancient Greek and Roman texts. The 15th century saw the first printed books, thanks to Gutenberg's movable type in 1452. The rest, as they say, is history.

Who Cares About Commas?

No one even knew what a comma was, much less the ever-vexing semicolon, for centuries. The earliest known use of punctuation is traced back to Aristophanes of Byzantium, a librarian at Alexandria, around 200 BC. Punctuation as we understand it today can be traced back to Aldus Manutius, a 15th-century Venetian grammarian.

Dissecting a Book

Books are a lot like people. They are made up of heads, joints, and spines. They may sport a headband or a jacket. Some of them have very nice tails. Like many people, you can recognize them by their signatures. What does this all mean?

Head: The margin at the top of a page of print.

Joint: The outside juncture of the spine and covers of a case-bound book.

Spine: The back of the book where the pages are sewn together.

Headband: A decorative strip of material between the head and tail.

Jacket: The paper cover of a book you can take off.

Tail: The bottom edge of a book.

Signature: A single printed sheet of paper ready for binding and trimming.

Book Quiz

Which of the following are found in the front of a book?

a. Frontispiece
b. Title page
c. Blank Leaf
d. Dedication page
e. Foreword
f. Introduction
g. Preface
h. All of the above

Answer:

H. All of the above

ISBN stands for International Standard Book Number. It's the number found above the barcode on the back cover of most books.

---

do we Dewey? *you bet we do*

· ·

Without the efforts of Melvil Dewey, books in libraries might be as chaotic as sock drawers. Here's a rundown of the Dewey Decimal System in all its glory.

Why We Dewey

All the knowledge in the world, from how to steam artichokes to the history of the War of the Roses, can be categorized thanks to the Dewey Decimal System. Ninety-five percent of public and school libraries in the United States use it. In fact, it is the most commonly used method of organizing books in the world (and probably the entire galaxy, but who can say for sure?). Prior to the system, books were organized by what random shelf they were placed on, or alphabetically by title. This method proved cumbersome as best. Something had to be done! Enter…

Mr. Dewey

Melvil Louis Kossuth Dewey was born in upstate New York in 1851. He was named after Hungarian revolutionary Lajos Kossuth. The spirit of revolution and courage coursed through his veins. When he was 17, his school caught on fire and young Dewey rescued as many books as he could. As a result of severe smoke inhalation, he was told he didn't have long to live. This lit a fire, of efficiency, in him. He wanted to streamline his life as much as possible, including dropping the last two letters off of his first name to simplify its spelling to Melvil.

Needless to say, he lived much longer than expected (80 years to be exact). He worked as an assistant librarian at Amherst College, where he received his B.A. and M.A. There he began developing his cataloging system. He created and edited the *Library Journal* and founded the American Library Association. In his spare time, he helped arrange the 1932 Winter Olympics in Lake Placid. To be fair, his life was far from perfect. He was also well known for his racism, anti-Semitism, and misogyny.

The basic plot S–U

• •

For this series of plot summaries, think X vs. Y. Whether sense is
opposed to sensibility or the young Stephen Dedalus is posed against
Leopold Bloom, we're taking a look at some great oppositional plots.

• • • • •

Sense and Sensibility

In this Jane Austen masterpiece, Elinor is all sense (reason) and
Marianne is all sensibility (feeling), or at least for most of the book
they are. However, once each feels the pain of desertion from the
man they love, they begin to see the wisdom in the other sister's
point of view. Older sister Elinor loves Edward Ferrars, but she is
too dignified and, well, sensible, to show it. He shares her restraint,
which keeps him from telling her one tiny, important fact—he has
been secretly engaged to Lucy Steele for, oh, about four years
now. Oops. Meanwhile, Marianne meets the love of her life, John
Willoughby, while running through a field in a storm. She twists
her ankle, and, like a knight in shining armor, he comes to the
rescue. Turns out, though, that this knight is a bit rusty. He harbors
a few secrets of his own, which make his competitor for Marianne's
affections, Colonel Brandon, all the more attractive, as Marianne
wises up and gets a little more sensible. Eventually everyone lives
happily ever after, once they learn to balance out their reason with
their emotions.

• • • • •

A Tale of Two Cities

In this oppositional plot line, Dickens contrasts Paris and London
during the French Revolution. The story begins when Dr. Alexander
Manette is released from the Bastille after 18 years, for having
knowledge about the Marquis de St. Evrémonde's assaulting of a
peasant girl. M. and Mme. Defarge take Manette back to London to

his daughter, Lucie. Years later they are asked to testify that they saw
Charles Darnay, the nephew of Evrémonde, flee to England to escape
trumped up charges of treason. Through a twin plot device, Darnay
is saved by Sydney Carton, who happens to look a lot like him. The
two young men become buddies, and while both love Lucie, Darnay
wins her hand. More years pass, and once again false charges affect
Darnay. He learns that a beloved old servant has been imprisoned
in Paris, so he goes to the war-torn city to help. He is imprisoned
and sentenced to die. Only his "twin," Carton, can save him, if he
is willing to take his place on the guillotine. Do Darnay and Lucie
live happily ever after, or does Darnay lose his head and Carton win
Lucie's hand? You'll have to read the book to find out.

• • • • •

Ulysses

Considered by many to be the greatest novel of all time, James
Joyce's *Ulysses* relies as much on a stream-of-consciousness style as
on plot to tell a riveting story of one day in the life of a man named
Leopold Bloom. Set on June 16, 1904, the novel is patterned after
The Odyssey, only it takes place in the city Joyce called "dear, dirty
Dublin." The ancient Greek character Ulysses becomes Leopold.
Penelope is his wife, Molly, and Telemachus becomes Stephen
Dedalus. Bloom and Dedalus are both in a condition of exile
throughout the novel. Bloom is estranged from his wife, who is
contemplating an affair. Dedalus is haunted by guilt for rejecting his
dying mother and her traditional views on religion. Each wanders
through Dublin over the course of the book, finally meeting each
other toward the end of the day. While Bloom represents the social
and political man, Stephen represents the spiritual artist. Their
oppositions find a kind of union in the final chapter when Molly gets
the last word.

some nice alliteration:
Pulitzer Prize for poetry 1991–2007

. . . .

1991: "Near Changes," Mona Van Duyn

1992: *Selected Poems,* James Tate

1993: "The Wild Iris," Louise Lock

1994: "Neon Vernacular," Yusef Komunyakaa

1995: "Simple Truth," Philip Levine

1996: "The Dream of the Unified Field," Jorie Graham

1997: *Alive Together: New and Selected Poems,* Lisel Mueller

1998: "Black Zodiac," Charles Wright

1999: "Blizzard of One," Mark Strand

2000: "Repair," C. K. Williams

2001: "Different Hours," Stephen Dunn

2002: "Practical Gods," Carl Dennis

2003: "Moy Sand and Gravel," Paul Muldoon

2004: "Walking to Martha's Vineyard," Franz Wright

2005: "Delights & Shadows," Ted Kooser

2006: "Late Wife," Claudia Emerson

2007: "Native Guard," Natasha Trethewey

affairs of the heart ...*and pen*

These literary lovers prove that the bond between soul mates can be as artistic as it is passionate.

. . . . .

Burning Their Candles at Both Ends: Edna St. Vincent Millay and Edmund Wilson
The same woman who wrote the famous lines "I burn my candle at both ends / It will not last the night" was, as one might imagine, quite notorious. She was well known for her multiple affairs with men and women. Sometimes she would sleep with two or three men in the same day. Nevertheless, she managed to find time for literary critic Edmund Wilson, who described falling in love with her as an "inevitable consequence" of knowing her. Their affair lasted until she moved on to her next conquest. No fading flower himself, Wilson managed to recover. He was married a total of four times in his life and, like Millay, had many affairs.

. . . . .

Mad, Bad, and Dangerous: Lady Caroline Lamb and Lord Byron
Lady Caroline Lamb came with quite a pedigree. She was the wife of William Lamb, who would later become Queen Victoria's first prime minister. She was wealthy and, well, a bit wild. When she met rock-star poet Lord Byron, it was lust at first sight for both of them. While some sweethearts exchange love poems or flowers, Lady Caroline and Byron exchanged locks of pubic hair after their first sexual encounter. Their tempestuous affair caused a scandal for many reasons, including the fact that she would frequently throw fits in public. Her antics quickly exhausted Byron. He scolded her for her "total want of common conduct." In turn, she called him "mad, bad, and dangerous to know." When he broke off the affair, Lady Caroline, ever the drama queen, tried to stab herself. Years later she wrote a juicy roman à clef, *Glenarvon*, which told her side of their story.

Jungle Cats: Rebecca West and H. G. Wells

You might call Wells a bit of a cradle robber. At 44, he began an affair with Rebecca West, who was only 19 years old. Admittedly, she was already writing for the suffragist weekly *Freewoman* as well as the *New York Star, New York Daily News,* and the socialist magazine, *Clarion* so she was probably mature for her years. While she was busy covering such stories as that of the suffragist Emily Davidson, who threw herself in front of one of the king's horses, Wells was writing a book called *Marriage.* West trashed it in a review and sparks flew. Their affair lasted for a decade, fueled by their fondness for calling each other such pet names as Panther and Jaguar. Their affection for animal names continued when they had a son in 1914 whom they named Anthony Panther. West broke up with "Jaguar" when one of his lovers tried to kill herself in his apartment.

· · · · ·

No Longer Fonda Jane: Ted Turner and Elizabeth Dewberry

Elizabeth Dewberry, blonde and beautiful author of *His Lovely Wife* and *Many Things Have Happened Since He Died and Here Are the Highlights,* was the wife of Pulitzer Prize-winning novelist Robert Olen Butler. Apparently, living in the shadow of his Pulitzer darkened Elizabeth's world, until a beacon of light shone through in the form of billionaire Ted Turner. Their affair became public knowledge when Butler saw fit to e-mail the details of her romance to fellow colleagues and graduate students at Florida State University.

the bard's barbs »

· ·

No one can pen an insult like William Shakespeare. Here's a list of some of his best.

I do desire we may be better strangers.
  —*As You Like It*

'Tis such fools as you that make the world full of ill-favor'd children
—*As You Like It*

I must tell you friendly in your ear, sell when you can, you are not for all markets
  —*As You Like It*

He is deformed, crooked, old and sere,
Ill-faced, worse bodied, shapeless every where;
Vicious, ungentle, foolish, blunt, unkind;
Stigmatical in making, worse in mind.
  — *The Comedy of Errors*

Dissembling harlot, thou art false in all!
  — *The Comedy of Errors*

More of your conversation would infect my brain.
  —*Coriolanus*

Here, thou incestuous, murderous, damned Dane,
Drink off this potion
  —*Hamlet*

I have thought some of Nature's journeymen had made men, and not
made them well, they imitated humanity so abominably.
   —*Hamlet*

...this sanguine coward, this bed-presser, this horseback-breaker, this
huge hill of flesh
—*Henry IV, Part 1*

'Sblood, you starveling, you elf-skin, you dried neat's tongue, you
bull's pizzle, you stock-fish! O for breath to utter what is like thee!
you tailor's-yard, you sheath, you bowcase; you vile standing-tuck!
   —*Henry IV, Part 1*

There's no more faith in thee than in a stewed prune.
   —*Henry IV, Part 1*

His wit's as thick as Tewksbury mustard.
   —*Henry IV, Part 2*

Away, you cut-purse rascal! you filthy bung, away! By this wine,
I'll thrust my knife in your mouldy chaps, an you play the saucy cuttle
with me. Away, you bottle-ale rascal! you basket-hilt stale juggler,
you!
   —*Henry IV, Part 2*

You whoreson cullionly barbermonger!
   —*King Lear*

[Thou art] a base, proud, shallow, beggarly, three-suited, hundred-
pound, filthy worsted-stocking knave; a lily-liver'd, action-taking,
whoreson, glass-gazing, superserviceable, finical rogue; one-trunk-
inheriting slave; one that wouldst be a bawd in way of good service,

and art nothing but the composition of a knave, beggar, coward, pandar, and the son and heir of a mungril bitch.
—*King Lear*

When all that is within him does condemn itself for being there.
—*Macbeth*

O faithless coward! O dishonest wretch!
Wilt thou be made a man out of my vice?
—*Measure for Measure*

Some report a sea-maid spawn'd him; some that he was begot between two stock-fishes. But it is certain that when he makes water his urine is congealed ice;
—*Measure for Measure*

I had rather be married to a death's head with a bone in his mouth.
—*The Merchant of Venice*

Vile worm, thou wast o'erlook'd even in thy birth.
—*The Merry Wives of Windsor*

Therein do men from children nothing differ.
—*Much Ado About Nothing*

In our last conflict four of his five wits went halting off, and now is the whole man govern'd with one; so that if he have wit enough to keep himself warm, let him bear it for a difference between himself and his horse, for it is all the wealth that he hath left, to be known a reasonable creature.
—*Much Ado About Nothing*

Heaven truly knows that thou art false as hell.
—*Othello*

O gull! O dolt! As ignorant as dirt!
  —*Othello*

Thou lump of foul deformity!
  —*Richard III*

You peasant swain! You whoreson malt-horse drudge!
  —*The Taming of the Shrew*

Were I like thee, I'd throw away myself.
  —*Timon of Athens*

Thou sodden-witted lord! thou hast no more brain than I have in mine / elbows.
  —*Troilus and Cressida*

Go hang yourself, you naughty mocking uncle!
  —*Troilus and Cressida*

I hate thee, Pronounce thee a gross lout, a mindless slave.
  —*The Winter's Tale*

other literary insults

· ·

Shakespeare wasn't the only one who could cut you down to size.

You bloody old towser-faced boot-faced totem pole on a crap
reservation.
  —Kingsley Amis

You bloody little cowshed mountebank.
  —Kingsley Amis

I fart at thee.
  —Ben Jonson

What I gained by being in France was learning to be better satisfied
with my own country.
  —Samuel Johnson

Crrritic.
  —Samuel Beckett

Pushing forty? She's hanging on for dear life.
  —Ivy Compton-Burnett

I didn't attend the funeral, but I sent a nice letter saying I approved
of it.
  —Mark Twain

He looked as inconspicuous as a tarantula on a slice of angel food.
  —Raymond Chandler

He's completely unspoiled by failure.
  —Noel Coward

He's liked, but he's not well liked.
  —Arthur Miller

Fine words! I wonder where you stole them.
  —Jonathan Swift

Gee, what a terrific party. Later on we'll get some fluid and embalm each other.
  —Neil Simon

The trouble with her is that she lacks the power of conversation but not the power of speech.
  —George Bernard Shaw

Where others have hearts, he carries a tumor of rotten principles.
  —Jack London

Some folks are wise and some are otherwise.
  —Tobias George Smolett

Some men are born mediocre, some men achieve mediocrity, and some men have mediocrity thrust upon them.
  —Joseph Heller

That woman speaks eight languages and can't say "no" in any of them.
  —Dorothy Parker

She's the sort of woman who lives for others—you can tell the others by their hunted expression.
  —C. S. Lewis

So boring you fall asleep halfway through her name.
  —Alan Bennett

She plunged into a sea of platitudes, and with the powerful breast stroke of a channel swimmer, made her confident way towards the white cliffs of the obvious.
  —W. Somerset Maugham

I'd call him a sadistic, hippophilic necrophile, but that would be beating a dead horse.
  —Woody Allen

God was bored by him.
  —Victor Hugo

He is not only dull himself, he is the cause of dullness in others.
  —Samuel Johnson

Shakespeare *on the sweeter side*

On the flip side, here is a list of Shakespearean compliments.

What a piece of work is man! how noble in reason! how infinite in faculty! in form and moving how express and admirable! in action how like an angel! in apprehension how like a god! the beauty of the world, the paragon of animals!
  —*Hamlet*

I am glad thou canst speak no better English, for if thou couldst, thou wouldst find me such a plain king that thou wouldst think I had sold my farm to buy my crown. I know no ways to mince it in love, but directly to say "I love you." ... I cannot look greenly, nor gasp out my eloquence, nor I have no cunning in protestation; only downright oaths, which I never use till urg'd, nor never break for urging. If thou canst love a fellow of this temper, Kate, whose face is not worth sunburning, that never looks in his glass for love of any thing he sees there, let thine eye be thy cook. I speak to thee plain soldier. If thou canst love me for this, take me!
  —*Henry V*

My love's more richer than my tongue
  —*King Lear*

One half of me is yours, the other half yours Mine own, I would say; but if mine, then yours, And so all yours.
  —*The Merchant of Venice*

O, she doth teach the torches to burn bright!
  —*Romeo and Juliet*

See, how she leans her cheek upon her hand! O that I were a glove
upon that hand, that I might touch that cheek!
  —*Romeo and Juliet*

It seems she hangs upon the cheek of night like a rich jewel in an
Ethiope's ear
  —*Romeo and Juliet*

My bounty is as boundless as the sea, My love as deep; the more
I give to thee, The more I have, for both are infinite.
  —*Romeo and Juliet*

Shall I compare thee to a summer's day?
Thou art more lovely and more temperate:
Rough winds do shake the darling buds of May,
And summer's lease hath all too short a date.
  —"Sonnet 18"

I might call him A thing divine, for nothing natural I ever saw
so noble.
  —*The Tempest*

Admir'd Miranda, Indeed the top of admiration! worth What's dearest
to the world! Full many a lady I have ey'd with best regard, and many
a time Th' harmony of their tongues hath into bondage Brought
my too diligent ear. For several virtues Have I lik'd several women,
never any With so full soul but some defect in her Did quarrel with
the noblest grace she ow'd, And put it to the foil. But you, O you, so
perfect and so peerless, are created Of every creature's best!"
  —*The Tempest*

I love thee so, that, maugre all thy pride,
Nor wit nor reason can my passion hide.
Do not extort thy reasons from this clause,
For that I woo, thou therefore hast no cause;
But rather reason thus with reason fetter,
Love sought is good, but given unsought better.
— *Twelfth Night*

What you do
Still betters what is done.
When you speak, sweet,
I'd have you do it ever; when you sing,
I'd have you buy and sell so; so give alms;
Pray so; and for the ord'ring of your affairs,
To sing them too. When you do dance, I wish you
A wave o' th' sea, that you might ever do
Nothing but that; move still, still so,
And own no other function. Each your doing
(So singular in each particular)
Crowns what you are doing in the present deeds,
That all your acts are queens.
— *The Winter's Tale*

across the ages through the pages:
brit lit 7

1901–1914: The Edwardian Period

The Edwardian period, named for King Edward VII, encompasses literature written between Queen Victoria's death in 1901 to the beginning of World War I in 1914. This was a time when the British Empire was flourishing, thus widening the gap between the wealthy upper class and the majority of the English population who lived in poverty. Edwardians were keenly aware of these economic disparities, as their writing reflects. In his plays, George Bernard Shaw dramatized social injustice. Joseph Conrad displayed the dark side of British imperialism.

George Bernard Shaw: The Least You Need to Know

- Irish playwright and critic, George Bernard Shaw lived from 1856 to 1950. As a socialist, he championed many causes, including public sanitation, vegetarianism, and equitable distribution of capital. His sympathies with the working class are evident in his numerous plays and essays.
- Fans of the musical *My Fair Lady* would recognize its source material in Shaw's 1913 play *Pygmalion*. Based on Ovid's tale of the sculptor who falls in love with his statue, Shaw's version of the story focuses on Professor Henry Higgins, a professor of phonetics who takes Eliza Doolittle, a Cockney flower girl, as his pet project. He helps transform her into a refined lady, but ultimately she rejects him romantically in favor of someone from a lower class.
- *Mrs. Warren's Profession*, written in 1893, dealt with the issue of prostitution, but the public outcry against the topic was so strong that the play was banned by Britain's theater censor. When it was produced in New York in 1905, the New York police arrested the cast and crew. The play was only allowed to be produced in England after 1925.

Joseph Conrad: The Least You Need to Know

- Born in Poland in 1857, Conrad did not learn to speak English until he was in his 20s, and yet his English novels are some of the most highly regarded in British literature.

- *Lord Jim* (1900) deals with issues of courage and cowardice. Jim, a young British seaman, is first mate on a ship traveling to Mecca. During an accident, he abandons the ship and its 800 Muslim passengers. He is charged with dereliction of duty and remains haunted by his cowardice. He flees to Patusan, a fictional country in the South Seas, where he becomes leader of the native inhabitants. When a group of white men murder Lord Jim's best friend, the son of a chief, Jim takes the burden of the crime upon himself to win back the honor he lost at sea so many years ago.

- Conrad critiqued the perils of colonialism and humankind's capacity for evil in his 1902 novella *Heart of Darkness.* In the story, the narrator, Marlow, describes a trip to the Belgian Congo, where he meets the maniacal white trader, Kurtz, who exploits the indigenous people of the jungle in his pursuit of absolute power. Kurtz's last words, "The horror! The horror!," reveal the potential for evil that lies within the human heart. The story will be familiar to film lovers as the basis for Francis Ford Coppola's 1979 film, *Apocalypse Now.*

across the ages through the pages:
american lit 5

1910–1939: The American Modernist Period

Between 1914 and 1939, American literature became what scholars refer to as modernist, which is to say, experimental in style and subject. Poet Ezra Pound coined the defining phrase of modernism when he urged fellow writers to "Make It New!" Other famous American modernist writers include poets Robert Frost and W. E. B. DuBois and fiction writers Djuna Barnes and Willa Cather.

Ezra Pound: The Least You Need to Know

- Considered the spokesman for the new era of literary experimentation in American writing, Pound was reacting against what he called "Victorian slither." Although his early poems were written in an Edwardian style, he quickly moved to reinventing poetic language as an imagist. According to Pound, the imagist movement, which he developed along with the poets H. D. (Hilda Doolittle) and Richard Aldington, should avoid long, abstract poetry. Instead, poems should treat their subjects directly, "use no word that does not contribute to the presentation," and write in a rhythm more like "the sequence of the musical phrase, not in a sequence of a metronome." His most famous imagist poem, " A Station in the Metro," consists of only two lines: "The apparition of these faces in the crowd / Petals on a wet, black bough."

- Pound knew he wanted to become a poet as a teenager. He studied at the University of Pennsylvania, where he met not only poet H. D. but also poet William Carlos Williams. For a while he taught at Wabash College, until he was fired for keeping a "lady-gent impersonator" in his private room. His termination prompted him to move to Europe, where he lived the rest of his life, meeting other famous authors such as James Joyce, W. B. Yeats, Marianne Moore, Gertrude Stein, Ernest Hemingway, and T. S. Eliot, who asked him to collaborate on *The Waste Land.*

- In 1924, he moved to Italy to work on his largest collection of poems, *The Cantos*, a group of radically different poems. Some incorporate Chinese characters, others include phrases in Latin, Greek, and other languages. As a whole, they illustrate his eccentric views on everything from usury and economics to poetry and philosophy. He began to develop an interest in fascism and anti-Semitism. During World War II, he made hundreds of fascistic propaganda broadcasts. As a result, he was indicted for treason and imprisoned for six months in a wire cage in Pisa before being sent to trial in the United States. The judge declared him mentally insane and committed him to a Washington, D.C., mental hospital for 12 years, until writers Archibald MacLeish, Robert Frost, and Ernest Hemingway persuaded authorities to release him.

Robert Frost: The Least You Need to Know

- Frost was born in California in 1874, but he is best known as a New England poet. He attended Dartmouth and Harvard and even farmed in New Hampshire for a few years before collections such as *North of Boston* and *New Hampshire* solidified his East Coast reputation. Of course, he became beloved nationwide for his delivery of a poem at the inauguration of John F. Kennedy and for winning four Pulitzer Prizes.
- While some readers see in Frost's writing as kind of anti-modernism, particularly in his rural themes and simple language, there remains in his poetry a thread of irony and ambiguity that aligns him with other early modernist experimenters. Poetry, for him, is " a momentary stay against confusion." As such, a famous poem like "The Road Not Taken," which is traditionally read as a work about nonconformity, reveals an underlying pessimism and ambiguity, as Frost admits that the two roads one can choose to walk down are not really all that different: "both that morning equally lay in leaves no step had trodden black." As such, the paths we can take in life are not as clear-cut as we might wish them to be.

- Unlike that of the modernists, Frost's poetic style was not very experimental overall. He thought writing in free verse was "like playing tennis without a net." However, like his fellow modernists, he preferred plain, conversational diction to ornate Victorian language. Simple moments of dialogue become powerful turning points in his work as this line from "Mending Wall" reveals: "Good fences make good neighbors."

W. E. B. DuBois: The Least You Need to Know

- Du Bois was an intrepid, powerful civil rights activist at the turn of the century. Born in 1868, he received his Ph.D. from Harvard in 1896, with a dissertation on "The Suppression of the Slave Trade in the United States of America," in which he argued that "the problem of the twentieth century is the problem of the color line." As the result of his beliefs, in 1909, he cofounded the National Negro Committee, which later became the NAACP.
- At a time when most scholars ignored the contributions of African-American writers, Du Bois, like other modernists, gained attention through his experimentation with literary forms that would try to describe as accurately as possible the distinctiveness of African-American culture. He published experimental poems, plays, and stories in the literary journals he edited. Such poems as "The Song of the Smoke," published in 1907, used the repeating refrain, "I am the smoke king, / I am black" in order to celebrate ethnicity. In a final, celebratory note, Du Bois alters the repetition slightly, "Hail to the smoke king, / Hail to the black!"
- His 1903 collection of essays *The Souls of Black Folk* indicts Reconstruction-era social programs for failing to provide equality for African-Americans. He argues that African Americans see themselves through a "double-consciousness"; on the one hand, they have a clear sense of their own culture and heritage, but they are also constantly aware of white prejudice. He disagrees with Booker T. Washington's call for vocational education; instead, Du

Bois argues for an educated class of African Americans to provide leadership.

Djuna Barnes: The Least You Need to Know

- Born in 1892 in Cornwall-on-Hudson, New York, Barnes is the prototypical, turn-of-the-century New Woman. She led a bohemian lifestyle as a bisexual, who, at times, used the pseudonym Lydia Steptoe to suggest that she wasn't afraid to step on people's toes if they objected to her nonconformity.
- Like many women writers in the modernist period, she moved to Paris, where she befriended Natalie Barney and founded the *Ladies Almanack*, a satirical look at Parisian lesbian life. The breakout of World War II forced her to leave the Left Bank for Greenwich Village, where she battled alcoholism and grew increasingly reclusive in her later years, dying in 1982.
- Barnes' 1936 novel *Nightwood* is one of the very first lesbian novels. It revolves around the ill-fated homosexual and heterosexual romances of five characters. Part of the material for the novel was based on Barnes' affair with the artist Thelma Wood. Many readers, including T. S. Eliot, find Barnes' writing style to be more poetical than prosaic. The plot is difficult to follow, but the rich language of the book highlights all of the passion and turmoil of its characters.

Willa Cather: The Least You Need to Know

- Although she was born in Virginia, Cather grew up in and spent most of her life in Nebraska. She worked for *McClure's Magazine* and began writing fiction in the style of Edith Wharton.
- However, in 1913, she published a novel that radically departed from her early style. *O Pioneers!* made Cather famous as an experimental writer who incorporated strong female characters and a blend of realism and aestheticism. The plot centers on the daughter of an immigrant, Alexandra Bergson, who, despite the fact that she is female, works on a farm with all of the creativity and enthusiasm of an artist. While the men in the community expect her

to fail, Alexandra, like Cather herself, exceeds social expectations of what a woman can achieve.

- *My Ántonia* (1918) continued Cather's focus on the stark beauty of prairie living. The character Jim Burden, who stands in as a substitute for the author herself, narrates the novel. He develops a strong interest in Ántonia, the daugher of a local immigrant. Through five volumes, the novel depicts Ántonia's life, her struggles with love and self-definition, and Jim's fascination with her as a bold, free-spirited pioneer.

Cather's birth certificate confirms her birthday, and her father mentions her in a letter of January 22, 1874. However, later in life Cather, claimed both 1875 and 1876 as her birth year, and the latter is carved into her gravestone.

laughing with the bard

The Merry Wives of Windsor

Plot

The boisterous Sir John Falstaff shows up in the quiet town of Windsor and turns everything upside down. He knows that Mrs. Ford and Mrs. Page manage the finances in their respective households, so he decides to woo them. However, the two women see through his attempts at seduction and vow to make a bigger fool of him than he is already making of himself. Mrs. Ford's husband disguises himself as a suitor to Mrs. Ford and asks Falstaff to help him win her affections. In his efforts, Falstaff is beaten and dunked in the Thames. Eventually Mr. Ford realizes that his wife is, and always has been, faithful to him, and he, Mrs. Ford, and Mrs. Page forgive the foolish Falstaff. In a moment of self-awareness, Falstaff agrees, "I do begin to perceive that I am made an ass."

Themes

1. Payback is hard. Falstaff tries to trick the two wives, but they are the ones who have the last laugh.
2. The love of money is the root of all evil, or at least embarrassment. Falstaff pretends to love Mrs. Ford and Mrs. Page, but really all he wants is access to their pocketbooks.

crying with the bard

. . . .

Othello

Plot

The Moor general, Othello, chooses Cassio over the evil Iago, his
ensign, to be his lieutenant. In his jealousy, Iago plots to destroy
Cassio and Othello, who thinks Iago is still his loyal friend. Othello
has recently wed Desdemona, the daughter of a Venetian senator. Iago
preys upon Othello's insecurities to suggest that Desdemona has been
unfaithful to him with Cassio. At first, Othello insists upon his trust
in Desdemona, but after he finds a handkerchief he had given her
among Cassio's possession (a handkerchief planted by Iago, of course),
Othello succumbs to jealous rage and strangles his wife. When Iago's
wife, Emilia, learns about his evil machinations and tells Othello, Iago
kills her for revealing the truth. Then the Moor, overcome with grief,
kills himself. For his crimes, Iago is sentenced to torture, and Cassio
becomes the new governor of Cyprus.

Themes

1. Jealousy is a "green-eyed monster which doth mock the meat it feeds
   on." Iago's jealousy of Cassio's appointment inspires his already
   wicked heart to commit more evil deeds. Similarly, Othello's jealousy
   about his wife's alleged love of Cassio causes him to murder her.
2. Racial prejudice unleashes larger troubles. Because he is a Moor,
   Othello is treated with some suspicion by most of the characters in
   the play, save Cassio and his wife. Desdemona's father, in particular,
   is upset that she has married a dark-skinned man. Always feeling like
   an outcast made Othello particularly susceptible to Iago's suggestion
   that he was unworthy of Desdemona's love.

learning with the bard

. . . .

The Famous History of the Life of King Henry VIII

Plot

King Henry VIII was the second king from the House of Tudor, ruling 38 years after King Henry VI. In the intervening years, the House of York had gained control, as we saw in *The Third Part of King Henry VI.* This play begins, as most of the history plays do, with a power struggle. Cardinal Wolsey has become more powerful as King Henry VIII returns to England from his travels. The Duke of Buckingham tries to warn the king, but Wolsey accuses him of treason and has him killed. Henry VIII is married to Katharine of Aragon, but he has fallen in love with Anne Bullen. With Wolsey's assistance, he persuades the pope to allow a divorce, but once Wolsey learns that Henry then wishes to marry Anne, he tries to stop it. The Archbishop of Canterbury, without permission from the Vatican, annuls Henry's marriage to Katharine to earn the king's favor. Wolsey is arrested for treason and dies, as does Katherine. Henry marries Anne, and they have a child, Elizabeth.

Themes

1. Too single-minded a pursuit can bring ruin. Henry VIII so longs for a male heir that he leaves Katherine to marry Anne. Later he would go on to marry Jane Seymour, Anne of Cleves, Catherine Howard, and Catherine Parr.
2. Repentance is always possible. In the beginning of the play, Cardinal Wolsey's ambition threatens the king. However, once he begins to understand Henry's lustfulness, he regrets his help in invalidating the marriage to Katherine.

The Coretta Scott King Award: *1989-2008*

• •

1989: Text - Walter Dean Myers, *Fallen Angels*
Illustration - Jerry Pinkney, *Mirandy and Brother Wind*

1990: Text - Patricia and Frederick McKissack, *A Long Hard Journey: The Story of the Pullman Porter*
Illustration - Jan Spivey Gilchrist, *Nathaniel Talking*

1991: Text - Mildred D. Taylor, *The Road to Memphis*
Illustration - Leo and Diane Dillon, *Aida*

1992: Text - Walter Dean Myers, *Now Is Your Time! The African-American Struggle for Freedom*
Illustration - Faith Ringgold, *Tar Beach*

1993: Text - Patricia McKissack, *The Dark-Thirty: Southern Tales of the Supernatural*
Illustration - Kathleen Atkins Wilson, *The Origin of Life on Earth: An African Creation Myth*

1994: Text - Angela Johnson, *Toning the Sweep*
Illustration - Tom Feelings, *Soul Looks Back in Wonder*

1995: Text - Patricia and Frederick McKissack, *Christmas in the Big House, Christmas in the Quarters*
Illustration - James Ransome, *The Creation*

1996: Text - Virginia Hamilton, *Her Stories* (illustrated by Leo and Diane Dillon)
Illustration - Tom Feelings, *The Middle Passage: White Ships, Black Cargo*

1997: Text - Walter Dean Myers, *Slam!*
Illustration - Jerry Pinkney, *Minty: A Story of Young Harriet Tubman*

1998: Text - Sharon M. Draper, *Forged by Fire*
Illustration - Javaka Steptoe, *In Daddy's Arms I Am Tall: African Americans Celebrating Fathers*

1999: Text - Angela Johnson, *Heaven*
Illustration - Michele Wood, *i see the rhythm*

2000: Text – Christopher Paul Curtis, *Bud, Not Buddy*
   Illustration – Brian Pickney, *In the Time of the Drums*
2001: Text -Andrea Davis Pinkney, *Let It Shine! Stories of Black Women Freedom Fighters*
   Illustration – Bryan Collier, *Uptown*
2002: Text – Sharon G. Flake, *Money Hungry*
   Illustration – Jerry Pinkney, *Goin' Someplace Special*
2003: Text – Brenda Woods, *The Red Rose*
   Illustration – E. B. Lewis, *Talkie' About Bessie: The Story of Aviator Elizabeth Coleman*
2004: Text – Patricia C. and Frederick L. McKissack, *Days of Jubilee: The End of Slavery in the United States*
   Illustration – Ashley Bryan, *Beautiful Blackbird*
2005: Text – Toni Morrison, *Remember: The Journey to School Integration*
   Illustration – Kadir Nelson, *Ellington Was Not a Street*
2006: Text - Julius Lester, *Days of Tears: A Novel in Dialogue*
   Illustration - Tonya Bolden, *A Nineteenth-Century American Girl*
2007: Text – Sharon Draper, *Copper Sun*
   Illustration - Kadir Nelson, *Moses: When Harriet Tubman Led Her People to Freedom*
2008: Text – Christopher Paul Curtis, *Elijah of Buxton*
   Illustration – Ashley Bryan, *Let It Shine*

"from books to movies for 300, please, alex."

Category: Horror

1408, Stephen King (short story)
American Psycho, Brett Easton Ellis
From Hell, Alan Moore
Salem's Lot, Stephen King
The Haunting, Shirley Jackson
The Secret Window, novella titled *Four Past Midnight*, Stephen King

Category: Mystery

Mystic River, Dennis Lehane
Derailed, James Siegel
Deliverance, James Dickey
The Manchurian Candidate, Richard Condon
A Scanner Darkly, Philip K. Dick
Road to Perdition, Max Allan Collins

Category: Based on a True Story

A Beautiful Mind, biography of John Nash Jr., Sylvia Nasar
A Mighty Heart, Mariane Pearl
Blow, Bruce Porter
Frida, Hayden Herrera
Gorillas in the Mist, Diane Fossey
The Prize Winner of Defiance Ohio, Jane Anderson
The Hours, Michael Cunningham
Seabiscuit, Laura Hillenbrand
Riding in Cars with Boys, Beverly D'Onofrio

pen names of famous pen holders #2

Author: George Orwell
Famous Works: *Animal Farm, 1984*
Real Name: Eric Arthur Blair

Author: Dr. Seuss
Famous Works: *Oh, The Places You Will Go!, The Lorax*
Real Name: Theodore Geisel

Author: J. K. Rowling
Famous Works: The *Harry Potter* series
Real Name: Joanne Rowling

Author: Pablo Neruda
Famous Works: *España en el Corazón, Obras Completas*
Real Name: Neftali Ricardo Reyes Basoalto

Author: Woody Allen
Famous Works: *Play It Again, Sam* (the play)
Real Name: Allen Stewart Konigsberg

Author Stephen King tried to fool everyone by publishing four titles under the name Richard Bachman. The writing styles of Bachman's and King's novels were compared, and it was soon revealed that Bachman was, in fact, Stephen King..

---

in the big house: [*authors in jail*]

It's one thing to pen a story. It's another to spend time in the pen. Nevertheless, some of the world's great writers have spent a little time in the big house.

·····

John Milton

He may have written about Adam and Eve, but that didn't keep Puritan John Milton from experiencing his own, personal "paradise lost." At first, things were going well for the poet-essayist. Charles I had been overthrown and the Puritans were in power. Milton's first son was born in 1651. He and his family moved to Westminster. Then trouble crept into his little Eden. In 1652, he lost his sight. His propagandist writings were burned by followers of Charles II. In autumn of 1659, he was arrested and jailed. A few months later, he was released by order of Parliament, but he had to live the rest of his days under a type of house arrest.

·····

John Bunyan

It's ironic that the author of the most famous Christian allegory of all time, *The Pilgrim's Progress,* would land in jail, but such was the fate of John Bunyan. He described his younger days as wild, if you consider such antics as cussing, dancing, and bell ringing out of control, but it was his religious conversion that ultimately got him in trouble. He became a Baptist and immediately began opposing the Quakers. They may have been a peace-loving people, but they were not amused. In 1658, he was warned against preaching without a license, but that didn't stop him, so two years later they locked him up. Officials told him that if he would stop preaching he could go free. He refused and, as a result, was awarded 12 more years in the slammer.

Thomas Paine

Early American radical Thomas Paine was a likely candidate for jail because he was never afraid to speak his mind, and folks like that tend to find themselves on the wrong side of the law every now and then. In 1776, he wrote *Common Sense* to advocate American independence. Then, in 1791, he wrote *Rights of Man* to support the French Revolution. His sympathy with the Girondists and his opposition to execution of the king put him at odds with Robespierre, so in 1793, he was put behind bars in Paris. A year later, he was released but was hardly tamed. He went on to publish *The Age of Reason,* which stirred up all kinds of controversy in its defense of deism.

· · · · ·

The Marquis de Sade

Like any nice boy, he got married, but unlike nice boys, he quickly began having affairs and soliciting prostitutes. He was notorious enough to catch the attention of Paris police, who warned local brothels about his vicious behavior. In 1772, he was given the death penalty for an "unnatural crime." This didn't stop him, however. He escaped and moved on to other places, where he organized orgies, took girls as sex slaves, and tried to poison prostitutes. All in all, he spent over 25 years in and out of prisons, years which he was able to parlay into pornography and fame.

· · · · ·

Émile Zola

Zola is best known for spearheading the literary movement known as naturalism, which he defined as "nature seen through a temperament." However, Zola was looking at more than just nature when he ended up in jail. In 1898, he published an open letter titled "J'accuse," in which he claimed that the government falsified evidence against a Jewish military officer who, allegedly, had given military secrets to the Germans. Zola knew his defense of Alfred

Dreyfus would be considered libelous, but he spoke out anyway. He died four years later under suspicious circumstances. The official cause of death was carbon monoxide poisoning, but whether it was an accident or whether someone blocked the ventilation in his house's chimney was a matter of debate.

· · · · ·

Fyodor Dostoevsky

Fyodor fell in with the wrong crowd when he took up with a group of utopian socialists. They must have seemed fun to him at the time; one of the prominent members of the group once went to church cross-dressed as a woman. In 1849, however, the secret police cracked down on the "crackpots" and arrested Dostoevsky, sentencing him to death. They put a blindfold on him and tied him up as if they were about to shoot him. At the last second, they let him live, shipping him off to Siberia for four years of hard labor.

· · · · ·

Norman Mailer

Oh sure, he was drunk at the time, but that excuse didn't keep him out of jail. First, in 1960, he was arrested on the charge of disorderly conduct after a drunken argument over a nightclub bill of a measly $7.60. A week later he was arrested again for stabbing his wife, Adele. Later, in 1967, Mailer was arrested at the Pentagon during a protest march against the Vietnam War. He was sentenced to 30 days in jail but only spent one night since he got out on $500 bail.

· · · · ·

Ken Kesey

Oh sure, he was high at the time, but that excuse didn't keep him out of jail. In 1966, police arrested the *One Flew over the Cuckoo's Nest* writer for possession of marijuana. However, Kesey was a man with a plan. He ran away to Mexico and faked a suicide before he could stand trial. Ultimately he ended up back in the United States, serving five months at the San Mateo County Jail. With his wild days and prison time behind him, he moved to Oregon, where he bought a farm and raised four kids.

· · · · ·

O. Henry

Like Ken Kersey, the Beat Generation Pied Piper, the writer known as O. Henry also had a substance abuse problem and fled to a Spanish-speaking country to avoid trial. But only he managed all this years before Kesey had LSD to blame for his antisocial behavior. O. Henry was born William Sydney Porter in 1862. When he was working as a bank teller at the First National Bank in Austin, the manager found a lot of cash missing. Porter was supposed to return to Austin to stand trial, but instead he escaped to Honduras. A few years later, when he heard that his wife was dying, he returned to Texas and was sentenced to three years in the federal pen for embezzlement. Some say that he took the pseudonym "O. Henry" from a warden named Orrin Henry.

name that hippie!

· ·

Hippie #1:
Coined the phrase "the Beat generation"
Wrote *On the Road*

Hippie #2:
Prefers to eat his lunch "naked"
Shot and killed his wife in a game of "William Tell"
Wrote a book called *Queer*

Hippie #3:
The inspiration for Dean Moriarty in *On the Road*
Drove the Merry Pranksters on a bus trip across America
Nick Nolte played him in the 1980 film *Heart Beat*

Hippie #4:
Fell in love with books after being bedridden from an accident at the age of seven
Studied Zen Buddhism with Alan Watts
Publications include *The Back Country*, *Regarding Wave*, and *Turtle Island*

Hippie #5:
Threw LSD parties called "acid tests"
Legendary Merry Prankster

Hippie #6
Published Allen Ginsberg's poem "Howl" in 1967
Owner of City Lights Bookstore in San Francisco
Named poet laureate of San Francisco in 1998

Hippie #7
Coined the phrase "Flower Power"
Appears as Carlo Marx in *On the Road*
French Minister of Culture awarded him the medal of Chevalier des
Arts et des Lettres (the Order of Arts and Letters)

Answers:
1. Jack Kerouac
2. William Burroughs
3. Neal Cassady
4. Gary Snyder
5. Ken Kesey
6. Lawrence Ferlinghetti
7. Allen Ginsberg

More Wacky Writers

- *Victor Hugo ran for the French presidency in 1848.*

- *Norman Mailer ran for mayor of New York City in 1969.*

- *Samuel Clemens chose the pseudonym Mark Twain
  because it is a nautical term which means "two fathoms
  deep."*

- *Virginia Woolf was the granddaughter of William
  Makepeace Thackeray.*

- *Aldous Huxley is the great-nephew of Matthew Arnold.*

---

poetry survival manual 3

"The Love Song of J. Alfred Prufrock"

The Trick: Read the footnotes.

Tools You'll Need: A dictionary and the memory of any nerd you went to high school with.

Directions: If you're expecting the ol' "Roses are red, Violets are blue" action, then this particular "Love Song" might throw you for a loop. Fear not. The footnote is your friend. Yes, yes, we know that pausing for those little numbers and having to look down at the bottom of the page and then find where you left off can be a pain in the poetic posterior, but it pays off.

"The Love Song of J. Alfred Prufrock" is all about allusions (that's poetry-speak for words that refer to something else). So, for example, when Prufrock says, "I am not Prince Hamlet," you probably don't need a footnote to understand that what he means is that he isn't the hero of a Shakespearean tragedy. Instead, he says, if he were cast in a Shakespeare play, he'd be the minor character who merely steps on stage long enough to announce the arrival of a king or to hand someone a cup of tea. However, earlier in the poem, just to show how wimpy he thinks he is, Prufrock compares himself to Lazarus. Unless you're up on your Bible stories, you might need to check the footnote on this one to learn that Lazarus is the man Jesus raised from the dead. So Prufrock isn't just wimpy—he's practically a corpse. It's no surprise, then, that when he overhears women talking about Michelangelo (footnote tells you, in case you don't know, that Michelangelo is the great Renaissance painter of the Sistine Chapel, among other things), he feels excluded. Why would women talk to little Prufrock about someone so great?

Be careful about footnotes, though. When they gloss a particular fact or historical event, that's one thing, but sometimes they can fool you. The first line of the poem makes it clear that Prufrock is talking to someone: "Let us go then, you and I." In some printings of the poem, the "you" has a footnote which explains that Eliot once claimed that the "you" in the poem was a male friend of Prufrock. That's fine, if Eliot really said that, but most of the time we don't know what a poet said about his work. Frankly, even if we do, the work has to stand on its own; there must be room for interpretation, because you can't always ask the poet what he meant, and half the time he may not know. Critics have long debated just whom Prufrock is speaking to in the poem. It could be a male friend, but the poem becomes even more interesting if he is speaking to a woman, maybe someone he's in love with. Or, he could be talking to himself, as some folks do. Keep that image of the high school nerd in mind. When he grows up into an old man, who is he going to be talking to in a love poem? Look to the footnotes, but don't let them limit your imagination.

pop quiz #4

1. Which novel begins with the line "A screaming comes across the sky?"
2. Which book begins with the line "In our family, there was no clear line between religion and fly-fishing."
3. Academy Award-winning movies have been made from which of the following novels: *The English Patient, Ordinary People,* or *Tom Jones?*
4. Which Western writer has had the most screenplays based on his work?
5. What was the pseudonym of William Sidney Porter?
6. What is the pseudonym of Florence Anthony?
7. What is the pseudonym of Jude Gilliam White?
8. Who said, "Fiction is obliged to stick to possibilities. Truth isn't."
9. Who is the most prolific American author?

Answers
1. *Gravity's Rainbow* by Thomas Pynchon
2. *A River Runs Through It* by Norman Maclean
3. All of them
4. Zane Grey, with 109 movies based on his writing.
5. O. Henry
6. Ai
7. Jude Deveraux
8. Mark Twain
9. Lauran Paine (1916–1995), who wrote over 900 books under various pseudonyms

without a wink: *literary insomniacs*

Was it their overflowing creativity? Drug problems? Whatever the reason, these authors were often up all night.

· · · · ·

Alexandre Dumas

Sleep was just a stroll away for *Count of Monte Cristo* author Alexandre Dumas. Nothing he tried could help him get to sleep, so finally he consulted a famous doctor, who told him that if he wasn't falling asleep he should just get out of the bed. Beds were for sleeping, not lying there wishing he was sleeping. As a result, he began to take long walks every night, and eventually his sleep patterns returned to normal.

· · · · ·

Charles Dickens

When *Great Expectations* author Charles Dickens had great expectations of sleep, those expectations were not always fulfilled. Like Alexandre Dumas, he learned to take long nocturnal walks to bring sleep on. He would stroll the streets of London and, being the writer he was, would take notes along the way of details he could use later in his books. One result of these strolls was *The Uncommercial Traveller,* a collection of literary sketches.

· · · · ·

Barbara Kingsolver

The Poisonwood Bible might never have been written if Barbara Kingsolver had been able to sleep. She was already quite busy in her life, what with studying biology at DePauw University, protesting the Vietnam War, and living in France and Greece. However, when she became pregnant, a wicked case of insomnia struck, and she had to do something to pass the time. Always resourceful, she took up fiction writing. She published her first novel, *The Bean Trees,* in 1998, and from there went on to write *The Poisonwood Bible,* a book short-listed for the Pulitzer Prize.

• • • • •

Franz Kafka

It's probably no surprise that anyone who would write a famous story about a guy turning into a giant insect might have trouble sleeping. To keep track of his insomnia, Kafka kept a diary. On October 2, 1911, he wrote, "Sleepless night. The third in a row. I fall asleep soundly, but after an hour I wake up, as though I had laid my head in the wrong hole." He finally came up with a solution. He thought feeling heavy might help him "sink" into sleep, so he would assume a special position in bed. He crossed his arms and put his hands on his shoulders to feel like a soldier burdened with a heavy pack.

• • • • •

Mark Twain

The author of *Tom Sawyer* is universally known for his humor, but having trouble falling asleep made him particularly grouchy. Once when he was spending the night at a friend's house, he couldn't sleep. In a fit, he hurled a pillow at his bedroom window to let in a little fresh air. When he woke the next morning, he hadn't actually busted out a window in the house, which was the good news. The bad news was that he had broken a glass-enclosed bookcase.

• • • • •

The Brontë Sisters

Elizabeth Gaskell, biographer of the Brontës, described how Charlotte and Emily came up with an unusual plan to beat insomnia—they walked in circles around the dining room table until they were exhausted enough to sleep. Years later, after Emily died, Charlotte had more trouble sleeping than usual. She missed her sister so much that she revived the old dining room table ritual, walking in circles all alone night after night.

Joyce Carol Oates

Sleeplessness wasn't such a problem for novelist and critic Joyce Carol Oates. In a 1971 interview she confessed: "I have terrible nights of insomnia, when my mind is galloping along and I feel a strange eerie nervousness, absolutely inexplicable. What a nuisance! Or, maybe it isn't a nuisance? An ideal insomnia allows for a lot of reading. When the house is dark and quiet and the entire world turned off for the night, it's a marvelous feeling to be there, alone, with a book, or a blank piece of paper…Such moments of solitude redeem all the rushing hours, the daylight confusion of people and duties." For her, there is a kind of "secret pride of the insomniac" because it sets him/her apart, presumably from all the other lazy slobs catching a night full of ZZZs.

• • • • •

Amy Lowell

When it came to sleeping in hotels, poet Amy Lowell took what you might call an anti-rock star approach. When she checked in, the last thing on her mind was throwing wild parties and breaking furniture. Instead, she would book five hotel rooms. She slept in the center room and made sure that the two rooms beside her and the ones above and below her were empty, so that no noise would wake her up.

• • • • •

Emily Dickinson

Dickinson's love of poetry began at a young age. She would rather write than sleep. Often she asked her father if she could stay up really late to write poems. When she was old enough not to need permission, she continued giving up sleep for writing. The biographer Richard B. Sewall argues that the poem beginning, "A Spider sewed at Night / Without a Light / Upon an Arc of White" is really about Emily herself spinning a web of poetry late at night.

Ernest Hemingway

Characters in Hemingway's books often have trouble falling asleep. Stories like "Big Two-Hearted River" and "Now I Lay Me" show how Papa's own insomnia influenced his work. After critics panned *Green Hills of Africa* in 1935, he wrote to fellow insomniac F. Scott Fitzgerald: "No matter what time I go to sleep [I] wake and hear the clock strike either one or two then lie wide awake and hear three, four and five. But since I have stopped giving a goddamn about anything in the past it doesn't bother [me] much and I just lie there and keep perfectly still." He admitted that his own insomnia helped him feel compassion for other people's suffering. Perhaps that is why, in 1940, when he bought a home in Cuba called Finca Vigia, he kept a separate bedroom from his wife so he wouldn't inflict his wakefulness on her.

• • • • •

F. Scott Fitzgerald

Tender Is the Night might have been a good title for a Fitzgerald novel, but it certainly didn't describe his own nocturnal sufferings. In 1934, he wrote an essay, "Sleeping & Waking," in which he described how a tiny mosquito in a New York hotel room initiated a long bout of insomnia for him. He became terrified of not being able to sleep, so he began a careful, sleep-inducing ritual—he would make a nightcap, read a little, and make sure his bedside table was perfectly organized. Nevertheless, he still suffered: "The horror has come now like a storm—what if this night prefigured the night after death—what if all thereafter was an eternal quivering on the edge of an abyss, with everything base and vicious in oneself urging one forward and the baseness and viciousness of the world just ahead. No choice, no road, no hope—only the endless repetition of the sordid and the semi-tragic." In 1936, he penned the famous description of the horrors of insomnia: "at three o'clock in the morning a forgotten package has the same tragic importance as a death sentence, and the cure doesn't work—and in a real dark night of the soul it is always three o'clock in the morning, day after day." Eventually he turned to barbiturates to get 40 winks...well, maybe only 35 or so.

The Pulitzer Prize *1976–2007*

. . . .

1976: *Humboldt's Gift* by Saul Bellow

1978: *Elbow Room* by James Alan McPherson

1979: *The Stories of John Cheever* by John Cheever

1980: *The Executioner's Song* by Norman Mailer

1981: *A Confederacy of Dunces* by John Kennedy Toole (posthumously)

1982: *Rabbit Is Rich* by John Updike, the latest novel in a memorable sequence

1983: *The Color Purple* by Alice Walker

1984: *Ironweed* by William Kennedy

1985: *Foreign Affairs* by Alison Lurie

1986: *Lonesome Dove* by Larry McMurtry

1987: *A Summons to Memphis* by Peter Taylor

1988: *Beloved* by Toni Morrison

1989: *Breathing Lessons* by Anne Tyler

1990: *The Mambo Kings Play Songs of Love* by Oscar Hijuelos

1991: *Rabbit at Rest* by John Updike

1992: *A Thousand Acres* by Jane Smiley

1993: *A Good Scent from a Strange Mountain* by Robert Olen Butler

1994: *The Shipping News* by E. Annie Proulx

1995: *The Stone Diaries* by Carol Shields

1996: *Independence Day* by Richard Ford

1997: *Martin Dressler: The Tale of an American Dreamer* by Steven Millhauser

1998: *American Pastoral* by Philip Roth

1999: *The Hours* by Michael Cunningham

2000: *Interpreter of Maladies* by Jhumpa Lahiri

2001: *The Amazing Adventures of Kavalier & Clay* by Michael Chabon

2002: *Empire Falls* by Richard Russo

Proof

In David Auburn's Pulitzer Prize-winning play Proof, *Robert, a well-known mathematician, has recently died leaving behind two daughters, Catherine and Claire. He also leaves many protégés, Hal in particular, to mourn his death. This play is about relationships and how they change during times of stress and tragedy. Each relationship is held together by a feeling of loss.*

Having inherited her father's genius, Catherine has written a proof that top mathematicians have been trying to calculate for many years. However, Robert's former students and colleagues believe he wrote the proof, not Catherine. Hal searches Robert's office in hopes of finding the proof, which is hidden in a locked drawer. During Hal's search, he and Catherine become quite close. Once shut off from the world, Catherine lets Hal in and gives him the key to her heart, literally. The key actually fits the drawer containing Catherine's proof. Upon seeing the proof, Hal becomes focused on the importance of his discovery and forgets Catherine's feelings. He doesn't believe her when she says she wrote it.

The proof emerges as the central image. It is an actual mathematical proof that proves an actual theory, but also refers to the characters' relationships. Catherine feels that she must prove to Hal that she wrote the proof. Hal must then prove to her that he is worthy of being trusted. Catherine also feels that she must convince Claire that she can take care of herself and feels she must show her father that she will be fine and is a good mathematician. Catherine must also convince herself of these things.

peculiar *poetry anthologies*

Poetry, by its very nature, can be peculiar enough. What happens when editors select an unusual group of poems to publish together? Sometimes, as you can see, very peculiar poetry anthologies can result.

• • • • •

Bum Rush the Page: A Def Poetry Jam (2001)

Publishers Weekly calls this anthology "orally friendly," which might be the first time in literary critical history that that particular term has been used. If that alone doesn't inspire you to check out the book, imagine hearing the poems read aloud at poetry slams around the country, and you can begin to appreciate what the fresh, funky collection represents. The poems are organized under such headings as "Blood I Say, Study Our Song, Sing This Song," "Open Your Mouth and Smile," "Every Word Must Conjure," "Drums Drown Out the Sorrow," and "When the Definition of Madness Is Love," just to name a few.

• • • • •

A Little Book of Ping-Pong Verse (1902)

What do you remember about the turn of the 20th century? Flappers? Model T's? A raging table-tennis craze? If that last one throws you for a loop, don't be surprised. Folks in the early 1900s loved their ping-pong, and this anthology of verse proves it. It includes such memorable poems as "The Rubaiyat of Ping-Pong," "The Ping-Pong Ankle," and, of course, a bunch of poems simply called "Ping-Pong" just to get the point across. In "Only a Ping-Pong Ball," Thomas Beasley compares the joys of table tennis to chasing women:

> It will lead you then a merry race,
> As any maiden coy,
> And should it find a hiding-place,
> It hugs itself with joy.

The Outlaw Bible of American Poetry (1999)

If the words "outlaw" and "Bible" provide a contrast that intrigues you, then this anthology might be right up your alley. These are the poems you don't read in high school. From Walt Whitman to Tupac Shakur, the poets published in this anthology are renegades, outsiders, and, to say the least, nonconformists. Consider such titles as "William, I Giggled with Your Girlfriend" and "Marianne Faithfull's Cigarette" as typical of what you might find. It ain't exactly "holy" scripture, but it's the Word of outlaws, that's for sure.

· · · · ·

Verses That Hurt: Pleasure and Pain From the POEMFONE Poets (1997)

OK, what exactly is a "poemfone" poet? Apparently, around 1995, poets were organized to read poems into a voicemail message. Listeners could call the number, listen to the poem, and reply to it in a voicemail message of their own. Often comments got quite out of hand, as did the poems themselves. *Verses That Hurt* offers up these sometimes funny, sometimes painful poems to readers willing, at times, to be addressed as "careerist, slime bucket, gladhandling a**holes." If pain is your thing, then this is the anthology for you!

· · · · ·

The Vampire in Verse: An Anthology (1985)

There are thousands of publishers, from Random House to university presses, but did you know that the venerable and esteemed Count Dracula Fan Club also publishes works of literary merit? Consider this peculiar anthology, which boasts poems by Keats, Kipling, Yeats, and Baudelaire. Whether it's Halloween or just any night you feel like reading about bloodsucking undead, you can find such lines as these from Goethe:

> I seek his love to whom my teeth were given,
> And I have sucked the lifeblood from his hearth.

Poetry of Chess (1981)

If the word "Checkmate!" is poetry to your ears, you'll love this collection of chess-related verse. The poets represented range from Chaucer and Goldsmith to Yeats and Pound. No scrawny little poetic pawns in this bunch! Think how your own game will improve after meditating on such lines as:

> But chess to women is like everyday
> Only even more so, and Kings and Queens
> Are you and me, in an odd sort of way.
> (They think of knights as horses though, it seems.)
> —Simon Lowy, "On Her Taking My Queen at Chess"

•••••

The Poetry of Geology (1982)

This volume just goes to show that earthquakes and sex aren't the only things that can make you feel as if the earth has moved. Thrill to poems like "A Meditation on Rhode-Island Coal" by William Cullen Bryant which describes, er, black stuff from a really small state. Consider the possibilities of all you could say to a plant as you read "To a Fossil Fern." Or pour a strong cup of coffee, and brace yourself for all 1,145 lines of John Scafe's 1820 poem "King Coal's Levee," which reads, at times, like a geological recipe card:

> Of Feldspar and Quartz a large quantity take,
> Then pepper with Mica, and mix up and bake.

•••••

Mary, Queen of Scots: An Anthology of Poetry (1981)

Poets are naturally inspired by all kinds of topics: love, nature, immortality, and, of course, 16th-century monarchs beheaded by Queen Elizabeth I of England. Little wonder, then, that such writers as Robert Burns, Edith Sitwell, and Boris Pasternak would spring to verse at the mere thought of Mary. Consider these lines from William Wordsworth, who, when he wasn't writing about daffodils, imagines Mary saying:

> O be my spirit, like my thraldom, strait;
> And, like mine eyes that stream with sorrow, blind!

· · · · ·

Gems from an Old Drummer's Grip (1889)

Since a "drummer" is a traveling salesman, you might expect a book of off-color jokes. But this anthology, instead, provides a number of great little poems you can take along on your travels. On the other hand, you could also feel free to make up traveling salesman jokes based on poetic titles such as "The Battered Old Grip," "What Mrs. Ella Wheeler Wilcox Says of the Boys," "When the Check Is on the Kiester," and "Never Go Back on a Traveling Man."

Heteronyms G–I

Graduate *GRAJ-u-wait* - to complete an academic degree; *Graj-u-ut-* someone who has graduated

When I graduate, I want to go see the movie The Graduate.

House *HAUS* - a building in which someone lives; *HOWZ* - to provide with living quarters

You cannot house anyone in the House of Representatives. OK, I guess you could, but why would you?

Incense *INsens* - material burned to produce a nice smell; *inSENS* - to make angry

Bob was incensed when his roommate burned incense all night and made their apartment smell like a yoga studio on steroids.

---

like parent like child

Sometimes great writing just runs in the family, as these literary families prove.

Parent	Child
Kingsley Amis	Martin Amis
Robert Benchley	Nathaniel Benchley
John Cheever	Susan Cheever
Clive Cussler	Dirk Cussler
Nicholas Delbanco	Francesca Delbanco
Millicent Dillon	Wendy Lesser
Andre Dubus	Andre Dubus IV
Richard Ellmann	Lucy Ellmann
Constance Garnett	David Garnett
Nathaniel Hawthorne	Julian Hawthorne
Stephen King	Owen King
Elizabeth Longford	Antonia Fraser
Anne Rice	Christopher Rice
Carl Sagan	Nick Sagan
Carolyn See	Lisa See
John Steinbeck	Thomas Steinbeck
Frances Trollope	Anthony Trollope
Evelyn Waugh	Auberon Waugh
James Wright	Franz Wright

short story *masters*

· ·

Make no mistake. Novels may be the longer genre, but short stories are equally difficult to craft because they require a sophisticated ability to render an entire narrative in a short amount of space. Like the best novelists, the short story author has to make each word and each detail count. Here's a quick guide to a few masters of the form.

· · · · ·

Flannery O'Connor

The Story Behind the Stories:

In 1925, Mary Flannery O'Connor was born in Savannah but grew up in scenic Milledgeville, Georgia. She achieved early fame by teaching a chicken to walk backwards when she was five. From there she went on to Georgia State College and the University of Iowa, where she earned an M.F.A. Three years later, she was diagnosed with lupus, the same disease that had taken her father's life when she was only 15. She returned to the family farm in Milledgeville to write fiction and, strangely enough, to raise peacocks. A devout Roman Catholic, she gave lectures on faith and literature and corresponded with such writers as Elizabeth Bishop and Robert Lowell. After surgery in 1964, she grew increasingly ill and died on August 3 at the age of 39.

O'Connor said that what makes a story successful lies in a unique, surprising gesture of a character that reveals the true heart of the tale. Violence works for her as a writer because it gives characters a clear reality check and opens a space for grace to enter. She believed that extreme circumstances most clearly reveal our essential natures.

The Stories:

"Revelation"—It's Mrs. Turpin's world, and everyone else just lives in it, or so Mrs. Turpin thinks. Young Mary Grace sits in the waiting room listening to Mrs. Turpin's egotistical ramblings until she finally snaps. Maybe it ain't Mrs. Turpin's world after all.

"Everything That Rises Must Converge"—A smug young son accompanies his bigoted mother to her weight loss meeting on a newly desegregated bus. They learn a thing or two about the new South in a tale with the most troubled mother-son relationship since *Psycho.*

"Good Country People"—The symbolically named Joy Hopewell has lost all hope now that she has lost a leg. When a traveling Bible salesman asks her to give him her wooden leg, she learns a lesson or two about what makes people "good."

"A Good Man Is Hard to Find"—A more frightening family vacation is hard to find than in this short story about one holiday gone awry. One escaped murderer plus one cranky grandmother and her kin prove a great O'Connor story is easy to find.

• • • • •

Raymond Carver

The Story Behind the Stories:

Raymond Carver worked as everything from a janitor to a tulip-picker in a life that taught him to sympathize with the working class. Born in 1938 in Clatskanie, Oregon, he grew up in Washington and, at the tender age of 19, married a 16-year-old girl with whom he quickly had two children. He attended Chico State College and Humboldt State College, all the while holding down a series of odd jobs to support his family. In 1967, he met a man who would change his life, editor Gordon Lish. He taught Carver to streamline his fiction into the more minimalist style that would eventually become his trademark. His writing career flourished, but he continued to struggle with alcoholism until he became sober in 1977. He divorced his first wife in 1982 and married poet Tess Gallagher in 1988. Six weeks later, at the age of 50, he died of lung cancer.

Carver always said he hated sloppy, wordy fiction. He believed a simple story with simple characters could move a reader just as strongly as something more complicated. For him, the work had to be as honest as possible. If a writer consulted a thesaurus just to seem smart, then the story would instantly ring false. Carver looked at life as realistically as possible, portraying it with the same unforgiving frankness as a photograph. His characters were real people—folks who got drunk, who got divorced, or who were just plain down and out. Never has such plainness held such fascination.

The Stories:

"What We Talk About When We Talk About Love"—Four people discuss their different definitions of love deep into the night. The more intoxicated they get, the less easy it is for them to talk about love. By the end of the story it becomes clear that love would be equally difficult to define for them even if they were stone-cold sober.

"The Student's Wife"—Nan suffers from insomnia as her husband lies snoring beside her in bed. Over the course of a sleepless night, her life seems increasingly more horrible until dawn approaches in all of its lovely, rosy terror.

"Cathedral"—A complacent, disaffected man has to meet an old friend of his wife's who turns out to be blind. As a drunken evening unfolds and the husband tries to teach the friend how to draw a cathedral, it quickly becomes apparent who is truly blind in the story.

"A Small, Good Thing"—A young boy gets hit by a car riding his bike. As his parents struggle with grief, an anonymous man keeps calling their house about a cake. Are they losing their minds, or is there something they need to remember about their son?

Franz Kafka

The Story Behind the Stories:

Franz Kafka was born in a Jewish neighborhood in Prague in 1883. As a Jew and as a person with German-Austrian ancestry, he encountered hostility all of his life. He studied law and then worked for 14 years as a bureaucrat in a job he hated, all the while living with his domineering father, whom he described as huge and overbearing. Throughout his life, he suffered from tuberculosis, depression, and anxiety, which helps explain the troubled tone and religious/psychological questions of much of his writing. He never married but was twice engaged to a woman named Felice Bauer. He only published a few stories during his lifetime. In fact, he left instructions to his friend Max Brod to burn all of his unpublished material after his death, including three novels. When he died in 1924, Brod disobeyed Kafka's wishes and published his fiction and diaries.

Critics debate whether Kafka's symbolic, surreal, Freudian works are religious allegories or representations of his own troubled mind. He is often aligned with the existentialists because of the absurdity and hopelessness that permeates his fiction. His style is precise, dreamlike, and even humorous at times. He is the master of weird, so that even if people have never read any of his stories, they usually know what the word *Kafkaesque* means.

The Stories:

"A Hunger Artist"–The title of this short story refers to a man whose craft is that is starving himself to the brink of death. In the good old days, crowds used to gather around him as he wasted away in a cage. As the years go by and people lose interest in his art form, he has to come to terms with suffering, art, and what it means to sell out to the public. (Ironically, Kafka himself died from starvation as he was being treated for tuberculosis. His throat was so sore he could no longer eat.)

"A Country Doctor"—This surreal tale describes the events of one night when a rural doctor tries to find a horse to make a house call. Mysterious horses appear, but as he rides off, his maid is placed in danger. He arrives to discover a patient who may or may not be dying. Can he rescue the patient and his maid, or are forces working against him?

"The Metamorphosis"—Gregor Samsa wakes up one morning to the surprise of his life: he has turned into a giant insect! Will he be squashed underfoot by his family? Will he ever return to normal?

"In the Penal Colony"—A condemned prisoner is subjected to a unique torture device, a machine that carves the victim's punishment in words deep into his flesh. He is literally "sentenced" to death.

famous characters

· ·

Some literary characters have become so well known through the years that they feel like real people. Can you identify the book that these characters come from?

1. The name Uriah Heep first appeared in this Victorian novel about the inhumane treatment of children.
2. Dr. Pangloss, James the Antibaptist, and Cunegonde live in the "best of all possible worlds" in this Voltaire satire about the philosophy of optimism.
3. Bernard Marx and John the Savage appear in this Aldous Huxley satire about the a futuristic nightmare world.
4. The character Humbert Humbert obsesses over the title character of this novel, which was banned in France and part of the United States for its eroticism.
5. In this Russian novel, Vronsky and Levin live to find love again, but the title character of the book ends up committing suicide over a failed love affair.
6. Captain Ahab, Queequeg, and Ishmael learn that a whaling vessel is a great place to learn lessons about good and evil.
7. Edward Rochester and St. John Rivers compete for the love of a famous governess whose name is also the title of this book.
8. Basil Hallward and Sibyl Vane join the title character of this Oscar Wilde masterpiece about vanity and ego.
9. Catherine Earnshaw and Heathcliff are swept up in all consuming love in this romantic novel about the heights of passion.
10. This Irish novel records the wanderings of Leopold Bloom and Stephen Dedalus on June 16, 1904.
11. Can haughty Professor Henry Higgins transform Eliza Doolittle into a lady in this George Bernard Shaw play?

12. The character's name is Stella Kowalski, but if you scream her first name at the top of your lungs standing beneath a New Orleans balcony, you will most likely recognize this play's title.
13. Iago may just be the most evil character in all of Shakespeare. His intense hatred destroys the lives of the lovely Desdemona and the title character of this tragedy.
14. Celie, Harpo, and Shug Avery jumped from the pages of this Alice Walker novel and onto the Broadway stage.
15. The strangeness of the character names Ofglen and Offred is particularly appropriate in this futuristic novel about a world in which women serve no other social purpose than reproduction.

Answers:
1. *David Copperfield*
2. *Candide*
3. *Brave New World*
4. *Lolita*
5. *Anna Karenina*
6. *Moby Dick*
7. *Jane Eyre*
8. *The Picture of Dorian Gray*
9. *Wuthering Heights*
10. *Ulysses*
11. *Pygmalion*
12. *A Streetcar Named Desire*
13. *Othello*
14. *The Color Purple*
15. *The Handmaid's Tale*

drama queens:

Pulitzer Prize for drama 1983–2007

1983: *'Night, Mother,* Marsha Norman
1984: *Glengarry Glen Ross,* David Mamet
1985: *Sunday in the Park with George,* Stephen Sondheim
and James Lapine
1987: *Fences,* August Wilson
1988: *Driving Miss Daisy,* Alfred Uhry
1989: *The Heidi Chronicles,* Wendy Wasserstein
1990: *The Piano Lesson,* August Wilson
1991: *Lost in Yonkers,* Neil Simon
1992: *The Kentucky Cycle,* Robert Schenkkan
1993: *Angels in America: Millennium Approaches,* Tony Kushner
1994: *Three Tall Women,* Edward Albee
1995: *The Young Man from Atlanta,* Horton Foote
1996: *Rent,* Jonathan Larson
1998: *How I Learned to Drive,* Paula Vogel
1999: *Wit,* Margaret Edson
2000: *Dinner with Friends,* Donald Margulies
2001: *Proof,* David Auburn
2002: *Topdog/Underdog,* Suzan-Lori Parks
2003: *Anna in the Tropics,* Nilo Cruz
2004: *I Am My Own Wife,* Doug Wright
2005: *Doubt: A Parable,* John Patrick Shanley
2007: *Rabbit Hole,* David Lindsay Abaire

across the ages through the pages:
brit lit 8

1914–1945: The Modernist Period

Modernist literature covers the period from the beginning of World War I through 1945. Authors during this time experimented with style and form as they sought new ways to express the angst and disillusionment of their era. Such major poets as W. B. Yeats and T. S. Eliot and such revolutionary novelists as James Joyce and Virginia Woolf were key figures in the modernist movement.

W. B. Yeats: The Least You Need to Know

- Yeats' poetic career exhibits a range that stretches from early work written in the romantic style to later, more experimental modernist pieces, with varying topics of love, art, war, and Irish nationalism. His work was so respected that he won the Nobel Prize for literature in 1923. Some of his most famous poems include "Leda and the Swan," "A Prayer for My Daughter, "Among School Children," and "The Circus Animals' Desertion."

- In addition to writing poems, Yeats was intensely involved in the theater. In 1899, he helped found the theater society that would later become the Abbey Theater. One of his best-known plays, *The Countess Cathleen*, incited the Catholic audience to riot because of its depiction of a countess selling her soul to the devil.

- The poem that most clearly illustrates Yeats' concern with the new era is "The Second Coming." In it he utters a phrase that stands as a hallmark for the violence and despair marking the early, war-torn part of the 20th century: "Things fall apart; the center cannot hold."

T. S. Eliot: The Least You Need to Know

- Born in St. Louis, Missouri, and educated at Harvard, Eliot moved to London in 1915, where he met Ezra Pound, a poet who would greatly influence the experimental nature of his writing. Eliot believed poetry should rely upon what he called an "objective correlative," that is, a concrete image that evokes emotion instead of relying on vague, abstract terms that sound artificially poetic.

- The work that has come to symbolize modernism for most critics is Eliot's five-part poem *The Waste Land.* In it, he paints a picture of urban decay and degeneration that typifies the destruction of Europe after World War I. The poem is filled with literary and cultural allusions, making it very difficult to read, but such lines as "These fragments I have shored against my ruins" speak to the belief that art can save us even if nothing else can.

James Joyce: The Least You Need to Know

- Like Yeats, Joyce was born in Ireland, but unlike Yeats, he left in 1902, spending the rest of his life in exile in France, Italy, and Switzerland. His novel *A Portrait of the Artist as a Young Man* (1916) gives an autobiographical glimpse into Joyce's disillusionment with much of Irish culture and with the Catholic church. In a stream-of-consciousness style, it tells the story of Stephen Dedalus who, as an artist, realizes that the only way he can truly commit himself to his writing is to escape the narrow world he has grown up in.
- Stephen Dedalus reappears in Joyce's masterpiece, *Ulysses.* Many critics consider *Ulysses* (1922) to be the greatest novel in the English language. The story is loosely based on the mythical character Odysseus, but Joyce reinvents the Greek hero as Leopold Bloom, an Irish Jew. The book follows Bloom, Stephen, and Bloom's wife, Molly, on one day, June 16, 1904. Using various writing styles, from the epic to the romance, Joyce expanded the scope of what the novel genre could accomplish.

Virginia Woolf: The Least You Need to Know

- Like Joyce, Woolf is best known for her radical literary experiments, particularly her use of interior monologue to capture the way people really think as they move through the day. Along with other experimental writers, such as her husband Leonard Woolf, her sister, Vanessa, and Vanessa's husband, Clive Bell, she formed what became known as the Bloomsbury Group. Virginia and Leonard founded the Hogarth Press and published such authors as Katherine Mansfield, E. M. Forster, and T. S. Eliot, as well as the first English edition of the writings of Sigmund Freud. Much of Woolf's writing drew upon her own personal life experience, including the death of her brother, her marital difficulties, and the depression that resulted in her suicide in 1941.

- One of her best-known novels, *Mrs. Dalloway* (1925), centers on the events of one day in Clarissa Dalloway's life as she prepares to host a party. Throughout the day, Clarissa reflects on her hopes and dreams, her family, and a suitor whom she had rejected in order to marry the more financially secure Mr. Dalloway. In a subplot, a character named Septimus Smith also reflects on his life, but his musings lead him to commit suicide.

- Woolf was also an influential essayist. Her oft-cited essay "A Room of One's Own" was written in 1929 and serves as a powerful, early example of feminist writing. Woolf contends that women do not have the same access to education as men and that the education they do receive is often centered solely on male accounts of history. She argues that it is extremely difficult for a woman to develop as an artist because of the domestic duties and societal expectations that hold women back. In a famous assertion, she says women need a room of their own and £500 a year; in other words, women, like men, need privacy and financial security in order to have an equal opportunity to succeed.

across the ages through the pages:
american lit 6

1920s–1930s: The Jazz Age

Scholars recognize the Jazz Age, which is part of the modernist period and includes the Harlem Renaissance and the Lost Generation, as a particular literary movement. Also known as the Roaring '20s, it spans the years between World War I and the Great Depression, overlapping with some of the modernist writers. It was a time in which hemlines were rising and sexual morals were loosening. The literature reflected the reckless emotion of jazz in all of its improvisation and unconventionality.

F. Scott Fitzgerald: The Least You Need to Know

- Fitzgerald called the Jazz Age "a new generation grown up to find all the Gods dead, all the wars fought, all faiths in man shaken." As one of the age's key representatives, Fitzgerald lived a life much like his characters. He was born in a wealthy family, served in the army, and made a tempestuous marriage to Zelda Sayre, an alliance marked by the highs of worldwide travel and the lows of mental illness and alcoholism.

- *The Great Gatsby* (1925) is the quintessential Jazz Age novel, filled with hedonism, wealth, and, eventually, sorrow. He centers the story around the narrator, Nick, who moves to New York to be near his cousin Daisy Buchanan. Soon he becomes intrigued by a love triangle between Daisy, her philandering husband, Tom, and the true love of her life, Jay Gatsby, a self-made millionaire prone to throwing lavish parties. At first, Nick looks down on the jet set he is living among, but eventually he comes to admire Gatsby for the strength of his love for Daisy and for his commitment to securing the American Dream. When Gatsby is murdered, neither Daisy nor any of his friends attends his funeral. Disillusioned with the whole scene, Nick returns to the Midwest, leaving it all behind.

- Considered by many to be a record of "The Lost Generation," *This Side of Paradise* (1920) chronicles the life of Amory Blaine, a gorgeous, wealthy Princeton student. Like many college students, he doesn't have a clear career path in mind, so he drifts from class to class, dabbling in literary arts and basically having a good time. Eventually he falls in love with a girl named Rosaline, who leaves him for someone even richer. Poor Amory. He goes off to war, embarking on many adventures in France. Upon his return, he begins a career as an ad man, but already he is feeling the strain of "the real world." No longer a free and easy Princeton undergrad, he struggles with all of the pain and heartache that comes when the young and rich have to join the rest of the world.

The Age of Innocence: The Least You Need to Know

- Edith Wharton was born into a wealthy New York family. Using her sharp powers of observation, she draws on her experience in aristocratic circles by satirizing the wealthy.
- Wharton became the first woman to win the Pulitzer Prize with *The Age of Innocence* in 1921. The book portrays Manhattan social life in the end of the 19th century, as it tells the story of social butterfly Newland Archer who is engaged to the lovely May Welland. All is well in their beautiful world until May's cousin, Ellen Olenska, a countess no less, arrives on the scene. Ellen has been living in Poland with her estranged husband, a count, and on the continent, she grew comfortable with loose, revealing clothing and looser morals. Back in the States, though, cousin May and fiancé Newland befriend her out of politeness. Soon, however, Newland sees in Ellen all the free, eccentric abandon that May lacks. Surprise, surprise! But when he allows himself to fall in love with Ellen once she announces her decision to divorce her Polish husband, May's parents push him to marry their daughter as soon as possible. Poor Newland. He marries May but pines for Ellen. Years pass, but when Newland finally has the opportunity to unite with Ellen, after his wife has died and their kids have grown, he decides not to, happy instead to live on memories of a passion he could never have.

Main Street: The Least You Need to Know

- Sinclair Lewis was the first American writer to win the Nobel Prize for Literature, and it all started here. Before he wrote such great works as *Babbitt* and *Arrowsmith*, the Nobel winner had already established his reputation as a satirist with a keen eye for American life with *Main Street.*
- In *Main Street,* Carol Kennicott is a Midwest version of Madame Bovary, a bored and disillusioned wife of a physician. She devotes a great deal of her life to raising the cultural standards of her fellow Gopher Prairie townspeople, but often to little avail. In her restlessness, she begins flirting with attorneys and sailors and eventually moves to Washington, DC. However, the nostalgic pull of small-town Main Street proves more than Carol can resist. She returns home, wiser from her travels and ready, finally, to settle down.

Three Soldiers: The Least You Need to Know

- Critic H. L. Mencken claimed that John Dos Passos' novel *Three Soldiers* set the standard against which future war stories would have to be measured. Dos Passos learned a lot about the battlefield by serving in an ambulance service during World War I.
- In this gritty portrayal of the First World War, John Dos Passos tells the story, as the title indicates, of three soldiers. Chris Chrisfield, a farmer from Indiana, Dan Fuselli, an Italian American from San Francisco, and John Andrews, a pianist from New York, meet during basic training in the Army. Throughout the war, they struggle with temptations of deserting the armed forces, of wondering how they can be patriots in such a terrible time, and how they will ever return home with their youthful idealism. As three representatives of the soldier's life, Chris, Dan, and John symbolize all of the struggle and fortitude required to emerge victorious in any sense of the term from the hell of war.

The Weary Blues: The Least You Need to Know
- The 1920s saw African-American culture flourish, and nowhere is this more apparent than in the poetry of Langston Hughes. A representative writer of the Harlem Renaissance, Hughes traveled through Africa, lived in Paris, and eventually settled in Harlem. As a writer, he emphasized black history and the black experience as he battled against racial stereotypes.
- The title poem of *The Weary Blues* is the first important blues poem in the American canon. Hughes recreates the experience of listening to a blues singer. The rhythm, tone, and tempo of the poem reflect the syncopated sound of blues music. Such lines as "He did a lazy sway.../He did a lazy sway..." repeat throughout the poem to lend a musicality to the words on the page.

The Sun Also Rises: The Least You Need to Know
- This 1926 Ernest Hemingway work is the quintessential novel of the Lost Generation. It also marks the beginning of his career as a major American writer. In 1952, Hemingway won a Pulitzer Prize for *The Old Man and the Sea,* and he received the Nobel Prize for Literature in 1954, seven years before his suicide.
- *The Sun Also Rises* focuses on expatriate Americans who had fought in France in World War I and who now live under a shroud of cynicism and dillusion. The story is narrated by Jake Barnes, a soldier whose war wound has rendered him impotent. He is deeply in love with Lady Brett Ashley, a carefree, hedonistic woman in the process of divorcing her husband and having numerous affairs. Jake and Brett travel to Spain with Bill Gorton, a friend of Jake's, Michael Campbell, a man Brett wants to marry, and Robert Cohn, a Jewish writer who took up boxing to overcome his shyness. Brett becomes infatuated with Romero, a bullfighter, but eventually breaks off their affair to return to Michael. In the end, she and Jake wish they could have fallen in love, but with her love of sex and his impotence, it could never happen.

Nella Larsen: The Least You Need to Know

- Although she began her career as a nurse and then a librarian, Nella Larsen eventually found her way into literary fame with the publication of two novels, *Quicksand* (1928) and *Passing* (1929). In 1919, she received the Harmon Award for distinguished achievement among African Americans. Then, a year after publishing *Passing*, she became the first African -American female to win the Guggenheim Award.

- *Quicksand* is based, in many ways, on Larsen's own life. The main character, Helga Crane, is the daughter of a black father and a white mother. She spends most of the story searching for a community where she feels she belongs. Southern African Americans strike her as too complacent, but Helga's white Chicago relatives, in turn, reject her. In addition, following a series of failed romances, Helga never really finds what she is looking for.

- *Passing* tells the story of Irene Redfield and Clare Kendry, two childhood friends. As they grew up, Irene marries an African-American doctor and lives in Harlem. Clare, however, leaves home at a young age, marries a wealthy white man, and begins to "pass" as white in social circles. When she returns to Harlem, Irene becomes convinced that Clare is having an affair with her husband. Clare, having lived a life filled with conflict and ambivalence about her racial identity, meets a tragic end when she falls out of an open window to her death. Did she commit suicide, or did Irene push her?

The Sound and the Fury: The Least You Need to Know

- Many critics consider this to be William Faulkner's greatest novel. In fact, the Modern Library ranks it in the top ten greatest English language novels of the 20th century.

- Faulkner was descended from an old Mississippi family, with his great-grandfather being a writer as well. Before Faulkner embarked on his writing career, he enlisted in the Canadian Air Force.

Eventually he began composing such novels as *As I Lay Dying* and *Absalom, Absalom!*, going on to win Pulitzer Prizes for *A Fable* and *The Reivers* and then the Nobel Prize for Literature in 1949.

- Unlike *The Sun Also Rises* or *The Great Gatsby*, *The Sound and the Fury* has little to do with the alcohol-drenched partying of the Jazz Age. Instead, Faulkner focuses his southern gothic tale on a radical experiment with form and style, as he builds a story around an aristocratic family in Mississippi. Three of the book's four sections are told from the perspective of the Compson brothers: the mentally challenged Benjy; Quentin, a Harvard student; and the greedy brother, Jason. The brothers' mother is a hypochondriac, their sister, Caddy, has an illegitimate daughter, and all of them, in their selfishness, contrast with the one stable character of the book, Dilsey, a black cook whose faith and goodness serve to highlight the decline of the other Compsons.

More Wacky Writers

- *John Dryden was Jonathan Swift's cousin.*

- *Charlotte Perkins Gilman was the great-niece of Harriet Beecher Stowe.*

- *Oscar Wilde converted to Catholicism the day before he died.*

- Quotations from the Works of Mao Tse-Tung *is the second-best-selling book of all time.*

- *When Victor Hugo was in his 70s, he had an affair with the actress Sarah Bernhardt.*

laughing with the bard

· ·

A Midsummer Night's Dream
Plot

One of the most famous of Shakespeare's plays, *A Midsummer Night's Dream* draws its plot from such sources as Plutarch's *Lives*, Chaucer's "Knight's Tale," and Ovid's *Metamorphosis*. The comedy opens with plans for a wedding. In four days, Theseus, Duke of Athens, is to marry Hippolyta, an Amazon queen. In the meantime, young lovers everywhere are at odds. Hermia, the daughter of an Athenian, has been promised to Demetrius, but she loves Lysander. The duke orders her to marry Demetrius, so she and Lysander escape to the forest. Demetrius follows her and is, in turn, followed by a young woman named Helena, who loves him. In the forest, more romantic trouble is revealed. Oberon, king of the fairies, is fighting with Titania, his wife. Puck, a merry, mischievous sprite, offers to help Oberon, but instead his trusty love potion causes Demetrius to give up chasing Hermia in favor of Helena. Eventually they wed, as do the lovers Lysander and Hermia. In a comic subplot, a group of tinkers, tailors, and other workers try to put on a play to amuse the duke. The antics of these men, Bottom, Flute, Snug, Snout, Robin, and Peter mirror the crazy romantic escapades of everyone else in the play.

Themes

1. True love prevails. Theseus marries Hippolyta. Hermia weds Lysander. Helena wins Demetrius. Oberon and Titania kiss and make up.
2. Play the fool if you wish...onstage, that is. Bottom and his gang are silly to be sure, but their sincere efforts to put on a play show that theatricality does have its place.

crying with the bard

· ·

Romeo and Juliet

Plot

The Montagues and Capulets are two feuding families whose hatred
of each other eventually destroys their children. Romeo Montague
meets Juliet Capulet at a ball and falls in love with her instantly. They
marry in secret in the cell of Friar Laurence. In the meantime, Romeo's
friend, Mercutio, is killed by Juliet's cousin, Tybalt. The murder only
fans the flames of anger, so much so that Romeo goes out and kills
Tybalt to avenge Mercutio's death. As a result, he is banished from
Verona. The Capulets, grieving the loss of Tybalt, urge Juliet to marry a
young nobleman named Paris. They do not know that she has secretly
married their sworn enemy. To help Juliet escape the marriage to Paris,
Friar Laurence gives her a sleeping potion that will make it appear as
though she has died. When Romeo hears that his beloved is dead, he
drinks poison at her tomb, never learning that, in fact, Juliet was merely
asleep. She wakes up, discovers that Romeo is dead, and stabs herself.
The two families try to establish peace once they learn that their feud
has cost them the lives of two of their dearest children.

Themes

1. Love is not for the timid. The passion between Romeo and Juliet
   is deep, spiritual, romantic, and intense. They are overcome by love
   and, at times, seem powerless in its grasp. Although their marriage
   may seem hasty, it solidifies the seriousness of their commitment
   and shows how far they are willing to go to try to unite themselves
   against all odds.
2. The individual vs. family/society. The long-standing war between the
   Capulets and Montagues carries enough momentum to cause even
   the boldest to ponder an alliance, but Romeo and Juliet, collectively
   and as individuals, listen to their respective hearts over and against

social dictates. The patriarchal structure of society placed Juliet in a particularly vulnerable position, especially as her family tried to get her to marry against her wishes. Her passion, however, could not be contained within the mandates of social/familial obligation.

Jitney

Jitney, one of August Wilson's first plays, begins a series that recounts the African-American experience through the 1900s. It is about a gypsy cab company in Pittsburgh, Pennsylvania, in the 1970s. There is no real plot, as the play revolves around the relationships of the jitney drivers. These relationships, though enveloped in conflict, help the characters succeed in life. It is through Wilson's famous monologues and the drivers' car trips that the characters' personalities are revealed.

Main Relationships

- *Youngblood (young) and Turnbo (old)*
- *Becker (father) and Booster (son)*
- *Fielding (alcoholic) and Becker (boss)*
- *Doub (optimist; knows how the world works) and Youngblood (pessimist; thinks everyone is out to get the him)*
- *Men and Women (Rena, the only female present, symbolizes love and is the epitome of everything the men are searching for.)*

In the end, the play is about hope and forgiveness. Becker's unexpected death brings about a change in all the men, as they realize that life is short and unexpected circumstances can change one's life in a heartbeat.

learning with the bard

The Life and Death of King John

Plot

King John turns Shakespeare's focus to an earlier time. John was born in 1167, the third son of King Henry II and Eleanor of Aquitaine. In 1189, his brother, Richard the Lion-Hearted, gained the crown, but John tried to take over while Richard was fighting in the Crusades. He eventually inherited the throne after Richard's death. As the play opens, though, King Philip of France claims that the English crown rightfully belongs to John's nephew, Arthur, Duke of Brittany, who was the son of Richard the Lion-Hearted. John is a weak leader and eventually loses the support of the English nobility. When he opposes the pope's choice of Archbishop of Canterbury, he makes an enemy of the church as well. John and Philip go to war. Arthur is captured and John orders Arthur killed because he knows he is a threat to his power. Hubert de Burgh, King John's Chamberlain, protects Arthur by telling everyone that he has died. Believing her son to be dead, Arthur's mother dies of grief. Trying to escape from prison, Arthur dies as well. In the end, King John gets poisoned, and his son, Henry III, assumes the throne.

Themes

1. Mother knows best. Arthur's mother stands up to King John by convincing King Philip to form an alliance with her to make her son the king.
2. Debates about legitimate rule can turn deadly. Arthur's mother claims her son is the rightful king, but eventually his efforts to land the crown get him killed.

rhyme time 3: *poetry for children*

. . . .

Shel Silverstein

Silverstein holds the honor of being the first author to have a children's book hit the top of the *New York Times* best-seller list. *A Light in the Attic* (1981) sold over one million copies thanks to its hilarious blend of wordplay, drawings, and verse. He did not originally intend to write for children, however. In fact, after spending two years in the army, he became a cartoonist for *Playboy* magazine. He claims to have been dragged "kicking and screaming" into an editor's office by a friend who insisted he would be a great children's author. When he wasn't writing children's books, he wrote the lyrics to such songs as "A Boy Named Sue," sung by Johnny Cash.

. . . . .

Jack Prelutsky

In 2006, Prelutsky earned the distinction of being named the first children's poet laureate ever. He claims that he never liked poetry as a child because of a teacher who "left me with the impression that poetry was the literary equivalent of liver. I was told it was good for me, but I wasn't convinced." In fact, in his early years, he occupied many jobs that seem a far cry from poet, including photographer, truck driver, and folksinger. After a few months of sketching imaginary animals in his spare time, he began writing short poems to accompany the drawings. His editor loved the poems, but not the artwork. As a result, he has published more than 40 books of poetry, including *Tyrannosaurus Was a Beast* and *The Dragons Are Singing Tonight.*

The Newbery Medal: *1966–2008*

. . . .

1966: Elizabeth Borton de Treviño, *I, Juan de Pareja*

1967: Irene Hunt, *Up a Road Slowly*

1968: E. L. Konigsburg, *From the Mixed-Up Files of Mrs. Basil E. Frankweiler*

1969: Lloyd Alexander, *The High King*

1970: William H. Armstrong, *Sounder*

1971: Betsy Byars, *The Summer of the Swans*

1972: Robert C. O'Brien, *Mrs. Frisby and the Rats of NIMH*

1973: Jean Craighead George, *Julie of the Wolves*

1974: Paula Fox, *The Slave Dancer*

1975: Virginia Hamilton, *M. C. Higgins, the Great*

1976: Susan Cooper, *The Grey King*

1977: Mildred D. Taylor, *Roll of Thunder, Hear My Cry*

1978: Katherine Paterson, *Bridge to Terabithia*

1979: Ellen Raskin, *The Westing Game*

1980: Joan Blos, *A Gathering of Days: A New England Girl's Journal, 1830–32*

1981: Katherine Paterson, *Jacob Have I Loved*

1982: Nancy Willard, *A Visit to William Blake's Inn: Poems for Innocent and Experienced Travelers*

1983: Cynthia Voigt, *Dicey's Song*

1984: Beverly Cleary, *Dear Mr. Henshaw*

1985: Robin McKinley, *The Hero and the Crown*

1986: Patricia MacLachlan, *Sarah, Plain and Tall*

1987: Sid Fleischman, *The Whipping Boy*

1988: Russell Freedman, *Lincoln: A Photobiography*

1989: Paul Fleischman, *Joyful Noise: Poems for Two Voices*

1990: Lois Lowry, *Number the Stars*

1991: Jerry Spinelli, *Maniac Magee*

1992: Phyllis Reynolds Naylor, *Shiloh*

1993: Cynthia Rylant, *Missing May*

1994: Lois Lowry, *The Giver*
1995: Sharon Creech, *Walk Two Moons*
1996: Karen Cushman, *The Midwife's Apprentice*
1997: E. L. Konigsburg, *The View from Saturday*
1998; Karen Hesse, *Out of the Dust*
1999: Louis Sachar, *Holes*
2000: Christopher Paul Curtis, *Bud, Not Buddy*
2001: Richard Peck, *A Year Down Yonder*
2002: Linda Sue Park, *A Single Shard*
2003: Avi, *Crispin: The Cross of Lead*
2004: Kate DiCamillo, *The Tale of Despereaux*
2005: Cynthia Kadohata, *Kira-Kira*
2006: Lynne Rae Perkins, *Criss Cross*
2007: Susan Patron, *The Higher Power of Lucky*
2008: Laura Amy Schlitz, *Good Masters! Sweet Ladies! Voices from a Medieval Village*

Literary Gossip

. . . .

Lewis Carroll and Queen Victoria

Rumor: British author Lewis Carroll once presented Britain's Queen Victoria with a mathematics textbook as a joke after she had requested a copy of one of his classic novels. Queen Victoria was apparently highly impressed with *Alice in Wonderland* and *Through the Looking Glass*, written by the mathematician Charles Dodgson, under the pseudonym Lewis Carroll. According to myth, the queen requested a copy of his next work, and he responded mischievously by delivering a copy of *An Elementary Treatise on Determinants*.

The Truth: Dodgson held a high respect for the British Court and was extremely honored by the queen's appreciation for his work. When confronted 30 years later with the rumor of the prank, he stated that "it is utterly false in every particular: nothing even resembling it has occurred." By this point of course, the story had become legend and the myth busted.

> *From Carroll's famous novel* Alice in Wonderland *came the name for Alice in Wonderland syndrome, a rare psychological disorder characterized by micropsia and macropsia. A person with the syndrome has trouble understanding relative size, sometimes believing that objects in front of them are either exaggeratedly large or extremely small, much like the character Alice in Carroll's famous story.*

the 411 *on a few more short stories*

• •

"The Ransom of Red Chief" – O. Henry

Two criminals, Bill and Sam, head to the South in search of petty ways to raise the $2,000 they need to pull off a scheme involving land fraud in Illinois. Landing in Summit, Alabama, the two quickly decide that the fastest way to make the money is by kidnapping the son of the well-to-do Ebenezer Dorset. They capture the boy and send a ransom note to Dorset demanding $2,000 for the release of his son. However, the young redheaded boy, who calls himself Red Chief, actually enjoys being kidnapped and seems to believe that he is on a trip. To make matters worse, the kidnappers hear no response from Dorset about the release of his son. The two soon realize that they are growing weary of Red Chief, as he continuously pulls pranks on Bill and Sam and insists that they entertain him. They lower the ransom price and try once again to solicit the money from Dorset. Finally, Dorset offers a mere $250 to have his son released, and the two kidnappers eagerly hand him back over and flee the town as quickly as possible. The story has been adopted for several films and television programs since its first publication in 1910.

• • • • •

"The Telltale Heart" – Edgar Allan Poe

An unnamed narrator begins the story with a first-person insistence of his own sanity, after revealing that he has murdered an old man that drove him crazy. The narrator has cut the old man's body into many pieces and hidden them beneath the floorboard of his house, ridding himself of any evidence. But soon, the authorities come to the narrator's home to question him about the disappearance. As he attempts to deliver the facts, the narrator hears a rhythmic sound growing louder and louder and believes that the sound is in fact the beating heart of the old man below. In a panic-stricken terror, the narrator confesses, believing that the authorities can also hear the heart and have him pinned for murder. In a shrieking fit, he screams at the officers to tear up the floorboards and find the "hideous heart," not realizing that the hard thumping sounds are actually those of his own panicked heart. The story was first published in 1843 in the Boston magazine *The Pioneer*. It has been reprinted many times in anthologies and was adapted for film in the 1950s.

"The Fall of the House of Usher" – Edgar Allan Poe

"The Fall of the House of Usher" begins as the narrator has received a chilling letter from a childhood acquaintance. Being a good friend, the narrator tries to console him. The friend, Roderick Usher, has a dying twin sister, Madeline. Roderick's mental disorder and Madeline's baffling illness lead you to assume that their birth was the result of an incestuous relationship, and they are the last remaining Ushers. The narrator moves in with his friend to help him through this difficult time. The sister dies and is entombed in a vault in the house. During the following week, both the narrator and Roderick are strangely unnerved and agitated. They determine the noises they hear and the strange lights they see are the result of Madeline being buried alive. She returns from the grave and dies, falling on her brother and killing him. Terrified, the narrator runs out of the house, looking back in time to see the structure crumble to the ground

playwright potpourri

If all the world's a stage, who are the writers staging our world? Here are some fun facts about playwrights through the ages.

. . . . .

Sophocles

- He wasn't merely a writer of such great works as *Antigone* and *Oedipus the King.* He also excelled as a musician, an athlete, a military advisor, and a politician.
- At the tender age of 16, he was chosen as the *choragos,* or leader of the chorus, in a recitation of a poem about the Greek victory over the Persians.
- He was very prolific. He wrote 123 plays, but only 7 tragedies still remain.
- One of his contributions to drama was introducing a third actor into scenes.

. . . . .

Euripides

- Fellow playwright Aristophanes used to mock the high-class Euripides by claiming that his mother sold vegetables.
- He wrote between 80 and 90 plays, including *The Trojan Women, Medea,* and *Electra,* but he won prizes only four times.
- Rumor had it that his daughter was killed by a rabid dog, but this may have just been another sick joke of Aristophanes'.

. . . . .

Aeschylus

- He was a warrior as well as a writer. He fought against the Persians in the battles of Marathon and Salamis. He must have been more proud of his military achievements than of his literary ones since he didn't even list his success as a playwright in his epitaph.

- Maybe it was all that exposure to wine, but as a young man he worked in the vineyards outside of Athens until, he claimed, the god Dionysus appeared to him in a dream and told him to begin writing plays.
- He wrote about 70 plays, but only 7 still exist, including *Seven Against Thebes* and the *Oresteia* trilogy.
- He was the first playwright to use a second actor in addition to the chorus. He was also well known for his elaborate costume designs.
- According to legend, he died when an eagle dropped a tortoise on his head.
- The Athenians held him in such high esteem that every year, at the Dionysia festival, they would let other playwrights reproduce his plays instead of presenting original works.

· · · · ·

William Shakespeare

- He married Anne Hathaway, who was 26 years old and pregnant, when he was only 18.
- In his will, he left his "second-best bed" to his wife.
- His sonnets were published without his permission in 1609.
- There are only seven known specimens of his signature.
- He was the first author to use the words "bump," "assassination," "lovely," and "hurry."
- More than 400 films have been made from his plays.
- Some critics claim that Shakespeare could not possibly have written all of his plays. Over the years, they have attributed his writing to authors as diverse as Sir Philip Sidney, John Donne, Christopher Marlowe, Ben Jonson, Cardinal Thomas Wolsey, Sir Walter Raleigh, Francis Bacon, and Edward de Vere.
- The earliest defense that Shakespeare single-handedly composed all of his own plays came in 1592, when a playwright named Robert Greene wrote *Groatsworth of Wit, Bought with a Million of Repentance*, in which he called the Bard "an upstart crow" for trying to compete with him.

- Shakespeare coined such phrases as "Neither a borrower nor a lender be," "Brevity is the soul of wit," and "All that glisters [glitters] is not gold."

Shakespeare's comedies, listed in chronological order of first performance, are:

Taming of the Shrew, 1593
Comedy of Errors, 1594
Two Gentlemen of Verona, 1594
Love's Labour's Lost, 1594
Midsummer Night's Dream, 1595
Merchant of Venice, 1596
Much Ado About Nothing, 1598
As You Like It, 1599
Merry Wives of Windsor, 1600
Troilus and Cressida, 1602
Twelfth Night, 1602
All's Well That Ends Well, 1602
Measure for Measure, 1604
Pericles, Prince of Tyre, 1608
The Tempest, 1611
Cymbeline, 1611
Winter's Tale, 1611

Shakespeare's tragedies, listed in chronological order of first performance, are:

Titus Andronicus, 1594
Romeo and Juliet, 1594
Hamlet, 1600
Julius Caesar, 1600
Othello, 1604
Antony and Cleopatra, 1606
King Lear, 1606

Coriolanus, 1607
Timon of Athens, 1607
Macbeth, 1611

Shakespeare's histories, listed in chronological order of first
performance, are:
King Henry VI, Part 1, 1592
King Henry VI, Part 2, 1592
King Henry VI, Part 3, 1592
King John, 1596
King Henry IV, Part 1, 1597
King Henry IV, Part 2, 1597
King Henry V, 1598
Richard II, 1600
Richard III, 1601
King Henry VIII, 1612

• • • • •

Christopher Marlowe
- He served as a spy for Queen Elizabeth I, who hired him to
  investigate Catholic plots against her.
- He was known for his quick temper. In 1589, he was charged with
  murder and sent to Newgate Prison, but he was acquitted two
  weeks later. Three years later, an injunction was brought against him
  because of a street fight, in which a man was killed.
- Marlowe was deported from Netherlands for counterfeiting gold coins.
- Fellow playwright Thomas Kyd confessed, under torture, that
  Marlowe denied the divinity of Christ.
- Like William Shakespeare, he wrote plays for Lord Strange's acting
  company.
- His public reputation suffered throughout his life because of
  accusations of homosexuality, blasphemy, and atheism.
- He died at the age of 29, when was stabbed above the right eye in a
  bar fight.

Ben Jonson

- He was a contemporary of Marlowe and Shakespeare and was best known for his plays *Volpone, Every Man in His Humour,* and *The Alchemist.*
- In 1598, he was jailed in Newgate Prison for killing fellow actor Gabriel Spencer in a duel.
- In 1605, he landed in prison again for libeling the Scottish in his play *Eastward Ho.*
- When he was 45 years old, he set out on foot to Scotland to learn about his ancestry.
- He is buried in Westminster Abbey, along with fellow British authors Geoffrey Chaucer, Charles Dickens, Thomas Hardy, Samuel Johnson, Robert Browning, and Alfred, Lord Tennyson.
- One of his best friends was William Shakespeare.

• • • • •

Anton Chekhov

- He attended Moscow University Medical School and became a physician.
- Just like playwrights Bertolt Brecht, Neil Simon, Arthur Miller, and Sam Shepard, he married an actress. He wed Olga Knipper in 1901, but their marriage only lasted until he died in 1904.
- He had a pet crane.
- He wrote the play *Swan Song* in one hour.
- After his play *The Wood Demon* failed, he took a break from writing and returned to medical research. He went to Siberia to a remote penal colony, where he conducted a census of 10,000 prisoners.

• • • • •

Henrik Ibsen

- One of his favorite hobbies was fishing.
- He wasn't fond of journalists. He once said, "It is inexcusable for scientists to torture animals. Let them do their experiments on journalists instead."

- His father went broke when Ibsen was a child. The family had to move into a farmhouse that their creditors provided.
- He hoped to become a doctor, but his grades weren't good enough.
- James Joyce's first published work was an essay praising Ibsen.

• • • • •

Oscar Wilde
- His full name was Oscar Fingal O'Flahertie Wills Wilde.
- His mother was able to satisfy some of her monetary debts by reciting *Aeschylus*.
- His father was surgeon oculist in ordinary to the queen.
- In college he collected peacock feathers.
- He had three rules for playwriting success: "The first rule for any young playwright to follow is not to write like Henry Arthur Jones. The second and third rules are the same."
- Although he was known to be homosexual, he married Constance Lloyd. They had two children, but eventually their sex life dwindled to nothing because of his recurring bouts of syphilis.
- He once bragged that he had had sex with five boys at the same time.
- He went to a French brothel with poet Ernest Dowson and later asked Dowson to tell everyone in England about it in order to restore his character.
- He was a bitter rival of novelist George Moore, who accused Wilde of plagiarism. Wilde, in turn, said that Moore "leads his readers to the latrine and locks them in."
- He spent two years in Reading Jail for being gay. In prison he wrote *De Profundis*.
- After battling an ear infection, he contracted meningitis and died at the age of 46.
- The day before he died, he converted to Catholicism.
- His last words were, "Either that wallpaper goes, or I do."

Tennessee Williams

- He was born with the name Thomas Lanier Williams, but he changed it to Tennessee to dissociate himself from his earlier, failed literary efforts.
- His father disapproved of Williams' writing goals, so he forced him to go to business school. After taking a night job in a shoe warehouse, Williams succumbed to a nervous breakdown in 1935.
- He converted to Catholicism in 1968.
- Truman Capote dedicated *Music for Chameleons* to Williams.
- He had a very unusual writing habit. He drank wine and spoke his words out loud as he wrote.
- The 1956 film *Baby Doll* was written by Williams, directed by Elia Kazan, and condemned by *Time* magazine as "just possibly the dirtiest American-made motion picture that has ever been legally exhibited."
- Williams' longtime companion was World War II veteran Frank Merlo. When Merlo died in 1961, Williams fell into a depression that lasted almost ten years.
- Williams choked to death on a bottle cap in a Manhattan hotel room in 1983, although his brother claimed he was murdered.

· · · · ·

Eugene O'Neill

- O'Neill was a busy man in the world of matrimony. He married three different times. His first marriage lasted 2 years, his second lasted 11, and his third lasted 24 years.
- He and his third wife, Carlotta, purchased a home in California that they named Tao House, after their mutual interest in Eastern thought.
- In 1909, he went prospecting for gold in Honduras. He didn't have much luck finding gold, but he did manage to catch malaria.
- When his 18-year-old daughter, Oona, married 54-year-old Charlie Chaplin, O'Neill disinherited her.

- He won a whopping total of four Pulitzer Prizes for *Beyond the Horizon, Anna Christie, Strange Interlude,* and *Long Day's Journey into Night.*

• • • • •

Arthur Miller

- Thanks to Fyodor Dostoevsky, Miller began his writing career. When he was in high school, Miller read *The Brothers Karamazov* because he thought it was a detective story. While he was wrong about that, he was right about discovering his love of literature.
- His first Broadway production, *The Man Who Had All the Luck,* received such bad reviews that it closed after only four performances.
- After a rough start on Broadway, Miller quickly became his own version of "the man who had all the luck." *Death of a Salesman,* became the first play to win "the triple crown": the New York Drama Critics Circle Award, the Pulitzer Prize, and the Tony Award.
- In 1956, he married Marilyn Monroe. Their marriage lasted five years.
- His daughter married actor Daniel Day-Lewis.
- His plays were banned in the Soviet Union because Miller spoke out for the rights of dissident writers.
- He died in 2005 on the 56th anniversary of the Broadway debut of *Death of a Salesman.*

• • • • •

Eugene Ionesco

- He was addicted to success and once said, "I detest and despise success, yet I cannot do without it. I'm like a drug addict. If nobody talks about me for a couple of months, I have withdrawal symptoms."
- As a child, he was fascinated by Punch and Judy puppet shows, which are humorous but extremely violent forms of entertainment. He would sit for hours watching the puppets club each other.
- He did not write his first play until he was 40 years old.
- Kenneth Tynan, drama critic for the *London Observer,* lambasted Ionesco as a possible "messiah" of antirealism. Tynan claimed that if

other writers copied Ionesco's style and distrust of language, that the future of theater would be very bleak.

- He tried his hand at acting, portraying the character Stepan Trofimovich in an adaptation of Dostoevsky's novel *The Possessed*. At first Ionesco was worried about losing himself in the character, but he soon realized that being "possessed" by a character was a great way to find out who he really was.
- He was a master at absurd plot lines. Consider the story of his 1955 play *The Submission*. The main character, Jack, wants to marry a girl with three noses. Roberta Robert has two noses, but that's not enough for Jack, so he marries her sister, Roberta II, who wins his love with her three noses and her dream visions of guinea pigs crawling out of her mother.

· · · · ·

Neil Simon

- He began his literary career while serving in the US Army, writing for the newspaper.
- He collaborated with his brother Danny Simon as a TV comedy writer on such shows as *The Phil Silvers Show* and *Your Show of Shows*.
- You might call 1966 his annus mirabilis. He had four Broadway shows being staged at the same time: *Sweet Charity, The Odd Couple, Barefoot in the Park,* and *The Star Spangled Girl.*
- He wrote an autobiographical trilogy, consisting of *Brighton Beach Memoirs, Biloxi Blues,* and *Broadway Bound.*
- The Alvin Theater on Broadway was renamed the Neil Simon Theater in 1983.
- His publicist, Bill Evans, donated a kidney to Simon in 2004.
- *Barefoot in the Park* had the longest original run of all of Simon's plays, with a total of 1,530 performances. Second place goes to *Brighton Beach Memoirs,* with a total of 1,299 performances.

Sam Shepard

- His full name is Samuel Shepard Rogers. He was the seventh-generation first-born son to bear the name.
- In the 1960s, he played drums for the band the Holy Modal Rounders. His bandmates had no idea he was a playwright too.
- He studied agriculture at San Antonio Junior College.
- In addition to writing plays, he wrote a rock drama called *The Tooth of Crime.*
- Thirty must be his lucky number. He had over 30 plays produced in New York before he was 30 years old.

Children's author Gary Paulsen was a regular competitor at the Iditarod. He had to give up sledding and sold his dogs in 1990 because of heart problems. However, after more than a decade in retirement sailing throughout the Pacific Ocean, he returned to the sport in 2003. He was supposed to compete in the 2005 Iditarod tournament but withdrew shortly before the race began.

The basic plot *V–Z*

We come to the end of the alphabet in our survey of great literary plots. Last but certainly not least, these stories will leave you wishing for more.

• • • • •

Vanity Fair

When William Thackeray was writing this 1848 masterpiece, he said he wanted to create a cast of characters who were thoroughly greedy, haughty, and self-righteous. Only a few characters would exemplify any real humility, and we could learn from them. He succeeded in this book, whose subtitle is *A Novel Without a Hero*. Becky Sharp and Amelia Sedley are two friends from boarding school with vastly different backgrounds. The wily and scheming Becky was born into poverty, but she tries to seduce Amelia's wealthy, stupid brother, Joseph. When he won't marry her, she weds Rawdon Crawley, the son of her employer. Crawley's father disinherits him, but Becky still manages to live a life of luxury through her "friendship" with Lord Steyne. Eventually Crawley leaves Becky, and she is left with nothing but her wits to sustain her.

Meanwhile, Amelia marries George Osborne, who gets killed in battle. Living in poverty, she has to give up her only son, Georgy, to her father-in-law. When Mr. Osborne dies, he leaves little Georgy a fortune. Amelia finds happiness through her faithful son and through William Dobbin, who has, for years, loved her from afar.

• • • • •

War and Peace

How do you sum up such a huge book? In a nutshell, the novel covers the years between 1805 and 1820, when Napoléon invaded Russia. Although Tolstoy plants over 500 characters in the book, the main ones follow the same path, growing from youthful naiveté to maturity. Natasha Rostova matures from belle of the ball to wife and mother. Prince Andrey Bolkonsky matures in his search for the meaning of life by means of reason and logic. On the other hand, Pierre Bezukhov lives in peace as a liberal Freemason who respects the peasant ways of living naturally (Tolstoy most identified with Bezukhov). Both fight for the love of Natasha; eventually she becomes Pierre's wife.

· · · · ·

Die Xenien

First things first. A xenion is a satirical couplet similar to the classical epigram. Johann Wolfgang von Goethe, along with his friend Friedrich von Schiller, made them famous in *Die Xenien* (German for "The Xenions"), a collection of biting couplets comparing religion to a darkened chamber that leaves ghosts and bogeymen in the mind.

· · · · ·

"Young Goodman Brown"

This 1835 short story by Nathaniel Hawthorne has fascinated readers for its depiction of the dark side of the Puritan mentality. The story begins with the symbolically named Goodman venturing into the forest one night, leaving his symbolically named wife, Faith, behind. He meets a mysterious, devilish-looking man carrying a staff shaped like a snake (symbolism anyone?). He learns that he is not the first person to sneak off into the woods in the otherwise traditional, religious village he lives in. When he gets to the center of the forest, he discovers a terrible secret that will leave him "stern, sad, and gloomy" for the rest of his life.

· · · · ·

The Zoo Story

Edward Albee's first play is the last in our list of plot summaries, but what a great note to end on! A one-act play, it focuses on only two characters, Peter and Jerry. Peter is your basic middle-class working man and husband. In Central Park one day, he meets a loner named Jerry who strikes up a conversation with him. Peter gets trapped listening to Jerry's life story and answering his questions, until Jerry, in a final desperate act, gets Peter's attention in a way no one would expect.

Edward Albee chose to use his plays as a way to work out his feelings and beliefs about life. He started by expressing ideas and then expanding them in order to deal with them in depth, developing them over time by continuing the same ideas throughout each play, starting with his earliest and ending with his latest. Each play is a continuation of the previous, and as we read them, we can see his ideas taking shape.

He first introduces us to his thoughts on life in The American Dream *and* The Sandbox. *These plays are about the same characters and are extensions of each other. In these plays Albee merely begins to develop his thoughts on life. Albee says that the older we get, the more childish we become. He also says that the "middle" generation only cares about earthly rewards.*

In The Death of Bessie Smith, *Albee embraces the topic of social inequality. During the time of this play, social inequality is a major issue the facing American people.*

Who's Afraid of Virginia Woolf? *is perhaps Albee's greatest play. In it he embraces two more themes: satisfaction and control. Martha has found satisfaction in other people and places; she doesn't need George all the time, she only wants him. George has found control in his life. He knows how to tell Martha no. It is the balance between them that makes it work and brings up the next play,* A Delicate Balance. *Here Albee continues his ideas of balance in life. Tobias and Agnes have a set balance that makes their marriage work, but it is broken because of selfishness and self-preservation. The equilibrium between these two forces makes this play a complete extension of Albee's previous plays.*

Nobel Prize Winners *1981–2006*
• •

1981: Elias Canetti, for writings as rich and various as you could ever ask for.

1982: Gabriel García Màrquez, who does magical realism better than anyone.

1983: Sir William Golding for novels with what the Swedish academy calls the "perspicuity of realistic narrative art."

1984: Jaroslav Seifert for sensuous, invigorating poetry which depicts the "indomitable spirit" of folks.

1985: Claude Simon, who blends the creativity of a poet and a painter for some very descriptive writing.

1986: Wole Soyinka, who masters in his writing "the drama of existence."

1987: Joseph Brodsky, who manages to write both clearly and poetically.

1988: Naguib Mahfouz, who revitalizes Arabian fiction.

1989: Camilo José Cela for strong writing that shows our weaknesses and vulnerabilities.

1990: Octavio Paz for some darn powerful poetry. Erotic. Lyrical. And he started publishing when he was only 19.

1991: Nadine Gordimer, who sums up all that Alfred Nobel had in mind—literature that greatly benefits humanity.

1992: Derek Walcott for beautiful poetry at once historical and multicultural.

1993: Toni Morrison for poetically describing the historical forces and contemporary realities facing African Americans.

1994: Kenzaburo Oe who blends myth with everyday life to develop a "disconcerting picture" of life as we know it.

1995: Seamus Heaney for gorgeous Irish poetry that blends the past with the wonders of the present.

1996: Wislawa Szymborska for poetry of "ironic precision."

1997: Dario Fo, who, like "jesters of the Middle Ages," skewers authority brilliantly.

1998: José Saramago, who shows that the best way to understand reality is through a good parable.

1999: Günter Grass, whose dark fables that are just way too much fun.

2000: Gao Zingjian for forging new paths in style and substance for Chinese writing.

2001: V. S. Naipaul for describing various histories that might otherwise get overlooked.

2002: Imre Kertész for proving that man + random forces of history = Nobel.

2003: John Maxwell Coetzee, who depicts the impact of an outsider better than anyone.

2004: Elfriede Jelinek for her "musical flow" of voices in both plays and in novels.

2005: Harold Pinter, who shows us that underneath everyday conversation lurks all kinds of weird stuff we might rather not think about.

2006: Orhan Pamuk, who captures the "melancholic soul"of Istanbul and can write about culture clash in fresh new ways.

2007: Doris Lessing, whose "scepticism, fire, and visionary power" scrutinizes a divided civilization.

Heteronyms J–M

Job *Jobe* - a book in the Bible; *(rhymes with Bob)* - an occupation

If I had to suffer like Job did in the Bible, I might be tempted to sing that old country classic, "Take this job and shove it."

Lead *LEED* - to direct the way or to guide; *LED* - metal

The EPA leads the way in lead-based paint removal.

Minute *MINNit* - 60 seconds; *myNOOT* - tiny

"Why, you're so tiny and minute that you ain't no bigger than a minute!" the farmer exclaimed to his petite girlfriend.

---

writers *at the movies*

When Hollywood takes on the subject of writers, the results range from idealization to flat out mockery, but either way, there is something about the writing life that brings folks, and their popcorn, coming back for more at the movies.

· · · · ·

Barton Fink

The writing life, in the eyes of the Coen Brothers, ain't no good life, but it's John Turturro's life in this 1991 Cannes Film Festival winner. Turturro stars as a playwright tormented by the need to produce a good script and by an obnoxious neighbor played by John Goodman. That's enough to make anyone sit back and watch the wallpaper peel, don't you think?

· · · · ·

Bullets over Broadway

Who else but Woody Allen could make hilariously brilliant statements about writers in the context of Jazz Age gangsters? This 1995 film features John Cusack as a struggling Broadway playwright who gets a little help on his script from none other than a gangster-turned-author played by Chazz Palminteri. Leave it to the mob to solve the question of whether life imitates art or art imitates life!

· · · · ·

Deconstructing Harry

If the title of the film alludes to a term from literary theory, you know, once again, it has to be Woody Allen. Writers are often his favorite subject, but they get a slightly darker treatment in this 1997 movie. Like Luigi Pirandello before him, Allen explores the possibilities of what happens when a fictional character comes to life to meet its author. The main character, Harry Block, suffers from a typical writer's malady. You can figure it out from his last name. Will his friends ever forgive him for writing about them in his latest novel, or will he be doomed to be "blocked" forever?

$$\bullet\ \bullet\ \bullet\ \bullet\ \bullet$$

Mrs. Parker and the Vicious Circle

The title of this 1994 film might seem a bit insulting, but any movie about the woman who coined such memorable lines as "If all the girls who attended the Yale prom were laid end to end, I wouldn't be a bit surprised" couldn't be called *Mrs. Parker and the Really Polite Circle*. This biopic about Dorothy Parker and the Algonquin table gives you a great glimpse into the witty literati.

$$\bullet\ \bullet\ \bullet\ \bullet\ \bullet$$

Capote

What really inspired Truman Capote to move from the delightful *Breakfast at Tiffany's* to the horrifying *In Cold Blood?* As an actor, Philip Seymour Hoffman knocks it out of the ballpark in his portrayal of the glamorous and manipulative Capote. The film also highlights the friendship between the toast of Manhattan and his good friend, southern author Harper Lee.

$$\bullet\ \bullet\ \bullet\ \bullet\ \bullet$$

The Squid and the Whale

Just because you write well doesn't mean you parent well. This is the lesson played out in all of its uncomfortable detail in this 2005 drama. Jeff Daniels plays a novelist whose career is in the toilet. He grows more and more estranged from his increasingly successful writer-wife, played by Laura Linney. After they divorce, the only thing more split than their infinitives is the loyalty of their children.

Adaptation

This 2002 comedy turns the writing life inside out as it explores two brothers who want to be writers. One struggles for originality. The other just wants to follow all the rules he learned in a creative writing class. Characters write themselves into their own stories, and all kinds of other mind-boggling plot twists ensue as they journey on the road to original adaptation, if such a thing even exists.

More Movies About Writers

Impromptu	George Sand
Henry and June	Henry Miller
Shadowlands	C. S. Lewis
Il Postino	Pablo Neruda
In Love and War	Ernest Hemingway
Tom and Viv	T. S. Eliot
Finding Neverland	J. M. Barrie
Quills	Marquis de Sade
The Hours	Virginia Woolf
Sylvia	Sylvia Plath

the write stuff:
a glossary of literary terms from R to V

OK, there are no literary terms beginning with Z, so we'll just have to stop a few letters short of an alphabet. But fear not! This list gives you the lowdown on every word you need to sound smart in your book club.

Rhyme–The repetition of identical or similar sounds in different words. *Cat, hat,* and *rat* all rhyme. Sometimes words look like they should rhyme, but they don't, such as *though* and *cough.* These are examples of eye rhyme because the eye sees similarities but the ear doesn't hear them. If you see the phrase *masculine rhyme,* it doesn't mean rhyming macho words, like muscle and tussle. Instead, it describes the rhyming of single-syllable words or sounds, such as *big* and *fig* or *restore* and *deplore. Feminine rhyme* happens when a rhymed stressed syllable is followed by unstressed syllables, as in *butter* and *clutter* or *reaction* and *subtraction.*

Setting–The time and place of a work of literature. Nebraska, 1901. China in the fourth century. You get the picture.

Simile–A comparison using *like* or *as.* "She is as pretty as a picture" is a good, although trite, example.

Soliloquy–A character sometimes talks out loud to himself. In real life, we call this mental illness. In drama, we call it a soliloquy. The most famous soliloquy of all time has to be when Hamlet's speech which begins: "To be or not to be."

Stream-of-consciousness technique–A type of narration that takes a reader inside a character's mind. What you read on the page seems like the random thoughts of someone as they stream through. Stream-of-consciousness writing is often written without punctuation or capitalization, because most folks don't think in grammatically perfect sentences. James Joyce and Virginia Woolf are two novelists who used this technique a lot.

Symbol—A person, thing, or place that suggests meaning beyond and usually more abstract than its literal meaning. A crucifix is a symbol of Christ's death and/or Christian salvation. Spring is a symbol of rebirth. Some symbols only work within the context of a particular book. A big, fat, white whale may not mean much in most places, but in *Moby Dick* it symbolizes evil, natural forces, and Ahab's obsessive mania, just to name a few things.

Syntax—Word order. Here is syntax that makes sense: To be or not to be. That is the question. Here is syntax that doesn't make sense: Question to or be not to be that is the.

Theme—The underlying meaning of a literary work or a recurring idea throughout the work. One of the themes of *The Great Gatsby*, for instance, is the failure of the American Dream.

Tragedy—A story that describes important, serious stuff and ends in disaster for the main characters. Aristotle said that the purpose of tragedy is emotional purging. The reader feels pity and fear and gets it all out. Usually the protagonist of a tragedy begins in a high place (king, prince) and falls in some way, which makes the situation all the more, um, tragic.

Villanelle—A fixed form of poetry consisting of 19 lines divided into six stanzas: five tercets (a group of three lines) and a concluding quatrain (a group of four lines). To make things more complicated, the first and third lines of the first tercet rhyme; these rhymes are repeated in all of the following tercets and in the final quatrain. Read Dylan Thomas' poem "Do not go gentle into that good night" and you'll see a villanelle in action.

fiction *into film*

It's hard to decide which is better, the book or the movie, when you consider these outstanding adaptations. You be the judge.

· · · · ·

Sense and Sensibility

Hard-core Jane Austen fans might gasp to think that a film could ever outdo one of her novels, and they're probably right. However, this 1995 Ang Lee adaptation boasts a screenplay by Emma Thompson, who won the Oscar for Best Screenplay Based on Material from Another Medium, and who also played the role of Elinor. The film captures the stuttering sense of Elinor and Edward as well as the high-strung sensibility of Marianne and Willoughby to such an extent that it feels like Austen herself directed it.

· · · · ·

Jaws

Peter Benchley already had a best-selling novel when the young Steven Spielberg turned it into one of the first summer blockbusters ever to hit the silver screen. Benchley came up with the idea of a man-eating shark wreaking havoc on a beachside community after reading about a 4,550-pound great white shark caught in 1964. That big shark meant big profits for Universal Pictures. *Jaws* grossed more than $470 million worldwide and helped launch Spielberg's career.

· · · · ·

Schindler's List

Steven Spielberg finally won an Academy Award for the breathtaking job of bringing Thomas Kenneally's book about Oskar Schindler to life. Spielberg avoided the sentimentality characteristic of much of his work as he gave us a glimpse into Nazi atrocities in haunting black and white.

The shot of the one little girl in a red jacket there amid the masses dying is an image that will haunt you for the rest of your life.

••••••

Jurassic Park
Once again, Steven Spielberg looks to the written word for cinematic inspiration. Michael Crichton published his techno-thriller in 1990, as a Frankenstein-type tale warning us of science running amok. By the time Spielberg brought incredibly lifelike dinosaurs onto the screen, we were all convinced that some scientific experiments are best left alone.

••••••

Raise the Red Lantern
Nominated for an Oscar for the Best Foreign Language Film in 1992, Zhang Yimou's masterpiece is an adaptation of *Wives and Concubines* by Su Tong. Tong's book is a collection of novellas that expose all of the poverty, prostitution, and crime seething beneath a lovely exterior in 1930s China. Yimou focused on one particular novella, *Raise the Red Lantern,* and found in its story a searing portrait of one woman's loneliness and despair as she is forced to become a concubine.

••••••

Stand by Me
Stephen King has never seemed so loveable. His novella *The Body* was the basis for this 1986 Rob Reiner drama about four young boys who venture into the woods near the town of Castle Rock to search for a dead body. Both the novella and the film illustrate King's masterful gift for painting memorable characters who can withstand great difficulty, whether it's typical Stephen King horror or, in this case, the trials of simply coming of age.

Smoke Signals

Chris Eyre based this 1998 independent film on Coeur D'Alene Indian writer Sherman Alexie's book *The Lone Ranger and Tonto Fistfight in Heaven*. Alexie's collection of stories brilliantly paints a realistic picture of modern life on an Indian reservation. *Smoke Signals* faithfully brings the characters to life in a movie with a Native American director, writer, and actors.

Quotes on Dogs

The dog was created especially for children. He is the god of frolic.

—Henry Ward Beecher, *Proverbs from Plymouth Pulpit*

...judiciously show a cat milk, if you wish her to thirst for it. Judiciously show a dog his natural prey, if you wish him to bring it down one day.

—Charles Dickens, *A Tale of Two Cities*

The greatest pleasure of a dog is that you may make a fool of yourself with him and not only will he not scold you, but he will make a fool of himself too.

—Samuel Butler, *Higgledy-Piggledy*

It's funny how dogs and cats know the insides of folks better than other folks do, isn't it?

—Eleanor H. Porter, *Pollyanna*

a lot *of Aesop*

What better way to teach a lesson to misguided humans than to tell stories about smart animals? Such was the thinking of the most famous fable spinner in all of history, Aesop. Read on and gain a little wisdom yourself.

· · · · ·

Biography:

We don't know a lot about Aesop's life, but scholars agree he was born around 620 BC in either Sardis, Mesembria, or Cotiaeum or on the Greek island Samos. Born a slave, he was owned by two men in Samos, first Xanthus and then Jadmon. Aesop was so clever that eventually Jadmon released him from slavery. Once free, he traveled the world until he came to Sardis, where he met the king of Lydia. Like Jadmon, the king was also impressed with Aesop's wit, so much so that he appointed Aesop to an ambassador position, which allowed him to travel all over Greece.

Through most of his travels, his diplomacy was well received. Heck, who wouldn't like the guy and all of his great stories about foxes and birds and so forth? However, when he was sent to Delphi, his life took a turn for the worse. The king wanted him to distribute funds to the citizens, but Aesop found them to be so greedy that he was disgusted. He sent the funds back to the king, saying there was no way the people of Delphi deserved them. Needless to say, this angered the Delphians, so they hatched a plan. They decided to accuse Aesop of sacrilege, a crime punishable by death. According to Plutarch, the Delphians threw him off a cliff.

Aesop left many memorable phrases in his wake, including such gems as "familiarity breeds contempt" and "sour grapes." In his death, one final phrase was added to the canon: "the blood of Aesop." According to legend, after Aesop's death (read "murder"), the Delphians endured a series of troubles and tragedies until they finally confessed their crime. Thereafter, "the blood of Aesop" referred to the fact than wrongdoing will always be punished somehow.

· · · · ·

Influence:

Aesop's influence on the world was far-reaching. Bigwigs from Plato and Aristotle to Cicero and Shakespeare were inspired by his tales. His name became synonymous with wise fables, so much so that many fables that he probably never told were later attributed to him. Bear in mind that he never actually wrote any of his stories down. They were passed on in the oral tradition, which makes it all the more remarkable that they have survived over 2,000 years.

Fables, by their very definition, are short, often funny stories told to illustrate a moral or lesson. Characters in fables usually represent human characteristics. For instance, foxes are crafty, bees are diligent, and lions are regal. In keeping with the genre, Aesop's fables are short and simple. They are told in plain language that anyone can understand. Don't be fooled, though. Beneath the elementary exterior lies some really deep stuff. Lessons like "birds of a feather flock together" tell us a lot about politics, prejudice, and social organization. Aesopic fables may be short and sweet, but they also represent the earliest stage of literary art. They are carefully crafted to combine naiveté and sophistication. They appeal to listeners and readers of all ages and across all cultures.

· · · · ·

A Few Fabulous Fables:

The North Wind and the Sun

The North Wind and the Sun fell into a terrible argument. Each was convinced that he was the strongest. To settle the debate, they tested their strength on a passing traveler. Their goal was to see who could be the first to get the man to take off his coat. The North Wind took the first turn. He marshaled all of his force and let out a howling gust. The man's coat twisted about him as the gale-force winds increased, yet the harder the North Wind blew, the more tightly the man drew his coat around himself. Next, the Sun took his turn. At first, he bathed the man in warm rays. The man took his coat and tossed it lightly over his shoulder. Then the Sun shone more strongly. Under the burning rays, the man took off his coat altogether. The Sun won the argument.

The moral of the story? Persuasion is always better than force.

• • • • •

The Fox and the Crane

One day Fox invited Crane to dinner. Thinking he was funny, Fox cooked up some soup, but he served it in such a shallow dish that the crane, with his long beak, couldn't sip any of it.

Fox asked sweetly, "Crane, don't you like the soup? Why aren't you eating it?"

Crane replied, "I like it just fine. In fact, why don't you do me the honor of dining at my house?"

When Fox arrived at Crane's for dinner, he sat down in front of a flagon with a tall, narrow mouth. There was no way Fox could get his nose into it. However, with his long neck, Crane was able to enjoy the soup without any effort at all.

"I am happy to be able to return your kindness," quipped Crane as he continued slurping his soup. "I hope you enjoy your dinner as much as I enjoyed mine at your house."

The moral of the story? What goes around, comes around.

• • • • •

The Fox and the Grapes

One day, a Fox was taking a walk when he saw a bunch of grapes just ripening on a vine. They were sweet and tasty looking, but they were growing on a vine just above his reach. He thought, "Those are just the thing to quench my thirst!" Determined to eat them, he took a running jump at the bunch, but he missed. He tried again, but to no avail. There they hung, tempting him, but he couldn't reach them. Over and over he tried, but at last he had to give up. As he walked away, he said smugly: "I am sure they are sour."

The moral of the story? It is easy to dislike what you cannot have.

• • • • •

The Lion and the Mouse

One day a Lion was sleeping when suddenly a little Mouse began running up and down his body. The Lion woke up furious and put his huge paw on the Mouse, ready to eat him alive.

"Pardon me, King," cried the little Mouse: "If you will forgive me just this once, I will never forget it. Who knows? One day I may be able to repay your kindness."

The Lion was so amused at the idea of this little Mouse being able to help him, that he let him go. Months later, the Lion got caught in a trap set by hunters. They wanted to take the Lion back to their king, so they tied him to a tree while they went searching for a cage. Who should show up just then but the little Mouse! Seeing the Lion's desperate situation, he immediately approached him and began gnawing at the ropes tying the King of the Beasts to the tree. In no time, the Lion was free. "What did I tell you?" asked the little Mouse. "One day I could repay your kindness."

The moral of the story? Little friends may prove great friends.

• • • • •

The Ant and the Grasshopper

One summer day, a Grasshopper was hopping about a field, enjoying himself immensely. An Ant passed by, carrying a giant ear of corn to his nest

"Why not come and talk to me," said the Grasshopper, "instead of working so hard?"

"I am helping to store up food for the winter," said the Ant, "and I would suggest that you do the same."

The Grasshopper replied, "Why bother about winter? We have plenty of food right now." The Ant turned away and kept working. When winter came, the Grasshopper, with no food, was dying of hunger. Starving, he watched the ants sharing corn and grain every day from the stores they had collected during their hard work in the summer.

The moral of the story? It is wise to prepare for the days of necessity.

· · · · ·

The Tortoise and the Hare

The Hare was once bragging in front of the other animals about how fast he was. "No one has ever beaten me in a race," he boasted. "I hereby challenge anyone to race me."

No one was willing to take on the Hare. Finally, a Tortoise said quietly, "I will accept your challenge."

The Hare laughed. "That's hilarious," he said. "I could run circles around you."

"Why don't you just hold off on your boasting until you've lost the race," replied the Tortoise. "Shall we race?"

They decided on a course and began. Immediately, the Hare ran almost out of sight. He was far ahead, so, to show his scorn for the Tortoise, he stopped and took a nap. Meanwhile, the Tortoise just kept plodding along. When the Hare woke from his nap, he saw the Tortoise approaching the finish line. Running as fast as he could, the Hare couldn't catch up in time. The Tortoise won the race.

The moral of the story? Slow and steady wins the race.

· · · · ·

The Fox and the Crow

One day a Fox saw a Crow fly by with a piece of cheese in its beak. The Crow landed on the branch of a tree.

Desiring the cheese, the Fox thought, "That cheese should be mine since I am a Fox." He approached the tree and called up to the Crow:

"Good afternoon, Miss Crow! You look so lovely today. Your feathers are shiny; your eyes are bright. I bet you sing more sweetly than the other birds. You sure look prettier than they do. If you will sing one little song for me, I will greet you as the Queen of Birds."

Delighted, the Crow lifted up her head and began to caw. The second she opened her beak, however, the piece of cheese fell to the ground. Instantly, the Fox ate it.

"That's enough," he said. "The cheese was all I wanted. In exchange for this tasty morsel, I will give you a piece of advice: Do not trust flatterers."

· · · · ·

The Frogs Wanting a King

A group of Frogs lived happily together in a swamp. They spent their days splashing and croaking in peace. One day a few of them decided they needed a king and a proper constitution, so they decided to ask Jove to give them what they wanted.

They prayed to Jove, "Please send us a king who will rule over us and keep us in order." Jove laughed at their croaking pleas and tossed a log down into the swamp. The Frogs were terrified by the noise the log made, so they all hurried to the bank to see what kind of monster made such a sound. The log just floated there, so eventually a couple of brave Frogs snuck up on it and touched it. It still didn't move. Next, the bravest of all the Frogs jumped on the log and danced on it. Soon all the Frogs danced on it too. Eventually they spent their days splashing, croaking, and dancing on the log.

Eventually they grew restless again, so they asked Jove, "Could you please send us a real king, one who will really rule over us?" Jove grew furious, so he sent down a giant Stork that began eating all the Frogs. They repented, but it was too late.

The moral of the story? Better no rule than cruel rule.

The Wolf and the Dog

There once was a starving Wolf almost dead with hunger who met a Dog passing by.

"Ah, cousin," said the Dog. "I knew that one day your irregular life would be the ruin of you. Why don't you work steadily as I do and get your food regularly given to you?"

"I wouldn't oppose that idea," said the Wolf, "if I could only find a place to work."

The Dog replied, "No problem. I can arrange that for you. Come with me to my master, and you can share my workload."

The Wolf followed the Dog into town. On the way, the Wolf noticed some of the hair on the Dog's neck had been worn off, so he asked him what happened.

"Oh, that? It's nothing," said the Dog. "It is only where my collar goes. I wear one at night to stay chained up. It rubs off the hair, but you get used to it."

The Wolf turned away. "Good-bye, Dog," he said, leaving him for good.

The moral of the story? Better to starve and be free than to be a fat slave.

The Mystery of the Poe Toaster

Every January 19 since 1949, an unnamed man with a black hood and a silver-tipped cane has visited Edgar Allan Poe's grave. He toasts the deceased author with a glass of Martel cognac, then departs while it is still dark, leaving behind the half-full liquor bottle and three red roses—one for Poe, one for Poe's mother, and one for Poe's wife.

---

children's lit top 40

Teenagers get *Billboard* magazine's Top 40 countdown of pop songs, but this list takes a new spin on the old number. Here's a Top 40 list of great kids' books for the very young.

1. ***Alexander and the Terrible, Horrible, No Good, Very Bad Day***
   Judith Viorst
   Alexander isn't having the best of all possible days, as the title suggests. This book does a great job of voicing young kids' little frustrations.

2. ***Brown Bear, Brown Bear, What Do You See?***
   Bill Martin Jr.
   Illustrated by Eric Carle
   A catchy rhyme and all the colors of the rainbow make this an enduring favorite.

3. ***Click, Clack, Moo: Cows That Type***
   Doreen Cronin
   When Farmer Brown's cows find a typewriter in the barn, they threaten to give Shakespeare a run for his money.

4. ***Curious George***
   H. A. and Margaret Rey
   This books gives a whole new twist to the phrase "monkey on your back."

5. ***Dinosaur Roar!***
   Paul and Henrietta Stickland
   All kids love dinosaurs, even sick ones or grumpy ones, as this book proves.

6. *Fire Truck*
Peter Sís

Matt wakes up one morning to discover that he has turned into a fire truck. Consider it Kafka's "Metamorphosis" for little ones.

7. *Freight Train*
Donald Crews

A colorful train travels the countryside, taking kids on a journey they won't soon forget.

8. *Froggy Gets Dressed*
Jonathan London
Illustrated by Frank Remkiewicz

Hey, when you're little, getting dressed is a big deal. Froggy thinks so too.

9. *George and Martha*
James Marshall

Two hippopotamuses become friends and learn about life together, as only hippopotamuses can.

10. *Good Night, Gorilla*
Peggy Rathmann

The zookeeper thinks the animals are still in the zoo, but it turns out they have followed him home!

11. *Goodnight, Moon*
Margaret W. Brown
Illustrated by Clement Hurd

The all-time classic. You'll get sleepy even as an adult reading it at night.

12. *Horton Hatches the Egg*
Dr. Seuss
A lazy mama bird asks an elephant to sit on her egg until it hatches.
He proves to be faithful on his watch

13. *If You Give a Mouse a Cookie*
Laura J. Numeroff
If you give a mouse a cookie, all kinds of good things can result.

14. *Lilly's Purple Plastic Purse*
Kevin Henkes
Lily the mouse loves school, until her favorite plastic purse isn't
such a big hit with the teacher.

15. *The Little Red Hen: An Old Story*
Margot Zemach
A retelling of the traditional story about the little red hen whose
lazy friends don't want to help her grind wheat into flour but are
more than happy to help her eat the bread that she makes from it.

16. *Lyle, Lyle, Crocodile*
Bernard Waber
A happy crocodile causes a big stink in a Manhattan neighborhood.

17. *Madeline*
Ludwig Bemelmans
A delightful story of a schoolgirl in Paris.

18. *Maisy Goes Swimming*
Lucy Cousins
Maisy the mouse needs help from young readers as she tries to
dress for a dip in the pool.

19. *Make Way for Ducklings*
Robert McCloskey
Mr. and Mrs. Mallard look for a safe and quiet place to raise their babies.

20. *Mike Mulligan and His Steam Shovel*
Virginia L. Burton
Can Mike and his old-fashioned steam shovel land a big job? This story proves that the latest in technology isn't always the best thing.

21. *Mr. Gumpy's Outing*
John Burningham
Mr. Gumpy can't say no to all of the animals on his boat. Then things get tricky.

22. *No, David!*
David Shannon
"No" may be the word kids hear the most. This story helps them delight in the trials of another child used to hearing the word.

23. *Olivia*
Ian Falconer
Olivia is one peppy pig with energy to spare.

24. *So Much*
Trish Cooke
Illustrated by Helen Oxenbury
Relatives almost overdo it as they express their excitement about a new baby.

25. *The Polar Express*
Chris Van Allsburg
A boy takes a magical train ride to the North Pole to receive a special gift from Santa Claus.

26. ***Puss in Boots***
Charles Perrault
A miller dies and leaves his son an amazing gift in the form of a cat.

27. ***The Random House Book of Mother Goose: A Treasury of 386 Timeless Nursery Rhymes***
Arnold Lobel
An illustrated collection of Mother Goose nursery rhymes.

28. ***Rumpelstiltskin***
Paul O. Zelinsky
A weird little man helps a girl spin straw into gold for the king on the condition that she will give him her firstborn child.

29. ***The Snowy Day***
Ezra Jack Keats
A young boy explores the wonderful world of snow and all the crazy things he can do with it.

30. ***The Story of Ferdinand***
Munro Leaf
Not all bulls were born to fight. This is the story of one bull who would rather hang out peacefully.

31. ***Strega Nona***
Tomie De Paola
A modern version of an old Italian tale about an apprentice, his curiosity, and a magic pasta pot.

32. ***Swimmy***
Leo Lionni
Swimmy is one resourceful fish trying to find a safe way to live in the big, scary sea.

33. *The Tale of Peter Rabbit*
Beatrix Potter
The classic tale of a mischievous rabbit.

34. *There Was an Old Lady Who Swallowed a Fly*
Simms Taback
Crazy things happen when one swallows a fly.

35. *The Three Bears*
Paul Galdone
You can't go wrong with this tale of trying to find just the right thing for the right person.

36. *The True Story of the Three Little Pigs by A. Wolf*
John Scieszka
The story of the three little pigs is retold from the wolf's point of view.

37. *The Very Hungry Caterpillar*
Eric Carle
Children love following a little caterpillar as he eats his way through an entire book.

38. *The Wheels of the Bus*
Adapted and illustrated by Paul O. Zelinsky
Wheels go 'round, wipers swish, and a host of other sights and sounds thrill young readers in this adaptation of the popular kids' song.

39. *Where the Wild Things Are*
Maurice Sendak
After Max is sent to bed for misbehaving, he imagines that he sails away to a place with monsters as wild as he is.

40. *Yoko*
Rosemary Wells
Not everyone brings a boring old sandwich to school for lunch, as Yoko learns when her sushi causes quite a stir.

across the ages through the pages:
brit lit 9

1945–Present: The Contemporary/Postmodernist Period

Following World War II (1939–1945), the postmodernist period ushered in writing that echoed modernism's irony but abandoned its claim that order and stability can be found in the world. Instead, writers as vastly different as Stevie Smith and Harold Pinter illustrate the wide scope of contemporary literature.

Stevie Smith: The Least You Need to Know

- Stevie's pseudonym points to her concern with gender roles. From her early novels, such as *Novel on Yellow Paper* (1936) and *Over the Frontier* (1938), to her numerous books of poetry, Smith investigates how society dictates gender norms.

- Smith often adopted a falsely naïve posture in her poems as a way of speaking about serious concerns without igniting too much controversy. She would write, in the voice of a young girl, playful poems that betrayed very real concerns with inequality, religious doubt, war, and death. One of her most famous poems, "Not Waving but Drowning," describes, in a morbidly humorous way, how miscommunication can have devastating effects. Many of her poems included doodles and sketches, which seemed silly on the surface, but often undercut the playful appearance of the poem. For example, in one poem, "My Hat," she describes a young girl's fairy-tale dream of escaping a forced marriage, but the drawing attached to the poem hints at the fact that there is never really an option of freedom for women in patriarchal society.

Harold Pinter: The Least You Need to Know

- Winner of the 2005 Nobel Prize for Literature, Pinter is a playwright whose postmodernist techniques enable him, for instance, in *Betrayal* (1978), to tell the story of a love affair backwards, from the breakup of the couple to how they first met. His plays often suggest that life is largely unexplainable and that human motivations are beyond our understanding. Themes of domination and loneliness come across through Pinter's use of fragmented speech, silence, and non sequiturs.

- His first full-length play, *The Birthday Party* (1958), takes place in a run-down British boardinghouse, where Stanley Webber, an unsuccessful piano player, is taken care of by a kind landlady. On his birthday, two menacing characters, Goldberg and McCann, visit and torture him psychologically with questions and accusations, to the point that he assaults his landlady and ends up a broken man, silent and passive. The play is an example of theater of the absurd, a type of drama that challenges the audience's notions of reality.

Heteronyms O–R

Object *ubJEKT* - to complain or to disagree ; *AHBjekt* - a thing

Betty objects to being treated like an object.

Perfect *PERfekt* - exactly correct, not having any errors; *perFEKT* - to make correct

After reading this page, you will perfect your understanding of the perfect heteronym.

Row *ROH* - to propel a boat with oars; *ROUW* - a fight

Said one fishing buddy to his lazy friend, "Look, buddy, you better help me row, row, row this boat or we're gonna get in a big row, ya hear me?"

---

across the ages through the pages:
american lit 7

. . . .

1950–Present: The Contemporary Period

American literature in the second half of the 20th century is marked
by a wide diversity of writers from various ethnic backgrounds. From
the Civil Rights movement through the Vietnam era and height of
the youth counterculture, post–World War II American society gave
rise to a wealth of new voices struggling to be heard. Prior to this
time, Hispanic, Asian-American, and Native American writers had
little opportunity to publish, but such influential writers as Sandra
Cisneros, Maxine Hong Kingston, and N. Scott Momaday prove that the
American melting pot offers a rich and varied literary landscape.

Sandra Cisneros: The Least You Need to Know

- Born as the only daughter in family of seven children in 1954,
  Cisneros is in many ways a "borderland" writer. As a child, her
  family often moved between their Chicago home and her father's
  family home in Mexico. Cisneros attended the renowned University
  of Iowa Writer's Workshop and taught creative writing at several
  universities. She has received two National Endowment for the Arts
  awards and, in 1996, was named a MacArthur fellow.

- Her first book of stories, *The House on Mango Street*, received the
  Before Columbus American Book Award. In it, she draws on a
  Chicano/Chicana literary tradition of telling short, related tales that
  unify under a larger theme. The stories in the collection focus on
  Esperanza, a young girl growing up in Chicago. She struggles with
  racism and sexism as she develops over the course of the book into
  a creative, self-aware woman, who manages to escape Mango Street
  but is able to return later with a maturity of vision and a desire to
  help others succeed too.

- Cisneros' collection of poetry, *My Wicked, Wicked Ways*, uses the archetypal Chicana/Mexicana figure of La Malinche, a legendary "evil woman" who was historically blamed for selling out her people to conquerors. In Cisneros' retelling of her character, La Malinche underlies the numerous strong representations of women in the poems, women who are heroic, brave, and unafraid.

Maxine Hong Kingston: The Least You Need to Know

- Kingston was born in California in 1940 and studied at the University of California, Berkeley. She is a dominant voice in Asian-American literature; in fact, her book *The Woman Warrior* received the National Book Critics Circle award in 1976 and was named one of the top ten nonfiction works of the decade by *Time* magazine. Critics praise Kingston for her inventive blend of fact and memoir, imagination and history. She incorporates ancient Chinese legends alongside contemporary Asian-American experience in order to outline the difficulties of embracing one's cultural heritage in the modern world.

- *The Woman Warrior* is loosely based on Kingston's life and stands as an excellent example of postmodernism in its fusion of fact and fiction. The five stories in the collection focus on different women's struggles. In one, a Chinese ancestor gives birth to an illegitimate child and is so shunned by her community that she commits suicide. In another, the speaker's aunt suffers from a mental breakdown as she fails to adjust to life in the United States after leaving her home in China.

N. Scott Momaday: The Least You Need to Know

- As a Kiowa Indian, Momaday learned tribal storytelling traditions from his father's family. He grew up with different southwestern tribes and in non-Indian communities and was thus taught by his mother to appreciate English literature as well as native stories. His education ranged from reservation schools, to a Virginia military academy, to Stanford University, where he received an M.A. and a Ph.D. As a poet, essayist, novelist, and autobiographer, he has earned a Pulitzer Prize and a Guggenheim fellowship.

- *House Made of Dawn* (1969) opened the door for Native-American writers. Focusing on a young member of the Jemez Pueblo, the novel blends Hemingway's succinct writing style with Navajo ceremonial elements. The main character, Abel, a World War II veteran, returns home to the reservation as a lost and alienated young man. He has an affair with a white woman, kills a man outside of a bar, and is sent to jail. After prison he struggles with alcoholism and gambling in Los Angeles. When his grandfather is on his deathbed, Abel returns to the reservation and is finally able to connect to his family roots.

laughing with the bard

Much Ado About Nothing

Plot

Friends of Leonato, a well-respected nobleman of Messina, return from war. One of them, Claudio, falls in love with Leonato's daughter, Hero. Unfortunately, Claudio has an enemy in fellow soldier Don John, who tricks him into thinking Hero has been unfaithful. As a result, on their wedding day, Claudio rejects Hero at the altar, and she fakes her own death so that her family can discover who had led Claudio astray. He grieves her death, and once he discovers her true innocence, he grieves even more. As a punishment for slandering her, Leonato tells him he must marry his "niece," but to Claudio's delight, the niece turns out to be Hero. In a parallel subplot, another friend of Leonato named Benedick swears he will never marry, but he falls for the equally witty and headstrong Beatrice.

Themes

1. The course of true love never did run smoothly. Claudio is almost deceived into thinking Hero is an unworthy mate, and the pride of Benedick and Beatrice almost ensures they will remain sworn enemies forever.

2. True love accepts faults. Benedick knows that Beatrice is outspoken and frank, and she knows he is headstrong and controlling, but they accept these qualities in each other and fall deeply in love anyway.

crying with the bard

Titus Andronicus

Plot

One of Shakespeare's most grisly, violent plays, *Titus Andronicus* is heavily influenced by the bloody dramas of Seneca, a Roman philosopher and playwright who lived in the first century AD. Shakespeare's tale begins when the aging Roman general, Titus, comes back to Rome after waging war against the Goths. He has captured the Goth queen, Tamora, and her three sons, one of whom Titus kills as a human sacrifice in order to satisfy the bloodlust of his own killed family members' souls. Titus is offered the throne, but he refuses, claiming he is too old. Instead, he insists that Saturnius become emperor and that his daughter, Lavinia, should become the emperor's wife. However, Lavinia is kidnapped by Bassanius, so Saturnius marries Tamora, who has vowed revenge for the death of her son. Her two remaining sons kill Bassanius, rape Lavinia, and cut off her tongue and hands. The horrors continue as two of Titus's sons are executed and one is banished. To repay Tamora for her latest acts of revenge, Titus kills her sons, cooks them in a pie, and serves them to her. He then kills his daughter, Lavinia, and stabs Tamora. Saturnius kills Titus, and Titus' banished son kills Saturnius.

Themes

1. Revenge produces revenge. Just consider the final scenes of the play to see how one act of revenge spurs more revenge and so forth. In fact, the word "revenge" appears 34 times in the play to underscore how central it is to the driving force of the conflict.
2. The body of the state mirrors the body of its citizens. As citizen turns on citizen, the cohesiveness of the political and social order unravels.

learning with the bard

Richard II

Plot

Historically, Richard II ruled as King of England from 1377 to 1399.
He had become king when he was only ten years old, so he ruled
under the guidance of John of Gaunt, Duke of Lancaster, and Thomas
of Woodstock, Duke of Gloucester. Gaunt's son, Henry Bolingbroke
and Thomas Mowbray, the Duke of Norfolk, were part of a group that
tried to control the young king. When the play begins, Bolingbroke
and Mowbray are vying for power, but King Richard banishes them
both from the kingdom. When John of Gaunt dies, Richard steals
Bolingbroke's inheritance in order to wage war against the Irish. While
Richard fights in Ireland, Bolingbroke returns to England, takes control,
and imprisons Richard. Bolingbroke becomes King Henry IV and has
Richard killed. The play concludes with King Henry IV pretending to
be outraged by Richard's death.

Themes

1. When is it just to usurp the throne? Richard believes that his
   authority is God given, but Bolingbroke believes that Richard is a
   weak king and that, in the best interests of England, he should be
   overthrown.
2. Overspending spoils the goodwill of the people. Richard is not frugal
   enough to guard the kingdom's wealth wisely. Once he confiscates
   Bolingbroke's inheritance to fight the Irish, the people turn to
   Bolingbroke's side.

from dogs and frogs to cheshire cats #3:
animals in children's literature

Lassie Come Home

In 1948, Eric Knight published this story of what would become one of the most famous dogs in popular culture. The collie, Lassie, makes a journey from Scotland to Yorkshire, England, to rejoin her original owner. Knight and his wife raised collies on their farm in Pennsylvania, but the fictional Lassie lived on the silver screen, starting with the 1943 production of *Lassie, Come Home*.

· · · · ·

The Tale of Peter Rabbit

Beatrix Potter wrote and illustrated this beloved children's book in 1901, and it has sold more than 40 million copies worldwide. Peter has three sisters, Flaps, Mopsy, and Cotton-tail, but Peter is the most adventurous of all the rabbits. He gets trapped in a garden where his father had lost his life, but he is saved by a group of birds. He returns home exhausted, and his mother makes him a cup of chamomile tea. The story, while simple, appeals to young readers' desires to explore the world within the safety of a mother's love. Other adorable animals in Potter's collection include Hunca Munca, Squirrel Nutkin, Mrs. Tiggy-Winkle, Jemima Puddle-Duck, and Mr. Tod the Fox.

· · · · ·

Stuart Little

This was the first children's story by E. B. White, the author of *Charlotte's Web*. It is the tale of a young New York mouse, Stuart, who is raised by humans. White said that the character first appeared to him in a dream he had while on a train, in the 1920s, but he didn't publish it until 1945. It was the first book illustrated by famous artist Garth Williams, who once quipped that "it is terribly difficult to draw

ATTRACTIVE mice." White gave ideas to Williams for the illustrations, including recommending a picture from the Sears catalog for one of the female characters. When the book was published, some critics thought it was too mature for children. White said it is about "the continuing journey that everybody takes—in search of what is perfect and unattainable. This is perhaps too elusive an idea to put in a book for children, but I put it in anyway." One angry reader with the actual name of Stuart Little wrote the author and said that he was writing a children's book about a rat named E. B. White.

• • • • •

The Wind in the Willows

This 1908 classic was written by Kenneth Grahame, an orphan who grew up to be a wealthy banker. He enjoyed telling bedtime stories to his son, Mouse. In fact, his son so loved his stories that when the boy was sent on vacation with his nurse, he complained that he would miss his father's nighttime tales. He begged him to mail him a story every day, and thus *Wind in the Willows* was born. Each chapter of the book describes the adventures of four animal friends, Water Rat, Mole, Toad, and Badger, each of whom embodies human characteristics: Water Rat is relaxed and loves the river; Mole is a homebody; Toad represents conceit and wealth; and Badger is a wise hermit. They live together happily along the river but must resist the urge to explore the Wild Wood and, beyond that, the Wide World.

• • • • •

Winnie-the-Pooh

The writer A. A. Milne wrote the story of this "silly old bear" in 1926 for his son, Christopher Robin, who wanted to hear stories about his toy animals. Since then, the book has been translated into over 25 languages as children all over the world relate to the idea that their stuffed animals could, somewhere else, have a real life of their own. The lovable bear, Pooh, derived part of his name from Winnipeg, a bear that the real Christopher Robin saw at the London Zoo, and another part form Pooh, a swan he and his father saw on vacation. The other animals—naïve Piglet, melancholy Eeyore, wise Rabbit, and the maternal Kanga—were drawn from Christopher's collection of toys as well. Interestingly, Pooh is such a beloved character worldwide that there is a street in Warsaw, Poland, named after him. Pooh was also awarded a star on the Hollywood Walk of Fame in 2006.

Murder on the Orient Express: The Least You Need to Know

An enticing story of murder and deceit, Murder on the Orient Express *is perhaps one of Christie's greatest novels. M. Hercule Poirot is in Syria working on a case for the French government. He finishes his case and decides to head back to England. Before he can depart, he is called to immediately return to London, where a very important case awaits his attention. His old friend, M. Bouc offers him a spot in the usually empty Calais Coach on the Orient Express.*

Poirot begins talking to a passenger named Ratchett. This American's life has been threatened, and he begs Poirot to act as his bodyguard during the remainder of the trip. Poirot refuses, and several hours later, Ratchett is murdered. When the body is found, Poirot is immediately called upon to work on the case. As an added twist, the Orient Express is stuck in a snowstorm in the countryside of Yugoslavia. Therefore, no one can get off the train.

Poirot begins to search Ratchett's quarters for clues while Dr. Constantine examines the body to determine the cause of death. Poirot finds an abundance of clues—too many, in fact. Who does Poirot determine killed Ratchett? You'll have to read the book to find out.

The Caldecott Medal *1971–2008*

. . . .

1971: Gail E. Haley, *A Story: A Story*

1972: Nonny Hogrogian, *One Fine Day*

1973: Blair Lent, *The Funny Little Woman* (text by Arlene Mosel)

1974: Margot Zemach, *Duffy and the Devil* (text by Harve Zemach)

1975: Gerald McDermott, *Arrow to the Sun: A Pueblo Indian Tale*

1976: Leo and Diane Dillon, *Why Mosquitoes Buzz in People's Ears: A West African Tale* (text by Verna Aardema)

1977: Leo and Diane Dillon, *Ashanti to Zulu: African Traditions* (text by Margaret Musgrove)

1978: Peter Spier, *Noah's Ark* (text by Jacob Revius)

1979: Paul Goble, *The Girl Who Loved Wild Horses*

1980: Barbara Cooney, *Ox-Cart Man* (text by Donald Hall)

1981: Arnold Lobel, *Fables*

1982: Chris Van Allsburg, *Jumanji*

1983: Marcia Brown, *Shadow* (text by Blaise Cendrars)

1984: Alice and Martin Provensen, *The Glorious Flight: Across the Channel with Louis Blériot*

1985: Trina Schart Hyman, *Saint George and the Dragon* (text by Margaret Hodges)

1986: Chris Van Allsburg, *The Polar Express*

1987: Richard Egielski, *Hey, Al* (text by Arthur Yorinks)

1988: John Schoenherr, *Owl Moon* (text by Jane Yolen)

1989: Stephen Gammell, *Song and Dance Man* (text by Karen Ackerman)

1990: Ed Young, *Lon Po Po: A Red-Riding Hood Story from China*

1991: David Macaulay, *Black and White*

1992: David Wiesner, *Tuesday*

1993: Emily Arnold McCully, *Mirette on the High Wire*

1994: Allen Say, *Grandfather's Journey*

1995: David Diaz, *Smoky Night* (text by Eve Bunting)

1996: Peggy Rathmann, *Officer Buckle and Gloria*

1997: David Wisniewski, *Golem*
1998: Paul O. Zelinsky, *Rapunzel*
1999: Mary Azarian, *Snowflake Bentley* (text by Jacqueline Briggs Martin)
2000: Simms Taback, *Joseph Had a Little Overcoat*
2001: David Small, *So You Want to Be President* (text by Judith St. George)
2002: David Wiesner, *Three Pigs*
2003: Eric Rohmann, *My Friend Rabbit*
2004: Mordicai Gerstein, *The Man Who Walked Between the Towers*
2005: Kevin Henkes, *Kitten's First Full Moon*
2006: Chris Raschka, *The Hello, Goodbye Window*
2007: David Wiener, *Flotsam*
2008: Brian Selznick, *The Invention of Hugo Cabret*

Ian Fleming wrote Casino Royale *and his other famed James Bond books in Jamaica, in a house he called Goldeneye, where he wouldn't be distracted by busy London life. He awoke at 7:30 a.m., went skinny-dipping in the ocean, ate scrambled eggs, laid in the sun, and then got to work.*

---

ya lit: suspense/mystery

Down the Rabbit Hole: An Echo Falls Mystery, Peter Abrahams
When 13-year-old Ingrid Levin-Hill accidentally leaves her soccer shoes
at the scene of a murder, she gets involved in an investigation that,
coupled with soccer practice, homework, and acting in a play, makes
her one busy young lady.

. . . . .

Chasing Vermeer, Blue Balliett
Eleven-year-olds Calder and Petra, classmates at the University of
Chicago lab school, are brought together through a series of unusual
coincidences, landing them in the unique position of recovering a
valuable Vermeer painting that is missing from the Art Institute. Can
they solve a mystery that has stumped even the FBI?

. . . . .

Another Kind of Monday, William Coles
"The hundred dollar bills were so new that Mark had had to pinch
them apart." So begins this exciting 1999 novel about a high school
senior who, along with a female friend, is led into a treasure hunt
throughout Pittsburgh.

. . . . .

The Hardy Boys, Franklin W. Dixon
This series is one of the earliest and most popular detective books in
American publishing history. Produced between 1927 and 1979, the
books were composed by a number of ghostwriters, most notably,
Leslie McFarlane, who wrote under the pseudonym Franklin W. Dixon.
The stories feature two brothers, Frank and Joe Hardy, ages 17 and
18, respectively, who are amateur detectives following in the footsteps

of their detective father. The first 58 stories form what is known as the official *Hardy Boys* canon.

· · · · ·

Where It Stops, Nobody Knows, Amy Ehrlich

Nina has spent her life moving all around the United States with her mother in their Chevy van. She would like to stay in Vermont, but when her mother keeps taking her to new places, Nina realizes that they are not so much seeking new adventures as running from an old, shocking secret.

· · · · ·

The Trouble with Lemons, Daniel Hayes

Winner of an American Library Association Best Book for Young Adults, this novel tells the story of an eighth-grader, Tyler, who, with his one friend, Lymie, finds a body in a quarry. When they learn who put the body there, the adventure begins.

· · · · ·

Nancy Drew, Carolyn Keene

The Stratemeyer Syndicate, which started the *Hardy Boys* series, began the *Nancy Drew* series in the 1930s, publishing a variety of authors who all used the pseudonym Carolyn Keene. The title character, Nancy, is a plucky, independent teenage girl who lives with her father, lawyer Carson Drew. Armed with her trusty flashlight, Nancy relies on her avid reading to help her solve mysteries. The original series were written between 1930 and 1979.

· · · · ·

Someone Was Watching, David Patneaude

A mystery in the style of the Hardy Boys books, *Someone Was Watching* outlines the adventures of Chris and his best friend, Pat, who fly to Florida to rescue his three-year-old sister, presumably drowned, whom Chris believes is still alive.

Uncovering Sadie's Secrets, Libby Sternberg
Nancy Drew fans will love 15-year-old Bianca Balducci, who investigates why her new classmate, Sadie, is being stalked. Bianca's older sister, Connie, is a private investigator, but leave it to Bianca to uncover secrets about Sadie's past.

· · · · ·

The Beekeeper's Apprentice, Laurie R King
The "retired" Sherlock Holmes teams up with a bright, orphaned, teenage girl named Mary Russell to solve a kidnapping case. The relationship between the famous old detective and the spunky American girl enlivens the adventure, as they solve crimes no one else can solve.

The First 5 Nancy Drew Books

1. *The Secret of the Old Clock*
2. *The Hidden Staircase*
3. *The Bungalow Mystery*
4. *The Mystery at Lilac Inn*
5. *The Secret of Shadow Ranch*

The First 5 Hardy Boys Books

1. *The Tower Treasure*
2. *The House on the Cliff*
3. *The Secret of the Old Mill*
4. *The Missing Chums*
5. *Hunting for Hidden Gold*

"from books to movies for 400, please, alex."

Category: Romance

Cold Mountain, Charles Frazier
The Notebook, Nicholas Sparks
The English Patient, Michael Ondaatje
Terms of Endearment, Larry McMurtry
The Bridges of Madison County, Robert Waller
The Prince of Tides, Pat Conroy

Category: Science Fiction

War of the Worlds, H. G. Wells
Stardust, Neil Gaimon
The Time Machine, H. G. Wells
Andromeda Strain, Michael Chriton
Contact, Carl Sagan
A Clockwork Orange, Anthony Burgess

Common Phrases and Their Origins

Phrase: Diamond in the rough
Meaning: A person or thing that has potential or value but lacks outward polish, appearance or credentials.
Origin: The first recorded usage of the phrase was in John Fletcher's *Wife for a Month* in 1624. The phrase was used to describe a "rough" woman with the potential for becoming as valuable and cherished as a diamond.

• • • • •

Phrase: Upper crust
Meaning: The more desireable or valuable part of something.
Origin: During the 1500s, bread was divided according to social class and status. Workers were allotted the burnt bottom of the loaf, family was given the middle, and guests were offered the top of the loaf, or the upper crust.

• • • • •

Phrase: Under the weather
Meaning: Feeling ill or sickly.
Origin: During rough seas and bad weather, passengers on seaborne ships often became seasick. Passengers would head below deck (or underneath the weather), both to escape the elements and to move to a more stable part of the ship, near the keel.

The Newer CLASSICS

The term "classic" doesn't necessarily have to mean 100 years old or written in Old English. There are many books written in the last few decades that are already being deemed as "classics" by the great critics and snobs of the literary world.

· · · · ·

Beloved, Toni Morrison (1987)
A densely written story of two slaves is representative of the slave narrative tradition but also covers themes such as sexual abuse.

· · · · ·

Kafka on the Shore, Haruki Murakami (2002)
A twist on popular culture and Shintoism recounts the story of one young man fleeing from an Oedipal curse and another with a strange capacity for locating cats.

· · · · ·

Middlesex, Jeffrey Eugenides (2002)
The novel spans eight decades of a family and tackles the subject of intersexuality, as well as growing up as a first-generation American.

· · · · ·

A Confederacy of Dunces, John Kennedy Toole (1980)
Following the experiences of an unemployed and obese protagonist who finds himself forced to comply with modern life, the novel provides readers with one of America's most memorable characters. The book wasn't published until 1980, over a decade after the author's suicide.

zoetrope: all-story
a literary link to the world of film

Launched in 1997 by Francis Ford Coppola, *Zoetrope: All-Story* is published quarterly and showcases only short stories and one-act plays by writers such as Mary Gaitskill, Elizabeth McCracken, Don DeLillo, Salman Rushdie, and Woody Allen. The caliber of the contributors has gained the magazine wide recognition in the literary world. In each edition of the journal is a feature called Classic Reprint, which reproduces a previously published story that inspired a modern film, for instance, Steven Millhauser's "Eisenheim the Illusionist," which inspired Neil Burger's film *The Illusionist*. In addition, the magazine invites a new contemporary artist to design every issue. Past issues have been designed by Gus Van Sant, Tom Waits, and Chip Kidd.

Online Literary Magazines

Popping up in cyberspace, many literary magazines are now showcasing literature online in the form of literary "web-zines", magazines that can either be viewed entirely on a webpage or downloaded in PDF form. This method cuts the cost of printing and distributing magazines, making the material more accessible to a larger number of readers.

One notable web-zine, McSweeney's Internet Tendency, *is one of four online publications produced by McSweeney's Publishing House, which was started by Dave Eggers, author of the best-selling novel* A Heartbreaking Work of Staggering Genius. *Updated regularly, the web-zine is a hub for humor in the form of essays, sestinas, lists, short fiction, and letters to the editor and has featured the likes of Stephen King, Joyce Carol Oates, and Robert Coover.*

pangrams, lipograms, palindromes *oh my!*

Wordsmiths like to play with words and letters and in doing so can sometimes come up with interesting combinations. Concocting pangrams, lipograms, and palindromes is one way that writers manipulate words to their own satisfaction. Through this play, sets of rules have evolved about letters of the alphabet and their unique arrangements.

• • • • •

Pangrams

A pangram is a grammatically correct sentence that uses all of the letters of the alphabet. The most common example of a pangram is the following sentence: The quick brown fox jumps over the lazy dog. This sentence uses each letter of the alphabet at least once, though it does repeat the *e, h, o, r, t,* and *u.* Wordsmiths attempt to craft sentences using each letter of the alphabet only once, but it becomes more and more difficult to make a coherent sentence when less letters are used.

In case you might be wondering how many words are *possible,* the 26 letters of the English alphabet can be combined in 403,290,000,000,000,000,000,000,000 different ways. Some words, such as *quick* and *quiz,* which utilize several uncommon letters, often pop up in pangrams. Here are a few to consider.

Two driven jocks help fax my big quiz.
Cozy sphinx waves quart jug of bad milk.
Jack quietly moved up front and seized the big ball of wax.
A quick movement of the enemy will jeopardize six gunboats.

Lipograms

Writers who form lipograms intentionally leave out a letter, or more than one letter, to craft sentences or even paragraphs. Many times, in order to follow the rules, the writer must leave out common words, substituting lesser known or obscure words to avoid using the targeted letter. In the most challenging lipograms, wordsmiths attempt to leave out the letter *e*.

- Ernest Vincent Wright and Georges Perec are two writers both known for crafting novels that completely excluded the letter *e*.
- Wright's *Gadsby* was published in 1939, and Perec's *A Void* (*La Disparition*) was published in 1969.
- Perec was a member of the French literary group Oulipo, whose mission was to form constrained literary texts using techniques such as lipograms.

In a popular Simpsons *episode titled "Burns' Heir," Montgomery Burns forces Lenny Leonard to give an explanation of why he should be able to keep his job. This sounds common. However, Burns requires that Lenny deliver the entire proposal without using the letter e. Lenny's response is, "Um, I'm a good...work...guy." Though he succeeds at the lipogram challenge, he's fired anyway.*

... **And Palindromes**

Ben Jonson, a 17th-century writer, coined the word *palindrome* to describe a word, phrase, or number that reads the same from the left as it does from the right. Although they have been around since at least AD 79, wordsmiths still enjoy finding palindromes in all languages.

Some common word palindromes include:
- civic
- noon
- did
- kayak
- solos
- level
- radar

Some word sequences form palindromes, which may be read letter by letter, as in the first example, or word by word, as in the second example:

- A man, a plan, a canal—Panama
- Fall leaves after leaves fall

And some sentences form palindromes:

- Was it a rat I saw?
- Name no one, Man!
- I prefer pi.

Language purists say that palindromes must make coherent words or sentences. Giles Selig Hales created the world's longest palindrome that followed that rule in 1980. His famous palindrome consists of 58,795 letters. The longest palindrome word in the *Oxford English Dictionary* is *tattarrattat,* coined by James Joyce in *Ulysses,* meaning a knock on the door.

laughing with the bard

. . . .

The Two Gentlemen of Verona

Plot

Proteus and Valentine are the titular gentleman of the drama. They begin the story as good friends, but they become rivals for the lovely Silvia, daughter of the Duke of Milan. The duke wants her to marry the ridiculous and cowardly Thurio, but she would prefer not to. In his passion, Proteus leaves his old love, Julia, tricks Valentine, and eventually has him banished. Silvia runs away from her forced engagement to the forest, where she is joined by Valentine. Proteus follows in hot pursuit, along with his page, who is actually Julia in disguise. Proteus finds Silvia hiding out and is cruel to her, but Valentine rescues her and even forgives Proteus's violent tendencies. Silvia's father arrives in time to commend Valentine's bravery and to offer Silvia's hand in marriage. Proteus ends up marrying Julia after all.

Themes

1. Consistency is preferable to change. Proteus is named after a Greek prophet who could change his shape and appearance at will. In the play, Proteus changes his affections from Julia to Silvia and then back to Julia. Valentine's constancy is more admirable.
2. Father knows best, or does he? The Duke of Milan is wrong in expecting his daughter to marry a buffoon when someone worthy like Valentine is an available suitor.

quick & easy shakespeare

Troilus and Cressida

Plot

The play begins during the eighth year of the Trojan War. The Trojans and Greeks have called a cease-fire, and Troilus, a Trojan prince, seizes the opportunity to pursue the affections of Cressida, daughter of the soothsayer Calchas. At first she acts uninterested in Troilus, but soon her uncle, Pandarus, helps arrange a meeting, wherein the two lovers consummate their relationship. Elsewhere, Calchas has offered to exchange Cressida for a Trojan prisoner. The Greek warrior Diomedes takes her to the Greek camp and falls in love with her. Continuing with their truce, the Greeks and Trojans feast together, and Troilus learns that Cressida has been sleeping with Diomedes. The war rages again when Achilles' best friend is killed by the Trojan hero Hector. Achilles then kills Hector and drags his corpse around the city in a gesture of profound disrespect. Feeling disrespected as well by Cressida, Troilus returns to Troy after losing his horse to Diomedes.

Themes

1. Know thyself. The real tragedy of the play rests in the major characters' complete unawareness of who they are. Troilus, Cressida, and Achilles never recognize their own faults, nor does Troilus even recognize how fickle Cressida is.
2. Beware love at first sight. Although *Romeo and Juliet* attests to the power of immediate attraction, Troilus and Cressida do not love each other as deeply after the infatuation wears off. Cressida seems resigned to live with Diomedes. She even gives him a gift that Troilus had originally given her, describing Troilus as one "that loved me better than you will."

neologism:
a word coined for coined words

Neologisms refer to words coined to describe existing situations, sometimes for the purpose of modernizing older terms. New inventions or phenomena often require neologisms, since there are typically no preexisting simple terms that can quantify new developments.

> *The word* neologism *was coined in the early 19th century, becoming a neologism itself!*

E-mail as an example, describes a new form of communication for which older terminology applied to mail and written communication was considered inappropriate. Other, more technical terms are *radar* (1941) and *black hole* (1960).

Neologisms can be formed within a number of categories where developments and transitions of thought require new terminology.

In the field of science, the following words can be regarded as neologisms:

- Black hole: coined in 1960
- Prion: coined in 1982
- Radar: coined in 1941

In the field of science fiction writing, new concepts are created that require matter-of-fact names. Perhaps the most famous is the coining of the word *robot* in a play by Czech writer Karel Capek titled *Rossum's Universal Robots*. Other examples include: *ansible*, coined in 1966 by Ursula K. Le Guin in the novel *Rocannon's World*, a machine used for faster-than-light communication; *phaser*, coined in the original *Star Trek* series, for a fictitious laser weapon; and x*enocide*, coined in the 1990s by Orson Scott Card in his famous *Ender's Game* series, for describing genocide performed on aliens.

Neologisms abound in classical literature and have consistently enriched the English language, as these words demonstrate:

- quixotic – Miguel de Cervantes, *Don Quixote*
- serendipity – Horace Walpole, *The Three Princes of Serendip*
- moron – Jean Baptiste Poquelin, *La Princesse d'Elide*
- vulpine – Ben Johnson, *Volpone*
- gargantuan – Francois Rabelais, *Gargantua*
- ogre – Charles Perrault, *Contes*

Did You Know?

Jules Verne's publishers often told him his anti-Semitism and pessimistic views of human progress were too dark for his readers. Publisher Pierre-Jules Hetzel changed the endings of several of Verne's books to lighten the mood:

- Mysterious Island *(1874) – Verne's original ending for his tale of Americans stranded in the South Pacific described survivors as living the rest of their lives nostalgically, missing the island. Hetzel rewrote them as heroes who build a replica of the island so they can live happily ever after.*

- Twenty Thousand Leagues Under the Sea *(1870) – In Verne's first draft, the valiant Captain Nemo was introduced as a Polish noble, bitter that his family had been murdered under Russian oppression from 1863–1864. Hetzel feared Russia would ban the book and upset its ally, France, and instead described Nemo as a Hindu who resents the British for their conquest of India.*

leo tolstoy: *a literary surprise*

It might be surprising to find out that Leo Tolstoy was actually a failed student who eventually dropped out of his university after only a few short months. He did, however, become intrigued by such great authors as Charles Dickens, Rousseau, and Voltaire during his short studies, and he developed a further interest in reading and writing outside the setting of academia.

- Tolstoy's first book, *Childhood*, the first of his autobiographical trilogy, was published as a series in the magazine *Sovremennik* in 1852.
- Later, while fighting in the Crimean War, Tolstoy wrote *Sevastopol Sketches*, which was published in *The Contemporary*, another well-known magazine of the time.
- Perhaps one of Tolstoy's most well-known works, *War and Peace*, is said to have been written with much help from Tolstoy's wife, Sofia "Sonya" Andreyevna Behrs. Although she bore 13 children, Sonya still managed to help Tolstoy extensively in the business side of things, organizing and managing his drafts, corresponding with publishers and magazines, and taking care of the estate. Her help enabled Tolstoy to complete six volumes of commentary on war and aristocratic society, which were later published over a period of years between 1865 and 1869.
- Another famous Tolstoy novel, *Anna Karenina*, is considered by many literary scholars to be the greatest novel ever written. Tolstoy referred to it as his first real novel. The work is one of the earliest examples known of stream-of-consciousness writing, weaving fiction and real events together in a clever and innovative fashion.
- Tolstoy's biting commentary was not restricted to fiction and prose. He also wrote numerous articles criticizing the government and church, which eventually led to his excommunication by the Russian Orthodox Church. Despite the controversy Tolstoy stirred

with the church, his rants served to increase his popularity with the public. By the turn of the century, Tolstoy had a large following of admiring readers.

- Like many famous writers of the period, Tolstoy eventually turned to pacifism and embraced the teachings of Christianity near the end of his life. He gave up meat, tobacco, and alcohol, and his writing transformed drastically. In 1893, he wrote a long commentary based on the Gospel of Luke. The resulting work, *The Kingdom of God Is Within You,* helped to form a friendship between Tolstoy and Mahatma Gandhi.

- By 1910, Tolstoy had adopted extreme religious beliefs and alienated the majority of his family. In October of that year, he left his home and set out to make a new life for himself. However, only a month later, on November 20, 1910, he died of pneumonia. Thousands of admirers mourned the loss of an accomplished author. Nearly a century later, in a January 2007 issue of *Time* magazine, two of Tolstoy's novels, *Anna Karenina* and *War and Peace,* were named in a list of the ten greatest novels of all time.

Did You Know?

After flunking out of one private high school as a young man, author J. D. Salinger studied at Valley Forge Military Academy in Pennsylvania. One year he got an 88 in English, 88 in French, 76 in German, 79 in history, and 88 in dramatics. His IQ was tested as 115, and he was a member of the glee club, aviation club, and French club, as well as the literary editor of the yearbook. He began writing short stories by flashlight under the covers after 'lights out' and dreamed of one day selling them to Hollywood.

reading up on paper

The first paperlike substance was invented by the Egyptians around 4000 BC. Known as papyrus, it was made from a woven mat of reeds, pounded together into a thin sheet. Since then, of course, paper has evolved to become more efficiently mass-produced. A 2002 study showed that on average, the typical American office worker uses a sheet of paper every 12 minutes and disposes of around 100 to 200 pounds of paper per year.

- The word *paper* comes from the word *papyrus*.
- In AD 105, paper was made in China using mulberry bark, hemp, rags, and water.
- The first paper mill was established in North America in 1690. At this time, paper was made from old clothing and rags.
- Paper can be made from any plant, but some plants make sturdier and longer-lasting paper than others.
- In 1850, a method was created to make paper out of wood pulp.
- Brown paper bags, like the ones used to carry groceries, were invented in 1883. Today, more than 10 million paper bags are used each year.
- Though large machinery is now used to make paper, the process is still much the same as it was in AD 105.
- The United States is the biggest producer and consumer of paper worldwide, followed by Japan.
- To achieve a glossier look and to make printing easier, some papers are coated with clay, the first material used to make writing tablets.

william faulkner: *a side story*

It might be surprising to know that in the later years of his writing career, William Faulkner, author of such famous titles as *As I Lay Dying* and *Light in August,* worked in Hollywood as a motion picture screenwriter. Faulkner was in search of a way to improve his financial state, and moved to the starry city in the 1930s. In fact, his tenure there actually served as inspiration for the title character, screenwriter Barton Fink, in the Coen brothers film of the same name.

What might be more well known about William Faulkner is the struggle with alcoholism he endured throughout his career, a problem that interfered with his ability and success in the movie industry. However, during his time in Hollywood, Faulkner established a few notable relationships, such as acquaintances with Humphrey Bogart and Howard Hawks and a close friendship with Clark Gable, a relationship that was later documented in a biography by M. Thomas Inge.

During his Hollywood stay, Faulkner produced scripts for Ernest Hemingway's *To Have and Have Not* and Raymond Chandler's *The Big Sleep*. Howard Hawks, director of both films, worked closely with Faulkner—until the author was stricken with a case of writer's block that eventually resulted in his move back to Mississippi, where he focused again on more literary projects.

banning, burning, and burying...
almost: joyce's *ulysses*

Though it was long regarded as one of the most impressive novels ever penned in English, and though it was listed on one of the Radcliffe Publishing Course "Top 100 Novels of the 20th Century," James Joyce's *Ulysses* almost never made it into publication in this country. Banned by US customs in 1921, the book became one of the most commonly smuggled texts from Europe to North America. Customs agents eventually began ignoring the text completely, as they were so used to seeing contraband copies coming through customs.

Though today relatively anything can be published through publishing houses or online venues, this has not always been the case. Censorship in the early part of the 20th century was so rampant that publishing novels was something quite difficult to do without facing many obstacles. A group known as the New York Society for the Suppression of Vice attempted to censor anything they labeled as "immoral." The group prohibited all "sensualist" material, much of which later became part of the literary canon. *Ulysses* was caught by the society when printed in *The Little Review* by publishers Margaret Anderson and Kate Heap. The two were accused of obscenity, and the book was banned nationwide.

At the time, Joyce had already been blacklisted in Ireland, though the book became quite popular to the European audience as the book slid through the bars of censorship for illegal distribution. When the illegal distribution of the novel spread to the United States, readers eagerly consumed the unauthorized copies. Bennett Cerf, an editor at Random House, decided that something should be done about the contradiction between the public acceptance and desire for the novel and its illegality and censorship. In 1933, Cerf and his partner, Donald Klopfer, arranged to have a copy of *Ulysses* combined with favorable reviews from European journals and then snuck into the United States. However, they insisted that the copy be seized and brought to trial in order to gain widespread public attention. The result was a trial labeled *United States Southern District of New York v. One Book Called "Ulysses,"* in which it was concluded that the book was not, in fact, sensualist, and all bans were lifted. This important trial set a precedent for American publishing, opening the doors to freedom of speech and expression in print.

Did You Know?

While researching for In Cold Blood, *Truman Capote became pen pals with two criminals on death row. From him they requested a dictionary and a thesaurus and wanted their descriptions of prison life to be accurate and sound smart. But their verbage was superfluous, as one wrote that he had "many diverse subjects I am desirous to discuss."*

anagrams

. . . .

An anagram is formed by rearranging the letters of a word or phrase to produce new words or a phrase. For example, the phrase a *decimal point* can be rearranged to say *I'm a dot in place*, using every letter in the original phrase. A person who creates anagrams—and there are such people—is called an anagrammist. While a simple rearrangement of letters to create another word is referred to as an anagram, the goal of most anagrammists is to create a new word or phrase that actually relates to or reflects on the subject of the original. For instance, the word *army* can be arranged to spell *Mary*, but the anagram does not reflect on the subject of the original word. However, the word *dormitory* rearranged to make *dirty room* does.

A few notable anagrams follow:

> *The Morse Code* = *Here Come Dots*
> *Slot Machines* = *Cash Lost in 'em*
> *Mother-in-law* = *Woman Hitler*
> *Semolina* = *Is No Meal*
> *The Eyes* = *They See*

Some anagrams actually are designed to make a witty response or commentary about the original word, phrase, or person, as in:

Frequently asked questions = Quit! End one's flaky requests
George Bush = He bugs Gore

Novel, Novella, Novelette

Just like *novel*, the word *novella* comes from the Italian *novella*, meaning "tale." A novella typically refers to a work of fictional prose that is longer than a short story but shorter than what might be considered a novel. The exact definition or length is typically determined within a specific book genre. For instance, in science fiction writing, a novella is a fictional work that reaches a word count between 17,000 and 40,000 words, with anything over that being classified as a novel. In mainstream adult fiction, a full-length novel manuscript is generally considered to be at least 80,000 words or more, further blurring the lines. Most genres hold that a work that falls between 20,000 and 40,000 words is, indeed, a novella.

A Few Famous Novellas

> *A River Runs Through It*, Norman Maclean
> *Breakfast at Tiffany's*, Truman Capote
> *Anthem*, Ayn Rand
> *The Bicentennial Man*, Isaac Asimov
> *Animal Farm*, George Orwell
> *Heart of Darkness*, Joseph Conrad
> *Mrs. Dalloway*, Virginia Woolf
> *Of Mice and Men*, John Steinbeck
> *The Old Man and the Sea*, Ernest Hemingway
> *The Turn of the Screw*, Henry James
> *The Stranger*, Albert Camus

Much like a novella, a *novelette* is a short piece of prose fiction that is longer than a short story but shorter than a novella. A novelette can fall anywhere between 7,500 words and 20,000 words. The term can also be used in a negative way, to speak of novels or novellas that seem to "fall short" of standards, seeming trite or contrived. Novelettes tend to appear in the genre of science fiction more than in any other genre.

A Few Famous Novelettes

The Birds, Daphne du Maurier
Flat Diane, Daniel Abraham
A Colder War, Charles Stross

Heteronyms S–W

Sake *SAHkey* - Japanese rice wine; *SAYK* - a purpose
  For the sake of greater intoxication, let's order more sake.

Tear *TARE* - to rip apart; *TEER* - fluid in eye
  Bob, I know when I tear up your love letter, there will be a tear in your eye, but you'll get over me in time. If not, have some more sake.

Use *Yoost* - point or purpose, *YOOZ* - to employ
  "Luke, use the force," said Yoda. "What's the use?" asked a disaffected Luke.

Viola *vie-OH-la* - a purple flower; *vee-OH-la* - a stringed musical instrument
  Vivian played the viola with a viola in her hair.

Wound *WOOND* - to injure; *WOWND* - coiled up
  When the wound began to bleed, Bob wound a tourniquet around it.

shel silverstein
"recited, sung, and shouted"

Known for his poetry, illustrations, plays, screenwriting, and songwriting, Shel Silverstein is somewhat of an anomaly on the literary scene. Born in 1930 as Sheldon Allan Silverstein, he is often referred to as the most beloved children's author of all time, and his work has been distributed to tens of millions of readers internationally.

As a G.I. in Japan and Korea during the 1950s, Silverstein began drawing his first cartoons. Never planning to write for children, he took up other hobbies, such as guitar playing and songwriting. In the early 1960s, Silverstein was introduced to Harper Collins editor Ursula Nordstrom, which led to the publication of *The Giving Tree*. With more than five million copies sold, Silverstein's first book still tops best-seller lists in children's literature.

Where the Sidewalk Ends was published in 1974 as his first book of poems. Though the book was instantly popular, it was followed by *The Light in the Attic* in 1981 breaking records on the *New York Times* best-seller list, where it stayed for 182 weeks. Silverstein continued writing songs, poems, and stories until his death in 1999.

Successful at many arts, Silverstein's talents at songwriting paid him well. His song A Boy Named Sue *was a hit for Johnny Cash, and* I'm Checking Out, *which he wrote for the film* Postcards from the Edge, *was nominated for an Academy Award in 1991. Silverstein won a Grammy in 1984 for Best Children's Album with* Where the Sidewalk Ends. *Silverstein wrote songs for Waylon Jennings, Mel Tillis, and Jerry Reed as well.*

---

a poet to know: e. e. cummings

Edward Estlin Cummings, the self-styled e. e. cummings, was born in
1894 in Cambridge, Massachusetts, the son of a renowned political
science and sociology professor at Harvard University. It is said that
the "preaching voice" that he adopts in many of his poems is a voice
inspired by his father, who left Harvard in 1900 to become an ordained
minister. Attending Harvard himself to study languages—particularly
Greek—he was introduced to the writings of Ezra Pound, who became
one of his major influences. After college, he joined an ambulance
corps and met William Slater Brown, who was arrested for writing
incriminating letters and was sentenced to a concentration camp.
Cummings refused to be separated from Brown, and the two were
sent to the La Ferte Mace concentration camp together, but were later
freed because of the political pull of Cummings' father. As a result of
his experience, he wrote *The Enormous Room*, an account of his time at
the concentration camp. With its publication, along with many other
pieces of work over the next decade, he began to focus on his writing
and painting. After 1926, the year his father was killed in a car accident
and his mother gravely injured, Cummings moved to transform his
poetry to define more serious aspects of his life. After he himself died
in 1962 from a cerebral hemorrhage, three volumes of his poetry were
published posthumously. The poet left behind a considerable body of
work, at 25 books of poetry, prose, drawings, and plays.

a poet to know: langston hughes

When he was a mere eighth grader, Langston Hughes began writing poetry. His father discouraged poetry as a career but later agreed to pay Hughes' tuition to Columbia University, if he would pursue a career in engineering. Hughes soon dropped out of that program, but he continued writing poetry, publishing his first piece "The Negro Speaks of Rivers" in *Brownie's Book*. He later published poems, essays, and stories in many magazines. His essay titled "The Negro Artist and the Racial Mountain" appeared in the *Nation* in 1926, stirring controversy and gaining him widespread attention. The essay discussed the "false integration" of black writers or poets, arguing that many black writers wanted to write like white writers, and criticizing this trend. Hughes' controversial and outspoken attitude toward race in writing gained him popularity and acclaim, leading to over 16 books of poetry, three collections of short stories, four volumes of "documentary" fiction, 20 plays, two novels, three autobiographies and countless musicals, children's poems, and magazine articles. Some of his more famous collections of poetry include *The Big Sea*, *The Dream Keeper*, and *One Way Ticket*.

Langston Hughes died of cancer in the spring of 1967, leaving five plays to be posthumously published. His block of residence on East 127th Street in Harlem, New York, was renamed Langston Hughes Place in his honor.

what on earth is a KENNING?

Used to color or emphasize a theme or meaning, a kenning is a group of words used in the place of a noun, or a mundane object. That is, to strike a reader's attention, the writer might use the phrase *whale-road*, instead of *sea*, as the author of *Beowulf* did. Though most people use kennings at some point in conversation or in writing, they may not realize that they are utilizing a literary technique that began in the Norse and Celtic poetry of long ago, for the term derives from the Old Norse word *kenna*, "to know" or "recognize." Kennings are sometimes used to create very descriptive metaphors. For instance, the kenning *wound sea*, for *blood*, describes the blood in an almost violent way that suggests battle, or the spraying or pouring of the blood.

Kennings to Consider

Kenning: battle-sweat
Primary Meaning: blood

Kenning: feeder of ravens
Primary Meaning: warrior

Kenning: whale-road
Primary Meaning: the sea
    (Beowulf)

Kenning: sleep of the sword
Primary Meaning: death
    (Beowulf)

faulkner's first lines

- The jury said "Guilty" and the Judge said "Life" but he didn't hear them.
  - *The Mansion*
- Through the fence, between the curling flower spaces, I could see them hitting.
  - *The Sound and the Fury*
- For a full minute Jiggs stood before the window in a light spatter of last night's confetti lying against the windowbase like spent dirty foam, lightpoised on the balls of his greasestained tennis shoes, looking at the boots.
  - *Pylon*
- Long before the first bugles sounded from the barracks within the city and the cantonments surrounding it, most of the people in the city were already awake.
  - *A Fable*
- From beyond the screen of bushes which surrounded the spring, Popeye watched the man drinking.
  - *Requiem for a Nun*
- Grandfather said:
  This is the kind of man Boon Hogganbeck was. Hung on the wall, it could have been his epitaph, like a Bertillon chart or a police poster; any cop in north Mississippi would have arrested him out of any crowd after merely reading the date.
  - *The Bear*
- Sitting beside the road, watching the wagon mount the hill toward her, Lena thinks, 'I have come from Alabama: a fur piece. All the way from Alabama a-walking. A fur piece.'
  - *Light in August*
- Old man Falls roared: "Cunnel was settin' thar in a cheer, his sock feet propped on the po'ch railin', smokin' this hyer very pipe...."
  - *Flags in the Dust*

behind the scenes: **mark twain**

• •

- Radically against the dissection of living animals for scientific research, Mark Twain was known as a staunch vegetarian.
- Originally born Samuel Clemens, Twain had several pen names. These included Thomas Jefferson Snodgrass, Sergeant Fathom, Rambler, and W. Epaminondas Adrastus Blab.
- At age 14, Twain dropped out of John Dawson's school to concentrate on working for the *Hannibal Gazette* and later the *Hannibal Journal.*
- Twain frequently invested his money in inventions. He held three patents: an automatically self-adjusting vest strap, a memory-improving history game, and a self-pasting scrapbook.
- An outspoken opponent of organized religion, Twain wrote and posthumously published books on the subject, including *Letters from the Earth* and *The Mysterious Stranger.*
- Prior to starting his writing career, Twain, like many authors, held many jobs, including that of a steamboat pilot and a gold prospector.
- Although he briefly volunteered in the Confederate cavalry, Twain later became a staunch abolitionist.

closed for remodeling

George Bernard Shaw, author of *Pygmalion*, often vented his anger at social injustice through sardonic novels and plays. One of his famous plays, *Closed for Remodeling*, nearly ruined the Savoy Theatre in the London city of Westminster.

A loud opponent of Britain's involvement in World War I, Shaw had stirred controversy and lost readers because of his political dissent, and he had nearly been tried for treason. At this turning point, his plays had become consistently more critical of society and government. During World War I, theatres had been closed in London, leaving crowds eagerly waiting for the stage play to return. In a reaction to his recent public criticism, Shaw opened his new play, titled *Closed for Remodeling*, and waited. Everyone in the business was excited about the triumphant return of the theatre and the Savoy eagerly booked Shaw's newest piece. The show opened but, night after night, with little to no turnout. After three weeks of no revenue, Savoy managers realized the prank that had been pulled; the name *Closed for Remodeling*, posted all over London, had led would-be patrons to believe that the playhouse was in a state of renovation and therefore closed to the public.

When approached by the producers of the show, Shaw denied any malevolence on his part. He agreed to change the name of the show to *Heartbreak House*, and the Savoy opened to a still-eager, large audience. The show continues, to this day, to be billed by that name.

· · · · ·

Shaw's Sarcasm
- Beauty is all very well at sight, but who can look at it when it has been in the house three days?
- The fact that a believer is happier than a skeptic is no more to the point than the fact that a drunken man is happier than a sober one.

- Martyrdom…is the only way in which a man can become famous without ability (from *The Devil's Disciple*).
- It is dangerous to be sincere unless you are also stupid (from *Maxims for Revolutionists*).
- The reasonable man adapts himself to the world; the unreasonable one persists in trying to adapt the world to himself. Therefore all progress depends on the unreasonable man (from *Maxims for Revolutionists*).
- A government that robs Peter to pay Paul can always depend on the support of Paul (from *Everybody's Political What's What*).

Three Things You Never Knew About: Stephen King

- *When he was a child, his mom worked in the kitchen of a mental institution.*

- *Although he generally writes using an Apple computer, he wrote the first draft of* Dreamcatcher *with a notepad and a fountain pen.*

- *He reads for four hours a day and writes for four hours a day. It is the only way to become a good writer, he says.*

---

what is a copyright?

A copyright is a legal concept that gives a person full and exclusive rights to a piece of created work. That person may be the author of the work, a beneficiary, a company, or an organization.

Copyrights were originally intended as a way for governments to restrict the printing of material, but in most cases today, copyrights are used to ensure that authors have the ability to control and profit from their original work for a period of time. The length of a copyright is today standardized internationally and in most cases lasts for 50 to 100 years after the death of the creator.

- Ideas cannot be copyrighted; only written material is copyrightable.
- A person "owns" the rights to his or her written text even if that person has not filed for a copyright. By registering a copyright with the Library of Congress, the rights to your work can be upheld in any court.
- In the United States, copyright owners, to receive special benefits, are required to renew their copyright after 28 years have passed.
- Also, in the United States, any books or works published before 1923 are considered to be public domain, since their copyrights have expired.

Copyleft

A copyleft is the process of uncopyrighting a work, or making it free for use by the public, that is, making it part of the public domain.

---

charles dickens & *maria beadnall*

Biographies have exposed that young Charles Dickens experienced a severe heartbreak when the object of his affection, Maria Beadnall, discovered that he was not of wealthy heritage. Not yet a great writer, Dickens was hardworking but poor. When she realized his background, she rejected him and left in pursuit of more opulent enterprises. Dickens eventually became one of the most famous men in Europe and the Americas. He also married, but biographies suggest that his marriage was not stable. According to legend, Beadnall returned to pay Dickens a visit, knowing that he was now famous and quite wealthy. Dickens' wealth had exploded, and his reputation had become internationally known, but his old crush had grown herself, but in a different way. Over the years, Maria Beadnall had gained considerable weight, so much weight, in fact, that Dickens didn't recognize her when she darkened his doorway so many years after leaving him heartbroken.

Though Dickens is known as one of the great novelists, most of his stories were published in serials, rather than in the traditional novel format. The anticipation caused by the popularity of the 19th-century serial is comparable to that of the recent Harry Potter craze, and J. K. Rowling has often been publicly compared to Dickens for this very reason.

Thoughts on Charles Dickens

- "Dickens is one of those authors who are well worth stealing."
  – novelist and essayist George Orwell, from *Charles Dickens*
- "My mother read secondarily for information; she sank as a hedonist into novels. She read Dickens in the spirit in which she would have eloped with him."
  – novelist Eudora Welty, from *One Writer's Beginnings*

virginia woolf
and the dreadnought *hoax*

In the early 20th century, controversy surrounded the Bloomsbury collective of artists and writers, because of their suspected hedonistic lifestyle and antiwar sentiments. The members of the group, which included, most notably, Virginia Woolf, spent much of their time engrossed in cultural endeavors; however, they also occasionally gained attention with high-profile pranks. One famous incident made history. On February 10, 1910, the British navy received a telegram announcing the imminent arrival of a group of dignitaries who wished to tour a warship. Shortly thereafter, a group of well-dressed dignitaries from Abyssinia approached Britain's most secret warship, the HMS *Dreadnought*. After being introduced as princes of Abyssinia, the assembly embarked on an incredibly exclusive tour of the ship. In reality, the group consisted of Virginia Woolf and other Bloomsbury members dressed in fine costumes and phony beards and speaking in a mixture of Swahili and Latin, all without arousing suspicion from their tour guides. The pranksters immortalized their trick by having a photograph printed in the *Daily Mirror*. The picture embarrassed the navy and resulted in the caning of one of the participants and national attention for the Bloomsbury members.

> *Virginia Woolf has actually been mentioned in the lyrics of several rock songs, perhaps because of her restless spirit and tumultuous life. She appears in songs from bands including the Indigo Girls, Modest Mouse, and Assembly Now.*

laughing with the bard

. . . .

Twelfth Night
Plot

Twin siblings, Viola and Sebastian, are shipwrecked off the coast of Illyria. Each believes the other to be dead. Viola lands ashore, disguises herself as a boy, and takes the name Cesario. She becomes the page of Duke Orsino, who is desperately in love with Olivia, who has sworn off men while she mourns for her dead brother. When the duke sends Cesario to try to woo Olivia for him, she instantly falls in love with Viola in disguise, thinking that she is a man. At about this time, Sebastian comes to the island, and Olivia, thinking he is Cesario, marries him. Once Viola and Sebastian are reunited, Viola is free to marry the duke, who realizes that all along he has been in love with her. In a comedic subplot, Olivia's manservant, Malvolio, rules with an iron fist over the rest of the household. To pay him back for his pomposity, Olivia's maid and her uncle devise a scheme to humiliate him. He thinks Olivia is actually in love with him and wants him to wear ridiculous yellow stockings. Once her love for Cesario is revealed, Malvolio learns a lesson about humility.

Themes

1. Seize the moment. No one thinks it unusual that Olivia falls in love with Cesario at first sight or that she continues to stay married to Sebastian once she learns that she doesn't actually know him. As the Fool wisely says, "What's to come is still unsure. In delay there lies no plenty," so she and the other characters often act impetuously.
2. Appearance vs. reality. Many characters appear to be one thing but, in reality, are something else. Viola appears male. The Fool appears foolish. The wise characters learn to look beneath the surface of things to discern the truth.

quick & easy shakespeare

The Winter's Tale

Plot

King Leontes invites Polixenes, the king of Bohemia, to Sicilia, but he grows jealous when Queen Hermione asks Polixenes to stay longer. He orders a Sicilian lord named Camillo to poison Polixenes, but instead Camillo runs away with Polixenes to Bohemia. Furious, Leontes imprisons Hermione and orders her baby girl to be cast aside on a deserted shore. Hermione, fainting, is reported dead. Eventually Leontes grows remorseful of his harsh actions and sinks into grief. Sixteen years later, Polixenes' son, Florizel, falls in love with Perdita, Leontes' long-lost daughter, who was raised by a shepherd near Bohemia. When Polixenes, ironically, forbids Florizel to marry a shepherdess, the lovers run away to Sicilia. There the identity of Perdita is revealed and the couple marry. Polixenes and Leontes become friends again, and Hermione happily comes out of seclusion.

Themes

1. Beware jealousy. Leontes' terrible jealousy sets the plot in motion and is responsible for much suffering throughout the drama.
2. Social standing should not impede true love. Florizel and Perdita love each other and almost have to live apart because of his father's class snobbery.

some of the *most commonly misspelled words*

· ·

These words, spelled correctly here, can have the most seasoned of writers consulting their dictionaries.

cemetery	minuscule
conscience	occurrence
conscious	perseverance
definitely	privilege
embarrass	receipt
guarantee	separate
inoculate	sergeant
liaison	twelfth
maintenance	until

Common 2-Letter Words to Know

In the game of Scrabble, having an arsenal of two-letter words handy is a way to ensure a high score, since two-letter words allow a player to build two words at once, or to build words alongside others already on the board.

aa	jo
ar	mm
er	op
fa	om
hm	oy
id	wo

---

random *literary trivia*

Here is a chunk of trivia you can use to show your smarts and spice up your conversations.

- Author Robert May wrote "Rudolph, the Red-nosed Reindeer" in 1939. While brainstorming the story, he initially considered naming the famed reindeer Rollo or Reginald.
- At the age of 14, Anna Sewell fell while walking home from school in the rain, injuring both her ankles. The injury was likely not treated correctly, and she became lame for the rest of her life, unable to stand or walk for any length of time. For greater mobility, she frequently used horse-drawn carriages, which contributed to her love of horses and concern for the humane treatment of animals. As she wrote *Black Beauty*, she dictated the text to her mother or wrote on slips of paper that her mother later compiled.
- Ralph Ellison's favorite books as a child were *Wuthering Heights, The Last of the Mohicans,* and *Jude the Obscure.*
- "Tintern Abbey" was one of the only poems William Wordsworth ever wrote that he didn't completely change through revisions and editing.
- *Pride and Prejudice* author Jane Austen was so humble and shy about her writing that no one ever caught her with a pen in hand. "No matter how suddenly one arrives, she has heard the door close...and hidden the white sheets," writes biographer Virginia Moore.
- *Pride and Prejudice* was originally titled *First Impressions.*
- Pippi Longstocking's full name is Pippilotta Provisionia Gaberdina Dandeliona Ephraimsdaughter Longstocking.
- When *Treasure Island* author Robert Louis Stevenson died in 1894, he put in his will that his November 13 birthday be gifted to a friend who hated her Christmas birthday.

child prodigy: dorothy straight

Born in Washington, DC, in 1958, Dorothy Straight penned her first, and apparently last, masterpiece at the tender age of four. The book, *How the World Began,* started as a gift to her grandmother and ended up in print, thanks to publishing house Pantheon Books in 1964, just after Dorothy's sixth birthday. After the initial press run, the book lost its steam. Less than 50 libraries and special collection throughout the United States have the text in their catalogs, and although a copy has been retained in the collection of the Library of Congress, little Dorothy's entry has been excluded from their most recent catalog. There are so few of the books in circulation today, that sellers can actually command hundreds of dollars for a copy. Dorothy Straight has not published any books since her short-lived *How the World Began.*

Susan Eloise Hinton, writing as S. E. Hinton, began The Outsiders, *a novel about gangs and male rivalry, at age 15. She used her initials instead of her name so that boys wouldn't disregard it as a book for girls. Since its publication in 1967, it has become one of the most popular books for young readers.*

who wrote it?
try to match the author with the famous title
· ·

1. *A Tale of Two Cities*	A. Edgar Allan Poe
2. *Utopia*	B. Truman Capote
3. *1984*	C. Sir Thomas More
4. *The Grapes of Wrath*	D. Harper Lee
5. *The Great Gatsby*	E. Victor Hugo
6. *Gulliver's Travels*	F. Sophocles
7. *Wuthering Heights*	G. George Bernard Shaw
8. *The Old Man and the Sea*	H. Louisa May Alcott
9. *The Taming of the Shrew*	I. Ernest Hemingway
10. *Pygmalion*	J. F. Scott Fitzgerald
11. *Little Women*	K. Jonathan Swift
12. *Les Misérables*	L. Emily Brontë
13. *Oedipus the King*	M. Charles Dickens
14. *The Telltale Heart*	N. ohn Steinbeck
15. *In Cold Blood*	O. George Orwell
16. *To Kill a Mockingbird*	P. William Shakespeare

Answers: 1-M, 2-C, 3-O, 4-N, 5-J, 6-K, 7-L, 8-I, 9-P, 10-G, 11-H, 12-E, 13-F, 14-A, 15-B, 16-D

a poet to know: john ashbery

Born in Rochester, New York, in 1927, John Ashbery was a child of
the Great Depression and the oldest son of his family. His family was
well-to-do and was able to send him to Massachusetts at age 16 to
attend a boarding school. At an early age, Ashbery had begun writing
poetry, and he had two of his poems published in the prestigious
magazine *Poetry* while he was in boarding school at Deerfield Academy.
Publishing more poems while at Harvard, studying English, Ashbery
became acquainted with mentors and editors Robert Bly, Donald Hall,
and Kenneth Koch, who ran the *Harvard Advocate.* Soon, Ashbery
joined the editorial board of the magazine and then later became its
leader. Upon graduating from Harvard, he went to Columbia University
for his master's in English. He began a career in publishing, working as
a copywriter and then for a book company.

Ashbery had become acquainted with many New York artists
while at Columbia, and so when his first slender chapbook of poetry
was published, it was illustrated by artist Jane Frielicher, with whom
Ashbery had become friends. In the following years, Ashbery won
the prestigious Fulbright fellowship, which enabled him to go to Paris
for study. He later won awards from Yale University Press and two
Guggenheim fellowships, one of the most prestigious awards a poet
can gain.

Ashbery served as the New York State poet laureate from 2001 to
2003 and now lives in Hudson, New York, where he teaches at Bard
College.

c. s. lewis *(1898-1963)*

Born in Belfast, Ireland, Clive Staples Lewis was an imaginative child, often writing and illustrating adventurous stories about animals. With his brother, Warnie, Lewis created Boxen, a mythical world that was ruled by animals. As a teenager, he began to write operas and epic poetry and developed a serious interest in Norse mythology, which later influenced his most famous work, *The Chronicles of Narnia*. Lewis is well known for the Christian parallels in his works and is widely studied by scholars of literature and Christian symbolism. *The Chronicles of Narnia*, has been translated in over 40 languages, and portions have been adapted into several movies and animated cartoons.

Lewis was a close friend of J. R. R. Tolkien, the author of *The Lord of the Rings*. They taught together at Oxford University and led a literary group called the Inklings. During his friendship with Tolkien, Lewis returned to the church. He had been an atheist between the ages of 13 and 31, when his interests drifted toward the occult and pagan ideas. Under the influence of Tolkien, however, Lewis was reunited with Christianity. In 1931, he joined the Church of England, although Tolkien was a devout Catholic and had encouraged Lewis toward Catholicism. Afterward, he began doing radio broadcasts about Christianity and gained a wide following of listeners. Lewis died in November 1963 and was buried in the churchyard of Holy Trinity Church in Oxford.

The Inklings, Lewis and Tokien's famous literary group, met on weekday evenings at the University of Oxford between the 1930s and 1960s. Members included writers Owen Barfield, Adam Fox, Charles Williams, and C. E. Stephens. The Inklings were encouraged to write fantasy fiction, and although Christian values often appear in both Lewis and Tolkien's fantasy works, many of the members of the Inklings were in fact atheists.

what a way to go: literary deaths

Think of the tragic final swoons of Romeo and Juliet. Recall Desdemona's brutal murder at the hands of her jealous husband. Famous authors can imagine a host of interesting ways to die, but all too often their own deaths were a bit odd, to say the least.

· · · · ·

Sherwood Anderson

Best known for his 1919 collection, *Winesburg, Ohio*, Anderson did not meet his end in that fabled state. No, he died of peritonitis after swallowing a toothpick. Really. During a trip to the Panama Canal in the spring of 1941, the writer and author of many famous American short stories, Anderson swallowed the fatal toothpick, leaving behind a legacy of storytelling of small-town America.

· · · · ·

Tennessee Williams

Another writer to get "all choked up," major 20th-century playwright and Pulitzer-winner Tennessee Williams died of choking on the cap of an eyedrop bottle. It was said that he frequently placed the cap in his mouth while leaning back to insert the eyedrops, but still, his close friends and family were suspicious of foul play and believed that he could have been murdered. The police report showed that there were many prescription drugs found in the room, as well as alcohol, which could have contributed to his inability to recover from the choking. Williams left behind famous works such as *The Glass Menagerie, Cat on a Hot Tin Roof,* and *A Streetcar Named Desire.*

Francis Bacon

No doubt a genius of the 17th century, Francis Bacon laid the groundwork for the scientific method. However, no amount of logic can explain his unusual death. During a snowy night in 1626, he came up with what he thought was a great idea. What if he stuffed a dead chicken with snow? Would it preserve the bird for future cooking? Like Julia Child on a mission, he stuffed the carcass bare-handed, but unfortunately, he caught a chill. Within a week he died of pneumonia. Historian Thomas Macaulay summed up the whole sad situation best, "The great apostle of experimental philosophy was destined to be its martyr."

• • • • •

Arnold Bennett

In 1923, Bennett had this to say about fiction writing, "If the characters are real, the novel will have a chance; if they are not, oblivion will be its portion." Eight years later, Bennett met his own oblivion by trying to prove a different point. Seated in a Parisian café, he was trying to show that the water was safe to drink. A few sips later, he caught typhoid and died within weeks.

• • • • •

Molière (Jean-Baptiste Poquelin)

In 1673, French playwright Molière learned once and for all what the phrase "life imitates art" meant. On the night of February 17, he was performing the role of the hypochondriac Argan in his play *The Imaginary Invalid*. While legend has it he died on stage, the truth is that, despite suffering a hemorrhage, he continued his performance. "There are fifty poor workers who have only their daily wage to live on. What will become of them if the performance does not take place?" he asked. He died later that night, with priests refusing to take the confession of an actor.

Rainer Maria Rilke

Famous poet and essayist Rainer Maria Rilke died at the young age of 51 from possible blood poisoning. According to his own rumor, he was cut by the thorn of a rose he had picked for a woman. At any rate, shortly before his death, Rilke had already been diagnosed with leukemia, and his heath was deteriorating. He wrote his own epitaph and left behind over 400 poems and two very famous prose pieces, *Letters to a Young Poet* and *The Notebooks of Malte Laurids Brigge*.

• • • • •

D. H. Lawrence

Ashes to ashes, dust to dust…France to New Mexico. So it went for novelist D. H. Lawrence. After contracting malaria and tuberculosis, the writer died in Vence, France, in 1930. Years later, his wife, Freida, moved to Taos, New Mexico, and she had her third husband brought Lawrence's ashes to a private chapel they had.

• • • • •

Percy Bysshe Shelley

Romantic poet Percy Shelley led a tempestuous life, and his death was no different. He drowned in 1822 and was cremated, but people at the cremation tried to grab parts of his remains from the flames. Fellow poet and friend Lord Byron wanted his skull, but it had disintegrated. Wife Mary, author of *Frankenstein*, stayed true to her macabre nature; she kept part of Shelley's heart with her the rest of her life. She wrapped it in silk and placed it in her traveling desk.

• • • • •

John Milton

A gruesome game of lost and found followed the death of the author of *Paradise Lost*. In 1790, Milton's grave was ransacked, and people were charged sixpence to steal a look at his teeth and leg.

George Bernard Shaw

Playwright of *Pygmalion* and *Mrs. Warren's Profession,* Shaw was vexed his whole life at how difficult spelling was. In his will, he set aside a large amount of his wealth to fund a new alphabet with phonetic spelling. He also wanted someone to estimate the cost in man-hours of how much money was wasted writing and printing in English with an alphabet of only 26 letters instead of the 40 letters he would prefer to see used. Ultimately, £8,300 from Shaw's estate was given toward the development of the new alphabet, though the idea still hasn't caught on.

More Wacky Writers

- *To please his father, William Golding enrolled in Oxford's Brasnose College as a science major before finally switching to his true loves—English and poetry—after his junior year.*

- *Belgian writer Georges Joseph Christian Simenon was able to write 60 to 80 pages a day and published 450 novels and short stories during his career.*

- *Geoffrey Chaucer's father was kidnapped in 1324 by one of his aunts, who hoped he would force his son to marry her daughter. She was arrested and fined £250.*

- *In 1932,* Death of a Salesman *author Arthur Miller couldn't afford to go to college so he worked as a truck driver, a waiter, and in an auto-parts warehouse for $15 per week.*

- *The poet Lord Tennyson loved "tavern food," including steak, cheese, and new potatoes.*

---

famous LAST WORDS

Leave it to literary geniuses to manage to be eloquent even as they are dying. Here's a collection of some famous, and often funny, last words.

Lord Byron
  "Good night."

Anton Chekhov
  "It's a long time since I've drunk champagne."

Noel Coward
  "Goodnight, my darlings. I'll see you tomorrow."

Hart Crane
  "Good-bye, everybody!" (spoken just before jumping overboard a ship to his death)

Emily Dickinson
  "…the fog is rising."

Johann Wolfgang von Goethe
  "Open the second shutter so that more light can come in."

O. Henry
  "Turn up the lights. I don't want to go home in the dark."

Heinrich Heine
  "God will pardon me. That is His trade."

Victor Hugo
  "I see a black light."

Henry James
  "So it has come at last, the distinguished thing."

D. H. Lawrence
  "I'm getting better."

Wyndham Lewis
"Mind your own business." (his response to a nurse who asked him about his bowel movements)

Karl Marx
"Go on, get out. Last words are for fools who haven't said enough."

W. Somerset Maugham
"Dying is a very dull, dreary affair. And my advice to you is to have nothing whatsoever to do with it."

Alexander Pope
"Here I am, dying of a hundred good symptoms."

François Rabelais
"I am going to seek the Great Perhaps."

William Saroyan
"Everybody has got to die, but I always thought an exception would be made in my case. Now what?"

George Bernard Shaw
"Sister, you are trying to keep me alive as an old curiosity, but I'm done, I'm finished."

Gertrude Stein
"What is the answer?" (When no answer came, she laughed and said, "In that case what is the question?")

Dylan Thomas
"I've had 18 straight whiskeys. I think that's the record."

James Thurber
"God bless, God damn."

Voltaire
"This is no time to make new enemies." (in response to a deathbed request for him to renounce Satan)

goodbye cruel world

While many writers find death a fascinating literary topic, some succumb to suicide. Some theorize that writing is lonely work. Others think that the heightened creativity of writers might unbalance them. Here is a list of writers who ultimately chose "not to be."

• • • • •

Sylvia Plath

During college, Plath made her first suicide attempt. After failing, she wrote about her suicidal tendencies in her 1963 novel *The Bell Jar*. Years later, when her husband had left her and she was raising two young children alone in a cold, small apartment, she stuck her head in a gas oven.

• • • • •

Yukio Mishima

Author of philosophical novels and Japan's first homosexual autobiography, as well as a lot of cheap fiction, Mishima led an extraordinary life, which culminated equally dramatically. He went from being an author (and a star in gangster films!) to leading a paramilitary organization. During an occupation of the Japanese Self-Defense Force in Tokyo, as many watched, Mishima performed the ancient samurai ritual of seppuku—he disemboweled himself. In his death, he became nothing short of a legendary, and hotly debated, figure.

• • • • •

Ernest Hemingway

Fame, alcohol, and depression eventually became too much for Papa to bear. His writing style deteriorated and he began hearing voices. After two months of electroshock therapy, he ended his life with his favorite shotgun at home in Ketchum, Idaho, in 1961. His younger brother, who was down the hall and heard the shot, also committed suicide in 1982, as their father had done in 1928. Likewise, Hemingway's granddaughter, supermodel Margeaux Hemingway, killed herself in 1995.

• • • • •

John Kennedy Toole
His might be the most ironic suicide in literary history. Toole's book, *The Confederacy of Dunces,* couldn't get published in his lifetime, but won a posthumous Pulitzer Prize in 1981. Originally, Simon and Schuster rejected the book. After bouts of depression about his fate as a writer, Toole put one end of a hose in his automobile's exhaust pipe and one in his car window. After his death, his mother gave the manuscript to author Walker Percy, who saw it through to publication. Had he lived, Toole would have seen his novel sell over 1.5 million copies.

• • • • •

Primo Levi
While all suicides are tragic, Levi's seems even more tragic than most. He managed to endure unspeakable horrors in a concentration camp, as his memoir *Survival in Auschwitz* details. He then went on with strength and courage to write other memoirs, essays, and poems. His resilience seemed unquestionable until the morning of April 11, 1987, when a concierge delivered his mail to the third-floor apartment Levi had been born in 67 years earlier. By the time the concierge reached the ground floor, she heard Levi's body fall to the bottom of the stairs. Fellow Holocaust survivor Elie Wiesel offered an explanation of how a man who had survived so much could kill himself. He said that Levi did, indeed, die in Auschwitz, only 40 years later.

• • • • •

Cesare Pavese
Like Primo Levi, who died in Turin in 1987, the Italian poet and novelist Pavese had also killed himself in Turin 37 years earlier.

Frustrated by writing and tormented by unrequited love for American actress Constance Dowling, Pavese died by overdose in a Turin hotel room.

· · · · ·

Virginia Woolf

Woolf suffered bouts of mental illness throughout her life. Between the world wars, she grew increasingly fearful of bombings. She and her husband, Leonard, made an agreement to kill themselves should Nazis invade. In 1941, after further bouts of depression, Woolf loaded her pockets with stones and drowned in the River Ouse. She left a note for Leonard that said, "I have a feeling I shall go mad. I cannot go on longer in these terrible times. I hear voices and cannot concentrate on my work. I have fought against it but cannot fight any longer. I owe all my happiness to you but cannot go on and spoil your life."

Three Things You Never Knew About: Boris Pasternak

• *He worked at a chemical factory during World War I.*

• *He wrote a poetry collection titled* My Sister Life *after falling in love with a young Jewish girl, but he was too embarrassed to have it published for four years.*

• *After he wrote a collection of poems titled* The Second Birth, *his colleagues described him as "Emily Dickinson in trousers."*

---

and that's all she wrote

It ain't over till the fat lady sings. Sometimes she hits a sour note, but sometimes she's right on key. Here are some great last lines that leave readers always wishing for more.

.....

With the Gardiners, they were always on the most intimate terms. Darcy, as well as Elizabeth, really loved them; and they were both ever sensible of the warmest gratitude towards the persons who, by bringing her into Derbyshire, had been the means of uniting them.
—Jane Austen, *Pride and Prejudice*

.....

I lingered round them, under that benign sky; watched the moths fluttering among the heath, and hare-bells; listened to the soft wind breathing through the grass; and wondered how anyone could ever imagine unquiet slumbers, for the sleepers in that quiet earth.
—Emily Brontë, *Wuthering Heights*

.....

It is a far, far better thing that I do, than I have ever done; it is a far, far better rest that I go to than I have ever known.
—Charles Dickens, *A Tale of Two Cities*

.....

But that is the beginning of a new story—the story of the gradual renewal of a man, the story of his gradual regeneration, of his passing from one world into another, of his initiation into a new unknown life. That might be the subject of a new story, but our present story is ended.
—Fyodor Dostoevsky, *Crime and Punishment*

So we beat on, boats against the current, borne back ceaselessly into the past.
—F. Scott Fitzgerald, *The Great Gatsby*

They hand in hand, with wandering steps and slow,
Through Eden took their solitary way.
—John Milton, *Paradise Lost*

So thanks to all at once and to each one,
Whom we invite to see us crowned at Scone.
—William Shakespeare, *Macbeth*

Go hence, to have more talk of these sad things;
Some shall be pardoned, and some punished;
For never was a story of more woe
Than this of Juliet and her Romeo.
—William Shakespeare, *Romeo and Juliet*

Bitter that his parents made so little money when he was a child (his father was a mailman), Tom Clancy now believes that large bank accounts are the definition of success. When nasty critics scorn his work, he simply responds by pointing out the difference in their income levels. Now who's more successful?